The Saving Word

Michael Glazier, Inc.

1210   King Street, Wilmington, Delaware 19801

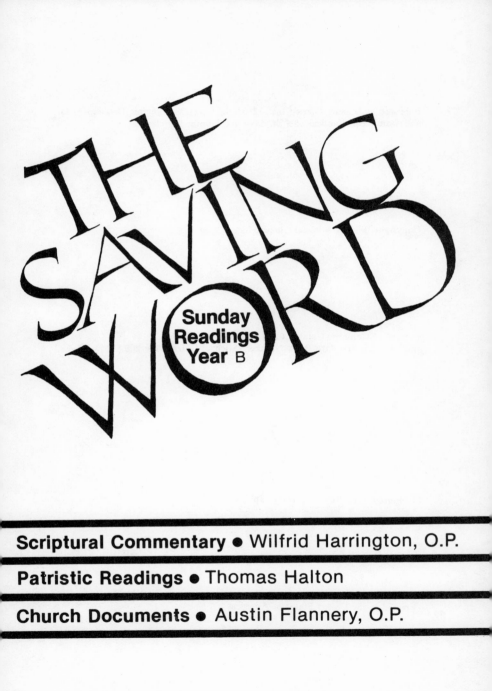

THE SAVING WORD

Sunday Readings Year B

Scriptural Commentary ● Wilfrid Harrington, O.P.

Patristic Readings ● Thomas Halton

Church Documents ● Austin Flannery, O.P.

Published by Michael Glazier, Inc., 1210 King Street, Wilmington, Delaware 19801 and Dominican Publications, St. Saviours, Dublin 1, Ireland

Library of Congress Catalog Card Number: 80-68395
International Standard Book Number (Michael Glazier, Inc.): 0-89453-266-9

Typography by Robert Zerbe Graphics

Printed in the United States of America

"Among the principal duties of bishops,
the preaching of the gospel occupies an eminent place.
For bishops are preachers of the faith
who lead new disciples to Christ." *Lumen Gentium*, 25.

To
THOMAS J. MARDAGA
Bishop of Wilmington
who
by word and deed proclaims
the presence of the
Lord Jesus
in
his people

LIST OF ABBREVIATIONS

NOTE

Certain Festivals (here indicated by asterisk) have the same scriptural readings in each of the three years of the liturgical cycle. We provide fresh commentary and texts—not reproducing the material of Year A but offering an alternative. Besides, first and second readings are the same in the following cases: The Holy Family, The Baptism of the Lord, Passion Sunday, The Ascension.

THE SAVING WORD

Editors
Scriptural Commentary: Rev. Wilfrid Harrington, O.P.
Patristic Commentary: Rev. Thomas Halton
Insights from the Documents of the Church: Rev.
Austin Flannery, O.P.

TABLE OF CONTENTS

LENT

EASTER

SUNDAYS OF THE YEAR

THE SOLEMNITIES OF THE LORD

ACKNOWLEDGEMENTS

The Bible quotes used by Wilfrid Harrington, O.P. are taken from the Revised Standard Version of the Bible, copyrighted in 1946, 1952, 1971, 1973 by the Division of Christian Education of the National Council of the Churches of Christ in the U.S.A., and used by permission.

The translations of the texts of the Fathers of the Church are used, with adaptations, from the following collections: *The Ante-Nicene Fathers; The Nicene and Post-Nicene Fathers; Ancient Christian Writers; Fathers of the Church;* and M.F. Toal's *The Sunday Sermons of the Great Fathers*, 4 vols., London, 1959.

The various editions of patristic texts differ greatly in scriptural translations and in syntactical usage; but it was decided to use, with necessary textual adaptations, the translations as they stood.

Extracts from *Ecclesiam Suam, Mater et Magistra, Pacem in Terris*, and *Populorum Progressio* are taken from the translations by the Catholic Truth Society of London and used with permission.

We wish to thank the Costello Publishing Company, Inc., of Northport, New York and Dominican Publications of Dublin for permission to use extracts from *Vatican II: The Conciliar and Post Conciliar Documents*, translated and edited by Austin Flannery, O.P.

ADVENT

FIRST SUNDAY OF ADVENT

Scriptural Commentary

First Reading Is 63:16-17; 64:1,3-8.

This first reading is taken from the long poem Is 63:7-64:11—a psalm of entreaty written by a returned exile not long after 538 B.C. Jerusalem lay in ruins; the task of re-building the temple had not yet been undertaken. The poem-prayer is typical of post-exilic prayers—the "prayers of the chastened"—in that it recalls God's past goodness to his people and candidly acknowledges the people's ingratitude and sinfulness. The dominant note, however, is serene confidence in God's loving-kindness. The opening statement, "I will declare the steadfast love of the Lord" (v.7), does not just introduce a chronicle of his mercies of the past; it is assurance that his steadfast love reaches into the present. There is, too, an urgency about the psalm as it strives to bring its hearers to a recognition of their plight from which God alone can deliver them. Not only recognition but acknowledgment: they are expected to make this prayer *their* fervent prayer.

"Thou art our Father"—the phrase occurs three times in our reading. God had become Father of his people by re-deeming them (Ex 4:22; Hos 11:1; Dt 32:5-6; Mal 1-6). Here the invocation of the Father is an expression of confidence: he can, and will, redeem this situation. There is a moving poignancy in this trustful "Father" on the lips of self-confessed sinners (64:6-6). No attempt at whitewash here; there are no extenuating circumstances.

God is the Father who redeemed his people—and the Shepherd who led his people from Egypt. His people abandoned him, to its great loss. Jerusalem, the holy city of his dwelling, lay in ruins. Israel proclaims its sin: it has become an unclean polluted thing. It had cut itself off from its life-giving source and has become a heap of withered leaves scattered to the winds [Compare, "If a man does not abide in me, he is cast forth as a branch and withers" (Jn 15:6)]. The psalmist begs his God to rend the veil of his heavenly abode and appear in a theophany more majestic than that of Sinai; he beseeches him to bring about a new exodus of salvation. Deliverance is readily within the power of the divine Potter as he moulds, to his will, the clay of his people. Potter, yes, but Potter who is *Father* of steadfast love. That is the truth that makes all the difference.

At the opening of the Advent season this gracious psalm shows us Israel's confident expectation—even in the midst of the ruins of catastrophe—of a new exodus. This new age was to dawn half a millennium after the time of the optimistic poet. And even though the Messiah has come we too, in the turmoil of our world, can look forward to the other coming of Christ when sin will be no more.

Second Reading 1 Cor 1:3-9.

In the early church, and it comes through in the earlier letters of Paul, there was lively expectation that the definitive coming of Christ, his *Parousia*, was imminent. This expectation was modified as the years went by but a looking to the day of our Lord Jesus Christ remained prominent in the New Testament. It was an attitude of joyful expectancy, a conviction that the Lord had not abandoned his people. He had gone to prepare for the day when he will finally gather his followers into the eternal kingdom. This positive picture of the goal of christian history was in time displaced by the more frightening image of the last day as a day of judgment and tribulation. For the faithful Christian, however, Christ will always come as redeemer, not as judge.

Of course, there is an aspect of truth in that other scene of judgment. It may be that our reading could make a nice balance. Here, as elsewhere, the clash of Corinthian enthusiasm and Pauline realism has served christian theology. Paul insists that the "grace"—God's gift of salvation—bestowed on this community must manifest itself. It will be seen in "all speech and all knowledge"—in the various "spiritual gifts" (vv.4-7). Paul is going to deal at length with these charismatic gifts in chs. 12-14. At this point he merely acknowledges their presence in this community. He will be at pains to show that the presence of these gifts of the Spirit in no way means that Corinth is an exemplary christian community—far from it!

The Corinthians may feel that they have already reached the goal—they are "not lacking in any spiritual gift" (v.7). Here lurks a warning, as the letter will show. The Lord will come, yes, but to reward fidelity and punish unfaithfulness (3:13; 4:3-4). The Corinthians must fight to retain what has been given (9:24-27). They can achieve this if they lean on the sustaining presence of the one who is to come! (v.8). A faithful God is active in the activity of his Son who calls Christians into "fellowship" (*koinonia*). "Christian existence is a shared mode of being; if it is only through love that we really exist (13:2), others are as necessary to our being as we to theirs. Such reciprocity on the level of being creates the organic unity of the New Man (Gal 3:28; Col 3:10) who is Christ (6:15; 12:12). The 'fellowship of the Son,' therefore, is quite different from the friendliness of a club" (J. Murphy-O'Connor, *1 Corinthians*, 5).

Gospel Mark 13:33-37.

Chapter 13 of Mark, which rounds off the ministry of Jesus, is his farewell discourse. More immediately, it faces up to an acute Marcan concern. It is written, most likely, just after the Roman destruction of Jerusalem in 70 A.D. Some Christians, seemingly, had looked to that event as the

moment of the End and were disillusioned when, afterwards, life went on as before. Mark is convinced that the
End is near—but is distinct from the fall of Jerusalem.
Following on a brief introduction (vv.1-4) he treats of the
signs of Parousia (5-23), the Parousia (24-27), and the nearness of the Parousia (28-37). Our reading is the conclusion
of this third part and of the whole discourse.

The exhortation of v.33 is Mark's introduction to the
parable of the Doorkeeper (34-36). "Take heed" (vv.5,9,23)
is the keynote of the farewell discourse. "Watch" means do
not permit yourselves to fall asleep! "Time" (cf. 1:15) is the
appointed time fixed in an ordered divine plan. In its
context the "time" refers to the incalculable "day or hour"
of v.32 (the End is near—but cannot be marked on a
calendar). The call to watchfulness in v.33 brings out the
exhortation latent in v.32.

The parable of the Doorkeeper, as Mark found it, had
already gone through a process of reshaping. It certainly
resembles the Watching Servants of Lk 12:35-38—indeed
both should be regarded as widely variant forms of the
same parable. The main sentence of v.35, "Watch therefore . . . lest he come suddenly and find you asleep," is the
application of the parable. Significantly, it is "the master
of the house" who will come, not the "man" of v.34: it is
Christ himself. The parable is now understood in christological terms. Christ is the departing Lord and the
parousia will mark his return. The doorkeeper represents
the waiting disciples, the community of believers, and
the divisions of the night are a symbol for the lapse of time
before the coming. This meaning is borne out by Mark's
care to bracket the first part of the parable with the warning,
"for you do not know when the time will come" (v.33b), "for
you do not know when the master of the house will come"
(v.35b).

The opening "Take heed" (v.5) and the final "Watch"
(v.37) emphasize that Mark's real interest in this passage
is centered in the exhortation, and his lesson is for all

Christians without exception: "I say to *all*." The repeated call to watchfulness indicates how he wanted, not only this parable but the whole discourse, to be understood: not as a guide in calculating a deadline, but as an inspiration and a warning, to live one's life at each moment in preparedness for the meeting with Christ.

Patristic Commentary

St. Basil (c. 330-379).
Homily: "Give heed to Thyself." PG 31, 201,
   FOTC 9.434-435.

"Give heed to thyself"—that is, examine yourself from all angles. Keep the eye of your soul sleeplessly on guard, for "Thou art going in the midst of snares." (Eccle 9:20). Traps set by the enemy lie concealed everywhere. Look about you in all directions, therefore, "that you may be saved as a swallow from the traps and as a bird from the snare." (Prov 6:5). The deer cannot be caught with traps because of the keenness of his vision; whence its name, deriving from its own sharpsightedness. A bird, if alert, easily flies out of the range of the huntsman's snare. See to it, then, that you are not more remiss than the animals in protecting yourself. Never let yourself be caught in the snares of the Devil and so become his prey, the captured plaything of his will.

"Give heed to thyself"—that is, attend neither to the goods you possess nor to the objects that are round about you, but to yourself alone. We ourselves are one thing; our possessions another; the objects that surround us, yet another. We are soul and intellect in that we have been made according to the image of the Creator. Our body is our own possession and the sensations which are expressed through it, but money, crafts, and other appurtenances of life in this world are extraneous to us. What, then, does the Scripture mean by this precept? Attend not to the flesh nor seek after its good in any form—health, beauty, enjoyment of pleasures, or longevity—and do not admire wealth and fame and power. Do not consider the accessories to your temporal existence to be of great consequence and thus, in your zealous concern for these things, neglect the life which is of primary importance to you. "Give heed to thyself," that is, to your soul. Adorn it, care for it, to the end that, by careful attention, every defilement incurred as a result of sin may be removed and every shameful vice expelled, and that it may be embellished and made bright with every ornament of virtue. Examine closely what sort of being you are. Know your nature—that your body is mortal, but your soul, immortal; that our life has two denotations, so to speak: one relating to the flesh, and this life is quickly over, the other referring to the soul, life without limit. "Give heed to thyself"—cling not to the mortal as if it were eternal; disdain not that which is eternal as if it were temporal. Despise the flesh, for it passes away; be solicitous for your soul which will never die.

Insights from the Documents of the Church

Liberation from Sin

This history of salvation is the history of liberation from sin. All of God's interventions . . . were to guide men and women in the struggle against the forces of sin. Christ's role in the history of salvation has to do with the destruction of sin and it was completed in the mystery of the cross. Saint Paul's reflections (Rom 5) on the reality of sin and on the work of justice performed by Christ must be numbered among the principal points of the Christian faith. (General Catechetical Directory, n. 62)

The Gifts of the Spirit

Jesus promised his disciples that the Holy Spirit would help them to bear witness fearlessly to their faith even in the face of persecution. The day before he suffered, he confirmed to his apostles that he would send the Spirit of truth from the Father, to remain with them for ever, helping them to be his witnesses. Lastly, after the resurrection, Christ promised the descent of the Holy Spirit: "You will receive power when the Holy Spirit comes upon you; and you will bear witness for me in Jerusalem." (Paul VI, Apostolic Constitution on the Sacrament of Confirmation)

"STAY AWAKE"

Since we know not the day nor the hour, we should follow the advice of the Lord and watch constantly so that, when the single course of our earthly life is completed, we may merit to enter with him into the marriage feast and be numbered among the blessed and not, like the wicked and slothful servants, be ordered to depart into the eternal fire, into the outer darkness where "men will weep and gnash their teeth" (Matt 22:1-3). (Vat. II, Constitution on the Church, no. 48)

SECOND SUNDAY OF ADVENT

Scriptural Commentary

First Reading Is 40:1-5, 9-11.

In the light of the historical situation in which these words were first uttered, one cannot but be impressed by the confidence of the anonymous prophet who spoke them. Humanly speaking, there seemed no grounds for optimism. Hope cast on the dynasty of David, bolstered by the oracles of Isaiah, had sputtered out in the catastrophe of Babylonian conquest. The cream of the survivors of Judah were in exile in Babylon. And it was there that this man of vision—we name him Second Isaiah—gave us chapters 40-55 of Isaiah, a work fittingly known as "The Book of

Consolation." God, this prophet assured his people, is about to come to lead his people once again out of slavery into their own land in a new exodus. Unlike the journey from Egypt to the promised land, this time there will be no straying. Israel, led by Yahweh, will journey in solemn pilgrimage along a *Via Sacra*, a processional way, across the Syrian desert.

In his poetic vision the prophet hears the voice of God bid a crier run speedily to Jerusalem to carry the good news as the Lord leads his people to freedom. "Good tidings": it is here the New Testament writers found their word "gospel"—Good News. The herald is urged to proclaim the good news openly in the towns of Judah. His message is to be: "Behold your God." By New Testament times this was paraphrased in the synagogues of Palestine as: "The kingdom of your God is revealed." The return from the exile, begun in 537, fell far short of the glowing picture painted here. Yet, all is not poetic imagery, for the restoration is a sign of salvation; it is, in its measure, a redemption, a new creation. Later generations of Jews had patiently to await the fulfilment of God's word. And the message could sometimes be reinterpreted in moral terms: the highway to be made straight was man's way of life; the kingdom was to be prepared for by repentance. It was still felt that the beginning of the messianic era would be associated with the desert. Thus did this biblical text and a later understanding of it prepare for the fulfilment that came in the person of Jesus and was ushered in by the Baptist.

Second Reading 2 Peter 3:8-14.

One of the problems faced by the early church was uncertainty as to the time-scale according to which God would conduct the history of salvation. We have already observed that, at first, Christians looked eagerly to an imminent return of Christ. Yet the End failed to materialize. On the whole, the church quietly adjusted to the situation. The perspective of the author of our epistle is that, since the resurrection, humanity lives in the last phase of its history and awaits the "Day of the Lord" which will mark the end of this present world. It is the confident view of a Christian of the early second century (2 Peter is generally dated about 120 A.D.). But there were some—as 2 Peter attests—who ridiculed the whole idea of the Lord's coming, thereby undermining the christian view of history. It is to the consequent danger to faith that the author of 2 Peter addresses himself in today's reading.

The "scoffers" had asked: "Where is the promise of his coming? For ever since the fathers [the apostles and first generation of Christians] fell asleep, all things have continued as they were from the beginning of creation" (v.4). They deny that history has any goal at all. Against their argument that the changeless nature of the universe forestalled the radical change demanded by the christian hope, the author shows from the Old Testament that once before the world had been destroyed—by the Flood—and that God could just as easily destroy it again by fire (vv.4-7).

Turning then to the "beloved" faithful, he points out that the apparent delay of the Parousia may be explained in part by the fact that God's measure of time differs from ours (cf. Ps 90:4) and in part by his forbearance: "not wishing that any should perish, but that all should reach repentance" (v.9). But the Day of the Lord will surely come, if unexpectedly (cf. Mt 24:43). The just have nothing to fear Expectation of the end will inspire them to live lives of holiness and godliness (3:11). Developing a Jewish idea that sin could delay the Coming (cf. Acts 3:19-20), the author suggests that righteousness can hasten the Parousia (vv.11-12), thus providing an added incentive for virtuous living. And the fiery end of this world of ours is not really destruction: it will mark the emergence of "the new heavens and a new earth in which righteousness dwells" (v.13). Cf. Is 65:17; 66:22; Rev 21:1,5.

Gospel Mark 1:1-8.

Mark states the theme of his gospel in his opening verse and then introduces the traditional prelude to the Good

News: "beginning from the baptism of John" (Acts 1:22).
The title (v.1) defines the whole work as "the gospel of
Jesus Christ": the gospel of the crucified and risen Lord—
the gospel that is Jesus himself (8:35; 10:29). For Mark the
gospel is somehow the presence of the saving power of
Jesus. Two of Mark's significant christological titles are
here at the start: Christ (Messiah) and Son of God. The
beginning and abiding source of this gospel lies in the
historical appearance of Jesus who, in the perspective of
the Easter faith of the church, was recognizable as the Son
of God.

John the Baptizer solemnly proclaims the coming of
the greater than he who will pour out the gift of the Spirit.
Vv.2-3 combine two scripture texts. John is the messenger
(Mal 3:1) and the prophet (Is 40:3). The good news which
concerns Jesus Christ begins with the wilderness prophet
John, clothed like Elijah (2 Kgs 1:8) and subsisting on
wilderness fare (v.6). John is the sign that in the wilderness
God is about to renew his covenant with Israel (Hos 2:14-23;
Jer 2:1-3). This mission explains his clarion call to repentance or *metanoia*, a radical conversion, finding symbolic
expression in baptism.

John who had uttered the call to repentance now proclaims the coming of the greater than he who will baptize
the people with the Holy Spirit (vv.7-8). His role of forerunner was already subtly intimated in v.3 where the
quotation from Is 40:3 is changed to read "his paths"
(instead of "the paths of our God"): "the Lord" is now Jesus
whose way John prepares. In contrast to the other synoptists who give a summary of the ethical preaching of
the Baptist, Mark focuses on him as the pointer to the
Coming One. Baptism "with the Holy Spirit" is the promised outpouring of the Spirit for the time of salvation (cf.
Joel 2:28-29; Is 44:3). In the parallel texts of Mt 3:11 and
Lk 3:16 this baptism is described as being "with the Holy
Spirit *and with fire*," that is, a baptism of judgment. It is
likely that the Baptist spoke only of baptism with fire.
Here a threat of imminent judgment has been transformed

into a prophecy of the outpouring of the Spirit, work of the risen Lord. In Mark, neither John nor Jesus preach judgment.

Patristic Commentary

St. Jerome (c. 347-c. 420)
Homily on Mk 1:1-12. CCL 78.454, FOTC 57.125.

Now with the guidance of your prayers, let us turn to the spiritual understanding of this passage. "John was clothed in camel's hair, with a leathern girdle about his waist." It is the same John who says: "He must increase, but I must decrease. He who has the bride is the bridegroom; but the friend of the bridegroom rejoices exceedingly if he sees the bridegroom." And again: "One mightier than I is coming after me, the thong of whose sandals I am not worthy to stoop down and loose." John, that is, the Law in John, was clothed, therefore, in the hair of a camel; he could not wear a tunic of the lamb of whom it is said: "Behold the lamb of God who takes away the sins of the world"; and again: "He is led like a lamb to the slaughter." In the Law, we cannot wear a tunic from that lamb.

In the Law John had a leather girdle because the Jews thought that to sin in act was the only sin. On the other hand, in the Apocalypse of John, our Lord Jesus, who is seen amidst the seven lamp-stands, also wore a girdle, a golden girdle, not about his waist, but about the breasts. The Law is girdled about the waist: but Christ, that is, the Gospel, is binding, not only in wanton passion, but also in mind and heart.

Insights from the Documents of the Church

Repentance and Atonement
The Father manifested his mercy by reconciling the world to himself in Christ, making peace by the blood of his cross

with all who are in heaven and on earth. The Son of God
became man and lived among men so that he might liberate
them from slavery to sin and call them out of darkness
into his wonderful light. Thus he commenced his task on
earth by preaching penance and saying: "Repent and
believe the Gospel" (Mark 1:15).

This invitation to penitence, which had often been issued
by the prophets, prepared the hearts of men for the coming
of the kingdom through the voice of John the Baptist, who
came preaching "a baptism of repentance for the forgiveness
of sins" (Mark 1:4).

But not only did Jesus exhort men to do penance, to give
up their sins and be converted to God with all their hearts.
He also received sinners and reconciled them to the Father.
He cured the sick as a sign of his power to forgive sins. He
himself even died for our sins and rose from the dead for our
justification. On the night he was betrayed, as he commenced his saving passion, he instituted the sacrifice of
the new covenant in his blood for the remission of sins, and
after his resurrection he sent his Spirit to the apostles that
they might have the power to forgive sins or to retain them,
and that they might accept the task of preaching penance
and the remission of sins to all nations in his name.

It was to Peter that the Lord said "I will give you the
keys of the kingdom of heaven, and whatever you bind on
earth shall be bound in heaven, and whatever you loose
on earth shall be loosed in heaven" (Matt. 16:19). In
obedience to the Lord's command Peter preached the
remission of sins by baptism on the day of Pentecost:
"Repent and be baptized, every one of you, in the name of
Jesus Christ for the forgiveness of your sins" (Acts 2:38).
From then on the Church has never ceased to call sinners
to conversion and to exhibit the victory of Christ over sin
in the celebration of penance.

This victory of Christ over sin is shown first in baptism,
by which the old man is crucified with Christ so that the
body of sin may be destroyed and we might no more serve

sin, but rise with Christ and live thenceforth. Thus the Church confesses its faith "in one baptism for the remission of sins." (Introduction to the Rite of Penance)

THIRD SUNDAY OF ADVENT

Scriptural Commentary

First Reading Is 61:1-2, 10-11.

In this reading we have the beginning and the close of a hymn (61:1-11) in which a post-exilic prophet declares that he has been sent by God to usher in the age of salvation for Jerusalem and all God's people. In the opening verses he speaks in his own name, while in the conclusion ("I will greatly rejoice . . .") he speaks in the person of the new Jerusalem. He is anointed with the Spirit of God to proclaim good tidings to the poor—the afflicted of every kind; to bring hope to the hopeless: to assure them of the care of their God. Luke tells us that Jesus found in this passage the programme of his own ministry. Coming, one sabbath, to the synagogue of his native Nazareth, he opened the scroll of Isaiah and read out:

The Spirit of the Lord is upon me,
because he has anointed me to preach good news
  to the poor.
He has sent me to proclaim relief to captives
and recovering of sight to the blind,
to set at liberty those who are oppressed,
to proclaim the acceptable year of the Lord.

And, having read the passage, he declared to his hearers: "Today this scripture has been fulfilled in your hearing" (Lk 4:16-21). In this way a passage, notable in its own right, has been given startling relevance. Who is the mysterious personage of the Isaian poem: the author? the Servant of Yahweh? a future bearer of good tidings? We cannot be sure. What matters for Christians is that Jesus made the prophecy his own. He was the Spirit-anointed one who preached good news to the poor. He manifested in his person the tender quality of the promised mercy. The saviour who was to come did show a gentle concern for people in their deepest need.

At the close of the reading Jerusalem is represented as exulting with joy in the good news brought to her. The church, the new Jerusalem, should, so much more, be characterized by joyful hope. Hope is always the measure of faith. *Gaudium et spes*—joy and hope—fittingly describe the role of the church and its message to our world. Any other message will not ring true.

Second Reading 1 Thes 5:16-24.

In 1 Thes 5:12-15 Paul had urged the Thessalonians to respect their leaders and live in peace with one another. He had exhorted them to admonish, encourage and help as the need arose—always in a spirit of patience. Then, in vv.16-22, he passes to the positive demands of christian love. Believers must "always seek the good"—and that not only within the community but "of all." In particular he exhorts to christian joy, to prayer and thanksgiving. "Rejoice always": this joy, of which Paul speaks more than once. is gift of the Holy Spirit (Gal 5:22). A characteristic of christian joy is that it can exist together with trials and sufferings; these can in fact give rise to joy in that they take one closer to Christ (cf. Acts 5:41). "Pray constantly" (cf. Lk 18:1)—constant prayer is a quality of christian life. Prayer will take the quality of thanksgiving: an eloquent way of praising God for his goodness.

It is clear from 1 Cor 12-14 that charismatic gifts, while being manifestations of the Spirit's presence in a community, could cause problems. The problem lay not in the gifts but in the fact that some could not cope with them. Charismatics tended to give themselves airs. The answer was not in trying to stifle the gifts—that is the meaning of the admonition, "do not quench the Spirit." What was needed was discernment: to know whether there is gift of the Spirit. In Corinth Paul had to defend the gift of prophecy, that is to say, inspired, forthright preaching, against those who had exaggerated the importance of tongues. We may suspect a similar situation in Thessalonica; at any rate, there were some who "despised" prophesying. In conclusion, Paul moves beyond the specific area of spiritual gifts and bids his readers hold fast to whatever is good and hold off from all that is evil.

We may see as the theme of the second reading that the salvation promised in Christ, the process of redemption already operative among us, is a source of present joy and peace. Even though the Christian is still preparing for the final coming of Christ, it is not an anxious worrying time, but a quiet confident waiting. Our prayer, to use the words of Paul (v.23) is that the God of peace will keep us safe and blameless, spirit, soul and body, for the coming of our Lord Jesus Christ. After all, he who has called us to salvation is the faithful Father (v.24).

Gospel John 1:6-8, 19-28.

The subject of the gospel reading is the same as the previous Sunday—the witness of John the Baptist. But, today, we view the Baptist and his message in the distinctive colours of the fourth evangelist.

The verses 6-8 are an insertion (as is v.15) into the hymn (1:1-18). More firmly even than Mark (1:7) John casts the Baptist in the role of witness: he came to testify, to witness. He is *not* the "light," the revealer; but he summons "all" to faith in Jesus.

Before embarking on his gospel proper, John brings forward (1:19-51) a series of witnesses who bear testimony to the Messiah in a variety of messianic titles. The first part of the passage (which constitutes our reading) is the Baptist's vehement negative testimony: *he* is not the Messiah! Nor is he Elijah—traditionally, on the basis of Mal 3:1; 4:5, expected to precede the Messiah. And he is not the prophet-like-Moses who was to come (cf. Dt 18:15, 18). He is a voice, only a heraldic voice—and yet the solemn voice of the wilderness prophet of Is 63. If he baptizes it is with water: a sign that one has repented. He is no more than a slave whose task it is to untie his master's sandal; and he feels unworthy even for that. There is polemic here. Not John himself, but disciples of the Baptist—who still claimed John as the Messiah—are being put in their place (cf. Acts 19:1-4).

What matters to us is that the sense of joy, which is the keynote of today's liturgy, should be based on a growing conviction that, in the words of the Baptist, there stands among us, perhaps unknown to us, the one who will finally come in glory. Our hope is not all in the future. The work of our salvation has already begun.

Patristic Commentary

St. Ambrose (c. 340-397).
The Holy Spirit. c.14, PL 16.737, FOTC 44.86.

But why should I add that just as the Father is light, so, too, the Son is light, and the Holy Spirit is light? This surely belongs to divine power. For God is light, as John said: "That God is light; and that in Him there is no darkness." (1 Jn 1:5).

But the Son also is Light, because "Life was the Light of men." And the Evangelist, that he might show that he spoke of the Son of God, says of John the Baptist: "He was not the light, but was to bear witness to the light. He was the true light, which enlightens every man that comes into this world." (Jn 1:8,9) Therefore, since God is the Light, and the Son of God is the true Light, without doubt the Son of God is true God.

You have it also elsewhere that the Son of God is the Light: "The people that dwelt in darkness and in the shadow of death have seen a great light." (Is 9:2) But what is more evident than this which says: "For with thee is the fountain of life; and in thy light we shall see light." (Ps 35:10) That is, that with Thee, God Omnipotent Father, who are the Fount of Life, in thy light the Son, we shall see the light of the Holy Spirit. Just as the Lord Himself shows when He says: "Receive ye the Holy Spirit," and elsewhere: "Virtue went out from Him." (Lk 6:19)

Moreover, who will doubt that the Father Himself is light, when it is read of His Son that He is the splendor of eternal light? (Heb 1:3) For of whom if not of the eternal Father is the Son the splendor, who both is always with the Father and always shines not with a dissimilar but with the same light?

And Isaiah points out that the Holy Spirit is not only light but is also fire, when he says: "And the light of Israel shall be as fire." (Is 10:19) Thus the Prophets called Him a burning fire, because in those three points we notice more readily the majesty of the Godhead, for to sanctify is of the Godhead, and to illuminate is proper to fire and light, and to be expressed and to be seen in the appearance of fire is customary with the Godhead; "for God is a consuming fire," (Dt 4:24) as Moses said.

Insights from the Documents of the Church

Liberty to Captives; Good News to the Poor

The prophetic mission of Christ "sent to preach the good news to the poor" (Luke 4:18) finds a strong echo in today's Church.

This is evident in numerous pontifical statements and in the clear and illuminating passages of the Pastoral Constitution on the Church in the modern World, *Gaudium et Spes*, which urge a closer relationship between the Church and the lives of the people. The 1971 Synod of Bishops, in its document "Justice in the World" emphasized the urgent need for awareness of this dimension of the Church's evangelizing mission.

The apostolic exhortation, "Evangelization Today," *Evangelii Nuntiandi,* drove the point home, calling on all of the People of God, to accept their own responsibility to reach out to the lives and situations of the "peoples . . . striving with all their power and energy to overcome all those circumstances which compel them to live on the border line of existence."

The themes of "evangelical liberation," based on the kingdom of God, ought therefore to be especially familiar to Christians.

In fact, the witness of Christians who have courageously taken part in the support of the lowly and in the defence of human rights, is an effective echo of the Gospel and of the voice of the Church.

The defence and promotion of justice ought to be particularly alert and active in those agonizing areas of "injustice without a voice" of which the Synod of 1971 speaks.

In fact, while certain categories of people are able to form their own vigorous structures for protest and support, there is also an immense amount of suffering and injustice which evokes little response in the hearts of many of our contemporaries. There is the plight of the refugees, of people persecuted because of their political ideas or for professing the faith; there is the violation of the right to be born; the unjustified limitations placed on human and religious liberty; the defective social structures which increase the sufferings of the old and of the marginalized.

The Church wishes to be, for these especially, voice, conscience, commitment. (*Religious and Human Advancement,* slightly adapted)

FOURTH SUNDAY OF ADVENT

Scriptural Commentary

First Reading 2 Sam 7:1-5, 8-11,16.

David, his days of brigandage and forced exile ended, became king, first of Judah and then of the united kingdom of Judah and Israel. He had won for himself the city of Jerusalem and made it his capital (2 Sam 5). By installing the ark of Yahweh there he turned it into the religious centre of his domain (ch.6). Then, adverting to the incongruity that he had a palace while the ark of Yahweh was still housed in a tent, he planned to build a temple.

David consulted the prophet Nathan. In their first dialogue we have a fascinating example of the need for discernment of spirits (7:1-3). (Note second reading of previous Sunday.) Nathan thought that David's proposal was great and enthusiastically gave the project his blessing: "Go, do all that is in your heart; for the Lord is with you" (v.3). "But that same night the word of the Lord came to Nathan . . ."! (v.4). The prophet had listened to his own heart; now he listens to the Lord. The Lord had pre-empted David's plan. The king had hoped to build a *house* (temple) for Yahweh; instead it is Yahweh who will build a house (dynasty) for David (7:4-17). It will be Solomon's task to build the temple. David receives the solemn promise that his dynasty would last forever: "Your house and your kingdom shall be made sure forever before me; your throne shall be established forever" (v.16). The temple liturgy kept this promise firmly before the people—notably Ps 88 which is read as the responsorial psalm today.

When Judah was overthrown and Jerusalem destroyed in 587 B.C., it seemed that this was one promise which had failed. Still, the Jewish people kept alive their hope that God would not renege on his promise and they continued to look forward to a Messiah who would be of the House of David. The expectation was fulfilled when Gabriel announced to Mary that she was to be the mother of the redeemer who, through Joseph, would be of the line of David. Gabriel's words echo the words of God's promise to David.

Second Reading Rom 16:25-27.

The doxology, which rounds off the letter to the Romans, may be a later addition by another than Paul. Authentic or not, it is certainly on all fours with the mind of Paul.

It stresses what God has done, and is doing, for Christians, how he has done it, and what their response should be. God strengthens Christians in their faith (v.25) and reaches out to others to bring them, too, into "the obedience of faith" (v.26). He achieves this through Paul's gospel—nothing other than Jesus Christ himself. This gospel is new but it has not sprung, unannounced, upon the world. God's "mystery"—his saving plan for Jew and Gentile—had been announced by the prophets. But it was not understood until the "now" of the era of salvation. Now, the good news can be proclaimed to all the world. The christian response is a fervent "thanks be to God!"—uttered, in christian fashion, through Jesus Christ.

"According to the command of the eternal God"—or, as JB has it, "the way the eternal God wants things to be done" (v.26). It is not difficult for Christians, with hindsight, to see in the person and life of Jesus the fulfilment and more than the fulfilment, of the promises made in Old Testament times. Yet the people to whom the promises had been first made could never have suspected that things would work out as they had. We too may have a very limited vision of what redemption is, and of how the coming of the Lord will be realized. Salvation history reassures us that God is faithful to his covenant—but in *his* way, for he is "the only wise" (v.27). Our hope is secure, but we must be sensitive and open to God as he works out his plan of redemption in his own mysterious time and manner.

Gospel Luke 1:26-38.

Luke asserts the basic fact that Mary was called, and knew herself to be called, to be the mother of the Messiah. It was, for her, a profound spiritual experience, a matter between herself and her God, something that took place in the depth of her being. In giving expression to this personal, spiritual experience, Luke spontaneously turned to the

Scriptures he knew so well. He brings before us the angelic messenger and his message: Gabriel, one of the "Angels of the Face," of Jewish tradition, who stand in the presence of God, and he provides the dialogue to bring out the significance of the call.

The angel describes the promised Son and his destiny (1:32-33) in terms borrowed from the Old Testament, especially from the oracle of Nathan (2 Sam 7:12-16) [first reading]. At this stage everything is still within the limits of the Old Law, but Luke will go on to explain that the intervention of the Holy Spirit will mean that Jesus must be named "Son of God" in a new sense. Mary's question (v.34) is a literary ploy, the evangelist's way of moving on to a new level. "The Holy Spirit will come upon you"—in Gen 1:2 the Spirit of God hovered over the waters, about to perform the great work of creation. Here, that divine power over-shadows Mary, about to perform a new and wonderful creation. This "Holy One" will be Son of God in a unique manner.

In Mary's consent (v.38) we may see the true pattern of her humility. If she had been troubled and if she had asked a question (and we can trust the delicate perception of Luke) it is because she had been perplexed. Now that she knows the divine purpose she accepts that purpose unhesitatingly and with perfect simplicity. If heroics would be out of place at such a moment so, no less certainly, would be a pro-testation, even a suggestion, of unworthiness. Mary was too completely God's to think of herself at all.

This final reading for Advent brings together the great themes of this season. Luke sees Mary as summing up in her person the deepest and purest traditions of Old Testament piety. She was one of those whose trust was not in an external, political redemption. Over the centuries the expectation of deliverance had been purified and spiritual-ized, and there was a class who yearned for a deeper and more personal salvation. Mary was of this tradition. [See *The Saving Word*, Year A, p.24]

Patristic Commentary

St. Ambrose (c. 340-397)
The Sacrament of the Incarnation. PL 16.831.
FOTC 44, 239-240.

Then Gabriel also declares this in proper words, saying: "The Holy which shall be born of thee shall be called the Son of God." (Lk 1:35) "Of thee," he says, that you might know that He was born of her according to man, for Mary produced from herself, in order that what was produced from her, in Him, the prerogative of the Lord's production being preserved, there might be the true nature of the body. But Paul also says that he was predestined for the Gospel of God. "Which he had promised before," he says, "by His prophets concerning His Son, who was made to him of the seed of David, according to the flesh." (Rom 1:2,3) And to the Galatians he says: "But when the fullness of time was come, God sent His Son, made of a woman." (Gal 4:4) And to Timothy he said: "Be mindful that the Lord Jesus Christ is risen from the dead, of the seed of David." (2 Tim 2:8)

So He received from us what He offered as His own for us, that He might redeem us from our own, and that He might confer upon us what was not our own from His divine liberality. According to our nature, then, He offered Himself, that He might do a work beyond our nature. From that which is ours is the sacrifice, from His is the reward; and many things will you find in Him both according to nature and beyond nature. For, according to the condition of the body He was in the womb, He was born, He was nursed, He was placed in the crib, but beyond this condition the Virgin conceived, the Virgin bore Him, that you might believe that it was God who renewed nature, and it was man who was born of man according to nature.

For not, as some have concluded, was the very nature of the Word changed, which is always unchangeable, as He himself said: "See me, see me, that it is I, and I am not changed." (Mal 3:6) But Paul also said: "Jesus Christ yesterday, and today, and the same forever"(Heb 13:8), that is, who is not changed according to the nature of the flesh, but who remained unchangeable even in the changeable quality itself of human condition.

Insights from the Documents of the Church

Our Lady in Advent

For example, during Advent there are many liturgical references to Mary besides the Solemnity of 8 December, which is a joint celebration of the Immaculate Conception of Mary, of the basic preparation (cf. Is 11:1,10) for the coming of the Saviour and of the happy beginning of the Church without spot or wrinkle. Such liturgical references are found especially on the days from 17 to 24 December, and more particularly on the Sunday before Christmas, which recalls the ancient prophecies concerning the Virgin Mother and the Messiah and includes readings from the Gospel concerning the imminent birth of Christ and his Precursor.

In this way the faithful, living in the liturgy the spirit of Advent, by thinking about the inexpressible love with which the Virgin Mother awaited her Son, are invited to take her as a model and to prepare themselves to meet the Saviour who is to come. They must be "vigilant in prayer and joyful in . . . praise." We would also remark that the Advent liturgy, by linking the awaiting of the Messiah and the awaiting of the glorious return of Christ with the admirable commemoration of his Mother, presents a happy balance in worship. This balance can be taken as a norm for preventing any tendency (as has happened at times in certain forms of popular piety) to separate devotion to the Blessed Virgin from its necessary point of reference— Christ. It also ensures that this season, as liturgy experts have noted, should be considered as a time particularly suited to devotion to the Mother of the Lord. This is an orientation that we confirm and which we hope to see accepted and followed everywhere. (Paul VI, To Honour Mary [*Marialis Cultus*])

God's Plan Revealed in Jesus Christ

We also are in a certain way in a season of a new Advent, a season of expectation: "In many and various ways God spoke of old to our fathers by the prophets; but in these last days he has spoken to us by a Son . . .", by 'the Son, his Word, who became man and was born of the Virgin Mary. This act of redemption marked the high point of the history of man within God's loving plan. God entered the history of humanity and, as a man, became an actor in that history, one of the thousands of millions of human beings but at the same time Unique! Through the Incarnation God gave human life the dimension that he intended man to have from his first beginning; he has granted that dimension definitively—in the way that is peculiar to him alone, in keeping with his eternal love and mercy, with the full freedom of God—and he has granted it also with the bounty that enables us, in considering the original sin and the whole history of the sins of humanity, and in considering the errors of the human intellect, will and heart, to repeat with amazement the words of the Sacred Liturgy: "O happy fault . . . which gained us so great a Redeemer!" (John Paul II, *Redemptor Hominis*)

THE IMMACULATE CONCEPTION OF MARY*

Scriptural Commentary

First Reading Gen 3:9-15,20.

In the theologically rich narrative of Genesis 2-3 the Yahwist faces up to the origin of sin and evil in our world.

He acknowledges that not God but mankind must shoulder responsibility—the mankind that would "go it alone" in vain quest of independence of God, the beneficent Creator. Our passage deals with the consequences of "the Fall."

Gerhard von Rad notes pertinently that, in dealing with this text, "one must proceed from the fact that it reflects quite realistically man's struggle with the real snake; but one must not stop there, for the things with which the narrator deals are basic." To the ancient biblical author, the snake seemed not only a dangerous creature but a mysterious one, the incarnation of evil and of cunning. He had gained one notable victory by deluding the woman under a guise of friendship. Henceforth she, and all her descendants, would wage unending struggle against evil—the snake and its offspring. The outcome of the struggle is none too clearly foretold by the text: while the serpent seems to come off worse, with its head trampled, it also presents a mortal threat to mankind, "snapping at our heels."

The patristic exegesis which hails this text as messianic prophecy (whereby Jesus crushes Satan's head through the power of the cross) reads far, far too much into what is, at best, a vaguely optimistic picture of man's struggle with evil. The interpretation which sees Mary, the "New Eve," in victorious combat with the devil is quite without foundation in the text. Yet, on the premise that "the New lies hidden in the Old," the church is entitled to nourish the Marian devotion of its members by such allusive use of the Genesis imagery.

Second Reading Eph 3:3-6,11-12.

The author elaborates on the theme enunciated in 1:3: "Blessed be the God and Father of our Lord . . . who has blessed us in Christ with every spiritual blessing." As servant of the Gospel, "Paul" sees that his task is to broadcast "the unsearchable riches of Christ." Indeed not only does he preach about "grace" (God's merciful plan for uniting mankind with himself through sending his Son as Saviour) but recognizes his ministry of preaching as itself a precious grace of God, to be strenuously exercised for others.

God's eternal purpose to "grace" mankind preceded the coming of Christ and prepared the way. In this light, the sinless holiness of Mary must be seen to prepare a fit dwelling-place for the Redeemer. "Paul sees all holiness as coming through Christ, indeed 'in Christ'; he does not reflect on the spiritual state of Mary, but had he wished to affirm her Immaculate Conception (as the church has done, *de congruo*), he would have enunciated the paradox: Before Jesus Christ was in Mary, according to the flesh (cf. Rom 1:3; Gal 4:4), she was in him according to the Spirit (cf. Gal 3:28; 4:6)" (P. Rogers).

Gospel Lk 1:26-38.

The full stream of divine favour is centred in Mary. The words of the angel evoke texts from the prophets, in particular Zephaniah and Zechariah. "Hail... the Lord is in your midst... have no fear... your Lord is in your womb" (Zeph 3:14-16; Zech 2:10; 9:9). The prophets speak to a personification of the people, the Daughter of Zion. Luke's use of this idea is instructive: Mary is presented as a corporate personality receiving and welcoming the Messiah. In the name of the people of Israel she received the announcement that the messianic age has come upon them. The coming of the Holy Spirit and his overshadowing of Mary highlight both the divine initiative and the beginning of the final process of salvation. It is also a way of presenting the idea of divine presence in Mary (cf. Ex 40:35). [See Fourth Sunday of Advent].

Patristic Commentary

Hesychius of Jerusalem (c.450), Hom. 5, PG 93.1464.
"Arise, Lord, into your rest and the ark of your sanctification (Ps 131:8), obviously the Virgin Mother of God. For if you

are a pearl, she is fittingly a treasure chest. Since you are the sun, the Virgin will necessarily be called the heavens. Since you happen to be the undecaying flower surely the Virgin will assuredly be the plant of incorruptibility, the garden of immortality, in regard to which, Isaiah, beholding these things immediately prophesied saying, "Behold the Virgin will conceive in her womb and bring forth a son, and they will call his name Emmanuel." (Is 7:14) Behold what kind of Virgin? The most select of women, the chosen one of the virgins, the venerable ornament of our nature, the glory of our clay, who has freed Eve from her shame and Adam from the threat of punishment, and cut to pieces the arrogance of the dragon. She whom the smoldering embers of concupiscence did not touch nor did the worm of soft living hurt her. "Behold the virgin shall conceive in her womb."

Insights from the Documents of the Church

Original Sin; Eve and Mary

Although set by God in a state of rectitude, man, enticed by the evil one, abused his freedom at the very start of history, He lifted himself up against God, and sought to attain his goal apart from him. Although they had known God, they did not glorify him as God, but their senseless hearts were darkened, and they served the creature rather than the creator. What Revelation makes known to us is, confirmed by our own experience. For when man looks into his own heart he finds that he is drawn towards what is wrong and sunk in many evils which cannot come from his good creator. Often refusing to acknowledge God as his source, man has also upset the relationship which should link him to his last end; and at the same time he has broken the right order that should reign within himself as well as between himself and other men and all creatures. (Vat. II, *Church in Modern World*, 13)

The Father of mercies willed that the Incarnation should be preceded by assent on the part of the predestined mother, so that just as a woman had a share in bringing about death, so also a woman should contribute to life. This is pre-eminently true of the Mother of Jesus, who gave to the world the Life that renews all things, and who was enriched by God with gifts appropriate to such a role. (Vat. II, *Church*, 56)

Not a few of the early Fathers gladly assert . . . "the knot of Eve's disobedience was untied by Mary's obedience: what the virgin Eve bound through her disbelief, Mary loosened by her faith." Comparing Mary with Eve, they call her "Mother of the living," and frequently claim: "death through Eve, life through Mary." (Vat. II, *Church*, 56)

Mary Pre-eminently Chosen and Holy

We believe that Mary is the ever-virgin mother of the Incarnate Word, our God and Saviour, Jesus Christ and that she was, in consideration of the merits of Christ, redeemed in a more exalted manner, preserved immune from all stain of original sin and by the gift of grace surpasses all other creatures. (Paul VI, *Profession of Faith*)

Redeemed, in a more exalted fashion, by reason of the merits of her Son and united to him by a close and indissoluble tie, she is endowed with the high office and dignity of the Mother of the Son of God, and therefore she is also the beloved daughter of the Father and the temple of the Holy Spirit. Because of this gift of sublime grace she far surpasses all creatures, both in heaven and on earth. (Vat. II, *Church*, 53).

Mary's Fiat and Divine Motherhood

This very mystery of the Redemption was effected—if we can thus express it—beneath the heart of the Virgin of Nazareth when she pronounced her "fiat." From that moment, under the special impulse of the Holy Spirit, her virginal and maternal heart was always involved in her Son's work and was open to all those whom Christ in his inexhaustible charity embraced and continues to embrace without ceasing. For this reason Mary's heart also must be endowed with inexhaustible mother's love. It is the mark of this maternal love by which the Mother of God is linked with the mystery of Redemption and the life of the Church that it is especially at hand to man and to all the needs. It is here that the mystery of the Mother lies.(John Paul II, *Redemptor Hominis*, 22)

CHRISTMAS

CHRISTMAS DAY: MASS AT MIDNIGHT

Scriptural Commentary

First Reading Is 9:1-7.

Isaiah speaks in prophecy of a Davidic son and heir—a prophecy made during a dark period in Israel's history, probably after the Assyrian king had conquered northern Galilee and annexed it to his own domain. Through that darkness Isaiah glimpses the advent of a son of David who will redeem his people, in a manner reminiscent of that earlier victory over the marauding Midianites (Jg 7:1; 8:21). The promise of the coming of the son of David and of a great light to shine upon "Galilee of the Gentiles" was fulfilled in Jesus (Mt 4:13-16).

Second Reading Titus 2:11-14.

A reminder that what started at Bethlehem is an ongoing process in which each of us must be involved. We must live lives worthy of our true selves in preparation for the second coming of Christ. Salvation is offered to *all*. Those who have experienced the gift of salvation will live as children of God. While christian hope is fixed on the certain coming of the "great God and Saviour," christian conduct will be shaped according to his way. The challenge of his way is formidable because *he gave himself*. Thereby he won a people for himself. In no different way can Christians win others to fellowship with his people.

Gospel Lk 2:1-14.

Throughout the first chapters of his gospel, while dealing with the annunciations of the births of John and of Jesus and with the birth of the Baptist, Luke's narrative has remained within the Jewish world. Now, at the beginning of the second chapter, when he comes to the birth of him who is "a light for revelation to the Gentiles" (2:32), his perspective opens, if only for a moment, on to the Gentile world. His eyes have glanced from the Jerusalem of the beginning of the gospel to the Rome of the last chapter of Acts. The birth of the Saviour of all mankind is fixed—though perhaps too vaguely for our taste—in the calendar of world history.

Mary gave birth to her "first-born son" (v.7). Since we are told that the newborn babe was laid in a manger, we learn that Joseph and Mary had found shelter in a stable of some sort. A tradition going back to the second century specifies a cave. These circumstances emphasize the lowliness and poverty that surrounded the birth of Jesus; nothing here suggests the power and glory of his divinity.

In Lk 7:22 we learn that one of the signs given to the Baptist whereby he might know that Jesus was indeed the Messiah was that "the poor have the good news preached to them." So it was that the first announcement of Jesus' birth was made to simple shepherds: these, the poor and humble, despised by the orthodox as non-observers of the Law, are granted and accept the revelation which the leaders of Israel will reject. The short canticle (v.14) is closely related to the acclamation of the crowd at Jesus' entry into Jerusalem (19:38). It would seem that "Glory to God" expresses not so much a wish ("let God be glorified") as a statement, a recognition of the significance of the hour, an acknowledgement of the saving act of God. The meaning of v.14 is that through the birth of the Messiah God is glorified in heaven (that is, his power and majesty are manifest) and, on earth, the people whom he loves receive the divine blessing of peace, the peace which the Saviour has brought.

Patristic Commentary

Ephraim the Syrian (c. 306-373)
Hymn of the Nativity. LPNF 13². 232.

With the weapon of the deceiver the First-born clad Himself, so that with the weapon that killed, He might restore to life again! With the tree wherewith he slew us, He delivered us. With the wine which maddened us, with it we were made chaste! With the rib that was drawn out of Adam, the wicked one drew out the heart of Adam. There rose from the Rib a hidden power, which cut off Satan as Dagon: for in that Ark a book was hidden that cried and proclaimed concerning the Conqueror! There was then a mystery revealed, in that Dagon was brought low in his own place of refuge! The accomplishment came after the type, in that the wicked one was brought low in the place in which he trusted! Blessed be He Who came and in Him were accomplished the mysteries of the left hand, and the right hand. Fulfilled was the mystery that was in the Lamb, and fulfilled was the type that was in Dagon. Blessed is He Who by the True Lamb redeemed us, and destroyed our destroyer as He did Dagon! In December when the nights are long, rose unto us the Day, of Whom there is no bound! In winter when all the world is gloomy, came forth the Fair One Who cheered all in the world! In winter that makes the earth barren, virginity learned to bring forth. In December, that causes the travails of the earth to cease, in it were the travails of virginity. The early lamb no one ever used to see before the shepherds: and as for the true Lamb, in the season of His birth, the tidings of Him too hasted unto the shepherds. That old wolf saw the sucking Lamb, and he trembled before Him, though He had concealed himself; for because the wolf had put on sheep's clothing, the Shepherd of all became a Lamb in the flocks, in order that when the greedy one had been bold against the Meek, the Mighty One might rend that Eater. The Holy One dwelt bodily in the womb; and He dwelt spiritually in the mind. Mary that conceived Him abhorred the marriage bed; let not that soul commit whoredom in the which He dwelleth. Because Mary perceived Him, she left her betrothed: He dwelleth in chaste virgins, if they perceive Him. The deaf perceive not the mighty thunder, neither does the heady man the sound of the commandment. For the deaf is bewildered in the time of the thunderclap, the heady man is bewildered also at the voice of instruction; if fearful thunder terrifies the deaf, then would fearful wrath stir the unclean! That the deaf hears not is no blame to him; but whoso tramples [on the commandments] it is headiness. From time to time there is thunder: but the voice of the law thunders every day. Let us not close our ears when their openings, as being opened and not closed against it, accuse us; and the door of hearing is open by nature, that it might reproach us for our headiness against our will. The door of the voice and the door of the mouth our will can open or close. Let us see what the Good One has given us; and let us hear the mighty Voice, and let not the doors of our ears be closed.

Glory to that Voice Which became Body, and to the Word of the High One Which became Flesh! Hear Him also, O ears, and see Him, O eyes, and feel Him, O hands, and eat Him, O mouth! Ye members and senses give praise unto Him, that came and quickened the whole body!

Insights from the Documents of the Church

Our Lady at Christmas

The Christmas Season is a prolonged commemoration of the divine, virginal and salvific Motherhood of her whose "inviolate virginity brought the Saviour into the world." In fact, on the Solemnity of the Birth of Christ the Church both adores the Saviour and venerates his glorious Mother (Paul VI To Honour Mary [*Marialis Cultus*])

A True Incarnation

Jesus Christ was sent into the world as the true Mediator between God and men. Since he is God, all the fullness of the divine nature dwells in him bodily (Col 2:9); as man he is the new Adam, full of grace and truth (Jn 1:14), who has been constituted head of a restored humanity. So the Son of God entered the world by means of a true incarnation that he might make men sharers in the divine nature; though rich, he was made poor for our sake, that by his poverty we might become rich (2 Cor 8:9). The Son of man did not come to be served, but to serve and to give his life as a ransom for many, that is for all (cf. Mk 10:45). The fathers of the Church constantly proclaim that what was not assumed by Christ was not healed. Now Christ took a complete human nature just as it is found in us poor unfortunates, but one that was without sin (cf. Heb 4:15; 9:28). Christ, whom the Father sanctified and sent into the world (cf. Jn 10:36), said of himself: "The Spirit of the Lord is upon me, because he annointed me; to bring good news to the poor he sent me, to heal the broken-hearted, to proclaim to the captive release, and sight to the blind" (Lk 4:8); and on another occasion: "The Son of man has come to seek and to save what was lost" (Lk 9:10).

Now, what was once preached by the Lord, or fulfilled in him for the salvation of mankind, must be proclaimed and spread to the ends of the earth (Acts 1:8), starting from Jerusalem (cf. Lk 24:27), so that what was accomplished for the salvation of all men may, in the course of time, achieve its universal effect. (Vat. II, The Church's Missionary Activity, No. 3)

CHRISTMAS DAY: MASS AT DAWN

Scriptural Commentary

First Reading Is 62:11-12.

Totally destroyed in 587 B.C., Zion, the holy city of Jerusalem, lay in ruins for more than half a century. The city's plight surely spoke the ruin of the Jewish nation and its abandonment by God—so it must have seemed. But the Lord had not abandoned his people. Israel, figured by Jerusalem, "the daughter of Zion," was his spouse; he was her redeemer who would rebuild the city and the nation. In our reading (the closing verses of the song 62:1-12), God solemnly proclaims that he is coming to save. Israel will once again be his people and a new Jerusalem will replace the old. The names given to both the nation ("the holy people") and the city ("sought out") express this new happy state of affairs. Note the contrasting names in an earlier part of the song: "You shall no more be termed Forsaken, and your land shall no more be termed Desolate; but you shall be called My-delight-is-in-her and your land Married" (v.4). God's saving visitation happens in the birth of Jesus, his coming to a new people and to a new Jerusalem, the Church.

Second Reading Titus 3:4-7.

In order to savour the refreshingly positive and downright optimistic tone of this passage, one should have in view the immediately preceding verse: "For we ourselves were once foolish, disobedient, led astray, slaves to various passions and pleasures, passing our days in malice and envy, hated by men and hating one another" (v.3). That is what we *were; now* God has lavished his goodness and his loving kindness upon us. The author is thinking of a change from paganism to new life in Christ. All of us can acknowledge that we stand in need of conversion, and the loving kindness of our Saviour can work wonders with us—if we would be open to him. The reading looks on the incarnation as a visitation of God's kindness and love—literally, of his "philanthropy," his love for men. This is seen in the fact that God first loved us, loved us while we were sinners. He cleanses us from our sins in baptism, in which we are given new life and become heirs of the kingdom of heaven.

Gospel Lk 2:15-20.

(Conclusion of the passage read at Midnight Mass). Marvelling at their strange experience (vv.8-14), stirred to excited anticipation by the angels' word, the shepherds set out in haste to Bethlehem. There they found that the facts were just as the angels had described. Naturally, they spoke freely of what they had seen and of the things that had been told them. If anything of this had come to the ears of "the wise" they put no stock in the "delusions" of these simple men. But one, at least, forgot none of these happenings: Mary kept in her heart the events and words and pondered over them (cf. 2:51). Her understanding of these events was not total; she had to ponder them in the quiet of her heart. In his customary manner, Luke winds up the episode by noting the return of the shepherds to their flocks. Despite the splendour of angelic manifestation and heavenly glory, they got down again to their humdrum task—but they went on their way "glorifying and praising God."

Patristic Commentary

St. Jerome (c.347-c.420)
On the Lord's Nativity. CCL 78.526, FOTC 57.224.

"The shepherds said to one another, 'Let us go over to Bethlehem'." Let us leave the deserted Temple and go over to Bethlehem. "And see the word which was made"(Lk 2:15). Truly alert, they did not say, Let us see the child, let us find out what is being announced; but: "Let us see the word that has been made." "In the beginning was the Word." "And the Word was made flesh." The Word that has always been, let us see how it was made for us. "And let us see this word which was made, which the Lord has made, and has made known to us." This same Word made itself inasmuch as this same Word is the Lord. Let us see, therefore, in what way this same Word, the Lord Himself, has made Himself and has made His flesh known to us. Because we could not see Him as long as He was the Word, let us see His flesh because it is flesh; let us see how the Word was made flesh.

"So they went with haste." The ardent longing of their souls gave wings to their feet; they could not keep pace with their yearning to see Him: "So they went with haste." Because they ran so eagerly, they find Him whom they sought.

Let us see what they find. "Mary and Joseph." (Lk 2:16) If she were truly wife, it would be improper to say, they found the wife and the husband; but the Gospel named the woman first, then the man, What does Holy Writ say? "They found Mary and Joseph": they found Mary, the mother, and Joseph, the guardian. "And the babe lying in the manger. And when they had seen, they understood concerning the word, what had been told them concerning this child. But Mary kept in mind all these words, pondering them in her heart." (Lk 2:16-19) What does pondering mean? It must have meant weighing carefully in her heart, meditating within herself, and, in her heart, comparing notes. A certain exegete explains, "pondering in her heart" thus: She was a holy woman, had read the Sacred Scriptures, knew the prophets, and was recalling that the angel Gabriel had said to her the same things that the prophets had foretold. She was pondering in her heart whether the prophets anticipated the words: "The Holy Spirit shall come upon thee and the power of the Most High shall overshadow thee; and therefore the Holy One to be born shall be called the Son of God." (Lk 1:35) Gabriel had said that; Isaia had foretold: "The virgin shall be with child, and bear a son." (Is 7:14) She had read the latter; she had heard the former. She looked upon the child lying before her; she saw in the manger the child crying; she saw there the Son of God, her Son, her one and only Son; she looked upon Him, and in her pondering, she compared what she had heard with what she had read and with what she herself perceived.

Since she was pondering in her heart, let us, likewise, meditate in our hearts that on this day Christ is born. There are some who think that He was born on Epiphany. We do not censure the opinion of others, but follow the conclusions of our own study. "Let everyone be convinced in his own mind and perhaps the Lord will reveal to each one." Both they who say the Lord is born then, and we who say He is born today, worship one Lord, acknowledge one Babe.

Insights from the Documents of the Church

God With Us
You are with us! Emmanuel!

In a way that really surpasses everything that man could have thought of you. You are with us as Man.

You are wonderful, truly wonderful, O God, Creator and Lord of the universe, God with the Father Almighty! The Logos! the only Son!

God of power! You are with us as man, as a newborn baby of the human race, absolutely weak, wrapped in swaddling clothes and placed in a manger, "because there was no place for them" in any inn (Lk 2:7).

Wonderful! Messenger of Great Counsel!

Is it not precisely because you became man in this way, came into the world in this way, without a roof to shelter you, that you became nearest to man?

Is it not precisely because you yourself, the newborn Jesus, are without a roof that you are nearest to those brothers and sisters of ours who are homeless or otherwise in need? And the people who really come to their aid are precisely the ones who have you in their hearts, you who were born at Bethlehem without a home.

Is it not precisely because from the first days of your life you were threatened with death at the hands of Herod that you are particularly close, the closest, to those who are threatened in any way, those who die at the hands of murderers, those who are denied basic human rights?

And still more: is it not for this reason that you are closer to those whose life is already threatened in their mother's womb?

O truly Wonderful! The God of power in his weakness as a child.

From all parts of Rome and of the world we are setting out towards you. We are being drawn by your birth at Bethlehem. Could you have done anything more than you have done, in order to be Emmanuel, God with us? Anything more than what our amazed eyes behold: the eyes of the people of the different parts of the world, the different countries and continents, the different parts of every geographical longitude and latitude, in the same way as once the eyes of Mary, of Joseph, and then the eyes of the Shepherds and of the Wise Men from the East beheld!

Truly blessed are the eyes that see what you see! (John Paul II, "Urbi et Orbi" Message from St. Peter's Basilica, Christmas Day, 1980, slightly adapted.)

CHRISTMAS DAY: MASS DURING THE DAY.*

Scriptural Commentary

First Reading Is 52:7-10.

"Good Tidings" or "Good News" was the message of hope addressed by the prophet to a people wilting under sadness, depression and despair. God's city was in ruins; his chosen people on the brink of extinction. They had reaped the dire harvest of sin. However—and this prophet is confidently sure of it—God is still in charge of his world. There is no cause for despair; Yahweh will restore his people to a better life. This "Old Testament Gospel" prepared for the coming of Christ, the Saviour.

Second Reading Heb 1:1-6.

The first four verses of the letter to the Hebrews (one sentence in the Greek) are an eloquent statement of what God has done in his Son. God had not been sparing of his revelation in the past ("in many and various ways"); but all his words through the prophets have been surpassed by his new word spoken in a Son. And, with the coming of that Son breaks the eschatological age ("in these last days"); Christians live in this new age. The Son is heir of all things; through him the world was made (cf. Jn 1:3). He is the reflection of God's glory and bears the very stamp of his nature—ideas suggested by Wis 7:25-26; he is the adequate expression of the Father (cf. Jn 14:9), one who alone knows the Father and can make him known (cf. Jn 1:18; 4:25, 14:9). High Priest of the New Covenant, he has made purification for sins by the offering of himself, and now takes his proper place at God's right hand. The name he has received—Son of God—and his exaltation to the throne of God, place him immeasurably above the angels.

The Gospel Jn 1:1-18.

John's prologue, like that of Hebrews, tells us of the eternal existence of Christ and of his incarnation. The Word who abode with God before creation took an active part in the creation of all things (1-3). The Word imparted a share in the divine life, and an illumination that would lead to God (v.4). Men rejected the illumination granted by the Word, but darkness, that is, a world estranged from God, did not fully overcome the light (v.5). It is incomprehensible, but sadly true, that when the Word who is the source of light and life came and lived among his own people they on the whole refused to believe in him (vv.10-11). But those who believed, he made to be children of God (vv.12-13).

The Prologue reaches its climax in v.14 with its un-equivocal statement of the incarnation. The Word who dwelt with God took on the lowliness of earthly existence in order to make revelation more accessible to humankind. Those who lived with Jesus witnessed the works which manifested the glory that rightly belonged to him as Son of God. They could say of him that he was "full of grace and truth." What could be said of the God of the Covenant may now be said of Jesus Christ. [See Second Sunday after Christmas].

Patristic Commentary

St. Augustine (354-430)
Hom 190. PL 38.1007, ACW15,102.

Let us, therefore, Brethren, keep this day with due solemnity; not, like those who are without faith, on account of the sun, but because of Him who made the sun. For He who was *the Word, was made flesh,* (Jn 1:14) that for our sakes He might be under the sun. Under the sun, to be sure, in His flesh; but in His majesty, over the whole universe in which He made the sun. And now, too, He, incarnate, stands above that sun which is worshipped as god by those who, intellectually blind, do not see the true Sun of Justice.

Let us, then, Christians, celebrate this day, not as that of His divine birth, but of His human birth, namely, the birth by which He was obedient to us, so that through the Invisible made visible, we may pass from visible things to the invisible. With our Catholic faith we ought to hold fast that the Lord has two births, the one divine, the other human; the one outside time, the other in time. Both, moreover, are extraordinary: the one without a mother, the other without a father. If we fail to grasp the latter, when shall we explain the first? Who can grasp this prodigy of prodigies, so unique and unprecedented in the world, this incredible thing made credible and, transcending belief, believed in the whole world: that a virgin conceived, a virgin gave birth, a virgin remained virgin when she gave birth?

What human reason cannot solve, faith comprehends; and where human reason fails, faith advances. Indeed, who would say that the Word of God through whom all things have been made, could not have made human flesh for Himself, even without a mother, just as He made the first man without a father and mother?

But because He Himself certainly had created both sexes, that is, male and female, even by His being born He wished to honor the sexes which He had come to free. Let both sexes, therefore, be reborn in Him who was born to-day. Let both sexes celebrate this day, the day on which Christ the Lord did not begin to exist, but on which He, who had always been with His Father, brought into the light of this world the flesh which He received from His Mother. Thus He gave fruitfulness to His mother, but He did not take away her virginity.

Insights from the Documents of the Church

How beautiful are the feet: evangelization the heart of the matter.

The church is keenly aware of this: she realizes that the words of the Saviour: "I must preach the good news of the kingdom of God" have a direct application to herself. And with St. Paul she freely declares: "If I preach the gospel, that gives me no cause for boasting. For necessity is laid upon me. Woe to me if I do not preach the gospel." It was accordingly for us a great joy and consolation at the close of the great assembly of bishops in the month of October 1974 to hear those inspiring words: "We wish to affirm once more that the essential mission of the church is to evangelize all men." It is a task and mission which the great and fundamental changes of contemporary society make all the more urgent. Evangelization is the special grace and vocation of the church. It is her essential function. The church exists to preach the gospel, that is to preach and teach the word of God so that through her the gift of grace may be given to us, sinners may be reconciled to God, and the sacrifice of the Mass, the memorial of his glorious death and resurrection, may be perpetuated.

Anyone who reads through the pages of the New Testament and reflects on the beginnings of the church, considering her amazing development and the nature of her life and activity, cannot fail to realize that evangelization is inherent in the very nature of the church.

The church takes its origin from the work of evangelization by Christ and the twelve apostles. Of this work she is the natural fruition. She is the end to which this work was directed, its immediate and most striking achievement: "Go, therefore, and make disciples of all nations." And further: "Those who received the word were baptized and there were added that day about three thousand souls . . . and the Lord added to their numbers day by day those who were being saved." (Paul VI, Evangelization Today [*Evangelii Nuntiandi*])

He has spoken through his son

Christ, then, reveals God who is Father who is "love," as Saint John will express it in his First Letter; Christ reveals God as "rich in mercy," as we read in Saint Paul. This truth is not just the subject of a teaching; it is a reality made present to us by Christ. *Making the Father present as love and mercy* is, in Christ's own consciousness, the fundamental touchstone of his mission as the Messiah; this is confirmed by the words that he uttered first in the synagogue at Nazareth and later in the presence of his disciples and of John the Baptist's messengers. (John Paul II, On the Mercy of God [*Dives in Misericordia*])

John came as witness

Finally, the man who has been evangelized becomes himself an evangelizer. This is the proof, the test of the genuineness of his own conversion. It is conceivable that a man who has received the word and surrendered himself to the kingdom should not himself become a witness and proclaimer of the truth. (Paul VI, Evangelization Today [*Evangelii Nuntiandi*])

THE HOLY FAMILY.
Sunday Within the Octave of Christmas
Scriptural Commentary

First Reading Ecclus 3:2-6, 12-14.

The author of Ephesians remarks that the commandment "Honour your father and your mother" (Ex 20:12) is the first commandment that carries a promise: "that it may be well with you and that you may live long on the earth" (Eph 6:2-3; cf. Ex 20:12). Our first reading, from one of the latest of the wisdom writings (about 180 B.C.), the work of Jesus ben Sirach, reminds us that God is the upholder of the rights of parents. He maintains that honour and respect for parents atones for sins and will cause one's prayers to be heard. Above all, Sirach insists that respect be shown them in their old age and that they be helped and supported. He asserts that kindness to parents is especially pleasing to God who, he repeats, will accept it as atonement for one's sins.

Second Reading Col 3:12-21.

Harmony in the family depends on the proper attitude of all its members, not just on the obedience of the children. The author speaks of the virtues proper to the christian family—which he considers within the larger context of the christian community: God's chosen people called to a life of holiness. In baptism Christians rise to a new life in Christ; and this reality should shine forth in their everyday living. Christ has died to bring unity and to remove hatred and every other obstacle that impedes harmonious relations. Unity can become a reality in living only if the basis for it exists in the human heart: love, kindness, forgiveness, humility, patience and gentleness. The new life proper to believers should be notably evident in the family, expressed in love between husband and wife, by reverence for parents on the part of children, and by deep understanding of

children on the part of parents—a christian understanding
that will permit them to develop as human beings and keep
them from feeling frustrated. "Paul" puts the ideal family
spirit very clearly before us—a spirit of love, compassion,
mutual forgiveness—and insists that we are called to this
high ideal, as God's chosen people.

Gospel Lk 2:22-40.

In 2:22-24 Luke has combined two distinct Israelite
customs: (1) consecration or presentation of the child to
the Lord (Ex 13:1, 11-16); (2) purification of the mother
after the birth of a child (Lev 12:1-8). Luke's text gives
evidence of his general knowledge of these customs and
of his inaccurate grasp of details.

It was fitting that the Lord, on entering his Temple for the
first time, be greeted by a representative of the prophets.
This role was filled by Simeon, the righteous and devout,
who awaited, with faith and patience, the fulfilment of
the hope of Israel, its "consolation" (cf. Is 40:1). The Holy
Spirit had moved him to visit the temple and had revealed
to him that the infant who was at this moment being
presented there was indeed the longed-for Messiah.
Simeon's Nunc Dimittis introduces the theme of salvation
for the Gentiles (cf. Is 42:6; 52:10). In the second oracle
(2:34-35) Simeon anticipates the rejection of Jesus by the
Jewish authorities and the rejection of the christian mission
to Israel as described in Acts. "Simeon announces the
sufferings which would accompany the unfolding of the
fulfilment, sufferings manifested in the passion of Jesus
but also in the life of the post-ascension community (2:34-
35). Luke's readers should thus be able to situate their own
sufferings with regard to their origins, which entailed the
fall and the rising of many in Israel (see 20:17-18). The sword
which pierced the soul of the mother of the first-born was
piercing that of the Church, the mother of all who shared
his life" (E.LaVerdiere, *Luke*, 36).

After a prophet a prophetess—the delicate hand of Luke—and yet again (implicitly this time) the Spirit of prophecy. Anna, now eighty-four, having lost her husband seven years after an early marriage, had preferred to remain a widow. She practically lived in the Temple, so uninterrupted were her prayers. Her prophetic instinct enabled her to recognize the infant Messiah and, gratefully, she spoke of him to those who, like Simeon and herself (typical saints of Judaism, the *anawim*, the "poor of Yahweh") looked for the salvation of Jerusalem (Is 52:9), that is, of Israel, God's people. The presence of Anna with her conviction of redemption permits Luke to close on a positive note. The conclusion of the episode (2:39-40) prepares the reader for the appearance of Jesus of Nazareth (ch. 4).

Patristic Commentary

St. Paulinus of Nola (353-431).
Poem 24, CSEL 30.234, ACW 40.241.

Just as Joseph, that holy man of God journeyed over the land of Memphis, stacked its luxuriant and fertile resources in enlarged granaries, and with the abundance of blessings from the years of plenty provided food for the era of famine, so this son of ours must traverse God's kingdom in the consecrated books. For the breath of the Holy Spirit breathes over Scripture, which is the mother of the eternal kingdom. I pray that the Spirit with His Spiritual care may make provision by erecting huge granaries within the boy's mind, so that he may store in distended heart abundant provisions for a lasting life. When he has made his land rich in life's sustenance, then you will enjoy as a second Israel in your old age to enjoy your son's dominion, and you will gladly enter there together with your retinue of relatives whom he has summoned (cf. Gen 42:1).

Your son will feed your aged frame with the bread he has obtained in the house of the King. Just so the eagle's young is said to feed and tend its parents in return when the onset of age has stripped them of their feathers and confines them to feeding in their nest. Then their bodies gain a covering of fresh feathers, and they blossom out with new wings. By a strange law of nature, the aged birds are transformed with the aid of their offspring into fledglings. Then, once their youth is purged of its senility and has made new birds of them, schooled by their offspring they learn afresh to use their unpractised wings as oars. They take pleasure in cutting serene paths through the bright heavens with lazy motion, fanning peacefully the translucent air. In line, their wings at rest, they alternately follow and lead each other, and group to form a circle.

How blessed a root is your saintly offspring, how fruitful a branch of a goodly tree! You gave your son to God to nurture, and God rears him for you in such a way that the boy in his turn nurtures his white-haired parents, so that the child is become your master in your old age. Through the wonderful mystery of love, he has become his parents' parent. So later all of you, the whole retinue of your holy family, will fly up to join the body of that Head in which the saints will gather like the eagles.

Insights from the Documents of the Church

The Family's Role in Christian Catechesis.

The family's catechetical activity has a special character, which is in a sense irreplaceable. This special character has been rightly stressed by the Church, particularly by the Second Vatican Council. Education in the faith by parents, which should begin from the children's tenderest age, is already being given when the members of a family help each other to grow in faith through the witness of their Christian lives, a witness that is often without words but which perseveres throughout a day-to-day life lived in accordance with the Gospel. This catechesis is more incisive when, in the course of family events (such as the reception of the sacraments, the celebration of great liturgical feasts, the birth of a child, a bereavement) care is taken to explain in the home the Christian or religious content of these events. But that is not enough: Christian parents must strive to follow and repeat, within the setting of family life, the more methodical teaching received elsewhere. The fact that these truths about the main questions of faith and Christian living are thus repeated within a family setting impregnated with love and respect will often make it possible to influence the children in a decisive way for life. The parents themselves profit from the effort that this demands of them, for in a catechetical dialogue of this sort each individual both receives and gives.

Family catechesis therefore precedes, accompanies and enriches all other forms of catechesis. Furthermore, in places where anti-religious legislation endeavours even to prevent education in the faith, and in places where widespread unbelief or pervasive secularism makes real religious growth practically impossible, "the Church of the home" remains the one place where children and young people can receive an authentic catechesis. Thus there cannot be too great an effort on the part of Christian parents for this ministry of being their own children's catechists and to carry it out with tireless zeal. Encouragement must also be given to the individual or institutions that, through person-to-person contacts, through meetings, and through all kinds of pedagogical means, help parents to perform their task: the service they are doing to catechesis is beyond price. (John Paul II, *Catechesis in our Time*, no. 68)

Our Lady at Christmas

On the Feast of the Holy Family of Jesus, Mary and Joseph (the Sunday within the octave of Christmas) the

Church meditates with profound reverence upon the holy life led in the house at Nazareth by Jesus, the Son of God and Son of Man, Mary his Mother, and Joseph the just man (cf. Mt 1:19). (Paul VI, To Honour Mary [*Marialis Cultus*])

SOLEMNITY OF MARY MOTHER OF GOD.*
Octave of Christmas.

Scriptural Commentary

First Reading Num 6:22-27.

In this first reading we have the formula used by the Jewish priests ("Aaron and his sons") when they called down God's blessing on Israel. Their prayer was that God would *bless Israel and keep it*: that he would bring it happiness and well-being and protect it through his divine providence. They prayed that God would *let his face shine* on his people by being gracious to them. To pray that his face shine on mankind was to ask God to let them experience his goodness, his loving providence. *And give you peace*: a prayer that God may bring peace to mankind, peace in the rich Jewish meaning of that word—happiness and well-being, both material and spiritual; in short, the good life that God has intended for mankind from the beginning. What the priest invoked in this blessing was really what revealed religion is all about: divine favour and friendship and the happiness and well-being flowing from these. At first sight, this blessing may not seem to fit the theme of today's celebration: Mary's divine motherhood. Yet, it can be shown that the combination of readings neatly gets the theme across. The priests, in blessing Israel, prayed that God would let his face shine on them and bring them peace (first reading: responsorial psalm); "in the fullness of time" this prayer was realized through the birth of the Son "born of a woman" (second reading); the shepherds, first witnesses of the fulfilment, found the Child "with Mary his mother" (Gospel).

Second Reading Gal 4:4-7.

With Christ and in Christ the appointed time has dawned. God who had spoken to Israel "in many and various ways" now speaks his final word "by a Son" (cf. Heb 1:1-2). Throughout Galatians Paul explains what that means for mankind. In Christ the promises made to Abraham have been fulfilled, promises intended for all, not for Israel only. Fulfilment means that we are children of God, brothers and sisters of Christ and co-heirs with him. Believers are made conscious of the reality of this new liberty and dignity by the Holy Spirit who leads them to address their Father in the same intimate way that Jesus did: *Abba*. We do need both the example of Jesus and the help of the Spirit to appreciate the dignity of our status. While, christologically this is a rich text it seems, mariologically, pale. It asserts that Jesus is true man because he was "born of woman" and true Son of God because God is his Father. Read against the infancy gospels of Matthew and Luke it implies that Mary is in truth Mother of God.

Gospel Lk 2:16-21.

The shepherds, hastening to Bethlehem, found that the splendour of angelic manifestation and heavenly glory (2:9-14) was not reflected in what they found there: a woman and a man gazing on a new-born babe lying in a manger. In contrast to the shepherds, bubbling over with tidings and praise (vv.17-18), the mother, Mary, pondered in silent meditation. Luke implies that she, more than any other, penetrated the mystery of Jesus' birth because she took it so much to heart. Down the centuries priests had prayed that God would look kindly on Israel and give his peace. The psalmist (Ps 66) prayed that all the earth would see the salvation of Israel's God. At Bethlehem it all happened. The divine light shone about the shepherds at the Saviour's birth and the angels brought the good tidings of peace and joy. Fulfilment had come of one born of a woman, born a subject of the law of Moses. And to show the reality of his subjection to the law, Jesus was circumcised on the eighth day—as the law prescribed (Lev 12:2-8).

Patristic Commentary

St. John of Damascus (c. 675-c.749)
Orthodox Faith. Book 4, c.6. PG 94.1112, FOTC 37.340.

Not as some falsely hold was the mind united to God the Word before the taking on of flesh from the Virgin and from that time called Christ. This absurdity results from the nonsense of Origen's teaching of the pre-existence of souls. We say that the Son and Word of God became Christ the instant that He came to dwell in the womb of the holy Ever-Virgin and was made flesh without undergoing change, the instant that the flesh was anointed with the divinity. For, as Gregory the Theologian says, there was such an anointing. Likewise, the most holy Cyril of Alexandria, in writing to Emperor Theodosius, said as follows: "I say that neither the Word of God as distinct from the humanity, nor the temple born of woman as not united to the Word, may be called Christ Jesus. The Word which is from God is considered to be Christ when ineffably brought together with the humanity in the union of the dispensation." And to the empresses he writes thus: "There are some who say that the name Christ properly belongs to the Word only as considered in Himself as existing begotten of God the Father. But we have not been taught to think or talk in that way, because it is when the Word was made flesh that we say that He received the name of Christ Jesus.

For, since He was anointed with the oil of gladness, that is to say, anointed with the Spirit by God the Father, for this reason is He called Christ, or Anointed. That the anointing was of the humanity no right minded person would doubt." And the renowned Athanasius says to this effect, somewhere in his discourse on the saving coming of Christ: "God (the Word) as existing before coming to dwell in the flesh was not man but God with God, being invisible and impassible. But, when He became man, He took the name Christ, because the passion and death are consequent upon this name."

Insights from the Documents of the Church

Our Lady and Peace

In the revised ordering of the Christmas period it seems to us that the attention of all should be directed towards the restored Solemnity of Mary the holy Mother of God. This celebration, placed on 1 January in conformity with the ancient indication of the liturgy of the City of Rome, is meant to commemorate the part played by Mary in this mystery of salvation. It is meant also to exalt the singular dignity which this mystery brings to the "holy Mother . . . through whom we were found worthy to receive the Author of Life." It is likewise a fitting occasion for renewing adoration to the newborn Prince of Peace, for listening once more to the glad tidings of the angels (cf. Lk 2:14), and for imploring from God, through the Queen of Peace, the supreme gift of peace. It is for this reason that, in the happy concurrence of the Octave of Christmas and the first day of the year, we have instituted the World Day of Peace, an occasion that is gaining increasing support and already bringing forth fruits of peace in the hearts of many. (Paul VI, To Honour Mary [*Marialis Cultus*])

Mary pondered in her heart

It was faith with which she, who played a part in the Incarnation and was a unique witness to it, thinking back on the events of the infancy of Christ, meditated upon these events in her heart (cf. Lk 2:19, 51). The Church also acts in this way, especially in the liturgy, when with faith she listens, accepts, proclaims and venerates the word of God, distributes it to the faithful as the bread of life and in the light of that word examines the signs of the times and interprets and lives the events of history. (Paul VI, To Honour Mary [*Marialis Cultus*])

SECOND SUNDAY AFTER CHRISTMAS*

Scriptural Commentary

First Reading Ecclus 24:1-2, 8-12.

The poem in praise of wisdom (24:1-31) is one of those rich and evocative Old Testament Wisdom texts which laid the groundwork for the Johannine theology of Jesus as the Logos—the Word. In Proverbs 8:22-31 and Job 28:12-27 Wisdom is personified: it existed before the visible world and was present with God at creation. Later texts like Ecclus 24 and Wisdom 7:22 - 8:1 attribute an active role to Wisdom in the creation of the world. The fact that Ecclus 24:23 explicitly identifies Wisdom with the Torah— God's "instruction" to Israel—helps us to understand today's reading which stresses the pre-existence of Wisdom ("from eternity, in the beginning, he created me") and its special presence in Israel ("make your dwelling in Jacob; I was established in Zion").

Because Wisdom (or the Torah) guided the lives of the people of Israel they were privileged above all peoples.

God had clearly made his will known to them and had pointed out the way that would lead to salvation. In spite of the fact that the sages of Israel personified Wisdom and seem to refer to it as something outside God and operating independently of him, it would be quite wrong to think that they ever regarded Wisdom as a divine person distinct from Yahweh. Such an idea would be incompatible with their strict monotheism. If they personified Wisdom and spoke of its pre-existence they did so only to depict poetically and vividly God's plan for the whole created world. Such speculation did, however, prepare for the christian doctrine of the pre-existence of Jesus (cf. Jn 1:1-18).

Second Reading Eph 1:3-6, 15-18.
    Our reading is formed of a blessing (1:3-14) and thanksgiving (1:15-16) leading into an intercession (1:17 - 2:22). The initial blessing is modelled on the Jewish *berakah*, a "blessing" of God in response to his previous "blessing." The blessing of Ephesians mentions the major themes of the letter and might be seen as a résumé of the letter. The God of Christians is the Father of our Lord Jesus Christ—the God who has revealed himself in Jesus. To acknowledge Jesus as Lord is to recognize God as Father (v.3). God has chosen Christians for a purpose: to be holy and blameless before him—in simple words, to be like him (v.4). We are predestined to be children of God, and we become God's children "through Jesus Christ." It is Jesus Christ who has revealed not only that God is Father but also how we are to realize our own divine sonship. If we Christians accept Jesus as "Lord," as the supreme influence in our lives, we must accept his view of God and acknowledge him as our Father.
    In vv.15-16 we have the writer's prayer of thanksgiving for his readers' faith and love, which runs, almost at once, into a prayer of intercession. He prays that his readers may really "know" the "hope" to which they have been called (vv.17-18). He thus implies that, despite their faith and

love, they still have to progress in their vocation. An understanding of the "mystery"—God's plan of salvation— is possible only as gift of God. (See Fifteenth Sunday of the Year).

Gospel Jn 1:1-18.

Whatever may be said about the origins of the Prologue (most likely a pre-existing hymn) it now forms a fitting introduction to the Fourth Gospel since it tells us about the divine and eternal origins of him whose ministry is described in the following chapters. One cannot understand the unique significance of Jesus' message of salvation unless one is aware of his mysterious provenance.

The first words of John's gospel recall Gen 1:1. In the Old Testament God's word manifested him: in creation, in deeds of power, in prophecy. John shows that Jesus Christ, the incarnate Word, is the ultimate revelation of God. The truth that all things were created through him is expressed first positively and then negatively. In vv.6-8 John introduces the Baptist. He is the first in a file of witnesses who testify to the event of the incarnation. Witness is a fundamental idea in John. He designates as "the world" those who refuse to accept Jesus and are hostile to him and to his disciples; they remain in darkness. Though his own people, on the whole, did reject him, those who had faith in the incarnate Word became children of God. To them he revealed his glory by his death, resurrection and ascension.

V.14 is the climax of the hymn. By the incarnation God is present visibly and personally to mankind and has become man in the fullest sense. In the expression "he pitched his tent among us" John recalls how Yahweh dwelt among the Israelites in the Tent of Meeting (Ex 33:7-11). "Glory" (*kabod*) is another expression of God's presence (cf. Ex 40:34; 1 Kg 8:11). In such terms John is expressing emphatically that in Jesus God is present among mankind.

The Prologue depicts Jesus primarily as the one who manifests the Father to men. Since he alone was with God (v.1) and since he alone had seen God (v.18), he alone could reveal the full truth about God. Unlike the synoptists who presented Jesus as the Messiah who inaugurates the kingdom of God, John will continue in the rest of the Gospel to present Jesus primarily as the Revealer of the Father and of the Father's plan of salvation.ı

Patristic Commentary

St. Jerome (c.347-c.420)
Homily on Jn 1:1-14, CCL 78.520, FOTC 57.217.

"The Word was made flesh, and dwelt among us." The Word was made flesh, but how He was made flesh, we do not know. The doctrine I have from God; the science of it, I do not have. I know that the Word was made flesh; how it was done, I do not know. Are you surprised that I do not know? No creature knows. It is a mystery which has been hidden for ages and generations, but now is clearly shown in our time. Someone may object: If it has been revealed, why do you say that you do not know? That it has been brought to pass has been revealed, but how it was brought to pass is hidden. Isaia even says: "Who can describe his generation?" (Isa 53:8) What has Isaia meant, then, by saying: "The virgin shall be with child and bear a son"? (Isa 7:14) He is telling us what has happened; but when he says: "Who can describe his generation," he is revealing to us the fact that He has been born, but how He has been born, we do not know. Holy Mary, blessed Mary, mother and virgin, virgin before giving birth, virgin after giving birth! I, for my part, marvel how a virgin is born of a virgin, and how, after the birth of a virgin, the mother is a virgin.

Would you like to know how He is born of a virgin and, after His nativity, the mother is still a virgin? "The doors were closed and Jesus entered." There is no question about that. He who entered through the closed doors was not a ghost nor a spirit; He was a real man with a real body. Furthermore, what does He say? "Feel me and see; for a spirit does not have flesh and bones, as you see I have."(Lk 24:39). He had flesh and bones, and the doors were closed. How do flesh and bones enter through closed doors? The doors are closed and He enters, whom we do not see entering. Whence has He entered? Everything is closed up; there is no place through which He may enter. Nevertheless, He who has entered is within and how He entered is not evident. You do not know how His entrance was accomplished, and you attribute it to the power of God. Attribute to the power of God, then, that He was born of a virgin, and the virgin herself after bringing forth was a virgin still.

Insights from the Documents of the Church

God chose us in Christ

Connected with the mystery of creation is the *mystery of the election*, which in a special way shaped the history of the people whose spiritual father is Abraham by virtue of his faith. Nevertheless, through this people which journeys forward through the history both of the Old Covenant and of the New, that mystery of election refers to every man and woman, to the whole great human family. "I have loved you with an everlasting love, therefore I have continued my faithfulness to you." "For the mountains may depart . . . my steadfast love shall not depart from you, and my covenant of peace shall not be removed." This truth, once proclaimed to Israel, involves a *perspective* of the whole history of man, a perspective both *temporal* and *eschatological* Christ reveals the Father within the framework of the same perspective and on ground already prepared, as many pages of the Old Testament writings demonstrate. At the end of this revelation, on the night before he dies, he says to the Apostle Philip these memorable words: "Have I been with you so long, and yet you do not know me . . .? He who has seen me has seen the Father." (John Paul II,, On the Mercy of God, *The Word was made flesh* [*Dives in Misericordia*])

The Word Made Flesh

After God had spoken many times and in various ways through the prophets, "in these last days he has spoken to us by a Son" (Heb 1:1-2). For he sent his Son, the eternal Word who enlightens all men, to dwell among men and to tell them about the inner life of God. Hence, Jesus Christ, sent as "a man among men," "speaks the words of God" (Jn 3:34), and accomplishes the saving work which the Father gave him to do (cf. Jn 5:36; 17:4). As a result, he himself—to see whom is to see the Father (cf. Jn 14:9)—completed and perfected Revelation and confirmed it with divine guarantees. He did this by the total fact of his presence and self-manifestation—by words and works, signs and miracles, but above all by his death and glorious resurrection from the dead, and finally by sending the Spirit of truth. He revealed that God was with us, to deliver us from the darkness of sin and death, and to raise us up to eternal life.

The Christian economy, therefore, since it is the new and definite covenant, will never pass away; and no new public revelation is to be expected before the glorious manifestation of our Lord, Jesus Christ (cf. 1 Tim 6:14 and Tit 2:13). (Vat. II, Divine Revelation, 4)

EPIPHANY*

Scriptural Commentary

First Reading Is 60:1-6.

This reading is the opening of a long poem (60:1-22) which is addressed to Jerusalem and promises and depicts its restoration after the Babylonian Exile. On the whole, the chapters Is 55-66 echo the euphoria that accompanied the rebuilding of the walls of Jerusalem and the restoration of the cult in the holy city. The resettled exiles saw in the return a proof that God had shown himself to be the undisputed Lord of history, and they believed that the establishment of his kingdom in Jerusalem would give Israel a privileged position among the nations. The holy city would become a gathering place, not only for scattered Jews, but also for all nations who would eventually be enlightened by the light of Yahweh.

Our passage is addressed directly to Jerusalem and it reminds her of her position as the religious centre of mankind. Her glory will come not from any achievements of her own but from the fact of Yahweh's presence in her midst. The light and the glory of God which illuminate the city will attract all nations to her. The author is so convinced that the Gentiles will come in pilgrimage to Jerusalem that he speaks of their arrival as a present reality: "Lift up your eyes round about and see; they all gather together; they come to you." The mighty ones of the world will be brought to recognize Israel's great King dwelling in his chosen city of Jerusalem. The text influenced Matthew in his Magi story, and other elements from it found their way into popular christian tradition.

Second Reading Eph 3:2-3, 5-6.

In the passage 3:1-6 the author describes the essence of the "mystery," in its biblical meaning of the "secret which has been revealed." God's saving plan is a "mystery" in that it is not accessible to the unaided human mind; but it is not a "secret" because it has been disclosed by God. In Christ God has fully revealed himself and his saving plan. In our reading, as v.6 makes clear, the aspect of the "mystery" envisaged is the salvation of the Gentiles. The truth that God was going to break down the barriers that separated Jew from non-Jew had not been made known even to the prophets. Now God has revealed to his apostles his hidden purpose of bringing all peoples into one body under one head, Jesus Christ. All those who are united in the one body of Christ, Jew or Gentile, are joint heirs of the divine gifts, sharing equally in the blessings once promised to Israel alone. A suitable text indeed for this feastday when we celebrate the epiphany of God to all peoples.

Gospel Mt 2:1-12.

In the Magi from the East, guided by the star (Num 24:17—"A star shall arise out of Jacob") and adoring Jesus in Bethlehem (Micah 2:6), Matthew sees the pagan world attracted by the light of the Messiah and coming to pay homage to the "king of the Jews" in the city of David. The homage is described with the help of the spiritual theme of the kings of Arabia bringing their presents to the King Messiah (Is 60:1-6). All the details—the strange visitors from the East, the mysterious star, the dream, the gifts—lead up to the final gesture of homage and worship. The adoration of the child by the magi fulfils Isaiah's prophecy (first reading) of the homage to be paid by the nations to the true Israel in the person of the Messiah.

Jesus, though born in obscurity, is truly Yahweh's messenger, the centre who unifies all nations in worship. The story of foreign magi worshipping the infant Christ, placed so early in the gospel, is a vivid hint that his message of salvation will be for the enlightenment of all mankind. The point is made explicit at the close of the gospel (28:19) in the command "make disciples of all nations."

Patristic Commentary

St. Leo the Great (d.461)
Tractatus 31, CCL 138.161, NPNF 12².144.

The last holy day which we celebrated was the day on which a pure Virgin brought forth the Savior of mankind. And now, dearly beloved, the venerable festival of the Epiphany gives us a continuation of joys, so that among these kindred solemnities, with their holy rites in close proximity, our heartiness of rejoicing and fervor of faith may be kept from cooling. For the salvation of all men is interested in the fact, that the infancy of the Mediator between God and men was already manifested to the whole world while He was still detained in an insignificant little town. As He was pleased to be born for all, He willed to be speedily recognized by all. Accordingly, there appeared in the East to three Magi a star of unparalleled brilliance that, being brighter and lovelier than the other stars, it might easily attract to itself the eyes and minds of those who gazed at it, and so they might at once observe that what seemed so strange was not without a meaning. Therefore He Who vouchsafed the sign gave intelligence to those who saw it; and that which He made them understand He made them seek after; and He, when sought, presented Himself to be found.

The Magi accomplish their desire, and being guided by the same star, reach a Child, the Lord Jesus Christ. In the flesh they adore the Word; in infancy, Wisdom; in weakness, Power; in man's true nature, the Lord of Majesty. And to manifest the sacred import of their faith and intelligence, they bear witness by gifts to what they believe in their hearts. They offer frankincense to the God, myrrh to the Man, gold to the King, consciously venerating the Divine and the human nature brought into unity; because, while the substances had their own properties, there was no diversity in power.

Insights from the Documents of the Church

Our Lady at Christmas

On the Epiphany, when she celebrates the universal call to salvation, the Church contemplates the Blessed Virgin, the true Seat of Wisdom and true Mother of the King, who presents to the Wise Men for their adoration the Redeemer of all peoples (cf. Mt 2:11). (Paul VI, To Honour Mary [*Marialis Cultus*])

Universality of call to salvation

In the closing words of the gospel according to Mark, Jesus invests the evangelization which he enjoins on the apostles with a universality which knows no frontiers: "Go into all the world and preach the gospel to the whole creation."

The twelve apostles and the first generations of christians fully appreciated the teaching of this and other similar texts and they developed from it a programme of action. The persecution by which the apostles were dispersed played its part in the dissemination of the gospel and the constant extension of the church to distant regions. The admission of Paul into the number of the apostles and his special mission to preach to the Gentiles rather than the Jews the coming of Jesus Christ gave further emphasis to this universality.

Generations of christians in the course of twenty centuries have overcome a variety of obstacles to his universal mission. For on the one hand the preachers themselves tended on various pretexts to restrict the field of their missionary activity and on the other hand those to whom they preached put up a resistance which could not be overcome by merely human resources. Moreover, sad to relate, the evangelical efforts of the church have been subject to virulent opposition, not to say actual obstruction, at the hands of governments. Even today the heralds of the divine word are deprived of their rights, harassed by persecution, threatened and even killed for no other reason than that they are preaching Jesus Christ and his gospel. It is our confident hope that, in spite of these trials, the zeal of these apostolic men will not fail in any part of the world.

Although she labours under these difficulties the church constantly renews that noble inspiration which comes to her directly from the divine Master as she recalls those words: "into all the world," "to the whole creation," "to the furthest ends of the earth." And she has reiterated this in the recent synod of bishops when they insisted that the evangelical message must not be restricted either to one section of the human family or to one social class or one form of human culture. Some examples may help to clarify this point. (Paul VI, Evangelization Today [*Evangelii Nuntiandi*]) nn.49,50)

THE BAPTISM OF THE LORD
[First Sunday of the Year]

Scriptural Commentary

First Reading Is 42:1-4, 6-7.

Our reading is the first of the Servant Songs of Second Isaiah. It is no longer possible for us to say who the poet had in mind: Israel, the Remnant, a king, a prophet? At any rate, the early Christians certainly took the Servant Songs as referring to Jesus. Most of the New Testament allusions to the Servant relate to the Passion. But the words spoken by the heavenly voice at the baptism of Jesus (see Gospel reading) are taken almost verbatim from Is 42:1. Jesus is identified at the beginning of his mission as the one who finally accomplishes the task of the Suffering Servant. According to today's reading, the Servant was endowed with the Spirit of God (cf. Is 11:1-3) to bring salvation to the world. He was to fulfil the kingly role of David by bringing justice to all nations. He was to continue the work of Moses by teaching to the nations the justice, law and religious principles for which they had been waiting. He was to exercise a prophetic role by pointing out to the peoples that they were blinded and imprisoned by their sins and that he could open their eyes and set them free. God will extend his plan of salvation to the world through his Servant who will accomplish his task peacefully and modestly, without violence and pressure. What is said about the Servant here was fulfilled in a most remarkable way by Jesus who came not to be served but to serve and to offer salvation to all mankind.

Second Reading Acts 10:34-38.

The passage 10:34-43, Peter's last discourse in Acts, is an example of early christian preaching to Gentile converts. Here, the theme of the universality of salvation that we remarked in Isaiah finds its first practical expression in the call of Cornelius and his family. God has no favourites and has extended his salvation to Gentile as well as Jew. Peter declares that anyone who fears God, that is, anyone who has a desire to serve God and to love him, is the object of his favour. Even if the people of Israel had God's message preached to them before others, the fact remains that Jesus is "the Lord of all." He came to announce the "good news of peace" (cf. Is 52:7), the news that the salvation promised by God is now made available to all men and women. Luke, who throughout his Gospel and Acts stresses the role of the Spirit in the life of Christ and of the early Christians, refers to Jesus' baptism as an anointing with the Spirit. In the résumé of Jesus' ministry which he places on Peter's lips he pictures Jesus as going about Palestine under the guidance of the Spirit doing good to all who needed his assistance. In saying that God was with Jesus in performing his good deeds he wishes to express the idea that God was present in him, in his preaching and in his works, manifesting the divine power to the world and offering salvation to all.

Gospel Mk 1:7-11.

This reading gives the Baptist's witness to Jesus (7-8) and the narrative of the baptism of Jesus (9-11). John, the

Elijah-like figure who had proclaimed the call to repentance (1:2-6) now proclaims the greater than he who will baptize the people with the Holy Spirit (7-8). [See Second Sunday of Advent.] Jesus comes from Nazareth of Galilee to be baptized by John. The description of the baptism is matter-of-fact. There is no trace of the embarrassment shown in Matthew's text (3:14-15); Mark ignores the difficulty raised by the fact of Jesus submitting to John's baptism "for the forgiveness of sins." In Mark's eyes, Jesus is not only the true Israelite whose repentance is perfect; he is the Son of God receiving the sign of repentance on behalf of the people of God. According to Mark, at the baptism Jesus alone saw and heard the heavenly happenings (10-11). "The Spirit" is the power of God coming upon Jesus, the Son, a consecration for his messianic mission: "how God anointed Jesus of Nazareth with the Holy Spirit and with power" (Acts 10:38). The phrase "like a dove" is found in all three synoptists; its symbolism, likely, has reference to the mission of Jesus, although its precise meaning escapes us.

The title "only Son" (for that is what "beloved Son" means) so solemnly attested (in terms echoing Ps 2:7) transcends messiahship and points to a unique relationship to God; it expresses the faith of the early church and marks a stage in christological thinking. The heavenly voice is for the christian reader, telling him the truth about Jesus. The baptism story, as we find it in Mark, was meant to assert that Jesus was constituted and declared Son of God at the time of his baptism by John. Mark's thought has not reached the concept of pre-existence and incarnation, and in this respect he joins hands with the other synoptists. Yet Jesus is for him formally Son of God and was so throughout his messianic career. Mark's christology is not fully rounded but it is a true christology, representing an intermediate stage in the growth of christological thought.

Gregory Nazianzus (c. 329-388)
Oration 39. on the Holy Lights, PG 36.349,
    NPNF 7².357.

At His birth we duly kept Festival, with the Star we ran,
and with the Magi we worshipped, and with the Shepherds
we were illuminated, and with the Angels we glorified
Him, and with Simeon we took Him up in our arms, and
with Anna the aged and chaste we made our confession.
Now, we come to another action of Christ, and another
mystery. I cannot restrain my pleasure; I am rapt into God.
Christ is illumined, let us shine forth with Him. Christ is
baptized, let us descend with Him that we may also ascend
with Him. Jesus is baptized; but we must attentively consider not only this but also some other points. Who is He,
and by whom is He baptized, and at what time? He is the
All-pure; and He is baptized by John; and the time is the
beginning of His miracles. What are we to learn and to be
taught by this? To purify ourselves first; to be lowly
minded; and to preach only in maturity both of spiritual
and bodily stature. The first has a word especially for those
who rush to Baptism off hand, and without due preparation, or providing for the stability of the Baptismal Grace
by the disposition of their minds to good. For since Grace
contains remission of the past (for it is a *grace*), it is on that
account more worthy of reverence, that we return not to the
same vomit again. The second speaks to those who rebel
against the Stewards of this Mystery, if they are their
superiors in rank. The third is for those who are confident
in their youth, and think that any time is the right one to
teach or to preside. Jesus is purified, and dost thou despise
purification? And by John, and dost thou rise up against thy
herald? And at thirty years of age, and dost thou before
thy beard has grown presume to teach the aged, or believe
that thou teachest them, though thou be not reverend on
account of thine age, or even perhaps for thy character?
But here it may be said, Daniel, and this or that other,
were judges in their youth, and examples are on your

tongues; for every wrongdoer is prepared to defend himself. But I reply that that which is rare is not the law of the Church. For one swallow does not make a summer, nor one line a geometrician, nor one voyage a sailor.

But John baptizes, Jesus comes to Him perhaps to sanctify the Baptist himself, but certainly to bury the whole of the old Adam in the water; and before this and for the sake of this, to sanctify Jordan; for as He is Spirit and Flesh, so He consecrates us by Spirit and water. John will not receive Him; Jesus contends. "I have need to be baptized of Thee" says the lamp to the sun, the Voice to the Word, the Friend to the Bridegroom; he that is above all among them that are born of women, to Him Who is the Firstborn of every creature; he that leaped in the womb, to Him Who was adored in the womb; he who was and is to be the Forerunner to Him Who was and is to be manifested. "I have need to be baptized of Thee"; add to this "and for Thee"; for he knew that he would be baptized by Martyrdom, or, like Peter, that he would be cleansed not only as to his feet. "And comest Thou to me?" This also was prophetic; for he knew that after Herod would come the madness of Pilate, and so that, when he had gone before, Christ would follow him. But what saith Jesus? "Suffer it to be so now," for this is the time of His Incarnation; for He knew that yet a little while and He should baptize the Baptist.

Insights from the Documents of the Church

To serve the cause of right

In our world the feeling of being under threat is increasing. There is an increase of that existential fear connected especially, as I said in the Encyclical *Redemptor Hominis*, with the prospect of a conflict that in view of today's atomic stockpiles could mean the partial self-destruction of humanity. But the threat does not merely concern what human beings can do to human beings through the means provided by military technology; it also concerns many other dangers produced by a materialistic society which—in spite of "humanistic" declarations— accepts the primacy of things over persons. Contemporary man, therefore, fears that by the use of the means invented by this type of society, *individuals* and the environment, communities, societies and nations *can fall victim to the abuse of power by other* individuals, environments and societies. The history of our century offers many examples of this. In spite of all the declarations on the rights of man in his integral dimension, that is to say in his bodily and spiritual existence, we cannot say that these examples belong only to the past.

Man rightly fears falling victim to an oppression that will deprive him of his interior freedom, of the possibility of expressing the truth of which he is convinced, of the faith that he professes, of the ability to obey the voice of conscience that tells him the right path to follow. The technical means at the disposal of modern society conceal within themselves not only the possibility of self-destruction through military conflict, but also *the possibility of a* "peaceful" *subjugation of individuals, of environments,* of entire societies and of nations, that for one reason or another might prove inconvenient for those who possess the necessary means and are ready to use them without scruple. An instance is the continued existence of torture, systematically used by authority as a means of domination and political oppression and practised by subordinates with impunity. (John Paul II, On the Mercy of God [*Dives in Misericordia*])

LENT

FIRST SUNDAY OF LENT

Scriptural Commentary

First Reading Gen 9:8-15.

It is rather a pity that the whole passage (Gen 9:1-17) has not been set as this reading. The changed situation after the Flood raises a basic question: did the first blessing of creation, "be fruitful and multiply" (1:28) still hold? The answer is that God has indeed renewed his blessing for the new generation. He has not abandoned humanity: he still wills procreation and increase (vv.1,7). Human life is sacred because man was made in God's image (v.5). The taking of human life (murder) is punished by death; God empowers man to avenge murder (v.6). This is an awesome responsibility. No more effectively could God express his abhorrence of murder. He grants to man, in this circumstance, to enter into his own preserve of life. Respect for human life was to take a giant step even beyond this for, in the ethic of Jesus, there is no place at all for the taking of human life. The contrary practice of Christians down the centuries has not made void this word of the Lord.

"My covenant" (vv.8-11)—the first in a series of patriarchal covenants that will serve as the preparation for the covenant at Sinai with the people of Israel. The term "covenant," which in its technical theological sense concerns the relations of man with God, was borrowed from the social experience of men, from the fact of treaties and alliances between individuals and peoples. In practice, the religious use of the term regards a special type of covenant, that in which one partner takes the initiative and imposes the conditions. Therefore, God lays down the terms, demanding of his people that it would keep the covenant (17:9; 19:5). See Sirach 44:18—"Everlasting covenants were made with him [Noah] that all flesh should not be blotted out by a flood." The most striking comment is that of Second Isaiah in his moving hymn to the New Jerusalem: "For this is like the days of Noah to me: as I swore that the waters of Noah should no more go over the earth, so I swore that I will not be angry with you and will not rebuke you. For the mountains may depart and the hills be removed, but my steadfast love shall not depart from you, and my covenant of peace shall not be removed, says the Lord, who has compassion on you" (Is 54:9-10).

God's covenants illustrate the way God deals with humankind—his justice, his mercy, and his readiness always to give another chance. God knows and understands the weakness of man; he asks only that he not turn away irrevocably. And that is the real significance of the new covenant made in Christ. It is God's complete and final answer to all those tentative beginnings and subsequent fresh starts made by man over the centuries. Christ is for those who need him—he is the saviour of humankind. That knowledge is, like the rainbow for Noah, our hope. And in it too we become more than ever aware that once "brought to life in Christ" our Christianity must issue forth in good works here and now. Therein lies our challenge.

Second Reading 1 Pet 3:18-22.

Peter is exhorting Gentile Christians to persevere in their faith in face of persecution. He points to Christ as the basis of their hope. Jesus may have been put to death "in the flesh," that is, as far as his earthly life was concerned. But that was beginning rather than end. In his resurrection he was "made alive in the spirit" and proclaimed to all his definitive victory over evil.

Christ's victory is communicated to men and women in baptism. Through it we share in his resurrection and are therefore assured of eternal salvation and ultimate triumph over all that is evil. Like Noah, the Christian is saved by passage through water. The baptized person has a firm ground of hope in time of trouble. Christ has already won the victory over the force of evil. The Christian who pledges himself to God with "a clear conscience" thereby professes faith in God's power and goodness and so can look, without fear or disappointment, to the living Lord for the grace and strength to keep the pledge he has given.

"This whole passage has taken us over a trajectory of salvation; from the death and resurrection of Jesus (v.18) to his descent into Sheol (v.19) to his triumphant exaltation at God's right hand (v.22). Although this 'journey' imagery (specifically the descent into Sheol) is unique in the New Testament, it is a theme picked up in the writings of the early Fathers and used in the creed. For 1 Peter, too, this saving journey was part of the 'creed' on which the energetic witness of the community must be based" (D. Senior, *1 & 2 Peter*, 73).

Gospel Mk 1:12-15.

With the emergence of the beloved Son (1:9-11) a new era has begun, the era of eschatological hope. An essential feature of this hope is the overthrow of evil. And thus it is that, confirmed in his divine Sonship and anointed with the Spirit for his task (vv.10-11), Jesus faces a trial of strength. The Spirit "drove"—a strong word—Jesus into the wilderness. In the setting of the temptation, a struggle with evil, the wilderness is the traditional haunt of evil spirits (symbolized by "wild beasts"); and there Jesus encounters Satan, the prince of evil, the enemy of God.

Jesus was tempted; the Greek word carries all the nuances of temptation, trial, tribulation, test. For Jesus, temptation did not end here (cf. 14:32-42), and the implied victory over Satan, reflected in his subsequent exorcisms, will have to be won all over again on the cross. Here we are doubtless to understand that the ministering angels supplied Jesus with food; Mark has no reference at all to a fast of Jesus. At this first struggle Jesus is not God-forsaken as he will be at his last (15:34).

Now that Jesus has been acknowledged as God's Son and has thrown himself into a totally committed struggle against evil, he can begin to preach the Good News (vv. 14-15). Mark's first words are ominous: "after John was delivered up." The fate of the Baptist was to be delivered up to his enemies in accordance with the divine will (6:17-29). The alert reader, conscious that Jesus suffered a like fate, will perceive in John a type of the suffering Messiah. Jesus came preaching "the gospel of God," the good news from God. It is the christian message of salvation (cf. 1 Thes 3:2,8-9; 2 Cor 11:7; Rom 1:1; 15:6). And the summary of that preaching uses early christian theological language. Like the Forerunner, Jesus calls for a thoroughgoing conversion: but, more urgently, he calls on men to embrace the Good News. While the sentence, "The reign of God has come; repent and believe the Good News" is an admirable summary of the preaching of Jesus, Mark himself undoubtedly understood the words "believe the gospel" in the christian sense of faith in the good news of salvation through Jesus Christ. And this is how his reader must take it.

Patristic Commentary

St. Augustine (354-430)
Sermon 210, PL 38.1051, FOTC 38.104.

The whole Body of Christ, diffused through the entire world, that is, the whole Church, practises penance as that corporate unity which says in the psalm: "To thee have I cried from the ends of the earth; when my heart was in anguish." (Ps 61:2). Hence, light begins to dawn upon us as to why the Lenten season was inaugurated as the solemnity of this humiliation. For the Church which cries from the ends of the earth when its heart is in anguish cries from those four regions of the earth which even the Scriptures often mention, that is, from the East and West, from the North and the South. Through the entire area the Decalogue of the Law has been promulgated, not merely to be feared in its literal expression, but to be fulfilled in the grace of charity. Hence, when four has been multiplied by ten, we see the number forty rounded out.

For forty days Moses, the guardian of the Law, fasted; for forty days Elias, the most excellent of the Prophets, fasted; for forty days the Lord Himself, to whom both the Law and the Prophets gave testimony, fasted. Hence, it was in company with these two that He revealed Himself on the mountain. Let us, however, who are not able to perform this long fast, as they did, taking no nourishment for so many days and nights, at least do as much as we can, so that, with the exception of those days on which, for certain reasons, the law of the Church forbids us to fast, we may please the Lord God by daily or frequent fasting.

Insights from the Documents of the Church

The Covenant

The Cross of Christ stands *beside the path* of that *admirabile commercium*, of that *wonderful self-communication of God to man*, which also includes *the call* to man to share in the divine life by giving himself, and with himself the whole visible world, to God, and like an adopted son to become a sharer in the truth and love which is in God and proceeds from God. It is precisely beside the path of man's eternal election to the dignity of being an adopted child of God that there stands in history the Cross of Christ, the only-begotten Son, who, as "light from light, true God from true God," came to give the final witness to the wonderful *Covenant of God with humanity, of God with man*—every human being. This covenant, as old as man— it goes back to the very mystery of creation—and afterwards many times renewed with one single chosen people, is equally the new and definitive covenant, which was established there on Calvary, and is not limited to a single people, to Israel, but is open to each and every individual. (John Paul II, On the Mercy of God [*Dives in Misericordia*])

The Waters of Baptism and the Covenant

Baptism, entrance to life and to the kingdom, is the first sacrament of the new law, offered by Christ to all, that they might have eternal life and afterwards entrusted, with the gospel, to his Church, when he commanded his apostles: "Go forth, therefore, and make all nations my disciples; baptise people everywhere in the name of the Father and the Son and the Holy Spirit." Baptism is, therefore, first and foremost the sacrament of that faith by which men and women, enlightened by the grace of the Holy Spirit, respond to the gospel of Christ. For the Church, therefore, there is nothing more important, nothing more in character, than to awaken all—catechumens, parents of children awaiting baptism, godparents— that true and active faith by which they give their allegiance to Christ and enter into the new covenant, or re-affirm their acceptance of it. . . . Baptism is the sacrament by which men and women are incorporated into the Church, assembled together into the house of God in the Spirit, into a royal priesthood and a holy nation. It is the sacramental bond of unity between all those who have received it. (*General Introduction to Christian Initiation*)

Lent: Baptism and Penance

The two elements which are especially characteristic of Lent—the recalling of baptism or the preparation for it, and penance—should be given greater emphasis in the liturgy and in liturgical catechesis. It is by means of them that the Church prepares the faithful for the celebration of Easter, while they hear God's word more frequently and devote more time to prayer.

(a) More use is to be made of the baptismal features which are proper to the Lenten liturgy. Some of them which were part of an earlier tradition are to be restored where opportune.

(b) The same may be said of the penitential elements. But catechesis, as well as pointing out the social consequences of sin, must impress on the minds of the faithful the distinctive character of penance as a detestation of sin because it is an offense against God. The role of the Church in penitential practices is not to be passed over, and the need to pray for sinners should be emphasized.

During Lent, penance should be not only internal and individual but also external and social. The practice of penance should be encouraged in ways suited to the present day, to different regions, and to individual circumstances. (Vat. II, Constitution on the Liturgy, 109, 110).

SECOND SUNDAY OF LENT

Scriptural Commentary

First Reading Gen 22:1-2, 9-13, 15-18.

It is clear, to us, that what took place in this episode was a test of Abraham's faith. But, for Abraham himself, it represents his agonizing effort to do what he thought God really wanted of him. Human sacrifice was known to the Canaanites, and the patriarch lived among them. It is not inconceivable that in his steady effort to find and do God's will he might have thought that God—the author of life—asked this deed of him. Rarely, if ever, was a man summoned to give greater proof of his faith and of his obedience. Ironically, it is Isaac, hitherto the reward of that faith, who becomes the focus of its supreme test. For Isaac, sole son of parents "past the age" and "as good as dead" (Heb 11:11-12), was the only possible way in which God's promises to Abraham could be fulfilled. Now God asks him to sacrifice his "only son"!

Abraham does not flinch. The story graphically describes the point of divine intervention as he "put forth his hand, and took the knife to slay his son." God forestalls him in the nick of time. Abraham had passed the test. And his extraordinary faith was rewarded in an extraordinary way. God (the "angel of the Lord" is God in person) swore "by his own self" to reward Abraham with the benefits of the Covenant.

There are two points of practical interest. If we read between the lines, we come face to face with the mysterious and absolute liberty of God's choice at all times. God gives and he takes away. He chooses whom he wills and as he wills. It is man's unending task to school himself to accept actively and always this gratuitousness. Then, the heroic example of Abraham is the standard against which we can measure our puny faith. Paul, surely a man of no mean faith, is lost in admiration of the faith of Abraham (Rom 4:1-12). The author of Hebrews gives Abraham star billing in his cast of champions of faith (Heb 11:8-10, 17-19). Abraham is indeed our father in faith.

Second Reading Rom 8:31-34.

The celebrant/reader should not be satisfied with this snippet but ought read on to v.39 or, preferably, read the whole passage 8:28-39. In the mind of Paul only the Christian has real reason for present assurance and future hope. Here are listed our reasons for an unshakable hope: the enormous realities in which we are immersed and by which we are surrounded. Sin is already condemned in the physical body of Jesus (8:3). The liberating Spirit of life "has made his home in us" (v.9). By the Spirit we can believe that we are God's children, coheirs with Christ (vv.14-17). The whole creation too is reaching out to us to be brought fully into God's plan (19-23). The fullness of that plan is not yet: we live in firm hope and patience (24-25). And we know that God is master: he turns everything to our good (28-30).

Today's passage is the beginning of a hymn of praise. Using the method and terminology of the law-court, Paul leads his readers to an inspiring and inescapable conclusion. There is no doubt that God is on the Christian's side—Jesus' sacrifice is eloquent proof of that: "God did not spare his own Son . . ." We recall that he spared Abraham's son (first reading). The fact that God is our judge is not a problem: in that he has already chosen us he has already pronounced in our favour. The only person who could claim the right to condemn us is Christ. But he is our *advocate*! Standing "at the right hand of God" he presents our needs to him and "intercedes for us." This passage is a celebration of assured victory for the Christian. "There is no arguing with such a certainty. Either you simply don't believe it or you recognize it as the word of God" (C. H. Dodd).

Gospel Mk 9:2-10.

While it is no longer possible to say what it was that transpired upon the mountain—was it vision? was it deep religious experience?—we must seek to understand what the episode means for Mark. Perhaps his pointer, immediately before (9:1), to an imminent parousia, and the presence of Elijah and Moses, may help us to understand his purpose. In ch. 13 Mark has to contend with some who, having pinned their parousia-hope on the destruction of Jerusalem and its temple in 70 A.D., were disillusioned because that hope had been dashed. Was Jesus after all no greater than Elijah and Moses who, too, had been rapt to heaven? He was not really the Messiah, then, and that is why their expectation had been disappointed.

In Mark the aspect of revelation made to Jesus (cf. Lk 9:28-32) yields wholly to the theme of revelation granted to the disciples. And now the entire first part of the narrative prepares for this. Jesus leads the three disciples "up a high mountain" where he was transfigured "before them" (v.2). Moses and Elijah appear "to them" and it was for the disciples' benefit that a heavenly voice was heard, speaking of Jesus in the third person (v.7). The "three booths," one each for Jesus, Elijah and Moses, would have put all three on an equal footing. Peter really "did not know what to say;" he has, yet again, wholly misunderstood The voice from heaven will set the matter straight. The cloud which now overshadows them is the cloud of God's *Shekinah* (the "presence" or "dwelling" of God) and the medium of his manifestation. "This is my beloved Son"—in contrast to 1:11 the words are here addressed to the disciples: they hear the divine approbation of Jesus as the messianic Son. Elijah and Moses have disappeared and he stands alone. "Listen to him"—the Beloved Son is also the prophet-like-Moses whose teaching must be heeded (cf. Dt 18:15-19).

The faith of the disciples in Jesus the Messiah had been confirmed. But this was only the beginning. Their problem remained—Jesus must die before he would be glorified. His mission was not that of a conquering hero; he was to be the Suffering Servant of Yahweh whose victory lay in apparent defeat on the cross. The disciples would have to work that one out for themselves and would find the solution only in the light of the resurrection. So it is with us. God's ways never seem to be ours. Unlike Peter we must resist the temptation to pick and choose—to build a tent—at any particular juncture. Rather we should strive to "listen to Jesus" in the whole of his teaching and make it effective in the whole of our lives.

Patristic Commentary

St. Jerome (c. 347-407)
Homily on Mark 9:1-7, CCL 78.480, FOTC 57.162.

"Now after six days Jesus took Peter, James and John."
"After six days." Pray the Lord that these words may be
expounded in the same Spirit in which they were uttered. It
came to pass six days later. Why not nine days later? Why
not ten, twenty, four, five? Why not some number before or
after; why six? "It came to pass after six days." They who are
standing with Jesus—of whom He says: "there are some of
those standing here"—will not see the kingdom of God
except after six days. Not until this world shall pass away—
that is the force of the six days—shall the new kingdom
appear. When the six days have passed, he who is Peter, that
is, he who, like Peter, has received his name from the Rock,
Christ, will merit to see the kingdom, for by the same token
that we are called Christians from Christ, Peter is named
from the Rock, "pétrinos."

Consider, too, that as long as Jesus is down below, He is
not transfigured; He ascends and is transformed. "He led
them up a high mountain off by themselves, and was transfigured before them. And his garments became shining, exceedingly white as snow." To this very day, Jesus is down
below for some and up above for others. They who are
below, the crowd who cannot climb the mountain, have
Jesus down below—only the disciples climb the mountain,
the crowd remains below—if anyone, I say, is one of the
crowd, he cannot see Jesus in shining garments, only in
soiled. If anyone follows the letter and is completely of
the earth and looks at the ground in the manner of brute
beasts, he is unable to see Jesus in a shining vestment, but
for him who follows the word of God and ascends the
mountain, climbs to the top, for him, Jesus is instantly
transfigured and His garments shine exceedingly.

"Now after six days Jesus took Peter, James and John, and led them up a high mountain off by themselves, and was transfigured before them." This, they say, is Christ ruling; the apostles saw what kind of king Christ was going to be. When they saw Him transfigured upon the mountain, they saw Him in the glory that would be His. This, therefore, is the meaning behind the words: "They shall not taste death, until they have seen the kingdom of God"—which came to pass six days later.   '

Insights from the Documents of the Church

God did not spare his own Son

The Paschal Mystery is Christ at the summit of the revelation of the inscrutable mystery of God. It is precisely then that the words pronounced in the Upper Room are completely fulfilled: "He who has seen me has seen the Father." In fact, Christ, whom the Father "did not spare" for the sake of man and who in his Passion and in the torment of the Cross did not obtain human mercy, has revealed in his Resurrection the fullness of the love that the Father has for him and, in him, for all people. "He is not God of the dead, but of the living." In his Resurrection Christ *has revealed the God of merciful love*, precisely because *he accepted the Cross as the way to the Resurrection*. And it is for this reason that—when we recall the Cross of Christ, his Passion and death—our faith and hope are centred on the Risen One: on that Christ who "on the evening of that day, the first day of the week, . . . stood among them" in the Upper Room, "where the disciples were, . . . breathed on them, and said to them: 'Receive the Holy Spirit. If you forgive the sins of any, they are forgiven; if you retain the sins of any, they are retained'."

Here is the Son of God, who in his Resurrection experienced in a radical way mercy shown to himself, that is to say the love of the Father which is *more powerful than death*. And it is also the same Christ, the Son of God, who at the end of his messianic mission—and, in a certain sense, even beyond the end—reveals himself as the inexhaustible source of mercy, of the same love that, in a subsequent perspective of the history of salvation in the Church, is to be everlastingly confirmed as *more powerful than sin*. The paschal Christ is the definitive incarnation of mercy, its living sign: in salvation history and in eschatology. In the same spirit, the liturgy of Eastertide places on our lips the words of the Psalm: *Misericordias Domini in aeternum cantabo*. (John Paul II, On the Mercy of God. [*Dives in Misericordia*])

THIRD SUNDAY OF LENT

Scriptural Commentary

First Reading Ex 20:1-17.

This reading is one of the two versions of the Decalogue—the other being Dt 5:6-21. The Ten Commandments should be viewed in their original Sinai setting. There they are clearly part of the covenant God made with his people; they are an expression of the profound and abiding nature of the covenant. They are not so much a set of laws to which God expected and exacted obedience as declarations of willing loyalty offered to God by his people.

It may be that commandments four to ten are the original seven commandments. They deal with the relations of man to man and are found in other codes of law since they are the core of "natural law." Crime in other ancient codes is against man. In the Bible it is seen as being against God himself. The distinctive commandments, one to three, make that point, dramatically. Morally and religiously, the decalogue is superior to other ancient codes. Yet we

Christians must be aware that we do *not* live by the ten commandments: we live by the "law" of Jesus (Mt 7:24).

Second Reading 1 Cor 1:22-25.

For Paul, Christianity was the message of the cross of Christ and he let nobody forget it. He proclaimed, without apology, a crucified saviour, knowing full well that this would shock the Jews and scandalize the Greek world of his time. For the Jews awaiting the advent of a Messiah who would inaugurate the sovereignty of Israel over the Gentiles, it was incredible that one who had been crucified as a criminal could be the Messiah. Did not their own law state clearly: "a hanged man is accursed by God" (Dt 21:23)! The fact of crucifixion automatically disqualified Jesus from being the Messiah. The Greek mind, consistently seeking for a philosophical system that would satisfactorily explain man and the world, found the idea of God becoming man repugnant. The incarnation, quite apart from crucifixion, was "madness."

It seems to be characteristic of God to confound human wisdom. He accomplishes by "foolishness" what the greatest human wisdom cannot achieve. And his wisdom and saving action are, paradoxically, revealed in Jesus Christ, crucified and risen. Those "who are called," that is, those who hear and heed the divine invitation, see in Christ "the power of God and the wisdom of God." For in him is salvation and new life.

The cross of Christ is hard to accept until we reflect on the fact that it is but the practical expression of "God so loved the world." The Israelite knew that God loved him— there was ample evidence of it. What he did not guess at was how much God loved him. Only the cross of Jesus would speak that. It was also a strangely fitting way of making the point.

Gospel Jn 2:13-25.

The cleansing of the temple which John has at an early stage of Jesus' ministry is, more credibly, put by the synoptists at the close of the ministry (Mk 11:15-18 and parr). What matters is not when it happened but what it means. Jesus passes judgment on the Jewish sacrificial system. By word and deed, in the fashion of the Old Testament prophets, (Jer 7:11; Mal 3:1), he protests against the profanation of God's house and signals that its messianic purification was at hand. "The Jews"—the hostile religious authorities—recognize that Jesus' action was deed of one who was a prophet and claimed to be Messiah.

John spells out the significance of the deed. He recalls the words of Psalm 69:10—"Zeal for thy house will consume me." The symbolic action had been predicted for the messianic age by Zech 14:21 ". . . there will be no more traders in the temple of Yahweh Sabaoth when that day comes." After the resurrection (vv.17,22) the full meaning of what Jesus did and said became clear to his followers. Jesus, the risen Messiah, had taken the place of the temple and all it stood for. The centre of God's presence among his people is no longer a place; it is henceforth a person. The new sanctuary is the risen body of Jesus. In this new temple dwells the fullness of the Spirit. And that Spirit comes to those who believe and dwells with them so that they too in their turn become temples of God.

Patristic Commentary

Origen (c.185-c.254)
Commentary on John, X, 137, SC 157.468,
    ANF IX.394.
When, therefore, the Saviour finds in the temple, the house of His Father those who are selling oxen and sheep and doves, and the changers of money sitting, He drives

them out, using the scourge of small cords which He has made, along with the sheep and oxen of their trade, and pours out their stock of coin, as not deserving to be kept together, so little is it worth. He also overturns the tables in the souls of such as love money, saying even to those who sell doves, "Take these things hence," that they may no longer traffic in the house of God. But I believe that in these words He indicated also a deeper truth, and that we may regard these occurrences as a symbol of the fact that the service of that temple was not any longer to be carried on by the priests in the way of material sacrifices, and that the time was coming when the law could no longer be observed, however much the Jews according to the flesh desired it. For when Jesus casts out the oxen and sheep, and orders the doves to be taken away, it was because oxen and sheep and doves were not much longer to be sacrificed there in accordance with Jewish practices. And possibly the coins which bore the stamp of material things and not of God were poured out by way of type; because the law which appears so venerable, with its letter that kills, was, now that Jesus had come and had used His scourge to the people, to be abrogated and rejected, the sacred office being transferred to those from the Gentiles who believed, and the kingdom of God being taken away from the Jews and given to a nation bringing forth the fruits of it. But it may also be the case that the natural temple is the soul endowed with reason, which, because of its inborn reason, is higher than the body; to which Jesus ascends from Capernaum, the lower-lying place of less dignity, and in which, before Jesus' discipline is applied to it, are found tendencies which are earthly and senseless and dangerous, and things which have the name but not the reality of beauty, and which are driven away by Jesus with His word plaited out of doctrines of demonstration and of rebuke, to the end that His Father's house may no longer be a house of merchandize but may receive, for its own salvation and that of others, that service of God which is performed in accordance with heavenly and spiritual laws. The ox is symbolic of earthly things, for he is a husbandman. The sheep, of senseless and brutal things, because it is more servile than most of the creatures without reason. Of empty and unstable thoughts, the dove. Of things that are thought good but are not, the small change.

Insights from the Documents of the Church

I am the Lord your God

Modern atheism often takes on a systematic form also which, in addition to other causes, so insists on man's desire for autonomy as to object to any dependence on God at all. Those who profess this kind of atheism maintain that freedom consists in this, that man is an end to himself, and the sole maker, with supreme control, of his own history. They claim that this outlook cannot be reconciled with the assertion of a Lord who is author and end of all things, or that at least it makes such an affirmation altogether unnecessary. The sense of power which modern technical progress begets in man may encourage this outlook.

Among the various kinds of present-day atheism, that one should not go unnoticed which looks for man's autonomy through his economic and social emancipation. It holds that religion, of its very nature, thwarts such emancipation by raising man's hopes in a future life, thus both deceiving him and discouraging him from working for a better form of life on earth. That is why those who hold such views, wherever they gain control of the state, violently attack religion, and in order to spread atheism, especially in the education of young people, make use of all the means by which the civil authority can bring pressure to bear on its subjects. (Vat. II, The Church in the Modern World, 20)

The Values of the Money Changers

Why fasting? It is necessary to give this question a wider and deeper answer, in order to clarify the relationship between fasting and "metanoia" that is between fasting and a spiritual change bringing man closer to God. We will try therefore to concentrate not only on the practice of abstention from food or from drink—which is the meaning of "fasting" in the usual sense—but on the deeper meaning of this practice which, moreover, can and must sometimes be "replaced" by another one. Food and drink are indispensable for man; he uses them and must use them, but he may not abuse them in any way. The tradition of abstention from food and drink is intended to introduce into man's existence not only the necessary balance, but also detachment from what might be defined as a "consumer attitude." *The consumer attitude!* In our times this attitude has become one of the characteristics of civilization and in particular of Western civilization.

We sometimes hear it said that the excessive increase of audiovisual media in the rich countries does not always aid the development of intelligence, particularly in children, and that, on the contrary, it sometimes contributes to checking its development. The child lives only on sensations, he looks for ever-new sensations . . . and thus he becomes, without realizing it, a slave of this modern passion. Satiating himself with sensations, he often remains passive intellectually; the intellect does not open to the search of truth; the will remains bound by habits which it is unable to oppose.

It is clear from this that modern man must *fast*, that is, abstain not only from food and drink, but from many other means of consumption, stimulation and satisfaction of the senses. To fast means to abstain, to renounce something.

Man, geared to material goods, multiple material goods, very often abuses them. It is not just a question here of food and drink. When man is geared exclusively to the possession and use of material goods—that is, of things—then the whole civilization is measured according to the quantity and the quality of the things with which it is in a position to supply man, and is not measured by a yardstick suitable to man. This civilization, in fact, supplies material goods not just to help man to carry out creative and useful activities, but more and more to satisfy his senses and give him momentary excitement. (John Paul II, At General Audience, 21 March, 1979)

FOURTH SUNDAY OF LENT

Scriptural Commentary

First Reading 2 Chr 36:14-16, 19-23.

The Chronicler's work (1,2 Chronicles, Ezra, Nehemiah) is a third century B.C. theology of history. The author brings to life again before the eyes of his contemporaries an (idealized) Davidic theocracy. This recalling of the glories of David is designed to make his readers ponder on their vocation as God's people. The story of the restoration (Ezra, Nehemiah), coming after the failure of the monarchy, would show how God had remained faithful to his people. As a new beginning it would turn their hope towards the full establishment of God's kingdom.

Our reading, the conclusion of 2 Chronicles, catalogues the sins of Zedekiah and his people and tells of the end of Jerusalem and its temple, and of the Babylonian exile. The candid confession of sin and the acknowledgment that the chastisement was richly deserved are typical of post-exilic writings. No less typical is the optimism: the book closes on the note of restoration (vv.22-23). Jerusalem is not destined for oblivion; God's promises are not nullified by his people's sins; his mercy overcomes his wrath.

Despite setbacks, the life of God's people will continue. Significantly, it is with this passage that the Hebrew canon of the Old Testament ends, pointing forward in hope towards an unforeseen future.

Second Reading Eph 2:4-10.

From the start the author of Ephesians writes with enthusiasm of God's gifts to mankind through Jesus the mediator. He elaborates on the gifts: "Blessed be the God and Father of our Lord Jesus Christ who has blessed us in Christ with every spiritual blessing in the heavenly places . . . . He has destined us in love to be his sons through Jesus Christ, according to the purpose of his will . . . a plan for the fullness of time, to unite all things in him, things in heaven and things in earth" (1:3,5,10). The power of God which was at work in Christ's resurrection and ascension has already been at work in us, in so far as we have been "raised" from the death of our former Gentile (and indeed Jewish) existence. To this extent we already share in Christ's dominion over the rest of creation (2:1-6). The description of our previous existence as a "death" and of our new life as a participation in Christ's resurrection and ascension reinforces the author's insistence that we have been saved only by grace (vv.7-9). God's saving grace is so radical, in fact, that even our good actions have been "prepared" by God (v.10). Man's part in the process of redemption is to be grateful, to trust in Christ, to accept the gift with all humility and begin to act in accordance with our new status—for we are "created in Christ Jesus, for good works . . . that we should walk in them."

Gospel Jn 3:14-21.

The dialogue with Nicodemus (Jn 3:1-21) treats of new birth. The phrase rendered "born anew" (vv.3,7) can equally well mean "born from above" and, typically, John intends both meanings. True to the procedure of the gospel Nicodemus understands the statement of Jesus at its surface level (v.4); Jesus then explains that he means spiritual rebirth from above; his baptism, which brings about this rebirth, is not in water only—as was the baptism of John—but in "water and the Spirit" (v.5). Then, in our reading, comes an enigmatic reference to the death of Jesus (vv.14-15) and a clear statement of the marvellous love of God (vv.16-18).

In v.14 John gives a double significance to the verb "to be lifted up." First, it is the physical fact of being elevated upon the cross, just as the bronze figure of a serpent was raised by Moses over the stricken Israelites (Num 21:4-9); but it also evokes the spiritual elevation of Jesus by the Father—that glorification which was granted him through his death. Like the bronze serpent of old, the raised-up Son of Man will be an effective sign of salvation for all who look on him with trust.

Verses 16-21 develop what has gone before. The hope of salvation offered through the descent and exaltation of the Son of Man is now traced back to its ultimate source: God's marvellous love. It was God who set the process in motion, wishing that the world be saved from sin. V.16 ("God so loved the world . . .") is the very foundation of the gospel; together with 1:14 ("the Word was made flesh") and 12:32 ("when I am lifted up from the earth, I will draw all men to myself"), it constitutes the "good news" proclaimed by John.

Yet, not everyone will benefit from the loving initiative of God; some, by hardening their hearts against belief in Jesus, will seal their own condemnation. Jesus brings judgment with him, necessarily; he is like a light that shines into the heart of each person, and the way we react to this light determines our destiny. If, loving darkness and deceit and selfish ways, we turn away wilfully from God's light, we cannot come to God; we renounce the right to be called his children. For John, salvation or damnation begins already, here on earth, according to one's acceptance or rejection of Jesus, the only Son of God. The essential judgment is not passed by Jesus (or by the Father) but is contained in the choice *we* make when we are confronted by him.

Patristic Commentary

St. Ambrose (c.340-397)
The Holy Spirit, BK 3, c.8, PL 16.787,
    FOTC 44.170.

Learn, also, that, while the Scripture said elsewhere that the Spirit was tempted, and that even God was tempted, the same Scripture says that Christ also was tempted, for you have the Apostle saying to the Corinthians: "Neither let us tempt Christ; as some of them tempted, and perished by serpents." (1 Cor 10:9). Just was the punishment, that the adversaries might feel the venom, who did not venerate the Author.

And when the brazen serpent was set up, well did the Lord order the wounds of the injured to be healed, (Num 21:9) for the brazen serpent is a representation of the Cross. For, although Christ was suspended in His flesh, yet in Him was the Apostle also crucified to the world, and the world was crucified to him, for he says: "The world is crucified to me, and I to the world." (Gal 6:14) So the world was crucified in its allurements, and thus not the true but the brazen serpent was set up, because in the truth of the body indeed, but without the truth of sin did the Lord take on the appearance of a sinner, that through the deceit of human weakness by imitating the serpent, throwing off the slough of the flesh, He might destroy the cunning of the true serpent. Thus through the cross of the Lord, which came to our aid in the vengeance of temptation, I, who accept the medicine of the Trinity, recognize the offence against the Trinity in the faithless.

Therefore, when you read in the book of Moses that the Lord being tempted sent serpents among the people of the

Jews (Num 21:6), either you must confess the unity in the divine majesty of the Father and the Son and the Holy Spirit, or certainly, when apostolic Scripture says that the Spirit was tempted, surely it pointed out the Spirit by the name of the Lord. Moreover, the Apostle, writing to the Hebrews, says that the Holy Spirit was tempted, for you have the following: "Wherefore, as the Holy Spirit saith: Today, if you shall hear his voice, harden not your hearts, as in the provocation, in the day of temptation in the desert, where your fathers tempted me, proved, and saw my works. Forty years was I near to this generation, and I said: They always err in heart; and they have not known my ways, as I have sworn in my wrath: If they shall enter into my rest." (Heb 3:7).

Insights from the Documents of the Church

Sin and Mercy

It is significant that in their preaching the prophets link mercy, which they often refer to because of the people's sins, with the incisive image of love on God's part. The Lord loves Israel with the love of a special choosing, much like the love of a spouse, and for this reason he pardons its sins and even its infidelities and betrayals. When he finds repentance and true conversion, he brings his people back to grace. In the preaching of the prophets *mercy* signifies a *special power of love,* which *prevails over the sin and infidelity* of the chosen people.

In this broad "social" context, mercy appears as a correlative to the interior experience of individuals languishing in a state of guilt or enduring every kind of suffering and misfortune. *Both physical evil and moral evil, namely sin,* cause the sons and daughters of Israel to turn to the Lord and beseech his mercy. In this way David turns to him, conscious of the seriousness of his guilt; Job too, after his rebellion, turns to him in his tremendous misfortune; so also does Esther, knowing the mortal threat to her own people. And we find still other examples in the books of the Old Testament.

At the root of this manysided conviction, which is both communal and personal, and which is demonstrated by the whole of the Old Testament down the centuries, is the basic experience of the chosen people at the Exodus: the Lord saw the affliction of his people reduced to slavery, heard their cry, knew their sufferings and decided to deliver them. In this act of salvation by the Lord, the prophet perceived his love and compassion. This is precisely the grounds upon which the people and each of its members based their certainty of the mercy of God, which can be invoked whenever tragedy strikes. (John Paul II, On the Mercy of God, [*Dives in Misericordia*])

FIFTH SUNDAY OF LENT

Scriptural Commentary

First Reading Jer 31:31-34.

Jeremiah's grim mission was "to pluck up and to break down, to destroy and to overthrow" (1:10). It was his hopeless task to try to bring his people to see that without a radical change of heart, a genuine conversion, they were living in a fool's paradise. Never could God permit his city to fall and his temple to be destroyed, they were convinced. In truth, the Babylonians were God's judgment on a grossly unfaithful people. Because there was not the slightest hint that the people were going to change their ways, Jeremiah has to insist that the nation is doomed. But, when Nebuchadnezzar had captured and destroyed Jerusalem did the prophet crow over it and call out: "I told you so!"? Far from it. The time for threats is over. Disaster has struck and here is a shattered people. His prophetic service had been to try and bring his people to their senses. His service now is to comfort them in their bewilderment.

Jeremiah saw that the old covenant would be replaced by a new one (31:31-34) when God would act directly on the human heart, when he would write his law on that heart, and when all men and women would know Yahweh. What is new about the covenant is not the *torah* (the "instruction," "guide of life") which it enshrines. The revelation at Sinai is not to be cancelled or withdrawn. The covenant itself was not inadequate—it was the people who had failed. What is new is that there is a change in the way in which the divine will is to be conveyed to men. Yahweh is to by-pass the process of speaking and listening and put his will straight into Israel's heart and Israel will hear and obey perfectly. Jeremiah's own experience is reflected here: he had preached to a hopelessly obdurate people; he is convinced that God must take a hand and change the heart of man (cf. 32:37-41). He glimpses the era of the Spirit as Paul will describe it—the "law of the spirit of life" (Rom 8:2); he beholds the new man led by the Spirit, moved from within.

The greatest tribute to Jeremiah was paid by the one whose way he had prepared. On that night before the Lord went to his death, he brought the most solemn promise of the prophet to fulfilment: "This cup is the new covenant in my blood" (Lk 22:20). God had set his seal on the life and message of his servant.

Second Reading Heb 5:1-9.

The priesthood of Christ is a central theme of the letter to the Hebrews and our reading is a key passage in the unfolding of the theme. It is well to look to the context (4:12-16) where it is urged that the demands of God's word spoken through Christ are stringent and there is no escaping them. We will be judged on how we have responded. This might seem to impose an impossible responsibility, but there is no need for discouragement. We have confidence in knowing that Jesus is our merciful high priest who will give us all the help we need to be faithful. He has entered heaven but he is united to us still in his perfect understanding of our trials and difficulties. The distance between us, abolished by the incarnation, has not been broadened again by the ascension. He is always ready and able to help us because he is always our compassionate High Priest.

The passage 5:1-10 falls naturally into two parts: (1) the qualities requisite for the priestly office (1-4); (2) Jesus possesses these qualities (5-10). A high priest is a man officially instituted as a mediator between God and humankind, who pleads the cause of men before God, who offers the gifts of men to God, especially sacrifice for sin. A true high priest must be compassionate, showing benevolence and indulgence to sinners and he must be chosen and called by God (1-4). In proving that Jesus has these qualities, the author proceeds in reverse order, dealing first with his vocation and then with his fellowship in human suffering. Christ did not take the dignity of high priesthood upon himself; God who, in Ps 2:7, hails the Messiah as his Son (cf. Heb 1:5), declares him in Ps 110:4 to be a high priest forever after the order of Melchizedek. If he possesses the premier condition of priesthood, divine vocation, he also possesses the fundamental quality of the priest, compassion towards sinners (7-10). These verses present the Son in an attitude of suppliance before the Father. At once priest and victim, he learned the difficulty of obedience; and, being perfected in suffering, he brought salvation to those who obey him. This long period falls into two principal propositions: the first (7-8) indicates the means (suffering) by which the saving mission of Christ is effected; the second (9-10) indicates the result for himself and for those who trust in him. Through his obedience Jesus gained an enriching experience, a practical comprehension of and appreciation of suffering which would enable him fully to sympathize with his brethren. "For we have not a high priest who is unable to sympathize with our weaknesses, but one who in every respect has been tempted as we are, yet without sinning" (4:15). [See Thirtieth Sunday of the Year]

Gospel Jn 12:20-33.

In the Fourth Gospel Jesus often speaks of his "hour," his supreme moment, when all that he has come to do on earth will be accomplished. (In 2:4; 7:30; 8:20 the "hour" has not yet arrived; in 13:1; 17:1 he knows that it has come at last). Twice, in today's gospel reading, he speaks of this fateful "hour" (vv.23,27). The time for his passion has come and he fears it and yet longs for it. His soul is troubled. Should he ask the Father to save him from the cross? No! He sets his mind to fulfil his task: "For this purpose I have come to this hour." Further, he is sure that in this hour of crisis and suffering he will be glorified. Here, in the attitude of Jesus to his coming passion, we find a close parallel to Heb 5:7-9. The high priest experiences the pain of obedience, yet offers himself up to it totally, and through it is glorified. Significantly, both in Heb 5:7-8 and Jn 12:27 we catch an unmistakable echo of the prayer of Gethsemane (cf. Mk 14:32-39).

Our passage is concerned with the relationship between death and life—between sacrificial death and fuller life. In vv.20-22 we hear that some Greeks wish to speak with Jesus. Surprisingly, instead of acceding to their request, he states a fundamental theme to guide all his followers: "unless a grain of wheat falls into the earth and dies, it remains alone; but if it dies, it bears much fruit" (v.24). Following Christ involves despising one's earthly life and possessions and being ready to yield up everything for his service. Jesus explains more fully in vv.32-33 the relation between his sacrificial death and the life of mankind. In his own person he exemplifies the general principle: life, through death—"And I, when I am lifted up from the earth, will draw all men to myself" (v.32). This *"lifting-up"* means, in the language of the fourth gospel, two things. It is both the physical posture of the crucifixion (cf. 3:14—"as Moses lifted up the serpent in the wilderness . . . .") and the divine act by which Jesus was glorified, on account of his obedient death. Just as he is lifted up in torment by sinful men, even so he is raised in immortal triumph, by the Father, to be the saviour of all. And through his death and glory, he will draw all humankind to himself, to give them faith and life and forgiveness.

Patristic Commentary

St. Leo the Great (d.461)
Tractatus LIX, CCL 138A.356, NPNF 12².170.

Accordingly, dearly-beloved, Christ being lifted up upon the cross, let the eyes of your mind not dwell only on that sight which those wicked sinners saw, to whom it was said by the mouth of Moses, "And thy life shall be hanging before thine eyes, and thou shalt fear day and night, and shalt not be assured of thy life. (Dt. 28:66)." For in the crucified LORD they could think of nothing but their wicked deed, having not the fear, by which true faith is justified, but that by which an evil conscience is racked. But let our understanding, illumined by the Spirit of Truth, foster with pure and free heart the glory of the cross which irradiates heaven and earth, and see with the inner sight what the LORD meant when He spoke of His coming Passion: "The hour is come that the Son of man may be glorified:" and below He says, "Now is My spirit troubled. And what shall I say? Father, save Me from this hour, but for this cause came I unto this hour. Father, glorify Thy Son." And when the Father's voice came from heaven, saying, "I have both glorified it and will glorify it again," Jesus in reply said to those that stood by, "This voice came not for Me but for you. Now is the world's judgment, now shall the prince of this world be cast out. And I, if I be lifted up from the earth, will draw all things unto Me."

O wondrous power of the Cross! O ineffable glory of the Passion, in which is contained the LORD's tribunal, the world's judgment, and the power of the Crucified! For thou didst draw all things unto Thee, LORD, and when Thou hadst stretched out Thy hands all the day long to an unbelieving people that gainsaid Thee, the whole world at last was brought to confess Thy majesty. Thou didst draw all things unto Thee, LORD, for the veil of the temple was rent, and the Holy of Holies existed no more for those unworthy high-priests: so that type was turned into Truth, prophecy into Revelation, law into Gospel. Thou didst draw all things unto Thee, LORD, for the veil of the temple was rent, one temple of the Jews in dark signs, was now to be celebrated everywhere by the piety of all the nations in full and open rite.

Insights from the Documents of the Church

The Obedience of Christ

The Son, accordingly, came, sent by the Father who, before the foundation of the world, chose us and pre-destined us in him for adoptive sonship. For it is in him that it pleased the Father to restore all things (cf. Eph. 1:4-5 and 10). To carry out the will of the Father Christ inaugurated the kingdom of heaven on earth and revealed to us his mystery; by his obedience he brought about our redemption. The Church—that is, the kingdom of Christ—already present in mystery, grows visibly through the power of God in the world. The origin and growth of the Church are symbolized by the blood and water which flowed from the open side of the crucified Jesus (cf. Jn 19:34), and are foretold in the words of the Lord referring to his death on the cross: "And I, if I be lifted up from the earth, will

draw all men to myself" (Jn. 12:32; Gk.). As often as the
sacrifice of the cross by which "Christ our Pasch is sacrificed"
(1 Cor. 5:7) is celebrated on the altar, the work of our
redemption is carried out. Likewise, in the sacrament of
the eucharistic bread, the unity of believers, who from one
body in Christ (cf. 1 Cor. 10:17), is both expressed and
brought about. All men are called to this union with
Christ, who is the light of the world, from whom we go
forth, through whom we live, and towards whom our whole
life is directed. (Vat. II, Constitution on the Church, 3.)

'I will draw all men to myself.'

In the human nature united to himself, the son of God,
by overcoming death through his own death and resurrection, redeemed man and changed him into a new creation
(cf. Gal. 6:15; 2 Cor. 5:17). For by communicating his
Spirit, Christ mystically constitutes as his body those
brothers of his who are called together from every nation.

In that body the life of Christ is communicated to those
who believe and who, through the sacraments, are united
in a hidden and real way to Christ in his passion and
glorification. Through baptism we are formed in the likeness of Christ: "For in one Spirit we were all baptized into
one body" (1 Cor. 12:13). In this sacred rite fellowship in
Christ's death and resurrection is symbolized and is brought
about: "For we were buried with him by means of baptism
into death"; and if "we have been united with him in the
likeness of his death, we shall be so in the likeness of his
resurrection also" (Rom. 6:4-5). Really sharing in the
body of the Lord in the breaking of the eucharistic bread,
we are taken up into communion with him and with one
another. "Because the bread is one, we, though many, are
one body, all of us who partake of the one bread" (1 Cor
10:17). In this way all of us are made members of his body
(cf. 1 Cor 12:27), "but severally members one of another"
(Rom 12:4). (Vat. II, Constitution on the Church, 7.)

PASSION SUNDAY

Scriptural Commentary

Processional Gospel Mk 11:1-10.

Bethphage and Bethany are the villages nearest Jerusalem on the road from Jericho. It is idle to speculate whether the precise directions of Jesus (vv.2-3) indicate a previous arrangement with the owner of the colt. Mark clearly presents Jesus as displaying supernatural knowledge in making these arrangements. "On which no one has ever sat" is a common requirement in a beast used for religious purposes. The garments (v.7) provide an improvised saddle; the spreading of garments on the road (v.8) was a form of royal homage (cf. 2 Kg 9:13). "Leafy branches" recall the procession on the feast of Tabernacles (or Dedication). Despite the "many" of v.8, Mark does not give the impression that the accompanying crowd is large; yet they walk behind and before Jesus, forming a procession. "Hosanna" is a transliteration of a Hebrew word meaning "Save now"; it became an acclamation (like Hallelujah). The entry as depicted here meant the coming of a Messiah who was poor, an advent in humility, not in glory. What is at stake, for Jesus, is the nature and manner of his messiahship. At this moment, coming to the city that will so soon see the passion and death, he can manifest himself. But he does not come as a temporal ruler or with worldly pomp. He comes as a religious figure, a prince of peace, "humble and riding on a donkey" (Zech 9:9).

The Servant of the Lord

In Luke's charming story of Jesus and the two disciples on the road to Emmaus (Lk. 24:13-35) we have Jesus himself "interpreting to them in all the scriptures the things concerning himself" (v.27)—a precious testimony to a christian reading of the Old Testament. Just before this he had reminded them that, in God's purpose, the way to glory was the path of suffering (v.26), a theme found in the Isaian texts known as the "Servant Songs." During Holy Week pride of place among the Old Testament readings goes to the four Songs of the Suffering Servant. These are Is 42:1-7 (read on Monday), 49:1-6 (read on Tuesday), 50:4-9 (read on Passion Sunday and on Wednesday) and, the most renowned of them, 52:13-53:12 (read on Good Friday).

In these passages of Second Isaiah (Is 40-55, work of a prophet of the Exile) the Servant is a mysterious figure who has been chosen by God and filled with his Spirit (42:1). Though he seems inseparable from the Israel whose name he bears, from the Remnant "in whom God will be glorified" (49:3), he must lead back Jacob (42:6) and reassemble (49:5-6) and teach (50:4-9) Israel. And he will be the light of nations. Patient (50:6) and humble (53:7) he will, through his suffering and death, accomplish the plan of God: the salvation of sinners from all nations (53:8, 11-12). While the identification of the Servant is a much-debated problem, there is general agreement that he is a messianic figure.

We may regard the poems as the reflection of Second Isaiah on the vocation of Israel. His reflection passes through different stages and the development may be traced in the songs. Israel is charged with the true religion for the whole world (first song). But a purified Remnant alone will be capable of this role, and the Remnant must first of all convert Israel (second song). The mission is difficult and painful for Israel (third song). These tribulations will not be incidental to the mission but the very means of its accomplishment—in the person of one who will surpass in stature and efficacy any historical figure (fourth song). The Servant is presented, with characteristics of Moses and Jeremiah as a Messiah-Prophet, and his death is described as a sacrifice of expiation. In him Israel is epitomized, but is not lost to sight—the situation foreshadows the mystery of Christ and his church.

At any rate, while we may argue over precise interpretation of the Isaian texts, we have no doubt that the New

Testament writers cast Jesus in the role of the Servant. He, meek and humble of heart (Mt 11:29), was among his disciples "as one who serves" (Lk 22:27)—though he was their teacher and Lord (Jn 13:12-15). He had not only given them the ultimate proof of his love (13:1; 15:13) but laid down his life for sinners (Mk 10:45; Mt 20:26). Treated like a common criminal (Lk 22:37), and condemned to death, he was raised up on a cross so that he might draw all to himself (18:31-33); for it was by passing through the suffering and death of the Servant that he entered into the glory of the Son of Man (24:26).

First Reading Is 50:4-7.

The third Song of the Suffering Servant opens with an assurance that God's word is a sure and strong support. The Servant, however, must prayerfully and rightly hear God's word before he can presume to proclaim it to others. If he is faithful, then the glory of God can be manifested even in suffering and rejection. That is because God himself is the strength of his faithful. The problem of who this Servant precisely is does not obscure the central point that he is one in tune with God who hears God's message. This is the challenge presented to us by the Servant whom we Christians, through the experience of salvation, know Jesus to be. We can see how perfectly well he was attuned to the will of the Father, knowing his word and bringing it to his people.

Second Reading Phil 2:6-11.

In this hymn of the early church we see Jesus in his three existent states: his life before the incarnation, his earthly life, and his glorification with the Father. He is shown leaving aside his divine dignity, taking on the servile state of the human condition with its inevitable termination in death, and being exalted and made "Lord." Jesus gives us the example of creative fidelity to God through self-abnegation. He set aside the status and glory that go with divinity to show us the way to the Father through openness to God's word and fidelity to his will. The form of human existence chosen by Jesus is that of the Servant of the Father, faithful, in his human condition, to the point of death. Paul was striving to correct the abuses of selfishness, conceit and disharmony that make a mockery of christian unity and love. He found a powerful argument in the example of his Lord.

Gospel Mk 14:1 - 15:47.

The final act of the drama of Jesus. The Son of Man *must* suffer many things. In this divine necessity Mark finds his reply to the question: Who, then, is this? The precise answer is spoken by the centurion: "Truly, this man was Son of God!" (15:39). But the whole gospel has prepared for that solemn declaration. We cannot here offer a detailed exegesis of these two chapters. We shall do no more than indicate certain distinctively Marcan stresses.

The opening section (14:1-11) affords an example of Mark's "sandwich" technique whereby he intercalates an episode between two parts of another: here the anointing (3-9) between decision to get rid of Jesus and betrayal (1-2, 10-11)—the "beautiful deed" of the woman shows up the malevolent activity of others. Again, in the Last Supper passage (14:12-25) the same technique serves to make a telling catechetical point. Between preparation for the Supper (12-16) and the Supper (22-25) comes the solemn warning to Judas (17-21). It is a chastening admonishment to the reader. Mark has studiously placed the betrayal episode in the setting of eucharistic fellowship. The Christian must ask: "Is it I? . . . am I a betrayer of the Lord Jesus?" One is reminded of Paul in 1 Cor 11:8—"Let a man examine himself . . ."

At Gethsemane Jesus prayed to be saved from the hour, prayed to have the cup removed (32-42). He is being tempted to eliminate suffering from his messianic way. It is the supreme test for evil is overcome not by violence but by loving obedience—"he was heard for his godly fear"

(Heb 5:7). Jesus, in Gethsemane, had come to terms with the necessity of suffering. It has seemed to him that the way of the cross was the path he was asked to walk. Now, through anguished prayer, it had become clear to him that what had seemed to be asked really was asked of him. In that certainty he had found peace. It is no longer a stricken Jesus (vv.34-35) but a serene Jesus, victor in temptation, who can call to his disciples, "Rise, let us be going" and walk resolutely to meet his betrayer and his fate. He has spoken for the last time of his suffering role (v.41). Now he undergoes that suffering.

The highlight of the Trial scene (55-65) is the high priest's question and Jesus' reply: "'Are you the Christ, the Son of the Blessed?' and Jesus said, 'I am'" (61-62) —and then he adds, "and you will see the Son of man sitting at the right hand of Power, and coming with the clouds of heaven" (v.62). Thoroughly Marcan, these verses are the culmination of his christology. Jesus himself, for the first and only time, positively and publicly acknowledges that he is the Christ, and that he is indeed the Son of God. But he does so on his own terms, in terms of "Son of Man." When he returns in glory as the victorious Son of Man his true identity will be revealed. Ironically, while Jesus is making his proclamation, Peter is denying him (53-54, 66-72).

Mark has firmly presented the crucifixion of Jesus as an enthronement (15:21-32); this appears at once in Pilate's opening question: "Are you the King of the Jews?" (15:2). Jesus accepts the designation but with the implication that he understands it differently. The soldiers pay homage to the "King of the Jews" (16-19) and the official super- scription. "The King of the Jews" is fixed on Jesus' cross. And priests and scribes mock him as "Christ, the King of Israel" (v.32). Jesus' royal status is wholly paradoxical.

Mark has Jesus die in total desolation (33-37). It would have seemed that, up to this point, Jesus' isolation could go no further: deserted by his disciples, taunted by his enemies, derided by those who hung with him, suffocating in the darkness of evil. But the worst is now: abandoned by God. His suffering is radically lonely. But his God is *"my* God" (v.34). Even in this, as at Gethsemane, it is "not what I will but what thou wilt." Now Jesus knows what it means to give his life as a ransom for many. Now the Son is wholly delivered into the hands of men.

The rending of the curtain of the temple (v.38) marks a transformation at the moment of Jesus' death. The temple has lost its significance; the privilege of Israel has come to an end; access to the divine presence is henceforth open to all. Far more important is the confession of the centurion (v.39). The centurion has looked upon the dead Jesus, and has seen the Son of God! Only one who can accept that paradox can, like him, make the full christian profession of faith. Only such a one can hope to see the Son of Man coming with the clouds of heaven.

Patristic Commentary

St. Jerome (c.347-c.420)
Homily on Mark 13.32f., CCL 78.497,
    FOTC 57.188.

This same lesson from the Gospel says: "When he was at Bethany, in the house of Simon the leper, and was reclining at the table, there came a woman with an alabaster jar of ointment, genuine nard of great value." She broke her alabaster jar that Christ may make you "christs," His anointed. Hear what it says in the Canticle of Canticles: "Your name spoken is a spreading perfume, therefore the maidens love you. We will follow you eagerly in the fragrance of your perfume!" (Cant 1.2) As long as the perfume was sealed up, as long as Christ was known only in Judea, in Israel alone His name was great, the maidens were not following Jesus. When His perfume spread throughout the world, then, maiden souls of believers followed the Savior.

"When he was at Bethany, in the house of Simon the leper." Bethany means house of obedience. How, then, is the house of Simon the leper in Bethany, the house of obedience? What is the Lord doing in the house of one who is leprous? That is exactly why He went into the house of a leper, in order to cleanse him. Leper implies, not one who is a leper, but who has been leprous; he was a leper before he received the Lord, but after he received Him, and the jar of perfume was broken in his house, the leprosy vanished. He retains his former identity, however, in order to manifest the power of the Savior.

"There came a woman with an alabaster jar of ointment." The Pharisees, the Scribes, and the priests are in the temple and they have no ointment. This woman is outside the temple and carries with her a jar of ointment containing nard, genuine nard, from which she has prepared the ointment; hence, you are called genuine [nard], or the faithful. The Church, gathered together from the Gentiles, is offering the Savior her gifts, the faith of believers. She has broken the alabaster jar that all may receive its perfume; she has broken the alabaster jar that was kept sealed in Judea. "She broke the alabaster jar." Just as the grain of wheat, unless it falls into the ground and dies, does not bring forth any fruit, so, also, unless the alabaster jar be broken, we cannot spread its fragrance.

Insights from the Documents of the Church

Christ emptied himself; Church called to follow

Just as Christ carried the work of redemption in poverty and oppression, so the Church is called to follow the same path if she is to communicate the fruits of salvation to men. Christ Jesus, "though he was by nature God . . . emptied himself, taking the nature of a slave" (Phil. 2:6,7), and "being rich, became poor" (2 Cor. 8:9) for our sake. Likewise, the Church, although she needs human resources to carry out her mission, is not set up to seek earthly glory, but to proclaim, and this by her own example, humility and self-denial. Christ was sent by the Father "to bring good news to the poor . . . to heal the contrite of heart" (Lk. 4:18), "to seek and to save what was lost" (Lk. 19:10). Similarly, the Church encompasses with her love all those who are afflicted by human misery and she recognizes in those who are poor and who suffer, the image of her poor and suffering founder. She does all in her power to relieve their need and in them she strives to serve Christ. Christ, "holy, innocent and undefiled" (Heb. 7:26) knew nothing of sin (2 Cor. 5:21), but came only to expiate the sins of the people (cf. Heb. 2:17). The Church, however, clasping sinners to her bosom, at once holy and always in need of purification, follows constantly the path of penance and renewal.

The Church, "like a stranger in a foreign land, presses forward amid the persecutions of the world and the con-solations of God," announcing the cross and death of the Lord until he comes (cf. 1 Cor. 11:26). But by the power of the risen Lord she is given strength to overcome, in patience and in love, her sorrows and her difficulties, both those that are from within and those that are from without, so that she may reveal in the world, faithfully, however darkly, the mystery of her Lord until, in the consummation, it shall be manifested in full light. (Vat. II, Constitution on the Church, 8.)

Prayer for Humanity

In the name of Jesus Christ crucified and risen, in the spirit of his messianic mission, enduring in the history of humanity, *we raise our voices and pray* that the Love which is in the Father may once again be revealed at this stage of history, and that, through the work of the Son and Holy Spirit, it may be shown to be present in our modern world and to be more powerful than evil: more powerful than sin and death. We pray for this through the intercession of her who does not cease to proclaim "mercy . . . from generation to generation," and also through the inter-cession of those for whom there have been completely fulfilled the words of the Sermon on the Mount: "Blessed are the merciful, for they shall obtain mercy." (John Paul II, On the Mercy of God, [*Dives in Misericordia*])

HOLY THURSDAY*

Scriptural Commentary

First Reading Ex 12:1-8,11-14.

The importance of this Old Testament text is not so much in its content as the fact that it situates Jesus' last supper in a tradition. Jesus was adopting as his own and transforming a rite which already existed and which celebrated annually the deliverance of the Israelites from Egypt and their formation into God's people.

In Jesus' time the Passover vigil (Ex 12:42) celebrated not only the deliverance from Egypt but also the creation of the world, the sacrifice of Isaac by Abraham (Gen. 22) and the future, final accomplishment of God's kingdom. All of these motifs figure in the Eucharist which is the Christian's Passover. Jesus' command to celebrate the Eucharist in his "remembrance" (1 Cor. 11:24-25) evokes the command given to Moses (Ex 12:14). "To remember," in this context, means not merely to "recall" to mind but to make really present. When the pious Jew today celebrates the Passover he considers that he is as really present to the event of the Exodus as were his ancestors over three thousand years ago. Likewise the Christian, in celebrating the Eucharist, knows that he shares in Jesus' "exodus" of his life, death and resurrection just as really as the first disciples.

Second Reading 1 Cor. 11:23-26.

This is the earliest reference in the New Testament to the institution of the Eucharist. Paul is quoting a piece of tradition which he has himself received and handed on to his readers. He reminds them of this tradition in order to correct an abuse in their celebration of the eucharist (11:17-22). He urges that "the Lord's supper" is more than the performance of a ritual; it concerns not only worship of God but also care for men. The eucharist is the "sacrament," that is, the expression, the sign or symbol, of Jesus' self-giving in his life and death for others. True communion with Christ involves a real sharing in his life and death for others. The Eucharist is both the source and the expression of this service.

Gospel Jn. 13:1-15.

Jesus' washing of his disciples' feet is the expression of the selfless love involved in his "Passover," that is, his departure "out of this world to the Father" (13:1). It is the function of a *slave* to wash his master's feet. Throughout his life, culminating in his death, Jesus has assumed the role of a slave (cf. Phil. 2:6-11), the one who is, essentially, for others. Like Paul before him (cf. 1 Cor. 11:17-34), John wishes to remind his readers that Jesus' mission is one of service, that he came not to show men what they should do for God but, rather, to reveal what God has done for them. Peter's reaction to Jesus' gesture (v.6) illustrates how difficult it is for us to accept the Lord's service. It is far easier for us to construct a religion based on service of the Lord in a way which by-passes our service of others. The firm point of John's lesson is that Jesus' behaviour towards us should serve as the example of our behaviour towards others (vv.12-17).

Patristic Commentary

St. Ambrose (c.340-397)
Holy Spirit, Book 1, c.12, PL 16.706,
    FOTC 44.40-41.

I find the Lord divesting Himself of His garments, and girding Himself with a towel, pouring water into a basin, washing the feet of His disciples. This water was that heavenly dew, which was prophesied: that the Lord Jesus would wash the feet of His disciples with that heavenly dew. And now let the feet of our souls be extended. The Lord Jesus wishes to wash our feet also, for not to Peter alone but to each one of the faithful does He say: "If I wash not thy feet, thou shalt have no part with me." (Jn. 13:8)

Come, therefore, O Lord Jesus, divest Yourself of Your garments which You have put on for my sake. Be You naked, that You may clothe us with your mercy. Gird Yourself with a towel for our sakes, that You may gird us with Your gift of immortality. Pour water into the basin; wash not only our feet but also the head, and not only the footprints of our body, but also of our mind. I wish to put off all the filth of our frailty, so that I, too, may say: "I have put off my garment, how shall I put it on? I have washed my feet, how shall I defile them?" (Song 5:3).

How great is that majesty! As a servant, You wash the feet of Your disciples, as God You pour dew from heaven. Not only do you wash the feet, but You also invite us to recline with You, and You exhort us by the example of Your graciousness saying: "You call me Master, and Lord; and you say well; for so I am. If I then, being Lord and Master, have washed your feet; you also ought to wash one another's feet."

I also, then, wish to wash the feet of my brethren; I wish to fulfil the mandate of the Lord; I do not wish to be ashamed of myself nor to disdain what He Himself did first. Good is the mystery of humility, because, while I wash the filth of others, I wash away my own. But not all were able to drink in this mystery. Indeed, Abraham also wished to wash feet, but because of a feeling of hospitality. (cf. Gen. 18:4). Gedeon, too, wished to wash the feet of the angel of the Lord who appeared to him; but he wished to do this to one; he wished to do it as one who was offering obedience, not as one who was offering fellowship. This is a great mystery, which no one knows. Then He said to Peter: "What I do thou knowest not now; but thou shalt know hereafter." (Jn 13:7). This, I say, is a divine mystery, which even they who have washed will need. It is not then the simple water of a heavenly mystery, by which we succeed in deserving to have a part with Christ.

Perpetuating the Cross

To perpetuate down the centuries the Sacrifice of the Cross, the divine Saviour instituted the Eucharistic Sacrifice, the memorial of his death and Resurrection, and entrusted it to his Spouse the Church, which especially on Sundays, calls the faithful together to celebrate the Passover of the Lord until he comes again. This the Church does in union with the saints in heaven and in particular with the Blessed Virgin, whose burning charity and unshakable faith she imitates. (Paul VI, To Honour Mary [*Marialis Cultus*])

Eucharist and Charity

Eucharistic worship constitutes the soul of all Christian life. In fact Christian life is expressed in the fulfilling of the greatest commandment, that is to say in the love of God and neighbour, and this love finds its source in the Blessed Sacrament, which is commonly called the Sacrament of love.

The Eucharist signifies this charity, and therefore recalls it, makes it present *and at the same time brings it about*. Every time that we consciously share in it, there opens in our souls a real dimension of that unfathomable love that includes everything that God has done and continues to do for us human beings, as Christ says: "My Father goes on working, and so do I." Together with this unfathomable and free gift, which is *charity* revealed in its fullest degree in the saving Sacrifice of the Son of God, the Sacrifice of which the Eucharist is the indelible sign, there also springs up within us a lively response of love. We not only know love; we ourselves *begin to love*. We enter, so to speak, upon the path of love and along this path make progress. Thanks to the Eucharist, the love that springs up within us from the Eucharist develops in us, becomes deeper and grows stronger.

Eucharistic worship is therefore precisely the expression of that love which is the authentic and deepest characteristic of the Christian vocation. This worship springs from the love and serves the love to which we are all called in Jesus Christ. A living fruit of this worship is the perfecting of the image of God that we bear within us, an image that corresponds to the one that Christ has revealed to us. As we thus become adorers of the Father "in spirit and truth," we mature in an ever fuller union with Christ, we are ever more united to him, and—if one may use the expression— we are ever more in harmony with him. (John Paul II, The Holy Eucharist.)

GOOD FRIDAY*

Scriptural Commentary

First Reading Is 52:13 - 53:12.

The close correspondence between the gospel narratives of the Passion and this fourth Servant Song is best explained by the recourse of the evangelists to this passage. The early Christians turned gratefully to the Suffering Servant in their coming to terms with the scandal of the cross and in their striving to understand the suffering and death of Jesus. Particularly helpful was the idea of vicarious suffering—"he was wounded for our transgressions . . . with his stripes we are healed."

The Servant's role is essentially that of mediator of the new covenant which would seal the return from the Babylonian exile, a return depicted by Second Isaiah as another Exodus. His willing acceptance of his (unmerited) suffering is interpreted as an expiation sacrifice for the people's sins

(53:10). And, because of his patient endurance, he is exalted by God (v.12). Is this mysterious Servant an individual? or a personification of the people? Perhaps it is best to combine both aspects. The Servant is an individual figure who stands in the person of Israel and accomplishes Israel's divine mission. The Servant's suffering is effective for the people only in so far as the people learn its lesson. (See Twenty-Ninth Sunday)

Second Reading Heb. 4:14-16; 5:7-9.

The author of Hebrews presents Jesus as our faithful and compassionate high priest. Already in 2:17 he had introduced Jesus as "a merciful and faithful high priest." Here (4:15-16) he stresses Jesus' solidarity with us ("one who in every respect has been tempted as we are" (cf. 2:17). He can share with us our disappointments and failures as well as our physical sufferings because he underwent the same experiences, and we can share ours with him. His sinlessness (because sin is self-seeking) makes him even more open to our needs. With confidence in our high priest we can unhesitatingly approach the "mercy seat" of God—to receive mercy and grace. As our high priest, Jesus is the one whom we must follow if we, like him, are to enter into God's presence. (See Twenty-Ninth Sunday)

Verses 1-4 of Ch. 5 establish two characteristics of the Old Testament high priest: as a man of his people he is able to understand their weakness and sympathise with them; he has not won for himself his role of mediator but has been appointed by God. In vv.5-10 we are shown that Jesus has these characteristics. Scripture (Pss 2:7; 110:4) makes clear that God has appointed Jesus his Son as "a priest for ever." He can sympathise with us because he knew suffering at first hand. His "prayer" was his sacrifice, an act of perfect love of the Father, of union with him. He grew through his suffering, learning by bitter experience what it may cost to obey God's will. The salvation that he wins for us is real because it is a salvation in and from our human lot.

If we wish to "receive mercy and find grace to help in time of need" (4:16) we, like Jesus, must pray and become obedient through our suffering (5:7-8). Jesus is indeed "the source of salvation" but only to those, "who obey him" (5:9). Hebrews is addressed to Christians who are gripped by profound psychological suffering. The author wishes to show them that these sufferings, far from being an obstacle to their union with God, are the very means by which they will arrive at maturity. They can be educative in that they permit us to rely progressively less upon ourselves and more upon God and thus become "perfect" children.

The Passion Jn. 18:1 - 19:42.

John presents the Passion as the triumph of the Son of God. The *dramatis personae* are sharply characterized. Despite appearances, *Jesus* is always in control. He is the Judge who judges his judge (Pilate) and his accusers ("the Jews"). He is the King who reigns, with the cross for a throne—"I, when I am lifted up from the earth, will draw all to myself." *The Jews* are not the whole Jewish people but its leaders who see Jesus as a danger to them, the Establishment, and who are determined to destroy him. *Pilate* recognizes, and three times acknowledges, the innocence of Jesus. He desperately tries to compromise but ends by yielding to political blackmail. He is a man who will not make a decision for or against Jesus—and finds himself trapped.

Jesus before Pilate (18:28 - 19:16). The synoptic accounts of the trial before Pilate tell us little whereas John's dramatic reconstruction does bring out the significance of it. Only John makes clear why Jesus was brought to Pilate in

the first place and why Pilate gave in to having him crucified. Only John shows the interplay of subtle (and not so
subtle) political forces on Pilate and indicates how Pilate's
original questioning of Jesus concerned a political charge
against him. Yet Mark, we now realize, has given the key
to the trial in the title "King of the Jews" (15:2); there-
after he stresses that it is as King of the Jews (Messiah)
that Jesus is rejected by the crowd and crucified. [See
Passion Sunday]

There is a theological reason for John's stress on the
Roman trial. We are to see Pilate in the light of the rest of
the Fourth Gospel. He provides an example of an attitude
to Jesus which is neither faith nor rejection: the typical
attitude of those who try to maintain a middle position
in an all-or-nothing situation. Pilate's refusal to make a
decision for or against the Light leads to tragedy. Because
Pilate will not face the challenge of deciding for the Truth
in Jesus and against the Jews, he thinks he can persuade the
Jews to accept a solution that will make it unnecessary for
him to declare for Jesus. This is the Johannine view of the
episodes of Barabbas, the scourging, and the delivery of
Jesus to the Jews as "your King." For John, this trial is our
own tragic history of temporizing and indecision. Pilate,
the would-be neutral man is frustrated by the pressure of
others. He failed to listen to the truth and decide in its
favour. He, and all who would follow him, inevitably end
up enslaved to this world.

Pilate yields to the Jewish demand for Jesus' crucifixion
(19:12-16). John's account of the passing of sentence of
death is detailed, dramatic and theological; the only points
of parallel with the synoptists are in the repeated cry for
crucifixion and the outcome of Jesus' being "handed over."
The Old Testament background to this verb used by all the
evangelists implies that Jesus was "delivered up" by "the
definite plan and foreknowledge of God" (Acts 2:23). The
real trial is over when the Jews utter the fateful words, "We
have no king but Caesar!" This is akin to the statement in

Matthew's account: "His blood be upon us and upon our children" (Mt. 27:25). Both evangelists are reflecting not history but apologetic theology. The tragedy of Jesus' death was viewed through the hostility between Church and Synagogue in the late first century A.D. The audience at the trial is made to voice a christian interpretation of salvation history.

John also tells us that it was noon on Passover Eve when the fatal renunciation of the Messiah was voiced. This was the hour when the Passover lambs were being sacrificed in the Temple. It is supreme Johannine irony: the Jews renounce the covenant at the very moment when the priests begin to prepare for the feast which annually recalled God's deliverance of his covenanted people. By the blood of a lamb in Egypt Yahweh had marked them off to be spared as his own. Now, they know no king but the emperor and they slay another Lamb. At this moment, just before the Passover, as Jesus set out for Golgotha to shed his saving blood, the trial of Jesus ends with the fulfilment of that proclamation at the beginning of the gospel: "Behold the lamb of God who takes away the sin of the world" (1:29).

The last word of Jesus—"It is fulfilled! (v.30)—is a cry of victory: now Jesus will draw all men to himself. "He gave up his spirit": Jesus dies, but his Spirit will take over his work of drawing mankind to himself. Jesus is now glorified in the completion of his "hour," the fulfilment of God's purpose—and so the Spirit now is given (cf. 7:39).

The final episode, the breaking of Jesus' legs and the flow of blood and water (31-37) is the only part of John's crucifixion narrative which has no parallel in the synoptics. The flow of blood and water is another proleptic reference to the giving of the Spirit. On a secondary level this flow symbolizes the sacraments of Eucharist and Baptism and points to their source in Jesus; through these sacraments the life of Jesus is communicated to the Christian. Blood and water flow from the *dead* Jesus. The drama of the cross does not end in death but in a flow of life that comes from death. The death of Jesus on the cross is the beginning of christian life.

Patristic Commentary

Lactantius (c.240-c.320)
Divine Institutes, Book 4, c.26, CSEL 19.382,
    FOTC 49.312.

Someone may say: "Why, if He were God and wanted to die, was He not visited with some honorable kind of death, at least? Why the extreme of the cross? Why this infamous kind of punishment which seems unworthy of a free man even, although he be dangerous? First, because He who had come in a lowly state to bring help to the lowly and weak and to show hope of salvation to all was afflicted with that type which is customary for the weak and downtrodden, lest there be anyone at all who could not imitate Him. Then, in order that His body be preserved entire, which He was to raise from the dead on the third day. For not anyone was to be ignorant of this, because He Himself, speaking beforehand about His Passion, also made it known that He had the power of laying down and of taking His life up again when He wished. So He was taken down from the cross after He had laid down His life. His murderers did not think it necessary to break His bones, as was their custom, but they only pierced His side. Thus His whole body was removed from the gibbet, and was carefully enclosed in a sepulchre. All these things were done for this reason, that a broken and diminished body might not be rendered unfit for His Resurrection. That was also a special reason why God preferred the cross, because it was necessary for Him to be exalted by it and for the Passion of God to be known to all peoples. For since He who is suspended on a gibbet is conspicuous to all and is higher than others, a cross was rather chosen, to signify that He would be so conspicuous and so exalted, that all the nations throughout the world would run together to know and serve Him. Finally, no nation is so unhuman, no region so remote, that His Passion or the sublimity of His Majesty is not known by it. Therefore, He extended His arms in the Passion and embraced the world, so as to show them that from the rising to the setting of the sun a great people gathered from every tribe and tongue would come, and gather under his wings and would take up that greatest symbol of all and bear it high on their foreheads.

Insights from the Documents of the Church

Our Lady and Calvary

The union of the Mother and the Son in the work of redemption reaches its climax on Calvary, where Christ "offered himself as the perfect sacrifice to God" (Heb. 9:14) and where Mary stood by the Cross (cf. Jn. 19:25), "suffering grievously with her only-begotten Son. There she united herself with a maternal heart to his sacrifice, and lovingly consented to the immolation of this victim which she herself had brought forth" and also was offering to the Eternal Father. (Paul VI, To Honour Mary [*Marialis Cultus*])

Christ dies for our sins

The events of Good Friday and, even before that, the prayer in Gethsemane, introduce a fundamental change into the whole course of the revelation of love and mercy in the messianic mission of Christ. The one who "went about doing good and healing" and "curing every sickness and disease" now himself seems to merit the greatest mercy and to *appeal for mercy*, when he is arrested, abused, condemned, scourged, crowned with thorns, when he is nailed to the Cross and dies amidst agonizing torments. It is then that he particularly deserves mercy from the people to whom he has done good, and he does not receive it. Even those who are closest to him cannot protect him and snatch him from the hands of his oppressors. At this final stage of his messianic activity the words which the prophets, especially Isaiah, uttered concerning the Servant of Yahweh are fulfilled in Christ: "Through his stripes we are healed."

Christ, as the man who suffers really and in a terrible way in the Garden of Olives and on Calvary, addresses himself to the Father—that Father whose love he has preached to people, to whose mercy he has borne witness through all of his activity. But he is not spared—not even he—the terrible suffering of death on the Cross: *"For our sake God made him to be sin who knew no sin,"* Saint Paul will write, summing up in a few words the whole depth of the Cross and at the same time the divine dimension of the reality of the Redemption. Indeed this Redemption is the ultimate and definitive revelation of the holiness of God, who is the absolute fullness of perfection: fullness of justice and of love, since justice is based on love, flows from it and tends towards it. In the Passion and death of Christ—in the fact that the Father did not spare his own Son, but "for our sake made him sin"—absolute justice is expressed, for Christ undergoes the Passion and Cross because of the sins of humanity. (John Paul II, On the Mercy of God [*Dives in Misericordia*])

Fasting

But the paschal fast must be kept sacred. It should be celebrated everywhere on Good Friday, and where possible should be prolonged throughout Holy Saturday so that the faithful may attain the joys of the Sunday of the resurrection with uplifted and responsive minds. (Vat. II, Constitution on the Liturgy, 110.)

EASTER

THE EASTER VIGIL

Scriptural Commentary

For the Easter Vigil there are seven Old Testament readings before the two New Testament readings of the Mass. These Old Testament readings may be reduced to three and, in special circumstances, even to two, with the proviso that the third, the narrative of the crossing of the Red Sea (Ex. 14:15 - 15:1), must be read. Where a selection needs to be made it is preferable to choose those readings which have a more direct bearing on the paschal theme and carry a message for Christians today. If three readings are selected, one would suggest the first, third and seventh.

A. Old Testament Readings

1. *Gen 1:1 - 2:2.* Though this passage is already a liturgical text and an eloquent and powerful statement of the truth of creation and its goodness, it is likely because of New Testament and patristic themes that it figures in our Easter liturgy. According to Paul, the work of Christ is a "new creation" (2 Cor 5:17). The spirit brooded over the primeval waters and they brought forth life; likewise, water and the Spirit give birth to the Christian. Light and darkness evoke the work of the Word (Jn 1:5) (given dramatic expression in the ritual of the paschal fire). The Word was in conflict with darkness and was present at the first creation; "all things were made through him" (Jn 1:3; Heb 1:2). As the new Adam the Word is a life-giving spirit (1 Cor 15:45).

2. *Gen 22:1-18.* The restoration of creation began with God's call of Abraham. The new relationship with God is based on total faith in him, symbolized here by Abraham's readiness to give up his only son Isaac. In the end it was God himself who gave his only Son to restore man to his friendship. The experience of Isaac has long been regarded as a type of the sacrifice of Christ. The total self-giving of Abraham as manifested in the event is the basis of his fatherhood of a people, the people of Israel. The death of Christ combined the sufferings of Isaac and the trust and obedience of Abraham and so was the event on which a new people of God was founded.

3. *Ex 14:15 - 15:1.* A description of the final act in the drama of the Hebrews' liberation from Egyptian slavery. The crossing of the Sea of Reeds and the defeat of the Egyptians became the great symbol of God's saving actions in history. That passage foreshadows the baptism of Christians (1 Cor 10:1-5).

4. *Is 54:5-14.* During the Exile, at a time when God seemed far away from her, Israel received this promise that God would take her back into his love and that the renewed relationship would last forever. The Church is the heir of this promise. The history of Israel stands as a warning. A loving and generous God looks for faithfulness.

5. *Is 55:1-11.* Virtually a continuation of the foregoing reading, this passage is an appeal to the exiles to turn from the ineffective things of this world to the word of God which alone achieves its purpose and can satisfy man's longing. Always, Israel must "seek the Lord"—calling for a humble turning to God. The transcendent God is near at hand, and man must play his part. "I can do all things in him who strengthens me." The word which comes from God is really heard only when it becomes part of us and finds human expression.

6. *Baruch 3:9-15,32—4:4*. A call to return to God who is source of true wisdom. Israel is privileged indeed to be the recipient of divine wisdom. If she will but live by it she will have life and peace.

7. *Ezek 36:16-28*. The traumatic experience of the Exile led Israel to doubt the power and protection of God. Ezekiel here reminds the exiles that the disaster had not come because of God's powerlessness but because of their sins. He promised that God would restore them by giving them his Spirit to be the unfailing source of obedience to his will. Thus he would show himself to be their God and they could again be truly his people. The ecclesial and baptismal reference of this reading is obvious: cleansing with water, the gift of God's own Spirit and the gathering together of God's people.

B. New Testament Readings
First Reading Rom 6:3-11.

In Romans 5:12-21 Paul has explained that we have been reconciled *through* Christ, thus stressing Christ's objective, mediatory role. But this insistence could give rise to a misunderstanding about our personal role in salvation. In 6:1-23 Paul notes the "subjective" aspect of salvation. Far from exempting us from death, Christ's death-and-resurrection "for us" involves us in a continual dying and rising "with" him and "in" him. This is symbolized by baptism: the descent into the water expressing death and the ascent from the font expressing life. Baptism is not only what is done to us but what we do. Christ's death and resurrection are made real in us not only by our resurrection from physical death (v.5) but also (and this is Paul's main point) through the continual "resurrection" from the "death" of sin by a way of life modelled on Christ's. The parallel in us to Christ's resurrection is our walking "in newness of life" (v.4). Thus Paul reminds his readers that their resurrection is not merely a future hope; it is also a present reality.

Gospel Mark 16:1-8.

The women (v.7) were given a message, the echo of a promise made by Jesus on the way to Gethsemane (14:28), a message for the disciples, and especially for Peter. Jesus is going before them to Galilee; they will see him there. At first sight this looks like an assurance that they will encounter the risen Lord in Galilee. The point is that Mark refrains stolidly from relating any resurrection appearances. Mark is writing for a community at a time when appearances of the Lord had long been a thing of the past. He has striven to get across the idea and the reality of a suffering Son of Man christology. He has no intention of spoiling the effect at the end.

There is a practical consensus that Mark's gospel ends, intentionally, at 16:8. If it were only a matter of the women's flight, of their trembling, astonishment and fear, it would appear to be an impressive end to his work. The snag is the statement "and they said nothing to anyone" (v.8). It is quite surprising in view of the clear-cut message they had received (v.7). There is no doubt that Mark has left us with a sense of incompleteness. He has omitted stories of Jesus' appearance to his disciples in order to emphasise the gratuitous character of faith. He reminds us that if we believe the gospel this is not because we have received it from a long chain of witnesses but because *God*, if indeed through those witnesses, has enabled us to believe. "Thus Mark, like Paul, holds that Jesus' resurrection is not merely an objective fact. It is also a subjective condition. For it is the gospel, the good news, the word—and a word which is not heard is not a word. Faith is as necessary to the resurrection as the resurrection is to faith (cf. 1 Cor 15:14)" (L. Swain).

Patristic Commentary

Asterius of Amasea (d. after 341)
Homily 19, PG 40.436.

As man he was slaughtered and as God he became alive, and gave life to the whole world. As an oyster he was trampled upon, and as a pearl he has adorned the Church. As a sheep he was slaughtered and as a shepherd with his cross for a staff he has expelled the flock of demons. As a light on a candelabrum he was extinguished on the cross, and as the sun he arose from the tomb. A double wonder could be seen: when Christ was crucified the day became dark, and when he arose the night became bright as day. Why was the day darkened? Because it was written concerning him, *he made darkness the cloak about him* (Ps 17:12). Why did the night become bright as day? Because the prophet said to him, *for you darkness itself is not dark and night shines as the day* (Ps 138:12).

O Night brighter than day; O Night brighter than the sun; O Night whiter than snow; O Night more brilliant than torches; O Night more delightful than paradise; O Night which knows not darkness; O Night which has banished sleep; O Night which has taught us to join vigil with angels; O Night terror of demons; O Night most desirable in the year; O Night of torchbearing of the bridegroom in the Church; O Night mother of the newly baptized; O Night when the devil slept and was stripped; O Night in which the Inheritor brought the beneficiaries into their inheritance; An inheritance without end.

Insights from the Documents of the Church

Baptism

It is recommended in order to set in relief its paschal character, that baptism be celebrated at the Easter vigil or on a Sunday, when the Church commemorates the Lord's resurrection. *Introduction to the Rite of Infant Baptism.*

Baptism is the sacrament by which men and women are incorporated into the Church, assembled together into the house of God in the Spirit, into a royal priesthood and a holy nation. It is the sacramental bond of unity between all those who have received it. This unalterable effect is symbolised in the Latin liturgy by the anointing of the baptised persons with chrism in the presence of God's people and because of it the rite of baptism is held in the highest esteem by all Christians. It is never lawful to repeat it if it has been validly celebrated, even by our separated fellow christians.

Baptism, which is washing with water accompanied by the living word, cleanses men and women of all stain of sin, original and personal, makes them sharers in God's life and his adopted children. As the prayers of the blessing of the water attest, baptism is water of heaven-sent regeneration of God's children and their re-birth. Readings from the Scriptures, the prayer of the community and a triple profession of faith prepare for the lead up to the culmination of the rite: the invocation of the blessed Trinity over those to be baptised. Signed with this name, they are consecrated to the blessed Trinity and enter into fellowship with the Father, the Son and the Holy Spirit.

Baptism, much more effective than the purification of the old law, produces these effects by the power of the mystery of the Passion and Resurrection of the Lord. When people are baptised, they share sacramentally in Christ's death, they are buried with him and lie dead, they are brought back to life with him and rise with him. For baptism recalls and actualises the very paschal mystery itself, since by its means men and women pass from the death of sin to life. For this reason it is fitting that the joy of the resurrection should be reflected when it is celebrated and especially during the Easter Vigil and on Sundays. (General Introduction to Christian Initiation)

EASTER SUNDAY*

Scriptural Commentary

First Reading Acts 10:34, 37-43.

This reading is part of Peter's sermon to the Roman centurion Cornelius and his family and friends (10:24); it presents the gospel in a nutshell. It stresses that the apostles are the accredited witnesses to the preachers of the gospel. It was because Christ had risen again from the dead that the apostles could preach the reality of redemption, of the forgiveness of sin. The risen Saviour continues to be with his church. In him the fulness of God dwells, the plentitude of divine power and goodness. It is an overflowing fulness, bringing divine life to all who believe in Christ.

Peter could speak with confidence of this divine power, having experienced the coming of the Holy Spirit at Pentecost. Two thousand years later our generation of Christians can proclaim, and must proclaim, the reality and the significance of the resurrection as confidently as Peter did. The church does so in a special way at Easter.

Second Reading Col 3:1-4.

According to the author, baptism is a participation in Christ's death and resurrection, symbolized by the ritual of being "plunged" into water (2:12). This real share in Christ's death and resurrection has profound and far-reaching repercussions in the Christian's present moral life. It entails the rejection of all that is "earthly" (3:2-5), that is, all that is opposed to God. It calls for the pursuit of the "good life"—not by the world's standards but as the good life has been lived by Jesus. Here we have the reality of *christian* freedom. Though, by his sacramental death in baptism, the Christian is liberated from past constraints, he is, nevertheless, bound to lead a new life in conformity with the gospel.

Alternative Second Reading 1 Cor 5:6-8.

The Jewish feast of Passover recalls the unleavened bread used for the festival. Householders were expected to get rid of the old leavened bread in preparation for the feast. Christians should celebrate the new christian Passover by getting rid of old attitudes and by living in sincerity and truth. The Easter feast is not just a calendar happening but a saving grace that should transform our lives. Like baptism (Col 3:1-4) the celebration of Easter is not a mere ritual. It is the symbol of a whole new way of life.

Gospel Jn 20:1-9.

As we had come to expect from the passion-narrative, the Johannine resurrection-narrative too is dramatic. It divides into two scenes: "at the tomb" (20:1-18) and "where the disciples were gathered" (20:19-29). Each scene has a definite time-setting at the beginning and in each there are two episodes: in the first, the disciples come to faith; in the second, Jesus appears to an individual and the recognition scene leads on to a larger audience. Our reading includes only part of the first scene.

In vv.3-10, disciples, notably Peter, visit the tomb on hearing the women's report. The disciples find the tomb empty then go away perplexed. Originally Peter was, in the tradition, accompanied by an unnamed disciple. In John he has become the "disciple whom Jesus loved" so that his coming to faith might interpret the significance of the empty tomb. In 20:8 the phrase, "he saw and believed" refers only to the Beloved Disciple: he is the ideal disciple whom all others should follow, he is *the* Christian. John's lesson is that love for Jesus gives the insight to perceive his presence. This disciple outdistances Peter because he loves Jesus more. Then, because he is closest to Jesus, he is also the first to look for him and to believe.

Patristic Commentary

St. Gregory Palamas (+ 1359)
Homily 20, PG 151.265.

John, the virgin, who by a singular grace received as a treasure the only virgin mother, the beloved disciple of Christ, the son of thunder, that thunder which reverberated when the Lord ascended into heaven, more deserving of the appellation "son" than any of the other evangelists in that his witness was more resounding than theirs, recounts for us the events of the resurrection of the Lord from the dead, and the manner of his subsequent appearances, heard in church in his Gospel pericope. These are his words: *Now on the first day of the week, Mary Magdalene came early to the tomb while it was still dark, and she saw the stone taken away from the tomb. She ran therefore and came to Simon Peter, and to the other disciple whom Jesus loved* (Jn 20:1). It is to himself that he refers. We have also heard his words: *But Mary was standing outside weeping at the tomb.* For when John himself and Peter heard from her, they ran to the tomb from which he had proceeded alive, saw what they saw, verified it through witnesses and departed home marveling.

But Mary stayed. She stood at the tomb weeping outside. It is plain that she had not yet received any clear testimony of the Lord's resurrection. And yet she had come to the tomb twice with the others, first with the Mother of God as Matthew narrates in the words: *Now late in the night of the Sabbath as the first day of the week began to dawn, Mary Magdalene and the other Mary came to see the sepulchre. And behold there was a great earthquake* (Mt 28:1,2). Secondly, she came with Peter and John who believed what they had seen and departed in a state of wonder and admiration. Twice, then, she came to the tomb with others and they all went away filled with faith and awe. But she alone, as if she got no reassurance, wept inconsolably.

One can see that this thing happens also in the struggles to be virtuous. For some get the help of grace immediately in their struggles, and the recognition of pledges is granted to them, giving them a foretaste of the promised rewards, as if a kindly hand were outstretched to receive them and anoint them for the future combat. The end of the contest finds others waiting, but the rewards of their patience have been fully prepared for them. One of the Fathers puts it like this: "Some receive their just recompense without pain, others in pain, and others only at the end." These things happen as a result of the complex disposition of our affairs by an all-wise Providence, which in its kindness allocates what is fitting and profitable to each in the practice

of virtue and the mysteries of faith. It is then in accordance
with his wise and providential disposition of Mary Magdalene's affairs that the Master has preferred to delay her
recognition of the certainty of his resurrection and at the
same time he converts through her those coming after by
inspiring them to perseverance.

Insights from the Documents of the Church

The Resurrection

The fact that Christ "was raised the third day" constitutes
the final sign of the messianic mission, a sign that perfects
the entire revelation of merciful love in a world that is
subject to evil. At the same time it constitutes the sign that
foretells "a new heaven and a new earth," when God "will
wipe away every tear from their eyes, there will be no more
death, or mourning, no crying, nor pain, for the former
things have passed away." . . . .

What does the Cross of Christ say to us, the Cross that
in a sense is the final word of his messianic message and
mission? And yet this is not yet the word of the God
of the Covenant: that will be pronounced at the dawn
when first the women and then the Apostles come to the
tomb of the crucified Christ, see the tomb empty and for
the first time hear the message: "He is risen." They will
repeat this message to the others and will be witnesses to
the Risen Christ. Yet, even in this glorification of the Son of
God, the Cross remains, that Cross which—through all the
messianic testimony of the Man-the Son, who suffered
death upon it—*speaks and never ceases to speak of God-the
Father, who is absolutely faithful to his eternal love for
man*, since he "so loved the world"—therefore man in the
world—that "he gave his only Son, that whoever believes
in him should not perish but have eternal life." Believing
in the crucified Son means "seeing the Father," means
believing that love is present in the world and that this love
is more powerful than any kind of evil in which individuals,

humanity, or the world are involved. Believing in this love means *believing in mercy.* For mercy is an indispensable dimension of love; it is as it were love's second name and, at the same time, the specific manner in which love is revealed and effected vis-à-vis the reality of the evil that is in the world, affecting and besieging man, insinuating itself even into his heart and capable of causing him to "perish in Gehenna." (John Paul II, On the Mercy of God [*Dives in Misericordia*]

Celebrating the Redemption

Holy Mother Church believes that it is for her to celebrate the saving work of her divine Spouse in a sacred commemoration on certain days throughout the course of the year. Once each week, on the day which she has called the Lord's Day, she keeps the memory of the Lord's resurrection. She also celebrates it once every year, together with his blessed passion, at Easter, that most solemn of all feasts.

In the course of the year, moreover, she unfolds the whole mystery of Christ from the incarnation and nativity to the ascension, to Pentecost and the expectation of the blessed hope of the coming of the Lord.

Thus recalling the mysteries of the redemption, she opens up to the faithful the riches of her Lord's powers and merits, so that these are in some way made present for all time; the faithful lay hold of them and are filled with saving grace. (Vat. II, Constitution on the Liturgy, 102)

SECOND SUNDAY OF EASTER

Scriptural Commentary

First Reading Acts 4:32-35.

A picture of a christian community ideally faithful to the gospel message. As in 2:42 "they devoted themselves to the apostles' teaching and fellowship, to the breaking of bread and the prayers." It is a community of shared faith and shared possessions: a faith in the resurrection and power of the Lord, and a distribution of goods now seen as common property. The motivation for the generous distribution is spelled out in 4:34—"there was not a needy person among them." There is no romantic glorification of poverty. Concern is for the poor—a preoccupation of Luke.

Second Reading 1 Jn 5:1-6.

Because through the Sundays of Easter (two to seven) the second reading is from the first letter of John, it seems helpful to give, in summary, the message of the letter. The author's primary purpose is not to exhort his readers to practise virtue or to fly sin, but to make them understand the sublimity of their condition as Christians. Christian existence is defined as a vital relationship to God. It is a matter of birth to the life of God, of fellowship with Father and Son: the faithful are born of God, they abide in God, they know God. In short, they have "eternal life"; and for John, eternal life is the very life of God. This life, possessed by the Christian, is a reality, but it is mysterious: what the faithful are now, as they will be hereafter, is attested only by faith. Therefore, the author multiplies the criteria by which the believer gauges the genuineness of his christian life; hence, the frequency of "by this" and the verb "recognize" (2:3,5; 3:10,14,19,24; 4:2,6,13,18,20). Since it is a participation in the divine life, christian life must reflect the qualities of God. If we are children of God, in fellowship with him, it is impossible that we should not be conformed to him.

God is Light (1:5) and Love (4:8): *Light* because he is the absolute good and because our moral conduct should be modelled on his justice and holiness (2:20; 3:7); *Love* because he is the source of all the tenderness and generosity that the verb "to love" suggests. The Christian is called to walk in the Light (1:6-7) and to abide in Love (4:16) by observing the commandments (2:3-7; 3:22-24; 5:2-3), summed up in the two precepts of faith in the name of Jesus and of fraternal charity (3:23). To believe in the divine Love which is incarnate in Jesus and, in turn, to love their brethren—such is the message addressed by John to Christians.

But John does also intend to recall—by implication at least—the fundamental norms of the christian life. In the realm of faith his readers must readily accept the apostolic witness (1:5; 3:21-24), as well- as the testimony of God (4:6,9,13) and the intimate word of the Spirit (2:20,27). Their relationship to their brethren is coloured by their care to observe the commandments, centred in the precept of charity (2:3-11; 3:11-24; 4:7 - 5:4). They must take their stand against the unbelieving world and face up resolutely to its allurements (2:12-17; 3:13; 4:1) bolstered by confidence in the person of the Saviour (2:1-2; 3:5,8; 5:6-7). The christian life makes demands and its sublimity is matched by a practicality that calmly accepts the realities of human existence.

John combats Gnostic tendencies, but it is true to say that the letter is fruit of an authentically christian *gnosis*, at once knowledge and fellowship. Its spiritual teaching is basically the same as that of Paul, but it is more theocentric than Paul and goes to the Father. Here the ideal is not to live "in Christ" but to "abide in God," in the "Father and Son." But this does not prevent John from emphasizing, just as strongly as Paul, the indispensable mediation of the incarnate Son of God: it is through the Son that the believer receives the very life of God. All the while, be it said again, a writing of such elevated spirituality, cast in the realm of Father and Son, keeps a close and constant grip on the world of humankind and testifies to a simple and demanding moral realism: fellowship with God, participation in the divine life, is impossible without absolute fidelity to the Commandment. This short writing has an abiding message for those far advanced in the Christian Way—and for all Christians.

5:1-6. A prominent theme of the letter is that the Christian is child of God—child of a Father who is Love. Our reading points out that the test of our loving lies in keeping the commandments. John really has one commandment in mind: that of love. The observation "his commandments are not burdensome" reminds us of Mt 11:30, "For my yoke is easy, and my burden is light." A prominent theme of Johannine preaching is the Christian's victory over sin or the evil one; here (vv.4-5) "world" is the same as the evil one. Victory is through faith in the Son of God who has already overcome the evil one (Jn 12:31; 16:33). John, typically, insists on the reality of the incarnation; Jesus came "by water and blood"—he is the Jesus of flesh and blood who was baptized and died on the cross (v.6).

Gospel Jn 20:19-31.

In this final scene of John's resurrection narrative (20:1-29), Jesus appears to the disciples, showing them his hands and his side and bestowing on them the peace he had promised them in the Farewell Discourse. As in the Synoptics, John then has Jesus entrust a salvific mission to those to whom he has appeared. Their mission is closely related to his breathing the new life of his Spirit upon them. The task of the spirit is to take Jesus' place by carrying on his work and being his presence in the world. He also gives the disciples power over sin: men are to be divided (by their self-judgment) into two groups—those who receive Jesus and those who do not recognize him. The most significant episode is that of Thomas' profession of faith. He provides the final example in this final chapter of the gospel (ch. 21 is appendix) of different attitudes of faith in the Risen Jesus. Thomas' cry, "My Lord and my God!" is the supreme christological statement of John's gospel. It is a liturgical confession, a response of praise to the God who has revealed himself in Jesus. And, of course, it leads to Jesus' blessing upon those who believe without having seen. When Jesus lived among his people, faith had to be found through the visible and tangible. Now the era of signs and appearances is passing away, for the Spirit, or invisible presence of Jesus, shall make possible another realm of believing.

In John's message what is important is to *believe* (vv.27-28), whether that faith comes through seeing or not. In this beatitude ("Blessed are those who have not seen yet believe") Jesus is contrasting two types of blessedness: they are the two different situations in which his disciples could find themselves. He is assuring all readers of his gospel, all Christians, that those who are coming later and who will not see Jesus are equal, in God's eyes, to those who lived with him, saw him and thus were, in a certain sense, privileged. "Blessed are those who have not seen and yet believe!" The words bear the stamp of the timeless Word spoken before the world was made. [See *The Saving Word*, Year A, 134-136].

Patristic Commentary

St. Augustine (354-430)
Sermon 247, On John 20.19-31, PL 38.1156,
    FOTC 38.297.

The account of the Resurrection of our Lord Jesus Christ according to the four Evangelists seemed to have been completed yesterday. For, on the first day the account of the Resurrection was read according to Matthew, on the second day according to Luke, on the third day according to Mark, and on the fourth day, according to John. But, since John and Luke wrote very many things about the Resurrection itself and the events which occurred after the Resurrection, accounts which cannot be read aloud in one reading, we heard some passages from St. John both yesterday and today; and still other readings remain. What, then, did we hear today? That on the very day on which He rose again, that is, on the Lord's Day, when it had become

late and the disciples were together in one place, with the
doors closed for fear of the Jews, the Lord appeared in the
midst of them. Hence, on that day, as John the Evangelist
is witness, He appeared twice to His disciples, once in the
morning and once in the evening. Also, a passage from the
account of His appearance early in the morning has been
read aloud to you; that He appeared again late on the same
day we have just heard when it was read aloud. There was no
need for me to mention these facts to you, but only for you
to note them. However, it was fitting for me to mention
them, by reason of the scant intelligence of certain persons
and the excessive negligence of others, so that you may
understand, not only what you have heard, but also from
what portion of the Scripture that which you have heard
was read to you.

Let us see, therefore, what today's reading presents to us
for discussion. Obviously, the passage urges us, and in a
certain manner tells us to say something as to how the Lord
was able to appear to His disciples when the doors were
closed, since He had risen so physically substantial that
He was not only seen by His disciples but even touched
by them. Some persons are so disturbed about this matter
that they endanger themselves, setting up the prejudice of
their own reasoning against divine miracles. In fact, they
argue in this fashion: "If there was a body, if there were
flesh and bones, if that body which hung on the cross rose
again from the tomb, how could it enter through closed
doors? If it could not do this," they say, "then it was not
done. If it could do this, how was it able to do so?" If you
understand the way, there is no miracle; and if there seems
to you to be no miracle, you are close to denying that He
rose again from the tomb.

Insights from the Documents of the Church

Believers united, heart and soul

The contemporary Church is profoundly conscious
that only on the basis of the mercy of God will she be able

to carry out the tasks that derive from the teaching of the Second Vatican Council, and, in the first place, the ecumenical task which aims at uniting all those who confess Christ. As she makes many efforts in this direction, the Church confesses with humility that only that *love* which is more powerful than the weakness of human divisions *can definitively bring about that unity* which Christ implored from the Father and which the Spirit never ceases to beseech for us "with sighs too deep for words." (John Paul II, On the Mercy of God, [*Dives in Misericordia*])

The spirit of collaboration and shared responsibility is spreading among priests also, as is confirmed by the many Councils of Priests that have sprung up since the Council. That spirit has extended also among the laity, not only strengthening the already existing organizations for lay apostolate but also creating new ones that often have a different outline and excellent dynamism. Furthermore, lay people conscious of their responsibility for the Church have willingly committed themselves to collaborating with the Pastors and with the representatives of the Institutes of consecrated life, in the spheres of the diocesan Synods and of the pastoral Councils in the parishes and dioceses. (John Paul II, *Redemptor Hominis*)

Whose sins you shall forgive

Our Lord Jesus Christ reconciled God and men through the mystery of his death and resurrection (see Rom 5:10). This ministry of reconciliation was committed to the Church through the apostles by our Lord (2 Cor 5:18ff) and the Church has executed the commission by bearing the glad tidings of salvation to men and by baptizing them in water and the Holy Spirit (see Matt 28:19).

Because of human weakness, however, it happens that Christians 'abandon the love they had at first' (see Apoc 2:4) and by sinning break the links of friendship that bind them to God. For this reason, the Lord instituted a special sacrament for the remission of sins committed after Baptism (see John 20:21-23). The Church has celebrated this sacrament through the ages, in various ways indeed, but always retaining its essential elements . . . . The Church has it at heart to call the faithful to continual conversion and renewal. It wishes that when the baptized should fall from grace they should acknowledge the sins they have committed against God and their brethren and should be truly penitent in their hearts. Anxious to prepare them for the celebration of the sacrament of Penance, it urges them to take part in penitential services from time to time. (Paul VI, Decree Promulgating Revised Order of Penance)

THIRD SUNDAY OF EASTER

Scriptural Commentary

First Reading Acts 3:13-15,17-19.

Peter and John's healing of a cripple (3:1-9) is followed by Peter's discourse (3:12-26). He begins by informing his hearers that the God of their fathers had raised up the Servant whom they had killed (v.13). They requested "a murderer" instead of "the holy and righteous one"—"the author of life."Yet, all had fallen within God's purpose (v.18). Ignorance accounted for much of their past sin; now they can, like many of their people already have done, repent and be forgiven. The reading is an early form of explanation of the Passion and an example of the early witness to the resurrection.

Second Reading 1 Jn 2:1-5.

"I am writing this to you so that you may not sin." Realistically, John anticipates that Christians, who are, like all humankind, prone to sin (1:8-10), will sin. If we sin. Jesus Christ comes to our assistance, for he, the Righteous One, is an advocate, a counsel for the defence. He is "the Lamb of God, who takes away the sin of the world" (Jn 1:29).

From the start John sees love as the criterion of the genuine disciple: "Whoever keeps his word, in him truly love for God is perfected" (v.5). The message is the same as in Jn 14:15,21,23-24—authentic love is proved by obedience, by the faithful observance of the commandments. Here we have the sign, the test, of the "love of God," that is, of properly divine and christian charity. In the obedient Christian this charity exists truly.

Gospel Lk 24:35-48.

In v.35, the concluding verse of the Emmaus story (24:13-35), Luke again draws attention to the "breaking of bread" (vv.30-31)—he is determined that his readers will not miss its significance. The breaking of bread together with him was the occasion of the two disciples' recognition of Jesus. The expression "breaking of bread" is a technical term for the eucharist. Luke has deliberately used eucharistic language: Jesus *took bread, blessed, broke, gave* to them. And his lesson is that as the two disciples recognized Jesus in the setting of a meal shared with them, so Christians, in the eucharistic meal, make the same real encounter with their Lord. This whole Emmaus passage, centred around the "liturgy of the word" (vv.19-27) and the "eucharistic" meal (vv.30-31), has a marked liturgical colouring. It is an early catechesis, in a liturgical setting, highlighting the encounter with the Lord in the Eucharist.

The appearance story immediately following (vv.36-42) has quite obvious apologetic motifs: Jesus shows that he is the same person whom the disciples had known prior to the crucifixion by pointing to his body, and by eating before them. As in all the appearance stories the risen Jesus is not immediately recognizable (v.37); a gesture or word is needed before the disciples recognize the risen Lord. This is quite a clever way of making the point that resurrection is *not* a return to earthly life; Jesus has risen to *new* life beyond death. He is the same—yet transformed. Here the point is firmly made that the risen Jesus is no "spirit." The assertion that he invited touching of his (wounded) hands and feet and that he ate in their presence is, in the apologetic of the time, a firm christian rejection of any challenge to the *reality* of the new life of their Lord.

At the close of his gospel (24:44-49) Luke summarizes the last commission of Jesus to his disciples; this he repeats at the beginning of Acts (1:3-8). More pointedly, the outline and words of this gospel passage echo the apostolic kerygma of Acts. Jesus recalls the occasions on which he had warned the disciples that he, in fulfilment of the will of God enshrined in the Scriptures, would have to suffer, die, and rise again (cf. 9:22,44; 17:25; 18:31-33; 22:37). "While I was still with you" (v.44): Jesus has entered into his glory (v.26) by his exaltation to the Father (Jn 20:17); his relations with the disciples are not what they were before his glorification.

The risen Lord gives his disciples a new understanding of the Old Testament (vv.45-48), an insight that will enable them to see how and where it "bears witness to him" (cf. Jn 5:39). This reinterpretation of the Old Testament is a basic element of the primitive kerygma: the dawning of the age of fulfilment (v.44; cf. Acts 2:16; 3:18,24); the suffering of the Messiah and his resurrection on the third day (v.46; cf. Acts 2:23-24; 3:13-15; 4:10). The kerygma always includes the proclamation of repentance and forgiveness of sins, a proclamation to all humankind—the universalist note is very much at home in Luke (Acts 2:38-39; 3:19-20; 4:12). The disciples are convincing witnesses and efficacious missionaries because they had seen the Lord and have believed in him; all who would, effectively, bear witness to Christ must have encountered him in personal and living faith. Today, when the call of the apostolate is urgent and the role of witness is seen as the obligation of every Christian, we are more keenly aware that religion is not the acceptance of a body of doctrine nor the adherence to a code of law, but attachment to a Person. Knowledge of Christ, in the biblical sense of acceptance and commitment, is the essence of christian life. It is obviously the first requirement of an apostle.

Patristic Commentary

St. Ignatius of Antioch (c.35-c.107)
Epistle to the Smyrnaeans, 1-4, SC 10.132,
   ACW 1.90.

I extol Jesus Christ, the God who has granted you such wisdom. For I have observed that you are thoroughly trained in unshaken faith, being nailed, as it were, to the Cross of the Lord Jesus Christ both in body and in soul, and that you are well established in love through the Blood of Christ and firmly believe in Our Lord: He is really *of the line of David according to the flesh*, (Rom 1.3) and the Son of God by the will and power of God; was really born of a virgin, and baptized by John *in order to comply with every ordinance.* (Matt 3.15)

Under Pontius Pilate and the tetrarch Herod He was really nailed to the cross in the flesh for our sake—of whose fruit we are, in virtue of His most blessed Passion. And thus, through the Resurrection, *He raised a banner* (Isa 5.26) for all times for His saints and faithful followers, whether among the Jews or the Gentiles, that they might be united in a single body, that is, His Church.

All these sufferings, assuredly, He underwent for our sake, that we might be saved.And He suffered really, as He also really raised Himself from the dead. It is not as some unbelievers say, who maintain that His suffering was a make-believe. In reality, it is they that are make-believes: and, as their notion, so their end: they will be bodiless and ghostlike shapes!

For myself, I know and believe that He was in the flesh even after the Resurrection. And when He came to Peter and Peter's companions, He said to them: *"Here; feel me and see that I am not a bodiless ghost.*" Immediately they touched Him and, through this contact with His Flesh and Spirit, believed. For the same reason they despised death and, in fact, proved stronger than death. Again, after the Resurrection, He ate and drank with them like a being of flesh and blood, though spiritually one with the Father.

I am urging these things on you, beloved, although I know that you are of the same mind. I am cautioning you betimes, however, against wild beasts in human form, whom you ought not only not to receive, but, if possible, even avoid meeting. Only pray for them, if somehow they may change their mind—a difficult thing! But that is in the power of Jesus Christ, our true Life.

Insights from the Documents of the Church

The sacrifice that takes our sins away

In the sacrifice of the Mass, the passion of Christ is re-presented. The body which is given for us and the blood which is shed for the remission of sins are offered to God by the Church for the salvation of the whole world. In the Eucharist Christ is present and is offered as "the sacrifice which had made our peace" and so that we might "be brought together in unity" by his Holy Spirit.

Further, when our Saviour Jesus Christ gave the power to forgive sins to the apostles and their successors, he instituted the sacrament of penance, so that the faithful who had committed sin after baptism could be restored to grace and reconciled to God. For the Church has both water and tears: the water of baptism, the tears of penitence. (Introduction to the Rite of Reconciliation)

Penance and Renewal

Christ "loved the Church and gave himself up for her, that he might sanctify her" (Eph 5:25-26). He united her to himself as a spouse. He fills her, his Body and completion, with his divine gifts and through her he distributes truth and grace to all.

The members of the Church are exposed to temptation, however, and it often happens that, unhappily, they fall into sin. Thus it is that "while Christ, 'holy, innocent and undefiled' (Heb 7:26) knew nothing of sin (2 Cor 5:21), but came to expiate only the sins of the people (see Heb 2:17), the Church, at the same time holy and always in need of purification, clasping sinners to her bosom, follows continuously the way of penance and renewal." (Introduction to the Rite of Reconciliation)

Understanding the Scriptures

The task of giving an authentic interpretation of the Word of God, whether in its written form or in the form of Tradition, has been entrusted to the living teaching office of the Church alone. Its authority in this matter is exercised in the name of Jesus Christ. Yet this Magisterium is not superior to the Word of God, but is its servant. It teaches only what has been handed on to it. At the divine command and with the help of the Holy Spirit, it listens to this devotedly, guards it with dedication and expounds it faithfully. All that it proposes for belief as being divinely revealed is drawn from this single deposit of faith.

It is clear, therefore, that, in the supremely wise arrangement of God, sacred Tradition, sacred Scripture and the Magisterium of the Church are so connected and associated that one of them cannot stand without the others. Working together, each in its own way under the action of the one Holy Spirit, they all contribute effectively to the salvation of souls. (Vat. II, Constitution on Divine Revelation, 10)

FOURTH SUNDAY OF EASTER

Scriptural Commentary

First Reading Acts 4:8-12.

The passage 4:1-22 presents the clash of "the apostles" and the sanhedrin, a little drama in three acts: arrest (1-4), discourse of Peter (5-12), and deliberation of the sanhedrin with Peter's response (13-22). Our reading gives Peter's discourse. What is really at issue, throughout the passage, is the separation of Christianity from the Jewish religion— an accomplished fact when Luke wrote. In the gospel, the authority of Jesus had been challenged: "By what authority do you do these things?" (Lk 20:2). The challenge had been uttered by "the chief priests, the scribes, and the elders," in other words, the sanhedrin. Now the same group challenges the apostles. And Peter responds.

By the time Luke wrote, the separation of Christianity from the Jewish religion was complete. Paul had watched the separation and agonized over the defection of the 'natural' heirs of God's promises (cf. Rom 9-11). For Luke, too, the community he belonged to was the fulfilment of the aspirations of Israel and the resurrection of Jesus inaugurated the era of the resurrection that was the characteristic hope of Israel's strictest practitioners, the Pharisees (Acts 4:2; cf. 23:6). Where Paul theologises, Luke tells the story. From its earliest days the christian community encountered hostility from the leaders of Israel as Jesus himself had" (J. Crowe, *The Acts*, 25).

The conflict surfaces in Peter's speech. For instance, the verse of Ps 118:22 "the stone which the builders rejected" was usually understood to refer to Israel, or to the temple which had been destroyed and rebuilt; Christians applied it to Jesus. Faith in Jesus finds an even more comprehensive expression in Peter's words: "there is no other name under heaven given among men by which we must be saved" (v.12). Christians are adamant that Jesus, God's only Son, is the one and only Saviour.

Second Reading 1 Jn 3:1-2.

We can speak of a person being *named* to an office or a job. In a Semitic context, to be named ("called") is a more forceful expression. Our text says we are named God's children and, in case there should be any doubt, John adds:

"and so we are." We *know*, that is, experience, our filial relationship to God. We have been born to a new life and share, mysteriously but really, in the life of God (1:29). The fact of being a Christian, of being born of God, is permanent assurance that one is loved by the Father; each carries in his or her person the attestation of this love. (John will, of course, insist that the Christian *live* as child of God, 3:4-23). The unbelieving world is incapable of recognising the true status of Christians because it has not come to know God. For John this means that it had failed to recognise Jesus. As for ourselves, we have to await the coming of the Lord, to see him "as he is," before we can arrive at full appreciation of our own christian reality. Only then shall we see clearly that our future state will be like the glorified state of Jesus. But the process of becoming like Christ has already begun—a familiar stress in John.

Gospel Jn 10:11-18.

The passage Jn 10:1-18 opens with two parables: on the right way of approach to the sheep (1-3a), and on the relation between shepherd and sheep (3b-5). The first parable is explained in vv.7-10; our reading is the explanation of the other. Jesus is the good shepherd who is willing to die to protect his sheep, his own sheep whom he knows intimately.

Our passage particularly brings to mind a passage from Ezek 34 where God promises his people, in the first place, that he himself would become their shepherd, and then that he would choose a shepherd for them in the messianic age. Jesus' assertion that he is the good shepherd indicates that this age has arrived and that he is the promised one. He is a shepherd so very different from those castigated by Ezekiel: "The weak you have not strengthened, the sick you have not healed, the crippled you have not bound up, the strayed you have not brought back, the lost you have not sought, and with force and harshness you have ruled them" (Ezek 34:4). In every point he stood in sharp contrast to them.

The second characteristic of the true shepherd is that he knows his sheep intimately and they know him. In John the mutual knowledge of Jesus and those who belong to him is an extension of the mutual knowledge of Father and Son (cf. Jn 17:25-26). Knowing Jesus and the Father means being of one mind and heart with them. But the goodness of this Shepherd reaches beyond his own sheep to invite others to join his flock (v.16)—"I, when I am lifted up from the earth, will draw all men to myself"(12:32). "All of Jesus' shepherd-task of guiding, caring for and uniting disciples together is the will of a Father and also the loving response of a Son. All this Jesus freely undertook out of love for mankind, since laying down his life was not imposed on him by any human being or power. This was the way he expressed his 'pastoral care' for disciples and it was also a loving response of a shepherd-Son to his Father (v.18)" (J. McPolin, *John*, 110-111).

Patristic Commentary

St. Peter Chrysologus, (c.406-450)
Sermon 40, CCL 24.226, FOTC 17.85.

Each year, when spring with its breezes begins to usher in the birth of so many sheep , and to deposit the numerous young of the fruitful flock about the fields, the meadows, and the paths, a good shepherd puts aside his feasts and songs. He anxiously searches for the tender sheeplings, picks them up and gathers them together. Happy to carry them, he places them about his neck, on his shoulders, and in his arms. He wants them to be safe as he carries or leads them to the protecting sheepfolds.

That is the case with ourselves, too, brethren. When we see our ecclesiastical flock gaining rich increase under the favoring smile of the spring of Lent, we put aside the resonant tones of our treatise and the customary fare of our discourse. Solicitous about our very heavy labor, we give all our concern to gathering and carrying in the heavenly sprouts.

But, since we see that the lambs have been returned to the flock and that all are now within the enclosure of Christ, we are called back in joy to the divine declamations. With full exaltation we set before you a life-giving abundance of the Lord's food, in order to have as sharers in our joy those whom we observed to be our companions in work.

Because this our preface, today's reading, has brought in mention of Him who alone is good, who alone is the Shepherd, and who alone is the Shepherd of shepherds, let the entire application of our discourse and treatise come to fulfillment and be deemed complete.

"The good shepherd," the text reads, "lays down his life for his sheep." The force of love makes a man brave, because genuine love counts nothing as hard, or bitter, or serious, or deadly. What sword, what wounds, what penalty, what deaths can avail to overcome perfect love? Love is an inpenetrable breastplate. It wards off missiles, sheds the blows of swords, taunts dangers, laughs at death. If love is present, it conquers everything.

But is that death of the shepherd advantageous to the sheep? Let us investigate. It leaves them abandoned, exposes them defenseless to the wolves, hands over the beloved flock to the gnawing jaws of beasts, gives them over to plunder and exposes them to death. All this is proved by the death of the Shepherd, Christ. From the time when He laid down His life for His sheep, and permitted Himself to be slain through the fury of the Jews, His sheep have been suffering invasions from the piratical Gentiles. Like prisoners to be slain in jails, they are shut up in the caves of robbers. They are torn unceasingly by persecutors who are like raging wolves. They are snapped at by heretics who are like mad dogs with savage teeth.

The martyred choir of the Apostles proves this. The blood of the martyrs shed throughout the whole world proclaims it. The members of Christians thrown to the beasts, or consumed with fire, or sunk in the rivers clearly display it. And truly, just as the death of the Shepherd brought all this in, so could His life have prevented it.

In the light of all this, does the Shepherd prove His love for you by His death? Is He proving His love because, when He sees danger threatening His sheep, when He cannot defend his flock, He prefers to die before He sees any evil done to the sheep?

But what are we to do, since the Life Himself could not die unless He had decided to? Who could have taken life away from the Giver of life if He were unwilling? He Himself said: "I have the power to lay down my life, and I have the power to take it up again. No one takes it from me." Therefore, He willed to die—He who permitted Himself to be slain although He was unable to die.

Insights from the Documents of the Church

God's Family

Men and women are delivered from the power of darkness through the sacraments of Christian initiation. They die with Christ, are buried with him and rise again with him. They receive the Spirit which makes them God's adopted sons and daughters and, with all God's people, they celebrate the memorial of the Lord's death and resurrection.

They are incorporated into Christ and are made God's people; with all their sins forgiven, they are delivered from the power of darkness and are made adopted sons and daughters. They are made a new creation through water and the Holy Spirit: they are called, and are, God's children.

Signed by the giving of the same Spirit in Confirmation, they become more like Our Lord and filled with the Holy Spirit. They are thus able to bear witness to him before the world and to help bring as close as possible the achievement of the fullness of the Body of Christ.

Finally, as part of the eucharistic assembly, they eat the flesh of the Son of Man and drink his Blood so that they may have eternal life and manifest the unity of God's people. Offering themselves with Christ, they share in the universal sacrifice which is all of redeemed humanity offered to God by the high priest. They pray that, with a great outpouring of the Holy Spirit, the entire human race would achieve the unity of God's family.

The three sacraments of Christian initiation are thus closely intertwined that they may bring Christians to their full stature, enabling them to carry out their mission in the Church and in the world. (General Introduction to Christian Initiation)

Priests

As I write, I think of the vast and varied human situations to which you are sent, dear brothers, as labourers into the Lord's vineyard (see Mt 20:1-16). But the parable of the sheep-fold (see Jn 10:1-16) is also applicable to you. Your priesthood imparts to you a pastoral charism, a special likeness to Christ, the Good Shepherd. This quality belongs to you in a very special way. All the laity, the great community of the People of God, our brothers and sisters, are expected to work for the salvation of others, as the Second Vatican Council stated so clearly (see *Lumen Gentium*, 11). You priests, however, are expected to have a concern and a commitment greater than and different from that of any lay person. And this is because you share in the priesthood of Jesus Christ in a way that differs "essentially and not only in degree" (*Lumen Gentium*, 10) from the manner in which they share. (John Paul II, Letter to Priests)

FIFTH SUNDAY OF EASTER

Scriptural Commentary

First Reading Acts 9:26-31.

Paul gives his own account of his visits to Jerusalem in Gal 1:18 - 2:10. The visit here mentioned corresponds to the first that Paul speaks of (1:18-24). Three years after his conversion he went to Jerusalem to see Peter and remained with him fifteen days. He also saw James. In our passages we are told that the Jerusalem Christians (not surprisingly, in view of his record—8:1-3; 9:1-2) were apprehensive of any trust with Saul—how could they trust him? Barnabas was able to persuade them that Saul the Pharisee had, indeed, become a true Christian. Once accepted, his charism was potent—so remarkably that it boomeranged on him. The hellenists (Greek-speaking Jews who had already engineered the death of Stephen) wanted to get rid of him too; in their eyes he was a traitor. The brethren had to hustle Paul to safety. In sharp contrast v.31, a typically Lucan summary statement, sums up the situation of christian communities able to live in peace. Luke notes in particular how the spread of the church and the joy which filled its members are the work of the Holy Spirit.

The role of Barnabas (v.27) is to be noted. It is thanks to this "son of encouragement" (4:36) that Paul was accepted by the Jerusalem community. Later, it is Barnabas who again rescued Saul from oblivion in Tarsus (11:25-26) and was the first companion of him who was to become the apostle of the Gentiles (13:1-3). Paul owed much to this discerning and magnanimous Christian.

Second Reading 1 Jn 3:18-24.

The passage 1 Jn 3:10-23 is a meditation on Jn 13:34-35, on the "new commandment": to love one another mutually *as* Christ has loved us. Jesus had declared that this would be the sign of the authentic Christian ("By this all men will know that you are my disciples," 13:35) and John reminds the disciples themselves of the criterion. For charity is not only a sign; it is also a test which divides true Christians from those who are such in name only. Love is not an action or a series of isolated actions, it is a permanent quality, a religious state. Here, however, the accent is on the manifestation of this love which is constantly active, which proves itself, gives itself and sacrifices itself. It is love "in deed and in truth" and it is by its fruits that it becomes an unmistakable criterion of divine sonship. Christ himself had set the example of brotherly love: his voluntary sacrifice is the highest example of authentic *agapē*. And so it is that the commandment of love includes faith in the Son: Christians are bidden to believe in the crucified Son of God and to love one another (v.23).

Of course, the Christian remains a sinner and his conscience may reproach him with many failings (v.20) but God is "greater than our hearts" and he will readily overlook the sins of one who is moved to pity by the plight of his neighbour and seeks to help him. Hardness of heart alone will provoke the severity of the sovereign Judge. In other words, the quality of fraternal relationship determines that of relations with God. But the sincere Christian, conscious of the disposition of God's heart—"we know" (v.24)—can and must approach God without fear and stand simply and even boldly before him (v.19). He can do so because God and he who loves his brethren are one: one abides in the other (v.24). Fraternal charity is the guarantee of the most direct and intimate loving relationship between God and the Christian.

Gospel Jn 15:1-8.

The image of the vine recalls the Old Testament designation of Israel as the vine of Yahweh (cf. Is 5:1-7; Jer 2:21; Ezek 15:1-8; Ps 80:8-19). Jesus declares that he himself, and not the Israel of old, is the real vine of God. But from this understanding of the image, we may move still further to stress the intimate relationship of branches and stock within the Vine. And Jesus does stress the union between himself and his disciples.

"I am the vine, you are the branches." We tend to regard this statement as no more than a figure of speech. Spontaneously, (for this is our way of thinking) we take the declaration about the vine to mean that the union of Christ with his own is *like* the link between the branches and the vine. The disciples are asked to think about a vine, to regard the vital link of branches and trunk. Jesus is thought to say, in effect: the union between us, between you and me, is something like that intimate unity of nature. What he really means is precisely the opposite! For him, the intimate union of vine and branches is only a *symbol* of the infinitely closer union of Jesus with his disciples. That is why Jesus can speak of himself as the *genuine* Vine: the sublime truth which the vine symbolizes is fully realized only in him. Understood in this way, the declaration of Jesus is emphatic and clear: we live by the life of the Vine, we live by the life of Christ.

The christian life is unthinkable except in terms of Christ. He and the Christian abide one in the other because they share a common life. The branches, however, while living by the sap of the vine, need to be tended. This is the work of the Father who, by trial and chastisement, guides and trains his children (cf. Heb 12:5-11). The Father tends the Vine, but its branches will bear fruit only if they are effectively attached to the Vine, only if his life flows in them: apart from him they can do nothing, they count for nothing. The Father expects the disciples, his children, to bear fruit. He is glorified in the Son, in his obedience and in the perfect accomplishment of his work. It is a short, inevitable, step to see the glorification of the Father also in the obedience and fruitfulness of those who are joined to the Son.

Patristic Commentary

St. John Chrysostom (c.347-407)
Hom. 76 on John, PG 59.411, FOTC 41.317.

Then He went on to declare: "I am the vine, you are the branches."

What did He wish to imply by the parable?

That it is not possible for anyone to have life if he does not pay attention to Christ's words, and also that the miracles that would later take place would be performed through the power of Christ.

"My Father is the vine-dresser."

What is this, then? Does the Son need assistance?

Perish the thought! For this illustration does not mean that. In fact, see how very carefully He developed the parable. He did not say that the root profits by the care of the vine-dresser, but the branches. Furthermore, in this context He made mention of the root in no other connection than that they might learn that nothing can be done without His power and that they must be united to Him by faith as the branch is to the vine.

"Every branch in me that bears no fruit the Father will take away." Here He was referring by implication to conduct, to show that it is not possible to be in Him without works. "And every branch that bears fruit he will cleanse," that is, will give it the benefit of much care. Even though in reality the root needs care before the branches do—to be dug around, to be dressed—He said nothing at all of it here, but confined Himself to the branches. He was showing that He Himself was sufficient to Himself, while His disciples were in need of much assistance from the vine-dresser, even if they were of very excellent virtue. That is why He said: "The one that bears fruit he will cleanse."

The other one, indeed, since it is without fruit, cannot be in the vine, while this one, since it bears fruit, is rendered more fruitful. Now, one might say that this statement was made with reference to the persecutions that were at that time about to descend on them.

Insights from the Documents of the Church

Love one another

The action of the Spirit of Christ is made clear when the peculiar characteristic of Christian moral teaching is brought to light; all precepts and counsels of this moral teaching are summarized in faith working through charity (cf. Gal 5:6), and this is as it were its soul.

Man is called to adhere freely to the will of God in all things; this is "the obedience of faith by which man entrusts his whole self freely to God" (DV,5). However, since God is love, and his plan calls for communicating his love in Jesus Christ and for uniting men in mutual love, it follows that adhering freely and perfectly to God and to his will is the same as following a way of life in which love reigns in the keeping of the commandments; in other words, it is identical with embracing and putting into practice the precept of charity as a new precept.

Man, therefore, is called to embrace, in Faith, a life of charity towards God and other men; in this lies his greatest responsibility and his exalted moral dignity. The holiness of a man, whatever his vocation or state of life may be, is nothing other than the perfection of charity (cf. LG, 39-42). (General Catechetical Directory, 64)

Images of the Church

In the Old Testament the revelation of the kingdom is often made under the forms of symbols. In similar fashion the inner nature of the Church is now made known to us in various images. Taken either from the life of the shepherd or from cultivation of the land, from the art of building or from family life and marriage, these images have their preparation in the books of the prophets.

The Church is, accordingly, a sheepfold, the sole and necessary gateway to which is Christ (Jn 10:1-10). It is also a flock, of which God foretold that he would himself be the shepherd (cf. Is 40:11; Ex 34:11f), and whose sheep, although watched over by human shepherds, are nevertheless at all times led and brought to pasture by Christ himself, the Good Shepherd and prince of shepherds (cf. Jn 10:11; 1 Pet 5:4), who gave his life for his sheep (cf. Jn 10:11-16).

The Church is a cultivated field, the tillage of God (1 Cor 3:9). On that land the ancient olive tree grows whose holy roots were the prophets and in which the reconciliation of Jews and Gentiles has been brought about and will be brought about again (Rom 11:13-26). That land, like a choice vineyard, has been planted by the heavenly cultivator (Mt 21:33-43; cf. Is 5:1f). Yet the true vine is Christ who gives life and fruitfulness to the branches, that is, to us, who through the Church remain in Christ without whom we can do nothing (Jn 15:1-5).

Often, too, the Church is called the building of God (1 Cor 3:9). The Lord compared himself to the stone which the builders rejected, but which was made into the cornerstone (Mt 21:42; cf. Acts 4:11; 1 Pet 2:7; Ps 117:22). On this foundation the Church is built by the apostles (cf. 1 Cor 3:11) and from it the Church receives solidity and unity. This edifice has many names to describe it: the house of God in which his family dwells; the household of God in the Spirit (Eph 2:19,22); the dwelling-place of God among men (Apoc 21:3); and, especially, the holy temple. This temple, symbolized in places of worship built out of stone, is praised by the Fathers and, not without reason, is compared in the liturgy to the Holy City, the New Jerusalem. As living stones we here on earth are built into it (1 Pet 2:5). It is this holy city that is seen by John as it comes down out of heaven from God when the world is made anew, prepared like a bride adorned for her husband (Apoc 21:1f). (Vat. II, Constitution on the Church, 6)

SIXTH SUNDAY OF EASTER

Scriptural Commentary

First Reading Acts 10:25-26, 34-35, 44-48.

Up to now the christian community had been exclusively Jewish. Now is a turning-point: the reception of the first Gentiles. The fact is so important that Luke has narrated

it three times (10:1-48; 11:5-18; 15:6-18). The first of the
three short excerpts from Acts 10 that make up our reading
(25-26) tells of Peter's arrival at Cornelius' house and his
refusal of a welcome befitting a heavenly messenger. The
significance of Peter's coming to a pagan home and accepting hospitality (v.48) is clearly brought out in the
objection of the "circumcision party": "Why did you go
to uncircumcized men and eat with them" (11:4). A Spirit-
guided Peter is taking the first practical step in breaking
down the ancient barrier between Jew and Gentile; both are
one in Christ. The verses 34-35 deal with the unlimited
goodness of God. For some time now Jews had welcomed
Gentiles who were prepared to take on full Mosaic observance (proselytes) and had tolerated "God-fearers"
(10:2). The Cornelius story touches on two basic problems
involved in the admission of Gentiles into a christian community. The first is whether or not they should be admitted
without being obliged to the law of Moses. The other is
whether a Jewish Christian might, without defilement, accept
hospitality from and share table with a gentile Christian.
The acuteness of this problem is evident in Gal 2:11-21.
"Luke's story provides answers to both of these problems.
What happens in Antioch after the breakthrough in
Casearea amounts to the foundation of a new community
of a universal type by an "alliance" between Jews and
pagans which will automatically involve table fellowship"
(J. Crowe, *The Acts*, 73).

In 44-48 we have Luke's "Gentile Pentecost." When
Peter had finished his outline of the gospel (34-43) the Holy
Spirit fell in his Gentile hearers, and they spoke in tongues
just as had the disciples at Pentecost (2:4). The Holy Spirit
produced directly, without human intervention, the effects
of baptism. Peter reacted to the situation by promptly
baptizing these Gentiles. In a sense, this incident brings
out the intimate connection between baptism and the Holy
Spirit. Normally, the rite of baptism is the occasion of the
gift of the Spirit, but a divine gift cannot be inexorably

bound to a rite, to a human element. The gift of the Spirit incorporates men into the christian community; baptism is the external sign of this invitation. The Holy Spirit had designated these Gentiles as members of the church; Peter had no option but to go ahead and formally enroll them.

Second Reading 1 Jn 4:7-10.

Paul had told us that *agapē* is poured into the hearts of Christians (Rom 5:5). John insists that love is closely linked to the "rebirth" of the believer, it is the proper attribute of his divine sonship: "he who loves is born of God." One loves because one has been born of God: this must be taken with great seriousness. God, in generating us, communicates to us his nature and his life. And, since "one born of God" and "one who loves" are equivalent designations of the Christian, we must take it that the one born of God has received a faculty of loving, a power of loving inherent in the divine nature in which he participates. This is the basis of brotherly love, which issues from the new nature. *Agape* is the fruit of the divine "seed" received at baptism.

The Christian must love because he has been born of God and because love comes from God; indeed, "God is love" (v.8). Is this to say that John is giving a definition of God? The context (4:7-9) is all-important. John is giving the fruit of his contemplation on the *manifestation* of God through history; above all, in the person, life and teaching of Jesus. In the Old Testament the relations of God with his people were marked by his *hesed,* his loving kindness. This characteristic is to be seen in the life and death of Jesus. As John meditates on the deeds of Jesus and on his teaching on love, he discovers that Christ is first and foremost the revealer of God as the only Son who reposes permanently in the bosom of the Father, who makes known the "mystery" of God (Jn 1:18).

John does not say that God is loving or that he has loved, but that he is *love*. Nor does he say that love is in God, but that God *is* love. And if this is not, strictly speaking, a definition of God, it points to the distinctive attribute of God: love is of God's essence. If God engenders children he necessarily makes them share in his love—since he communicates to them his own life—in such a way that they also should be all love towards their brethren (vv.7-8). It is Christ who has revealed and communicated to men the love of his Father (v.9). Verse 10 takes up and deepens this thought. God had shown what love is by the sending of his Son into the world, in the death of his Son, and by forgiving all our sins. These three great mysteries of salvation— incarnation, redemption, grace—sum up the Gospel (Jn 3:16; 1 Jn 3:16).

Gospel Jn 15:9-17.

This is the second part of the passage of the Vine and the Branches; the first part was the gospel reading of the previous Sunday. In this second part the image of the vine has slipped into the background to reappear, momentarily, in the metaphor of fruit: "that you should go and bear fruit and that your fruit should abide" (v.16). The intimate union of vine and branches, which the image had stressed, is now presented as a bond of love which should unite the disciples of Christ. His affection for them is a friendship which knows no limits; he asks that all of them should love one another as friends and bear outwardly the fruit of charity. To abide in him, to live with his life, is to abide in his love, in the love with which he loves his disciples as the Father has loved him. Jesus had loved his disciples before he had chosen them: they are to abide in that love which is his more than it is their own. He goes on to show what abiding in his love means. The love of Jesus is modelled on that of the Father. The fidelity of the disciples, in abiding in the divine life and under the divine care, should model itself on the Son: as he has observed the commandments of his Father, so they should observe his. The parallel shows that love and obedience are mutually dependent: love arises out of obedience, obedience out of love. It follows that authentically christian obedience can flourish only in an atmosphere of christian love.

The "commandments" of Jesus may be reduced to one: the commandment of love. Love is the sap of the Vine, the bond of existence within the unity of Father, Son and believers. Jesus had hitherto granted to his disciples, to his own, obvious marks of affection and that from the moment he had chosen them (cf. Jn 13:1). But now he is going to give them the supreme evidence of his love. Voluntary death, a life freely laid down, will be the characteristic proof of *agapē*, a force which moves one to sacrifice oneself for others. The statement that the greatest love is that which entails the supreme sacrifice is not, however, a definition of love; Jesus means that this sacrifice is the most expressive mark of it. The sense is: nobody can give a more convincing proof of love than he who offers his life for those whom he loves. And when Jesus adds: "You are my friends," in effect he is telling them: Nobody has a greater love than that which I have for you. But it is also clear that this status of friend is not one which precludes obedient service.

Jesus sketches for his disciples the programme of the christian apostolate: "You did not choose me, but I chose you, and appointed you that you should go and bear fruit and that your fruit should abide" (v.16). It is he who chooses, calls, and appoints them; the insistence is entirely his. The principle of the apostolate is union with Jesus, but the disciples have a task to perform. And, by bearing the fruit that Jesus expects of them (fruit, even in the apostolate, which may well be hidden from eyes of flesh) they are true children of their heavenly Father. Then they can indeed address him as *Abba*; then they can pray to him with absolute confidence.

As for Jesus himself, he does not draw up for his disciples an elaborate code of law; he has no wish to place a heavy burden on them. He desires to set them free, not to bind them. All that he commands them is reduced to one precept: "Love one another." But he is not thereby less demanding. Anyone who has seriously sought to obey this one commandment knows that there are no limits to its demands. The substitution of the rule of law for the rule of love is, in reality, a pandering to our human weakness. And our initial lack of generosity has its revenge: the rule of law can effectively stifle further generosity. At any rate, there is no getting away from the fact that the one thing Jesus has asked of us—the one thing that Jesus has *commanded* us to do—is to love one another.

Patristic Commentary

Cyprian (c.200-258)
On the Unity of the Church, 14 OECT, 80,
    ed. Bevenot.

This is the Apostle Paul's teaching and witness: *And if I should have faith so that I could remove mountains and have not charity, I am nothing. And if I should distribute all my goods in food, and if I should deliver my body to be burned and have not charity, I profit nothing. Charity is great-hearted, charity is kind, charity envieth not, is not puffed up, is not provoked to anger, dealeth not perversely, thinketh no evil, loveth all things, believeth all things, hopeth all things, beareth all things. Charity shall never fall away.*

"Never," he says, "shall charity fall away." It will persist in the kingdom for ever, it will continue for all eternity in the close union of the brethren together. Discord cannot lead to the kingdom of heaven; and Christ, who said: *"This is my commandment, that ye love one another, as I have loved you,"* cannot reward him who has violated the love of Christ by disloyal dissension. He who has not charity, has not God. Hear the voice of the blessed Apostle John: *God, he says, is love; and he that abideth in God abideth in love, and God abideth in him* (1 Jn 4:16).) Those who have refused to be of one mind in the Church of God cannot therefore be abiding with God. Though they be cast in the fire and burnt in the flames, though they be exposed to the wild beasts and lay down their lives, this will not win them the crown of faith, but will be the penalty for their unfaithfulness; not the glorious consummation of holy valour, but an end put to recklessness. Such a man may be put to death; crowned he cannot be. If he calls himself a Christian, the devil also often calls himself the Christ, and is a liar; the Lord Himself foretelling it: *"Many will come in my name, saying, 'I am the Christ,' and will deceive many."* Just as the devil is not Christ though he tricks people by the name, so a man cannot be reckoned a Christian who does not abide in Christ's true Gospel and faith.

Insights from the Documents of the Church

Universality of the Church

When I meditate in this way, together with you gathered here, on those words of the Gospel of Matthew, there comes into my mind the texts of the Constitution *Lumen Gentium* which speak of the universality of the Church. The day of the Epiphany is the feast of the universality of the Church, of her universal mission. Well, we read in the Council: "The one People of God is accordingly present in all the nations of the earth, since its citizens, who are taken from all nations, are of a kingdom whose nature is not earthly but heavenly. All the faithful scattered throughout the world are in communion with each other in the Holy Spirit so that "he who dwells in Rome knows those in most distant parts to be his members" (n.9). Since the kingdom of Christ is not of this world (cf. Jn 18:36), the Church or People of God which establishes this Kingdom does not take away anything from the temporal welfare of any people. Rather, she fosters and takes to herself, in so far as they are good, the abilities, the resources and customs of peoples. In so taking them to herself she purifies, strengthens and elevates them. The Church indeed is mindful that she must work with that king to whom the nations were given for an inheritance (cf. Ps 2:8) and to whose city gifts are brought (cf. Ps 71(72):10; Is 60:4-7; Apoc 21:24). The character of universality which adorns the People of God is a gift from the Lord himself whereby the Catholic ceaselessly and efficaciously seeks for the return of all humanity and all its goods under Christ the Head in the unity of his Spirit. (John Paul II, To General Audience, 24 Jan., 1979)

No greater love

In the eschatological fulfilment mercy will be revealed as love, while in the temporal phase, in human history, which is at the same time the history of sin and death, love must be revealed above all as mercy and must also be actualized as mercy. Christ's messianic programme, the programme of mercy, becomes the programme of his people, the programme of the Church. At its very centre there is always the Cross, for it is in the Cross that the revelation of merciful love attains its culmination. Until "the former things pass away," the Cross will remain the point of reference for other words too of the Revelation of John: "Behold, I stand at the door and knock; if any one hears my voice and opens the door, I will come in and eat with him and he with me." (John Paul II, On the Mercy of God, [*Dives in Misericordia*])

THE ASCENSION OF THE LORD

Scriptural Commentary

First Reading Acts 1:1-11.

Most books open with the introduction of the central characters. Acts of the Apostles, too, begins with Jesus

Christ—yet he departs the scene after eleven verses! But if the book is about the *church* of Jesus Christ the situation is different. With the Ascension it is over to his disciples who now continue Jesus' mission. The disciples are situated firmly at the centre of the stage. Their witness fans out from Jerusalem to the end of the earth (v.8). In the mind of Luke the Gospel dealt with "all that Jesus began to do and teach" (v.1); by implication, what follows describes the continuation of Christ's doing and teaching through the apostles and the church. Christ's presence in his flock is a well advertised fact in Acts (9:4; 22:8; 26:14). Jesus Christ and the church are one.

Luke, in Acts, does not delay introducing the subject of the Holy Spirit; it is almost forced into his opening statement. In his gospel (he tells us) he had dealt with what Jesus had begun to do and teach, up to the moment of his ascension (v.2). Now he concentrates on the preparation of the apostles for their special role in the church, and he seeks to emphasize the part played in this by the Spirit. The risen Lord had shown himself to them and had assured them that he was truly risen. He charged them to remain in Jerusalem, waiting for "the promise of the Father" (Acts 1:4; Lk 24:49). The Father's promise is the Spirit (v.5); its coming at Pentecost will empower the twelve to accomplish their mission.

For the twelve this raises the question of the parousia, when the risen Lord will restore the kingdom of Israel (v.6). That day is the secret of the Father: "but you shall receive power when the Holy Spirit has come upon you" (v.8)—the Spirit, in some sense, substitutes for the parousia. To Luke the Spirit is the principle of continued existence in the new age of salvation history, the era of the church and mission. He has come to terms with the delay of the parousia and the ongoing thrust of history: his answer is the dynamic presence of the Spirit in the church. So, there is a mission, a vast programme (v.8). The kingdom will not come as a spectacular heavenly event; it will come through the action of the Spirit-powered leaven of Christians on earth. The christian mission must be the achievement of the Spirit.

Second Reading Eph 1:17-23.

The author of Ephesians had hardly finished his prayer of blessing (1:3-14) when he launched into a prayer of thanksgiving for his readers' faith and love (15-16). But this prayer of thanksgiving turns almost inperceptively into a prayer of intercession. Despite digressions this prayer lasts to 2:22, after which the writer will begin to intercede again. He prays that his readers may really "know" the "hope" to which they have been called (17-18). He thus implies that, despite their faith and love, they still have to progress in their vocation. He also implies that, although he is attempting to explain the "mystery" to them, their grasp of it will come not from his clear exposition of it, let alone their own efforts, but only as a gift of God's grace. Indeed, believing itself is less man's effort than the expression of God's power at work in the believer (v.19). This is the same power as that which was at work in Christ's resurrection and ascension, that is, in the accomplishment of God's plan—described here with explicit introduction of the notions of church, body and fulness. By his death, resurrection and ascension Christ has realised his dominion in every sphere of reality, from the underworld to the heavenly places. In this sense, the whole of creation is "full" of him, is his "fulness." But this fulness is recognised and acknowledged only by the church which, to this extent, becomes his articulated "body."

Gospel Mk 16:15-20.

Today it is commonly accepted that Mark ended his gospel at 16:8. It is evident, however, that even early Christians had been disconcerted by such a seemingly abrupt ending. The most ambitious attempt to round the gospel off "satisfactorily" is found in the passage now commonly appended to the gospel—16:9-20. That passage is no help to a proper understanding of Mark. It is little other than a borrowing from the endings of the other gospels. For our reading look to Lk 24:36-49; Jn 20:19-23;

Mt 28:18-20. The passage is concerned with the missionary charge of the risen Christ. The preachers of the good news are described as people at home in the world. Their preaching was to have the same effect as Jesus' own: it was to challenge people of all times and places to take a stand on the gospel, either believing (and being baptised, that is, initiated into a christian community) or rejecting Christ through unbelief.

Patristic Commentary

St. Leo the Great (d.461)
Tractatus 73, CCL 138A.451, NPNF12².187.

Those days, then, dearly beloved, which elapsed between the Resurrection and Ascension of our Lord, did not pass away in an inactive course: but in them great and sacred truths were confirmed, great mysteries were revealed. In them is taken away the fear of terrible death, and the immortality not only of the soul, but also of the flesh, is displayed. In them, by means of the Lord's breathing, the Holy Spirit is poured into all the Apostles; and to the blessed Apostle Peter above the rest, after the keys of the kingdom, is entrusted the care of the Lord's flock. In these days, when two disciples are on their road, the Lord associates Himself as a third with them. Whence the most blessed Apostles, and all the disciples, who had been both trembling at the result of the crucifixion, and doubtful as to belief in the Resurrection, were so invigorated by the clear vision of the truth, that when the Lord was going up to the height of heaven, they were not only not affected by any sadness, but even filled with a "great joy." And a truly great and ineffable cause of rejoicing it was, when in the presence of a holy multitude the nature of mankind was ascending above the dignity of all celestial creatures, to pass above the Angelic ranks, and to be elevated above the

high seats of Archangels, and not to let any degree of lofti-
ness be a limit to its advancement, until it should be received
to sit down with the Eternal Father, and associated in the
throne with His glory, to Whose nature it was coupled in
the Son! Since, then, Christ's Ascension is *our* advancement, and whither the glory of the Head has gone before,
thither is the hope of the body summoned, let us, dearly
beloved, exult with befitting joys, and rejoice with devout
thanksgiving. For to-day have we not only been confirmed
in the possession of Paradise, but in Christ have even
penetrated the heights of heaven, having won, through
the ineffable grace of Christ, richer gifts than we had lost
through the devil's envy. For those whom the venomous
enemy cast down from the happiness of their first habita-
tion, has the Son of God made of one body with Himself,
and placed at the Father's right hand, with Whom He
liveth and reigneth, in the unity of the Holy Spirit, God,
through all eternity. Amen.

Insights from the Documents of the Church

When the Holy Spirit comes upon you

When man accepts the Spirit of Christ, he establishes a
way of life that is totally new and gratuitous.

The Holy Spirit, present in the soul of the Christian,
makes him a partaker of the divine nature and intimately
unites him to the Father and Christ in a communion of life
which not even death can break (cf. Jn 14:23). The Holy
Spirit heals man of his spiritual weaknesses and infirmities,
frees him from the slavery of his passions and of immoderate
self-love by giving him power to keep the divine law,
strengthens him with hope and fortitude, enlightens him
in the pursuit of the good, and infuses in him the fruits of
charity, joy, peace, patience, kindness, goodness, lon-
ganimity, humility, fidelity, modesty, continence, and
chastity (cf. Gal 5:22-23). This is why the Holy Spirit is
invoked as the guest of the soul.

Justification from sin and God's indwelling in the soul are a grace. When we say a sinner is justified by God, is given life by the Holy Spirit, possesses in himself Christ's life, or has grace, we are using expressions which in different words mean one and the same thing, namely, dying to sin, becoming partakers of the divinity of the Son through the Spirit of adoption, and entering into an intimate communion with the Most Holy Trinity.

The man belonging to the history of salvation is the man ordered to the grace of filial adoption and to eternal life. Christian anthropology finds its own proper character in the grace of Christ the Saviour. (General Catechetical Directory, 60)

Teach all Nations

The image of Christ the Teacher was stamped on the spirit of the Twelve and of the first disciples, and the command "Go . . . and make disciples of all nations" set the course for the whole of their lives. Saint John bears witness to this in his Gospel when he reports the words of Jesus: "No longer do I call you servants, for the servant does not know what his master is doing; but I have called you friends, for all that I have heard from my Father I have made known to you." It was not they who chose to follow Jesus; it was Jesus who chose them, kept them with him, and appointed them even before his Passover, that they should go and bear fruit and that their fruit should remain. For this reason he formally conferred on them after the Resurrection the mission of making disciples of all nations.

The whole of the book of the Acts of the Apostles is a witness that they were faithful to their vocation and to the mission they had received. The members of the first Christian community are seen in it as "devoted to the apostles' teaching and fellowship, to the breaking of bread and the prayers." Without any doubt we find in that a lasting image of the Church being born of and continually nourished by the word of the Lord, thanks to the teaching of the Apostles, celebrating that word in the Eucharistic

Sacrifice and bearing witness to it before the world in the sign of charity. (John Paul II, Catechesis in Our Time [*Catechesi Tradendae*])

SEVENTH SUNDAY OF EASTER

Scriptural Commentary

First Reading Acts 1:15-17, 20-26.

Jesus had chosen "twelve whom he named apostles" (Lk 6:13). "The Twelve" were the nucleus of the new Israel. Just as the Jews believed that their roots could be traced back to the twelve patriarchs, so the new Israel is rooted in the Twelve. The defection of Judas had left a gap which must be filled. In vv.21-22 we have an important statement of Luke's idea of what "apostles" are. The chief duty of the "apostle"—that is to say, of one of the Twelve— is to witness to the resurrection; but he is also to witness to the public life of Jesus. To do this he must have been associated with Jesus from his baptism until his ascension. Elsewhere Luke notes that knowledge of what happened in the ministry of Jesus must be allied with a clear understanding of its significance in the context of the divine plan of salvation (Lk 24:44-47).

The Twelve, therefore, provide continuity between the historical life of Jesus and the era of the church. The role of the Twelve in the early church is more important as symbolizing a principle of life than for their active contribution. For instance, Matthias is never again mentioned in the New Testament and, apart from Peter, we hear little, or nothing, of any of the others. Yet, the Twelve, with their specific qualifications, stand at the origin of the christian church and they have unique familiarity with the preaching Christ. The Twelve, as Twelve, have no successors.

Second Reading 1 Jn 4:11-16.
The section 4:7-21 is on the theme of brotherly love—
vv.7-10 form the second reading of the sixth Sunday of
Easter. Today's passage introduces us to another characteristic of *agapē*: initiative. In real love, the love of God for
us, it is he who takes the initiative. Jesus, in showing his love
for us, laid down his life. The love of Christians, that love
which is a sharing in the love of God, in the love of Christ,
must have this quality of initiative. But our love of God
cannot have the priority, the initiative, which is characteristic of *agapē*. God and Jesus have first loved us; we
cannot love them in the same way. But we can take a loving
initiative—towards our brethren. It is by loving his brethren
that the Christian can love *as* God loves. In so far as one
possesses, and puts into practice, love towards one's
neighbour, God abides in one—as the Lord had promised
(Jn 14:23).

For *agapē* does indeed mark the vital encounter of the
Christian with his God: "So we know and believe the love
God has among us. God is love, and he who abides in love
abides in God and God abides in him" (v.16). *Agapē* is an
object of apostolic faith: the "we" refers first and foremost
to the Twelve, the witnesses of the Son. These are committed witnesses who "know and believe"—who are fully
convinced, totally persuaded, who believe with all their
being. The object of such solemn assurance is *agapē* in its
biblical sense of *manifestation* of love, and especially in
its christian acceptance of a love properly divine, revealed
and committed to mankind. It is the "love which God has
among us" because the manifestation of the divine love,
object of the apostles' faith, is, in the concrete, the incarnate
and redeeming Christ. Faith discerns in the incarnate Word
the presence and the nature of God; and it discovers that
God is love. To believe in the love which God has among
us is not only to confess Christ the Saviour who manifests
this love; it is to accept it, to receive it, to be united to it
and to live by it. It is, consequently, to incorporate the

divine *agapē*—to "abide in love." For the Christian is one who adheres to the revelation of the true God in the person of Jesus, who enters wholeheartedly into his plan of salvation and who is faithful to his commandments—especially that of brotherly love (Jn 13:34-35).

Gospel Jn 17:11-19.

The most solemn prayer of Jesus in the New Testament is the priestly and royal prayer of Jn 17. Here, Jesus prays for himself (1-5), for his disciples (6-19) and for the community of the future who will "believe through their word" (20-26). Our reading gives most of the prayer for the disciples. Jesus prays for his disciples present at the meal (ch. 13); he had taken care to make his Father known to them. Indeed they were the Father's gift to him in the first place—they know that the Father is the source of all that Jesus has done for them. Jesus has given them "the words" of the Father: he has revealed the Father. Now he is the high priest.

Jesus had come into the world because God so loved the world that he gave his only Son (3:16), in order to save that world of men (v.17). But the world would not face the light; the saving gift had been turned into judgment (3:18-19). Jesus who is now sending his disciples into the world to speak again his word of salvation, cannot pray for that hostile world (17:6-10). The disciples are being sent, as Jesus was sent, to challenge the world so that men might, at last, turn from darkness to light. He prays for those whom he leaves behind to carry on his work. He commits them to the Father's care and prays especially that they may know among themselves the warm communion of Father and Son. He reminds the Father that he, on earth, had kept and guarded them (vv.11-12).

V.13 opens the theme of Jesus' return to the Father. He speaks, while he is still with them, so that the disciples he is leaving behind may find the joy which follows on the fulfilment of the commandment of love. In bearing witness to the world they must, as he, suffer the world's hate. But that is a feature of their task, as it was of his. The Father will "keep them from the evil one"—surely an echo of the Lord's Prayer (Mt 6:13).

The disciples will be consecrated in the truth, that is to say, in God's word—the truth that is Jesus' revelation of the unseen God. To be consecrated in the truth means to have a closer union with Jesus who is the Truth (14:6). They have accepted him and kept his word (17:6,14); now they must bring him and his word to others. Jesus sends them as he himself was sent; the mission of this community of the faith is to continue the mission of Jesus. By his death (his "consecration") Jesus will confirm and consecrate his disciples. His death is a sacrifice, the supreme high-priestly action on their behalf (vv.16-19).

Patristic Commentary

St. Caesarius of Arles (c.470-542)
Sermon 186, CCL 104.758, FOTC 47.490.

We ought to know, dearest brethren, that there are two cities in this world, Babylon and Jerusalem. Babylon is interpreted as "confusion," and Jerusalem as "the vision of peace." These two cities have their own people and their own citizens. Do not attach yourself to the Babylonians if you desire to reach the eternal country. When you see a man possess charity and seeking eternal joy, you have found a citizen, a fellow-citizen of the angels, a pilgrim sighing on the way. Join him, for he is your companion; run along with him.

We who are pilgrims and strangers in this world, dearest brethren, ought to understand that we are still on the way, and not yet in our true country. Truly, life is this road. When man is born he begins the road, when he dies he is known to have finished it. For this reason men are wise if they show anxiety about the salvation of their soul and do not lóve the road. By running along the road, they long for their true country. But lovers of dissipation, who love present things more than future ones for the sake of fleeting pleasures, love the road, and as long as they wish to rejoice on the road they do not merit to reach the eternal country. Therefore, is fulfilled in them what is written: "The burdens of the world have made them miserable."

Insights from the Documents of the Church

The Apostles
From the beginning of his ministry the Lord Jesus "called to himself those whom he wished and he caused twelve of them to be with him and to be sent out preaching" (Mk 3:13; cf. Mt 10:1-42). Thus the apostles were both the seeds of the new Israel and the beginning of the sacred hierarchy. Later, before he was assumed into heaven (cf. Acts 1:11), after he had fulfilled in himself the mysteries of our salvation and the renewal of all things by his death and resurrection, the Lord, who had received all power in heaven and on earth (cf. Mt 28:18), founded his Church as the sacrament of salvation; and just as he had been sent by the Father (cf. Jn 20:21), so he sent the apostles into the whole world, commanding them: "Go, therefore, and make disciples of all nations, baptizing them in the name of the Father and of the Son and of the Holy Spirit; teaching them to observe all that I have commanded you" (Mt 28:19ff); "Go into the whole world, preach the Gospel to every creature. He who believes and is baptized shall be saved; but he who does not believe, shall be condemned" (Mk 16:15 ff). Hence the Church has an obligation to proclaim the faith and salvation which comes from Christ, both by reason of the express command which the order of bishops inherited from the apostles, an obligation in the discharge of which they are assisted by priests, and one which they

share with the successor of St. Peter, the supreme pastor of the Church, and also by reason of the life which Christ infuses into his members: "From him the whole body, being closely joined and knit together through every joint of the system, according to the functioning in due measure of each single part, derives its increase to the building up of itself in love" (Eph 4:16). The mission of the Church is carried out by means of that activity through which, in obedience to Christ's command and moved by the grace and love of the Holy Spirit, the Church makes itself fully present to all men and peoples in order to lead them to the faith, freedom and peace of Christ by the example of its life and teaching, by the sacraments and other means of grace. Its aim is to open up for all men a free and sure path to full participation in the mystery of Christ. (Vat. II, The Church's Missionary Activity, 5)

The Holy Spirit and apostolic activity

To do this, Christ sent the Holy Spirit from the Father to exercise inwardly his saving influence, and to promote the spread of the Church. Without doubt, the Holy Spirit was at work in the world before Christ was glorified. On the day of Penance, however, he came down on the disciples that he might remain with them forever (cf. Jn 14:16); on that day the Church was openly displayed to the crowds and the spread of the Gospel among the nations, through preaching, was begun. Finally, on that day was foreshadowed the union of all peoples in the catholicity of the faith by means of the Church of the New Alliance, a Church which speaks every language, understands and embraces all tongues in charity, and thus overcomes the dispersion of Babel. The "acts of the apostles" began with Pentecost, just as Christ was conceived in the Virgin Mary with the coming of the Holy Spirit and was moved to begin his ministry by the descent of the same Holy Spirit, who came down upon him while he was praying. Before freely laying down his life for the world, the Lord Jesus organized the apostolic ministry and promised to send the Holy Spirit, in such a way that both would be always and everywhere associated in the fulfilment of the work of salvation. Throughout the ages the Holy Spirit makes the entire Church "one in communion and ministry; and provides her with different hierarchical and charismatic gifts," giving life to ecclesiastical structures, being as it were their soul, and inspiring in the hearts of the faithful that same spirit of mission which impelled Christ himself. He even at times visibly anticipates apostolic action, just as in various ways he unceasingly accompanies and directs it. (Vat. II, The Church's Missionary Activity, 4)

PENTECOST SUNDAY*

Scriptural Commentary

First Reading Acts 2:1-11.

Luke's dramatic Pentecost presentation of the coming of the Spirit upon the apostles (vv.1-4) takes on fuller resonance when we note its Jewish colouring. Certainly in later Judaism and, very probably, already in the first century, Pentecost was the feast of the giving of the Law on Sinai. According to a tradition attested by Philo, at the giving of the Law God sent out a mighty wind which turned into a fire while a voice proclaimed the Law. Another tradition has it that the voice split into seventy tongues so as to be understood by all the nations on the earth. Much of this seems to be reflected and sharpened in Luke's text. For instance, the nations listed in vv.9-11 represent all nations—"every nation under heaven" (v.5).

The declaration of v.4 is very important: "And they were all filled with the Holy Spirit and began to speak in other tongues, as the Spirit gave them utterance." This presents

the Holy Spirit as the great gift of the final age (v.17) and as
the fulfilment of the Risen One's promise (1:8). At once the
effect of the presence of the Spirit is manifest: the witnesses
begin to speak according to the dictates of the Spirit. Luke
has chosen to regard the happening as a speaking in "other
tongues," thus dramatically presenting the real significance
of the outpouring of the Spirit: this preaching of the Good
News, in their own languages, to representatives of the
known world is the inauguration of a world-wide mission.
The Spirit is the gift and power of God which directs the
growth of the christian community and enables the followers of Christ to carry out their witness of witnessing
to him.

Second Reading 1 Cor 12:3-7,12-13.

In chapters 12-14 of his first letter to the Corinthians,
Paul treats of the final question raised in a letter of the
Corinthians to him, one concerning the "charisms" or
spiritual gifts granted to members of the community.
Their variety, and the rather disturbing character of some
of these gifts, tended to cause confusion. Hence Paul inter-
vened and clarified the situation. All these gifts come from
the same Spirit; they are granted in view of the good of the
community; their relative importance is based on the importance of the services they render; charity stands far
above the gift of speaking in tongues (glossolalia) a gift of
which the Corinthians were inordinately proud.

Paul (12:4-11) begins by pointing out that the gifts of the
Spirit are far more varied than the Corinthians had
imagined. It becomes abundantly clear, in his development
in these chapters, that christian endowments are truly such
only if they edify, build up. Behind these specifically christian gifts stand Spirit, Lord, and God; the gifts are, im-
pressively, of divine provenance. The divine activity is
never dissipated but is necessarily unified. And so there is
unity in the diversity of charisms, for all come from the same
Holy Spirit, and are destined for the building up, the edifi-
cation of the community.

In 12:12-26 Paul introduces the analogy of the body with its members. The human body is one, yet is composed of many members. The Apostle would suggest that the body with its various members may be compared to the body of the church, with its many and varied Spirit-inspired ministries. We are not really dealing with metaphor or image: because Christians have been baptized, by one Spirit, into one body (13:13), this body is the body of Christ, it is Christ himself.

Gospel Jn 20:19-23.

In 7:39 John declares: "as yet the Spirit had not been given, because Jesus was not yet glorified." Fittingly, the glorified Lord does communicate the Spirit. On the evening of Easter Day he came where the disciples were and gave them their commission and their anointing (20:21-23). It is common gospel tradition that Jesus commissioned his disciples for a saving mission. In John, too, the gift of the Spirit is closely related to the sending of the disciples as missionaries into the world. John's distinctive contribution is that their misssion is modelled on the mission of the Son. But they can undertake and accomplish the apostolic task inherited from Jesus only if, like him, they are filled with the Holy Spirit. The risen Lord "breathed" on them— in Greek it is the same verb used in Gen 2:7 (Septuagint): ". . . and he breathed into his nostrils the breath of life"—a deliberate echo. What John is saying is that, as in the first creation God breathed a living spirit into man, so now, at the moment of new creation, the glorified Jesus breathes the Holy Spirit into his disciples, giving them eternal life.

But what is this forgiveness and retention of sins? Happily this is the Johannine gospel and the very last thing one would expect of John (and of Paul for that matter) is legalism in any guise. True, the formulation seems to be clearly juridical: "forgiving" and "retaining"—surely a matter of handing down a verdict? Yes—except that this is John's gospel! The disciples are being sent out, just as Jesus was; their attitude to sin should be the same as his. And, for John, Jesus is *not* a judge. He is light and, in his presence, men judge themselves. And some men turn to the light and seek and find forgiveness and salvation; some turn from the light and so are hardened in their sin. The one thing the Spirit is not is a Spirit of judgment. As the presence of the absent Jesus he is indeed our advocate: "if any one does sin, we have a Paraclete with the Father, Jesus Christ the righteous" (1 Jn 2:1). We interpret Jn 20:23 in the light of 1 Jn 2:1 and in the light of the whole gospel of John—or we misinterpret. What John says here, as he has said elsewhere, is that the Spirit-filled disciples are the witnesses of Jesus and carry on his work. They reflect his life and, in the presence of their testimony, men are judged: "If they persecuted me, they will persecute you; if they keep my word, they will keep yours also" (15:20). Herein is judgment.

Luke's setting of the gift of the Spirit at Pentecost (first reading, Acts 2:1-11) conflicts with the position of the fourth evangelist. In Jn 20:22 the risen Lord, on Easter day (20:19), came and breathed on the disciples and imparted the gift of the Holy Spirit. We must avoid any impression of a two-fold initial solemn bestowal of the Spirit: once on Easter day (John) and secondly at Pentecost (Luke). Both John and Luke agree that the gift of the Spirit was bestowed on the disciples by the risen Lord. That they differ in their dating is due to theological concern.

St. Ambrose (c.340-397)
The Holy Spirit, Book 3, 1, PL 16.777,
　　FOTC 44.154.
But if no credence is given the Son, let them hear the Father also saying that the Spirit of the Lord is upon Christ. For He says to John: "He upon whom thou shalt see the Spirit descending, and remaining on him, he it is that baptizeth with the Holy Spirit." (Jn 1:33). God the Father

said this to John; and John heard and saw and believed. He heard from God; he saw in the Lord; he believed that it was the Spirit who was descending from heaven. For not a dove, but like a dove He descended, for thus it is written: "I saw the Spirit coming down as a dove from heaven." (Mk 1:10).

Just as John said that he had seen, so too did Mark write. Luke, however, added that the Holy Spirit descended in a bodily appearance like a dove (Lk 3:22)., You should not think that this was an incarnation, but an appearance. But He put forth the appearance on this account, that through the appearance he might believe, who did not see the Spirit, and through the appearance He might declare that He had a share with the Father and the Son of the one honor in the authority, of the one operation in the mystery, of the one gift in the bath, unless, perchance, we believe it invalid for a mere servant to be baptized in that in which the Lord was baptized.

Well did he say: "Remaining on him," because with reference to the Prophets the Spirit, as often as He wished, inspired a word or acted, but always remained in Christ.

Let it not again disturb you that he said "upon Him," for he was speaking of the Son of Man, because He was baptized as the Son of Man. For according to Godhead the Spirit is not upon Christ but in Christ, because, just as the Father is in the Son, and the Son in the Father, so the Spirit of God and the Spirit of Christ is both in the Father and in the Son, for He is the Spirit of His mouth. For He who is of God abides in God, as it is written: "Now we have received not the spirit of this world, but the spirit that is of God. (1 Cor 2:12) And He abides in Christ, who has received from Christ; and He is in Christ, for again it is written: "He shall receive of mine," (Jn 16:14) and elsewhere: "For the law of the spirit of life, in Christ Jesus, hath delivered me from the law of sin and of death" (Rom 8:2). He is not, then, over Christ according to the Godhead of Christ, because the Trinity is not over Itself, but over all things; It is not over Itself, but in Itself.

Insights from the Documents of the Church

The Holy Spirit in Our Lives

In describing the mission that the Holy Spirit would have in the Church, Christ used the significant words: "He will teach you all things, and bring to your remembrance all that I have said to you." And he added: "When the Spirit of truth comes, he will guide you into all the truth . . . he will declare to you the things that are to come."

The Spirit is thus promised to the Church and to each Christian as a Teacher who, in the secret of one's conscience and one's heart, makes one understand what one has heard but was not capable of grasping: "Even now the Holy Spirit teaches the faithful," said Saint Augustine in this regard, "in accordance with each one's spiritual capacity. And he sets their hearts aflame with greater desire according as they progress in the charity that makes them love what they already know and desire what they have yet to know."

Furthermore, the Spirit's mission is also to transform the disciples into witnesses to Christ: "He will bear witness to me; and you also are witnesses."

But this is not all. For Saint Paul, who on this matter synthesizes a theology that is implicit in all of the New Testament, it is the whole of one's "being a Christian," the whole of the Christian life, the new life of the children of God, that constitutes a life in accordance with the Spirit. Only the Spirit enables us to say to God: "Abba, Father." Without the Spirit we cannot say: "Jesus is Lord." From the Spirit come all the charisms that build up the Church, the community of Christians. In keeping with this, Saint Paul gives each disciple of Christ the instruction: "Be filled with the Spirit." Saint Augustine is very explicit: "Both (our believing and our doing good) are ours because of the choice of our will, and yet both are gifts from the Spirit of faith and charity."

Growth in faith and the maturing of Christian life towards its fullness, is consequently a work of the Holy Spirit, a work that he alone can initiate and sustain in the

Church . . . . Consequently, it is clear that the Church—and also every individual Christian devoting himself to that mission within the Church and in her name—must be very much aware of acting as a living pliant instrument of the Holy Spirit. To invoke this Spirit constantly, to be in communion with him, to endeavour to know his authentic inspirations must be the attitude of the teaching Church and of every Christian. (John Paul II, *Catechesis in Our Time*, no. 72 [slightly adapted])

SUNDAYS OF THE YEAR

SECOND SUNDAY OF THE YEAR

Scriptural Commentary

First Reading 1 Sam 3:3-10,19.

God always filled the major role in the Hebrew view of history. Men played their part in the building up of Israel in response to a call of Yahweh. Samuel was the instrument through whom Israel received its first kings (1 Sam 8-12). Samuel, himself conservative, opened a whole new chapter in the development of Israel. Up to now there was a loose tribal confederacy; under the king the tribes were to be, for a while at least, built into a nation. This shift of history through the agency of Samuel could only happen by Yahweh's choice.

The boy Samuel, an answer to a mother's fervent prayer, had been, by her, in thankfulness, dedicated to the Lord and was brought up by the priest Eli at the sanctuary of Shiloh (1 Sam 1). Our reading gives the story of the boy's call to be a prophet. The insistent word of the Lord came through again and again until Eli was convinced that it was the Lord who called. This episode, charmingly related, is the model for all later prophetic vocations. The initiative is firmly with God; the "call" is his. And being a call it elicits a response, to be freely given. And since God always speaks with purpose, every word will have its effect. No authentic word of his prophet will God let "fall to the ground."

Man's response to God's call comes through willing obedience. Samuel will later remind Saul that obedience is better than sacrifice (1 Sam 15:22). The same sentiment is expressed in today's *Responsorial Psalm* (Ps 40). It is God's gift to furnish man with an "open ear"—a heart responsive to his will. Christ, true prophet, whose food was to do the will of the Father (Jn 4:34) was the model of joyous response (Heb 10:5-6). His followers are called to share in faithfulness to God's purpose. Through obedience the prophetic mission begun in Samuel and lived perfectly by Jesus, is kept alive in the world. It is noteworthy that this first reading and responsorial psalm are read in the liturgy of religious profession. The self-dedication of religious to "the affairs of the Lord" is a sharing in the obedience of Christ to the Father. And through this obedience their way of life bears prophetic witness.

Second Reading 1 Cor 6:13-15, 17-20.

Until the sixth Sunday of the year inclusively, second readings are from 1 Corinthians. Paul visited Corinth for the first time on his second missionary journey. There he founded a church and remained for eighteen months, from winter of 50 A.D. to the summer of 52. Later, at Ephesus (54-57), he was informed of rival parties and of scandals in the Corinthian church; and the Corinthians, in a letter to him, had submitted a number of questions. In 1 Corinthians he faced up to the unsettled situation of the community and answered its questions.

The problem which faces Paul in 1 Cor 6:12-20 is that of casual copulation with a prostitute. It arises because of a conviction of some Corinthians that they, possessing a special "wisdom," had been raised to a spiritual sphere in which everything material was irrelevant and where no corporeal action had any moral value. In their eyes, everything was permissible. They could eat what and where they pleased (even in pagan temples); they could sleep with whom they pleased. They flouted convention on principle.

Paul takes up in turn, and qualifies, three slogans of the Corinthians.

He begins with the slogan: "All things are lawful for me" (v.12). Taken literally this is destructive of community—and, for Paul, true christian community is all-important. He points out that "not all things are helpful": what *I* want may be hurtful to the community. And if the community breaks apart one is back in slavery to Sin (Rom 6:17-18) and Paul will not have this enslavement (v.12). To the slogan, "Food is meant for the stomach and the stomach for food" (v.13) he retorts that the body is not for immorality but for the Lord, and the Lord for the body. The proof is that God raised Jesus from the dead (v.14): God's deed refutes the Corinthians' assertion that the body is of no concern. The body *is* morally relevant. With his repeated "Do you not know" (vv.15,16,19) Paul draws out implications of his own authentic teaching. A Christian belongs *wholly* to Christ; and casual sexual intercourse is a manifestly un-Christlike act (v.15).

The third Corinthian slogan: "Every sin which a man may commit is outside the body" (not "every *other* sin," RSV) (v.18), reflects their view that sin can only be in the "spiritual" sphere. Paul has already reinstated the body and so can proudly declare that the immoral man sins against his own body (v.18) because he does not use it for the purpose intended by God. In casual fornication the other person is not empowered to grow but is used, as an object, for selfish gratification.

In conclusion Paul asks: "Do you not know that your body is a temple of the Holy Spirit within you?" (v.19) God's presence in Jesus was in and through the physical, historical existence of Jesus. Similarly, God's presence in his members (v.15) is in their bodily lives. Bought at a great price (v.20), the physical death of Jesus, Christians belong to Christ (3:23). They glorify God, do God's will, by living christian lives which cannot be lived otherwise than in the body.

Gospel Jn 1:35-42.

Before embarking on his gospel proper, John (1:19-51) brings forward a series of witnesses who bear testimony to the Messiah in a variety of messianic titles. John the Baptist calls him the "Lamb of God" (vv.29-36) and the "Elect of God" (v.34). Andrew speaks of him as the "Messiah" (v.41). For Philip he is "he of whom Moses in the Law and also the prophets wrote" (v.45): and Nathanael exclaimed: "You are the Son of God; you are the king of Israel" (v.49). Jesus himself rounds off the list by adding his own designation: Son of Man (v.51).

As John's account of the call of Andrew and Simon, this gospel reading is related to the call of Samuel (first reading). With Samuel, Israel had reached a turning-point in its history; Christ's coming was the turning-point of history itself. John the Baptist is still preaching his baptism of penance by the Jordan and points out Jesus, the Lamb of God, to two of his followers. The designation "Lamb of God" suggests the Passover lamb (cf. 1 Cor 5:7). More immediately, it seems we should look to the "Servant of Yahweh." In Is 53:7 the suffering servant is likened to a "lamb led to the slaughter" and it is noteworthy that the Aramaic word *talya* can be translated "lamb" or "servant." The Baptist points to the Lamb who is the Servant who suffers and dies for the sins of the world (Jn 1:29). John's fate and mission, in his own words, were that he should decrease, pass from the centre of the stage, so preparing the road for the Redeemer. Here we see him lose two of his followers to Jesus. This self-less type of witness characterizes the Baptist's testimony in the Fourth Gospel.

"What do you seek?" Jesus asks and bids the seekers "come and see." To "come to" Jesus (3:18-21) and to "see" him (14:9) is the active movement towards the person of the Lord and the understanding in faith of who he is. Though the first who answered the call was Andrew, attention focuses on the initiative of Jesus who designated (by a significant change of name) Peter for a future supportive role in the christian community.

Patristic Commentary

St. Cyril, of Jerusalem (c.315-386)
Catechesis 13, PG 33.772, FOTC 64.4

The Catholic Church glories in every action of Christ, but her glory of glories is the Cross. Knowing this, Paul says: "But far be it from me that I should glory, except in the cross of our Lord Jesus Christ." (Gal 6:14) The glory of the Cross has at one and the same time led into the light those blind through ignorance, has delivered all bound in sin, and redeemed all mankind.

Do not wonder that the whole world was redeemed, for it was no mere man, but the Only-begotten Son of God who died for it. The sin of one man, Adam, availed to bring death to the world; if by one man's offense death reigned for the world, why should not life reign all the more "from the justice of the one?" (Rom 5:7) If Adam and Eve were cast out of paradise because of the tree from which they ate, should not believers more easily enter into paradise because of the Tree of Jesus? If the first man, fashioned out of the earth, brought universal death, shall not He who fashioned him, being the Life, bring everlasting life? If Phinees by his zeal in slaying the evildoer appeased the wrath of God (Numb 25:8), shall not Jesus, who slew no other, but "gave himself as a ransom for all," (1 Tim 2:6) take away God's wrath against man?

Therefore let us not be ashamed of the Cross of our Savior, but rather glory in it; "for the doctrine of the cross" is "to the Jews a stumbling-block and to the Gentiles foolishness," but to us salvation, "foolishness to those who perish but to those who are saved, that is, to us, it is the power of God." (1 Cor 1:18) For as I said before, it was not a mere man who died for us, but the Son of God, God made man. If under Moses the lamb kept the destroyer away, did not "the Lamb of God, who takes away the sins of the world," (John 1:29) all the more deliver us from our sins? The blood of a brute sheep accorded salvation; shall not the blood of the Only-begotten much more save us? If any

man doubts the power of the Crucified, let him question
the devils; if any man doubts words, let him believe the
evident facts. Many have been crucified throughout the
world, but of none of these are the demons afraid. For
these died because of their own sins, but Christ for the
sin of others; for He "did not sin, neither was deceit found
in his mouth."

Insights from the Documents of the Church

All Christians called

The Church is a communion. She herself acquired a fuller
awareness of that truth in the Second Vatican Council.

Th Church is a people assembled by God and united by
close spiritual bonds. Her structure needs a diversity of gifts
and offices; and yet the distinctions within her, though they
can be not only of degree but also of essence, as is the case
between the ministerial priesthood and the common
priesthood of the people, by no means takes away the basic
and essential equality of persons. "The chosen People of
God is one: 'one Lord, one Faith, one Baptism' (Eph 4:5).
As members, they share a common dignity from their
rebirth in Christ. They have the same filial grace and the
same vocation to perfection. They possess in common one
salvation, one hope, and one undivided charity . . . . And
if by the will of Christ some are made teachers, dispensers
of mysteries, and shepherds on behalf of others, yet all
share a true equality with regard to the dignity and the
activity common to all the faithful for the building up of the
Body of Christ" (LG,32).

In the Church, therefore, every vocation is worthy of
honour and is a call to the fullness of love, that is, to holiness; every person is endowed with his own supernatural
excellence, and must be given respect. All gifts and charisms, even though some are objectively more excellent than
others (cf. 1 Cor 12:31; 7:38), work together for the good
of all members by means of the provident multiplicity of

forms, which the apostolic office must discover and co-ordinate (cf. LG,12). This holds also for all particular churches individually; for in each one, though it be small and poor or living in dispersion, "Christ is present, and by his power the one, holy catholic, and apostolic Church is gathered together" (LG, 26). (General Catechetical Directory, 66)

Decline in Moral Values

The Church, having before her eyes the picture of the generation to which we belong, *shares the uneasiness of so many of the people of our time*. Moreover, one cannot fail to be worried by *the decline of many fundamental values*, which constitute an unquestionable good not only for Christian morality but simply *for human morality, for moral culture:* these values include respect for human life from the moment of conception, respect for marriage in its indissoluble unity, and respect for the stability of the family. Moral permissiveness strikes especially at this most sensitive sphere of life and society. Hand in hand with this go the crisis of truth in human relationships, lack of responsibility for what one says, the purely utilitarian relationship between individual and individual, the loss of a sense of the authentic common good and the ease with which this good is alienated. Finally, there is the "desacralization" that often turns into "dehumanization": the individual and the society for whom nothing is "sacred" suffer moral decay, in spite of appearances. (John Paul II, On the Mercy of God [*Dives in Misericordia*])

THIRD SUNDAY OF THE YEAR

Scriptural Commentary

First Reading Jonah 3:1-5,10.

The book of Jonah is post-exilic, written likely in the fifth century B.C. Far from being a naive story of a man-eating "great fish," it is a sophisticated satire. It hits out at Jewish exclusiveness and boldly asserts that God is the God of all peoples. A Hebrew prophet is sent by God to Ninevah, capital of the Assyrian oppressor. The prophet, knowing the mercy of his God, and fearing that the Ninevites may repent and escape their fate (the last thing *he* wants) seeks to evade the task (ch.1). There is no escaping God and, the second time, Jonah obeys (ch.3). His worst fears are realised: the king of Nineveh and his people at once believe the word of the prophet and do penance (3:5-9). The irony is unmistakable: the preaching of the reluctant Jonah meets with an immediate and universal response in the pagan city, whereas the great prophets had, over the centuries, preached to the chosen people in vain! The book may be regarded as a dramatization of Jer 18:8 (alluded to in Jonah 3:10): "If that nation concerning which I have spoken turns from its evil, I will repent of the evil that I thought to do to it." The author not only demonstrates the possibility of a heathen city repenting and turning to God but draws attention also to the love, mercy, and forgiveness of God and, in the person of Jonah, strongly rebukes (4:9-11) those who would be unwilling to see God's mercy beyond Israel.

Second Reading 1 Cor 7:29-31.

In the second part of this letter (7:1 - 11:1) Paul answers the queries raised in the letter of the Corinthian community. In the first place (ch.7) the merits of marriage and celibacy. He favours the celibate state but he acknowledges that marriage is good and he insists on the mutual conferring of conjugal rights (7:1-9). Concerning divorce, he reiterates the Lord's teaching (vv.10-11) but, nevertheless, gives his own view on mixed marriages (vv.12-16). Then, by association of ideas, he turns to exhort Christians to remain in the way of life which the Lord has assigned to each (vv. 17-24).

In 7:25-40 he passes to a new question on "spiritual" marriages, that is, marriages in which the partners committed themselves to a celibate life-style. Paul is being asked what he thinks of the practice. He begins by stating his conviction that the Parousia of Christ was imminent (vv.29,31; cf. 1 Thes 4:13-18), and he assumes that the Corinthians share that view. They cannot, then, imagine that the realities of their present lives are going to go on for long. "This is the central thrust of vv.29b-31a whose individual phrases should not be taken out of this context. Paul is not recommending that husbands should cease to love their wives (v.29b), nor that they should put on a hypocritical show of sorrow or rejoicing, nor that they stop all commercial activity. His concern is to prepare them for the day when all these will change. He is asking for an attitude of detachment from the dear, familiar things which tend to absorb humanity. It is foolish to give too much importance to the impermanent" (J. Murphy-O'Connor, *1 Corinthians*, 73). Two things should be kept in mind for properly understanding this chapter of Paul: the eschatological perspective; and the fact that not marriage as such is being considered but marriage within a troubled Corinthian setting.

Gospel Mk 1:14-20.
From today until the thirty-third Sunday inclusive, Gospel readings are from the gospel of Mark. Now generally recognized as the earliest of our gospels, Mark is built up of two complementary parts. The first (1:14 - 8:30) is concerned with the mystery of Jesus' identity; it is dominated by the queston: "Who is Jesus?". The emphasis in this first part of Mark is on Jesus' miracles, while the little teaching that is contained in it is addressed to the crowds, and is largely parabolic. The second part (8:31 - 16:8) is concerned with the messianic destiny of Jesus: a way of suffering and death. The emphasis in this second half of

Mark is on Jesus' teaching which, now directed to his disciples, builds upon their recognition of him as Messiah, and is concerned mainly with the nature of his messiahship and with the suffering it will entail both for himself and his followers.

[For Mk 1:1-8 see Second Sunday of Advent; for 1:7-11 see The Baptism of the Lord].

(1:14-20). Mark intersperses his gospel with a series of summary statements which succinctly describe a period of activity and trace the course of events. His first summary (1:14-15) opens the public ministry and covers the initial period. The opening words are ominous: "after John was delivered up." The fate of the Baptist was to be delivered up to his enemies in accordance with the divine will (6:17-29)—he is a type of the suffering Messiah. The long shadow of the cross reaches to the beginning. And now begins the preaching of "the good news of peace" and Mark's sentence, "the reign of God is at hand; repent and believe the good news" is an admirable summing-up of the preaching and message of Jesus. Like the Baptist, Jesus calls for a thorough-going conversion; but, more urgently, he calls on men to embrace the Good News. The evangelist intended the words "believe in the gospel" to be taken in the christian sense of faith in the good news of salvation through Jesus Christ. (See First Sunday of Lent).

By the time of Jesus "kingdom of God" had come to represent particularly the expectation of an eschatological deed of God. What Jesus claimed was that this decisive intervention of God was happening in his ministry. The Kingdom is here and now present in history in that the power of evil spirits is broken, sins are forgiven, sinners are gathered into Jesus' friendship. The kingdom comes as a present offer, in actual gift, through the proclamation of the gospel. But it only fully arrives on condition of the positive response of the hearer.

The call of the first disciples (v.16-20) is a passage shaped to bring out the nature of Christ's call and the christian response, to show what "following Jesus" means. The decisive factor is the person of Jesus himself. In order to become a disciple of Jesus it is not necessary to be an exceptional person. It is the mighty, immediate impression of Jesus on Peter and his companions, reinforced by his personal word of call, which brought them into his following and made them his disciples.

Patristic Commentary

St. Jerome (c.347-c.420)
Homily on St. Mark 1.13-31, CCL 78.461,
    FOTC 57.133.

"After John had been delivered up, Jesus came into Galilee." (Mk 1:14) When we were commenting upon the Gospel last Sunday, we distinguished John in the Law and Jesus in the Gospel, for John says: "One mightier than I is coming after me, the strap of whose sandals I am not worthy to stoop down and loose." (Mk 1:7) And in another place, he says: "He must increase, but I must decrease." (Jn 3:30) He is drawing a comparision, therefore, between the Law and the Gospel. Farther, he says: "I have baptized you with water," that is, the Law; "but he will baptize you with the Holy Spirit," (Mk 1:8) that is, the Gospel. Jesus came, therefore, to open for us the inner chambers of the Gospel that we, too, may say with David: "Open my eyes that I may consider the wonders of your law."

"Preaching the gospel of the kingdom of God, and saying, 'The time [of the Law] is fulfilled,'" the Gospel has begun "and the kingdom of God is at hand." He did not say, the kingdom of God has already arrived, but the kingdom is at hand. Until I suffer and shed My blood, the kingdom of God is closed; it is near at hand, therefore, because not yet have I suffered the Passion. "Repent and believe in the gospel":

by no means in the Law, but in the Gospel; nay, rather through the Law into the Gospel, as it is written: "From faith unto faith." The faith of the Law has confirmed the faith of the Gospel.

"Passing along the sea of Galilee, he saw Simon and his brother Andrew, casting their nets into the sea (for they were fishermen)." Simon, not yet Peter—for not yet had he followed the Rock that he should be called Peter—Simon and his brother, Andrew, were at sea and were casting their nets. Scripture does not say that they cast their nets and caught fish. He saw Simon, it says, and his brother, Andrew, casting their nets into the sea, for they were fishermen. The Gospel reports, to be sure, that they were casting nets; still it does not say that they caught anything; hence, it is clear that before the Passion, they cast nets, but it is not recorded that they caught anything. After the Passion, however, they let down their net and drew up a catch, so great that it broke the nets. "Casting their nets into the sea, for they were fishermen."

"Jesus said to them, 'Come, follow me, and I will make you fishers of men.'" Happy exchange of fishing! Jesus fishes for them that they may become fishers of other fishermen. First, they become fish that they may be caught by Christ; afterwards, they will fish for others.

Insights from the Documents of the Church

Sin and Repentance

The people of God do penance continually in many and various ways. Sharing in the sufferings of Christ by their own suffering, performing works of mercy and charity, undergoing a constant conversion to the Gospel of Christ, they become to the world a symbol of conversion to God. This the Church expresses in its life and celebrates in its liturgy, when the faithful profess themselves sinners and ask pardon of God and their brothers—as happens in penitential services, in the proclamation of the word of God, in prayer, in the penitential elements of the Mass.

And in the sacrament of Penance, the faithful "obtain pardon from God's mercy for the offence committed against him and are, at the same time, reconciled with the Church, which they have wounded by their sins and which by charity, example and prayer labours for their conversion."

Since sin is an offence against God and breaks our friendship with him, penance "has for its ultimate objective that we should love God and commit ourselves wholly to him." When the sinner, therefore, by God's mercy takes the road of penance, he returns to the Father who "loved us first" (1 John 4:19), to Christ who gave himself up for us, and to the Holy Spirit who is poured out on us abundantly.

But, "because of a secret and loving mystery of dispensation, men are joined together by a supernatural necessity, in such wise that the sin of one injures the others, and the holiness of one benefits the others." In the same way, penance affords reconciliation with a man's brothers, who likewise are injured by sin.

Further, men often act together in committing sin. In the same way, they help one another when doing penance, so that, freed from sin by the grace of Christ, they might, with all men of good will, make peace and achieve justice in the world. (Introduction to the Rite of Reconciliation)

Vocations: Appeal to young people

Dear young people, on this occasion I would like to address to you a very special invitation: reflect. Understand that I am talking to you about very great things. It is about consecrating the whole of one's life to the service of God and the Church. It is about consecrating one's life with certain faith, mature conviction and a free decision, with generosity ready for any trials and without regrets. The words of Jesus: "I am with you always, to the close of the age" ensure the continuing of that "you." The Lord will always call, and there will always be responses on the part of the people who are ready and willing. You too must listen. With your minds enlightened by faith you must penetrate into the other-worldly dimension of the divine plan of universal salvation. I know that you are disturbed by many things of this world, many events of the present time. It is for this very reason that I invite you to reflect! Open your hearts to the joyous encounter with the Risen Christ. Let the power of the Holy Spirit work in you and inspire you with the right choices for your lives. Ask advice. The Church of Jesus must continue her mission in the world: she needs you, for there is so much work to be done. In speaking to you about vocation and in inviting you to follow this path I am the humble and earnest servant of that love by which Christ was moved when he called the disciples to follow him. (John Paul II, Message for World Day of Prayer for Vocations, 27 April 1980)

FOURTH SUNDAY OF THE YEAR

Scriptural Commentary

First Reading Dt 18:15-20.

In Dt 18:10-14 the Lord had warned the Israelites against the use of various magical techniques for discovering the will of God. Prophecy, Yahweh's gift to his people, is Israel's special means of communication with God (v.15). The Israelites on Sinai had begged to be spared the awesome ordeal of hearing the divine voice directly. They asked Moses to represent them in God's presence and to convey God's word to them. Yahweh granted their request and the office of prophetic mediator came into being.

"The Lord will raise up for you a prophet like me" (v.15); the verb implies "continually raise up" and refers to a line of prophets, to the prophetic office as seen by Deuteronomy. Biblical tradition represents Moses as the ideal prophet. Exodus 33:11 tells us that "the Lord used to speak to Moses face to face, as a man speaks to his friend." The prophet can never speak on his own authority. The prophet who proclaims as a divine word something that has not come from God is threatened with death (v.20). The prophet of lying vision and deceit is no successor of Moses.

Later Jewish tradition saw in v.18 not a promise of a line of prophets but a promise of a figure of the last days, a Prophet-like-Moses. It seems clear from Acts 3:22-23 (which quotes Dt 18:15-16,23) that the early Christians regarded Jesus as the awaited prophet. Jn 6:14 and 7:40 also hold reference to the people's expectation of the Prophet-like-Moses.

Second Reading 1 Cor 7:32-35.

Today's reading follows directly on last Sunday's excerpt from 1 Cor 7. It is clear that Paul himself believed that his celibate state was better than the married state (vv.7-8); it enabled him to give his undivided attention to the Lord (vv.32-35). He is clear that it is gift (v.7) and he will not impose practical acceptance of the ideal on all. This is what some at Corinth wanted to do. Again, properly to evaluate vv.32-35, one must appreciate the strained Corinthian situation; otherwise one must think Paul's remarks banal. At Corinth those who did marry would come under attack from the ascetics and have "worldly troubles." Paul stresses *anxieties* and wants Christians to be free of them. And he realistically notes the total absorption of the newly married (vv.33-34). His care to describe the unmarried man/woman as "*anxious* about the affairs of the Lord" would seem to hold a smack of irony, a challenge to the ascetics: are they really as concerned "to please the Lord" as they claim to be? When the whole of chapter 7 is taken into account, it is clear that though Paul regarded the single state (which was his own, v.7) as best, he did not glorify it, and finally refused to make it mandatory for any other (v.35). Throughout, his fundamental objection is to the presumption of those who claim to know what is best for others.

Gospel Mk 1:21-28.

"A day in the life of Jesus" (1:21-34) illustrates a feature of the early ministry: the authority of Jesus in terms of teaching and exorcism and healing. Two distinct episodes are set in the Capernaum synagogue: a teaching of Jesus which provokes the admiration of his hearers, and the expulsion of an unclean spirit which awakens reverential fear in the bystanders. Later, in 3:22-30, we learn that exorcisms are to be seen in terms of the struggle between the Spirit and Satan begun in the temptation (1:12-13). Each specific exorcism is a particular instance of the unrelenting hostility between Jesus and the spirits of evil, a struggle continued in the life of every Christian. In this case (v.22) what "astonishes" is the note of assurance and authority in Jesus' teaching. He speaks with prophetic authority in a manner very different from the traditionalism of the scribes. The spirit of the gospel stands out firmly against the spirit of legalism.

The extreme astonishment (v.27) of those present was occasioned by the authoritative teaching and the effortless exorcism. "With authority" is best taken along with "a new teaching" to mean "a new teaching with authority behind it." Expressions of astonishment at the actions of, or before the person of, Jesus are frequent throughout Mark. It is the evangelist's way of drawing the attention of the reader to a manifestation of Jesus' true nature. The crowds are astonished because they do not understand what is really taking place and who it is that stands before them. The christian reader should not miss the full message of the text.

Patristic Commentary

St. Irenaeus of Lyons (c.130-200)
Against Heresies, Bk. 4. c.6, SC 100.448,
    ANF 1.469.

For by means of the creation itself, the Word reveals God the Creator; and by means of the world does He declare the Lord the Maker of the world; and by means of the formation [of man] the Artificer who formed him; and by the Son that Father who begat the Son; and these things do indeed address all men in the same manner, but all do not in the same way believe them. But by the law and the prophets did the Word preach both Himself and the Father alike; and all the people heard Him alike, but all did not alike believe. And through the Word Himself who had been made visible and palpable, was the Father shown forth, although all did not equally believe in Him; but all saw the Father in the Son: for the Father is the invisible reality of the Son, but the Son the visible reality of the Father. And for this reason all spoke with Christ when He was present [upon earth], and they named Him God. Even the demons exclaimed, on beholding the Son: "We know Thee who Thou art, the Holy One of God." (Mk 1:24) And the devil looking at Him and tempting Him, said: "If Thou art the Son of God;"—all thus indeed seeing and speaking of the Son and the Father, but all not believing in them.

For it was fitting that the truth should receive testimony from all, and should become a means of judgment for the salvation indeed of those who believe, but for the condemnation of those who believe not; that all should be fairly judged, and that the faith in the Father and Son should be approved by all, receiving testimony from all, both from those belonging to it, since they are its friends, and by those having no connection with it, though they are its enemies. For that evidence is true, and cannot be gainsaid, which elicits even from its adversaries striking testimonies in its behalf; they being convinced with respect to the matter in hand by their own plain contemplation of it, and bearing testimony to it, as well as declaring it. But after a while they break forth into enmity, and become accusers [of what they had approved], and are desirous that their own testimony should not be regarded as true.

For the Son, being present with His own handiwork from the beginning, reveals the Father to all; to whom He wills, and when He wills, and as the Father wills. Wherefore, then, in all things, and through all things, there is one God, the Father, and one Word, and one Son, and one Spirit, and one salvation to all who believe in Him.

Insights from the Documents of the Church

Chastity

Chastity "for the sake of the kingdom of heaven" (Mt 19:22), which religious profess, must be esteemed an exceptional gift of grace. It uniquely frees the heart of man (cf. 1 Cor 7:32-35), so that he becomes more fervent in love for God and for all men. For this reason it is a special symbol of heavenly benefits, and for religious it is a most effective means of dedicating themselves wholeheartedly to the divine service and the works of the apostolate. Thus for all Christ's faithful religious recall that wonderful marriage made by God, which will be fully manifested in the future age, and in which the Church has Christ for her only spouse. (Vat. II, Renewal of Religious Life, 12)

Only the love of God—it must be repeated—calls in a decisive way to religious chastity. This love moreover makes so uncompromising a demand for fraternal charity that the religious will live more profoundly with his contemporaries in the heart of Christ. On this condition, the gift of self. made to God and to others, will be the source of deep peace. Without in any way undervaluing human love and marriage—is not the latter, according to faith, the image and sharing of the union of love joining Christ and the Church?—consecrated chastity evokes this union in a more immediate way and brings that surpassing excellence to which all human love should tend. Thus, at the very moment that human love is more than ever threatened by a "ravaging eroticism," consecrated chastity must be today more than ever understood and lived with uprightness and generosity. Chastity is decisively positive, it witnesses to preferential love for the Lord and symbolizes in the most eminent and absolute way the mystery of the union of the Mystical Body with its Head, the union of the Bride with her eternal Bridegroom. Finally, it reaches, transforms and imbues with a mysterious likeness to Christ man's being in its most hidden depths. (Paul VI, Apostolic Exhortation on the Renewal of Religious Life [*Evangelica Testificatio*])

Why does the Latin Catholic Church link this gift not only with the vocation to the religious life, but also with the vocation to the hierarchical and ministerial priesthood? It does so because celibacy "for the sake of the kingdom" is not only an eschatological sign, it also has great social relevance in this life for the service of the People of God. Through his celibacy, the priest becomes the "man for others" differently from the way that a married man becomes, as husband and father, a "man for others," especially within his own family: for his wife and, with her, for the children whom he begets. The priest in renouncing the fatherhood proper to married men seeks another fatherhood and even another motherhood, as it were, after the words of the Apostle concerning the children with whom he is "in travail" (see Gal 4:19, 1 Cor 4:15). (John Paul II, Letter to Priests)

FIFTH SUNDAY OF THE YEAR

Scriptural Commentary

First Reading Job 7:1-4, 6-7.

The book of Job (5th century B.C.) belongs to the stage when the idea of individual retribution (the traditional doctrine of retribution, in its simplest form, is that the good are rewarded and the wicked punished *in this life*) palpably ran up against insoluble practical difficulties. It is important to have in mind that, until the first half of the second century B.C., the Hebrews had a very vague notion of the afterlife.

At death a man did not quite disappear, he continued to exist in some dim, undefined way in Sheol; but in that dismal abode of the dead all, rich and poor, good and bad, were equal. Given this situation it is inevitable that, throughout most of the Old Testament, retribution of good and evil was seen in an exclusively earthly perspective, strictly within the confines of this life. In the dialogues Job wrestles with a tormenting problem: he is suffering, yet knows himself to be innocent. The inadequacy of the traditional position has become apparent, but men can close their eyes to a disturbing new truth. Here the three friends are the champions of "orthodoxy"; they have accepted the classic teaching without question and quite refuse to admit that it will not fit the facts of the present case. There position is very direct: suffering is punishment for sin; if a man suffers it is because he is a sinner—the facts must be made to fit the traditional viewpoint! Hence they proceed to comfort the sufferer by pointing out that he must be a sinner—and a great sinner at that, judging by his sufferings —and they grow insistent as he protests his innocence.

Our reading is a brief extract from Job's anguished response (chs.6-7) to Eliphaz's (the senior of the friends) assured insistence that Job is being rightfully punished for his sin. It is not surprising that, in face of his atrocious suffering and such cold comfort, Job takes a dim view of life. Later, in ch.29, he nostalgically paints a glowing picture of his former life. Manifestly, the author of Job is sensitive to the tragic predicament of humanity and he gives poignant expression to the pain and confusion that baffles the man who grapples with the problem of suffering and tragedy. We should not allow ourselves to forget the happy times. For, normally, life is not all drudgery and is something better than a dreary passing from hopeless night to weary day, as Job paints it. But we may surely ask what is the ultimate meaning of our transitory life and how we may give it meaning.

Second Reading 1 Cor 9:16-19, 22-23.

In 1 Cor 8 Paul has told his readers that it may be necessary to forego one's rights in order to avoid leading others astray. In our reading he shows how he himself lives it out; he does not insist on his right as an apostle to be supported by the Corinthians to whom he preaches. Though he had the support of the Law and the word of the Lord (1 Cor 9:13-14) to back up his claim to be supported by his converts, he did not wish to insist on his right. He preaches because he cannot resist the overwhelming power of Christ who has called him to be an apostle. He feels that by taking a reward from men he would be putting an obstacle in the way of the gospel. Paul finds the Corinthians jealous of their rights and wants to make the point that renunciation of rights can readily become a christian duty. To add further muscle to his own example, he carefully refrains from stressing that he had no objection to accepting support from a community *after* he had left it (cf. 2 Cor 11:7-9; 12:11-6; Phil 4:15-16). But he did make a principle of being independent of the community to which he ministered.

Paul, who was so proud of his freedom as a Roman citizen (cf. Acts 21:39) and as a Christian (1 Cor 9:1) was prepared to become a slave of all for the sake of the gospel. His aim is to make himself "all things to all men," to be at the service of all, to meet people on their own ground. He has special interest in the "weak." These were in the first place, the scrupulous brethren of ch. 8, converts from paganism, who wanted to remain free of their pagan past. But Paul's concern was wider and reached to others who laboured under any sort of weakness. He desired to help, but, above all, to be heard; and he knew that the preacher must win a sympathetic hearing.

Gospel Mk 1:29-39.

In healing Peter's mother-in-law (1:29-31) Jesus, who had cast out a demon (vv.23-26), is shown to have power over sickness. Like the exorcisms, the miracles of healing, too, are signs of salvation. The early christian community was not interested in miracles of Jesus as brute facts. It regarded them in a twofold light: as a manifestation of the power of God active in Jesus and as signs of the redemption which Jesus had wrought. Here the phrase, "he raised her up" (*egeirō*, "to life up" also means "raise from the dead"), has symbolic meaning. The woman "lifted up" from "fever" symbolises one formerly prostrate beneath the power of sin now raised up by the Lord and called upon to serve him.

At the close of this specimen day (1:21-34), "all" the sick and possessed of the town are brought to Jesus (vv.32-34). This summarizing passage describes Jesus' mission up to now and marks a transition to the further spread of his work. The demons (v.34) understood, as the crowds and the disciples do not, that Jesus is the envoy of God and are bidden to keep silent. This "messianic secret" has to do with the true status of Jesus. Mark is sure that what "Son of God" means can be understood only when Jesus had shown, through suffering and death, what it means. That is why Jesus cannot be proclaimed "until the Son of man should have risen from the dead" (9:9).

Reference to the prayer of Jesus (v.35) may give us a proper understanding of the episode of 1:35-39. Mark mentions Jesus' prayer on two further occasions: after the multiplication of loaves (6:46) and in Gethsemane (14:35, 39). Each time the true nature of Jesus' messiahship is in question and he has to contend with the incomprehension of his disciples (6:52; 14:10). So, here, the disciples have "hunted him out" because they feel that he, the wonder-worker, was missing a golden opportunity. This is not the attitude of true disciples; this is not the following of Jesus to which they had been called.

Patristic Commentary

Origen (c.185-c.254)
Comm. on John, X 53, SC 157.418,
ANF IX.386-387

And at Capernaum Simon's mother-in-law is cured of her fever. And Mark adds that when evening was come all those were cured who were sick and who were possessed with demons. Luke's report is very like Mark's about Capernaum. He says, "And He came to Capernaum, a city of Galilee, and He was teaching them on the Sabbath day, and they were astonished at His teachings, for His word was with authority. And in the synagogue there was a man having a spirit of an unclean demon, and he cried out with a loud voice, Ah! what have we to do with you, Jesus of Nazareth? Have you come to destroy us? I know who you are, the holy one of God. And Jesus rebuked him, saying, Hold your peace and come out of him. Then the demon having thrown him down in the midst, went out of him, doing him no harm." And then Luke reports how the Lord rose up from the synagogue and went into the house of Simon, and rebuked the fever in his mother-in-law, and cured her of her disease; and after this cure, "when the sun was setting," he says, "all, as many as had persons sick with divers diseases, brought them to Him, and He laid his hands on each one of them and cured them. And demons also went out from many, crying and saying, you art the Son of God, and He rebuked them and suffered them not to speak because they knew that He was the Christ."

Matthew for his part adds, that when the Lord had entered into Capernaum the centurion came to him, saying, "My boy is lying in my house sick of the palsy, grievously tormented," and after telling the Lord some more about him, received the reply, "Go, and as thou hast believed, so be it unto thee." And Matthew then gives us the story of Peter's mother-in-law, in close agreement with the other two. I conceive it to be a worthy ambition and becoming to one who is anxious to know more about Christ, to collect from the four Gospels all that is related about Capernaum, and the discourses spoken, and the works done there, and how many visits the Lord paid to the place, and how, at one time, He is said to have gone down to it, and at another to have entered into it, and where He came from when He did so. On the one hand, the sick are healed, and other works of power are done there, and on the other, the preaching, Repent ye, for the kingdom of heaven is at hand, begins there, and this appears to be a sign, as we showed when entering on this subject, of some more needy place of consolation, made so perhaps by Jesus, who comforted men by what He taught and by what He did there, in that place of consolation. For we know that the names of places agree in their meaning with the things connected with Jesus; as Gergesa, where the citizens of these parts besought Him to depart out of their coasts, means. "The dwelling of the casters-out." And this, too, we have noticed about Capernaum, that not only did the preaching, "Repent ye, for the kingdom of heaven is at hand," begin there, but that according to the three Evangelists Jesus performed there His first miracles.

Insights from the Documents of the Church

The Duty to Preach the Gospel - for the laity, too

From the day of Pentecost the church has recognized that her primary function, entrusted to her by her founder was to reveal Jesus Christ and his gospel to those who did not know him. The whole of the New Testament and especially the Acts of the Apostles show us that this time was ideally suited to evangelization and in a certain sense offers us a prototype for the accomplishment of this work, a work of which the whole history of the church furnishes a splendid counterpart . . . .

Laymen, whose vocation commits them to the world and to various temporal enterprises, should exercise a special form of evangelization.

Their principal and primary function is not to establish or promote ecclesial communities, which is the special function of pastors, but to develop and make effective all those latent christian and evangelical possibilities which already exist and operate in the world.

The special field for their evangelical zeal is the wide and complex arena of politics, sociology and economics. They can be effective also in the spheres of culture, the sciences, the arts, international relations and the communications media. There are certain other fields which are especially appropriate for evangelization such as human love, the family, the education of children and adolescents, the practice of the various professions and the relief of human suffering. If laymen who are actively involved in these spheres are inspired with the evangelical spirit, if they are competent and determined to bring into play all those christian powers in themselves which so often lie hidden and dormant, then all these activities will be all the more helpful in the building up of the kingdom of God and in bringing salvation in Jesus Christ. And in this their effectiveness in the temporal sphere will be in no way diminished; on the contrary new fields of higher achievement will be opened up to them.

We must not fail to draw attention to the role played by the family in the sphere of the apostolate which is proper to the laity. It has rightly been called the *domestic* church and this title has been confirmed by the second Vatican council. It declares that in every christian family the various features and characteristics of the universal church should be found. And accordingly the family, just like the church, must always be regarded as a centre to which the gospel must be brought and from which it must be proclaimed.

Therefore in a family which is conscious of this role all the members of the family are evangelizers and are themselves evangelized. Not only will the parents impart the gospel to their children's lives. Such a family will bring the gospel to many other families and to the whole social circle to which it belongs. Families of mixed marriages must teach Christ to their children, stressing the significance and efficacy of a common baptism. There is also incumbent on them the difficult task of making themselves the architects of unity. (Paul VI, Evangelization today, 64, 70, 71)

SIXTH SUNDAY OF THE YEAR

Scriptural Commentary

First Reading Lev 13:1-2, 45-46.

The whole of chapter 13 of Leviticus is concerned with "leprosy"—a term not confined to Hansen's disease but which includes different kinds of infectious skin diseases. Whatever the actual nature of the disease may have been, the person afflicted with it was considered ritually unclean, as was anybody or anything that came into contact with him. It was the duty of the priests to diagnose the disease. Once they had confirmed that someone was a leper no compassion was shown the unfortunate sufferer. He was forbidden to live in any town or village. His clothes were to be distinctive and he had to let his hair grow loose. Since contact with a leper rendered a person "unclean," the leper was obliged to cry out: "Unclean!" when he saw anybody approach. Although the rabbis maintained that the healing of leprosy was "as difficult as raising the dead," it was believed that the disease sometimes healed spontaneously. When a leper was pronounced cured and had undergone a purification rite, he was readmitted to the community

(Lev 14). Since lepers were such outcasts and their disease so feared, we can imagine how surprised and even shocked the people were when they saw Jesus go so far as to touch them in the manner described in today's Gospel reading.

Second Reading 1 Cor 10:31 - 11:1.

In 1 Cor 10:23 - 11:1 Paul turns his attention to "the weak." Coming from a pagan background, they could not as readily come to terms with the eating of idol-meat (8:7) as could "the strong," mostly Jewish converts with supreme contempt for "idols" (8:4). Where in chapter 8 he had urged on the Strong their obligation of delicate christian consideration for the Weak, he now (10:23-30) reminds the Weak that they should show consideration for the Strong and strive to appreciate their viewpoint. Our reading gives Paul's conclusion to the whole lengthy (and, for our day, rather tiresome) debate. This conclusion is a thoroughly positive principle, one susceptible of very wide application indeed: "do all to the glory of God" (v.31).

A Christian gives glory to God by being what he or she is meant to be: a manifestation of the love of Christ. Hence one must give no offense *to anyone*. One must never do anything that would make it difficult for the Jew or the pagan to see the beauty of Christianity. One's action should never lead a Christian to reject his church or be the reason of his failure to grow in holiness. Paul himself had always been guided by his consideration for the good of others and he urges the Corinthians to follow his example. The ultimate norm, for him and for them, is Christ "who did not please himself" (Rom 15:3). In order to assure them that the ideal is not beyond the reach of humankind Paul can say to the Corinthians: "Be imitators of me, as I am of Christ" (11:1). The implication is awesome. To demonstrate to others that the love of God in Christ is a present reality a preacher should be able to point to himself. Paul, at least, would hold that, if he cannot do so, if he cannot show forth in his person "the life of Jesus" (2 Cor 4:10), he really has no right to speak.

Gospel Mk 1:40-45.

The significance of the cure of a leper lies in the fact that (as we have seen in our first reading) leprosy is the ultimate uncleanness which made one socially, and in the religious sphere, wholly an outcast. The Law was helpless in face of leprosy; it could only defend the community against the leper. But what the law could not achieve, Jesus accomplishes. Cf. Rom 8:3.

In v.41 "moved with anger" (and not "moved with pity") should be taken as the original reading. The anger of Jesus is his reaction to the disease which brings him face to face with the power of evil. He is shocked by the fact that the community has to *defend* itself against this poor wretch and does so by branding him as a pariah. *He* reaches out to the man a loving and healing hand. This is how a christian community should deal with sinners and down-and-outs.

In v.45 we read that the former leper began to tell his tale to everyone he met. Significantly, "to talk" also means "to proclaim" and "the news" is *ho logos*, "the word." These terms carry christian overtones which Mark's readers would not have missed. A Christian is one "cleansed" by Christ in baptism; one who then ought to "preach" and "spread abroad the Good News."

Patristic Commentary

Origen (c.185-c.254)
Ex Diversis Hom. in Matt, Toal, Patristic Homilies 1.346.

Lord, if you will, you can make me clean. To me the gain, to you the praise; to all who behold your wonder an increase in knowledge of the truth.

Lord, if you will, you can make me clean. You Who by your servant Eliseus did cleanse of leprosy Naaman, the prince of Syria, bidding him wash in the Jordan, now, if you will, you can make me clean.

To whom in reply the Lord says: Believing, you confess that I can, and that if I will it comes to pass; accordingly, I will: be thou made clean. Wondrously hast thou believed, and wondrously art thou healed; without measure thou hast confessed, without measure art thou made joyful. I will: be thou made clean. You faltered not in believing: I am quick to heal. You delayed not to confess your faith: I delay not to cleanse thee. I will: be clean. That I may show thee great favour, I stretch forth my Hand to thee; *and stretching forth His hand, touched him, saying: I will; be clean.*

And why did He touch him, since the Law forbade the touching of a leper? For this did He touch, that He might show that *all things are clean to the clean.* Because the filth that is *in* one person adheres not to others; neither does external uncleanness defile the clean of heart. But wherefore, in this circumstance, does He touch him? That He might instruct us in humility; that He might teach us that we should despise no one, or abhor them, or regard them as pitiable, because of some wound of their body, some blemish that is sent by God, for which it is He that will give reason, and render an account. I am the heavenly physician, He says, I can cure bodies as well as souls. And so I touch all, not that their infirmities may adhere to me, but that I may drive them from those who are afflicted.

Insights from the Documents of the Church

Suffering, pain-killers, euthanasia

By the sacred anointing of the sick and the prayer of the priests the whole Church commends those who are ill to the suffering and glorified Lord that he may raise them up and save them (cf. Jas 5:14-16). And indeed she exhorts them to contribute to the good of the People of God by freely uniting themselves to the passion and death of Christ (cf. Rom 8:17; Col 1:24; Tim 2:11-12). (Vat. II, Constitution on the Church, 11)

Physical suffering is certainly an unavoidable element of the human condition; on the biological level, it constitutes a warning of which no one denies the usefulness; but, since it affects the human psychological makeup, it often exceeds its own biological usefulness and so can become so severe as to cause the desire to remove it at any cost.

According to Christian teaching, however, suffering, especially suffering during the last moments of life, has a special place in God's saving plan; it is in fact a sharing in Christ's Passion and a union with the redeeming sacrifice which he offered in obedience to the Father's will. Therefore one must not be surprised if some Christians prefer to moderate their use of painkillers, in order to accept voluntarily at least a part of their sufferings and thus associate themselves in a conscious way with the sufferings of Christ crucified (cf. Mt 27:34). Nevertheless it would be imprudent to impose a heroic way of acting as a general rule. On the contrary, human and Christian prudence suggest for the majority of sick people the use of medicines capable of alleviating or suppressing pain, even though these may cause as a secondary effect semiconsciousness and reduced ludicity. As for those who are not in a state to express themselves, one can reasonably presume that they wish to take these painkillers, and have them administered according to the doctor's advice . . . .

It is necessary to state firmly once more that nothing and no one can in any way permit the killing of an innocent human being, whether a foetus or an embryo, an infant or an adult, an old person, or one suffering from an incurable disease, or a person who is dying. Furthermore, no one is permitted to ask for this act of killing, either for himself or herself or for another person entrusted to his or her care, nor can he or she consent to it, either explicitly or implicitly. Nor can any authority legitimately recommend or permit such an action. For it is a question of the violation of the divine law, an offence against the dignity of the human person, a crime against life, and an attack on humanity.

It may happen that, by reason of prolonged and barely tolerable pain, for deeply personal or other reasons, people may be led to believe that they can legitimately ask for death or obtain it for others. Although in these cases the guilt of the individual may be reduced or completely absent, nevertheless the error of judgment into which the conscience falls, perhaps in good faith, does not change the nature of this act of killing, which will always be in itself something to be rejected. The pleas of gravely ill people who sometimes ask for death are not to be understood as implying a true desire for euthanasia; in fact it is almost always a case of an anguished plea for help and love. What a sick person needs, besides medical care, is love, the human and supernatural warmth with which the sick person can and ought to be surrounded by all those close to him or her, parents and children, doctors and nurses. (Declaration on Euthanasia)

SEVENTH SUNDAY OF THE YEAR

Scriptural Commentary

First Reading Is 43:18-19, 21-22, 24-25.

In Is 40-48 we have a series of hymns to the Lord Redeemer. Today's reading is taken from one of them, on the redemption and restoration of Israel (43:1 - 44:23). The author is encouraging the exiles in Babylon, assuring them that all is not lost despite the recent disaster of the destruction of Jerusalem and of the exile. On the contrary, there is prospect of a glorious future. Israel was conscious of her past, of the great things that the Lord had done for her from the time of the Exodus onwards. These great deeds were recalled in song and story. Now, the prophet proclaims, a greater deed was about to be performed in comparison with which past history would appear a small thing. There would be a new exodus (this time from Babylon), a new

journey through the desert, a new settlement in the home-
land. This new age would be a pure act of grace, totally
unmerited by Israel who had only burdened her God with
her sins. The new order of things would be characterized by
the forgiveness of sins, thus ensuring reconciliation and
friendship between God and mankind. In making the
forgiveness of sin a characteristic of the new age, Second
Isaiah is in the tradition of Jeremiah: "I will forgive their
iniquity and remember their sin no more" (Jer 31:31-34) and
Ezekiel: "I will sprinkle clean water upon you and you
shall be clean . . ." (Ezek 36:25-29).

Second Reading 2 Cor 1:18-22.

From today until the fourteenth Sunday inclusive
second readings are from 2 Corinthians. In Macedonia,
towards the close of 57 A.D., Paul learned from Titus
(2 Cor 2:12-13; 7:5-16) that the turbulent Corinthian
community, in the meantime shaken by further crises,
was at last reasonably tranquil. Second Corinthians
expresses his satisfaction at this turn, but is also very much
of an apologia. The writing is, in large measure, a defence
of the apostolic ministry and reveals the deeply human side
of Paul. We find in him the model of a pastor: a fusion of
love and of justice, of prudence and of energy in the ani-
mating and guiding of a community.

Paul seeks to re-establish the warm relationship that had
existed between the Corinthian community and himself
(cf. 1 Cor 4:14-16). Rivals of his, "travelling preachers,"
more eloquent than he, less demanding in their moral
standards, had attempted to come between him and the
community. They accused Paul of promising a great deal by
letter and doing little in person. He had been accused of
vacillating; of saying one thing to them and of doing (or
meaning) something else. They instanced his failure to visit
Corinth as arranged. He explains why he had changed his
travel plans. It was to spare their feelings of the community
that he had not come: one painful visit was more than
enough (1:23 - 2:1). Refuting the charge of duplicity, he

declares himself to be not a man who answers "yes" and "no" in the same breath. He is very conscious that he is a sign of Christ, and Christ was fidelity itself. Paul plays on the fundamental idea behind the Hebrew word "Amen" ("to stand," "to be [or make] firm") and on the meanings of the word itself: "So it is," "Yes". The word brings to mind fidelity. Christ is the Amen, the Faithful One (Rev 3:14; 19:11). He is God's "Amen" to his promises, he fulfils them. We make our Amen through him. It is an Amen which says "yes" to all that God has done for us, which expresses a conviction that he will continue to help us and ensures a constancy in our own christian living. Such confidence gives glory to the Father. It is he who has brought about our union with Jesus and has anointed us for mission. He has sealed us as his very own and given us his Spirit who is the pledge of future fulfilment.

Gospel Mk 2:1-12.

Up until now Jesus had been carrying out his mission in Galilee, teaching, healing, casting out demons. At this point (ch.2) comes his first explicit confrontation with official Judaism. It is documented in a series of five controversies: on forgiveness of sins (2:1-12), on eating with tax-collectors and sinners (2:13-17), on fasting (2:18-22), on grainfields and the sabbath (2:23-28), and concerning healing on the sabbath (3:1-6). At the same time, the section sets the teaching of Jesus in relief: the section is not only apologetic but is markedly cathetical as well. The fact is that each of the separate units which make up the complex is not only a conflict story, a debate with adversaries, but is, too a pronouncement story. We can see that the saving message of each is to be found in a saying of the Lord—the stories are so many illustrations of that "new teaching with authority behind it" (1:27). If we set out the five climactic sayings one after another we can readily perceive how valuable they are for an understanding of the christian gospel:

The Son of man has authority on earth to forgive sins.
I came, not to call the righteous but sinners.

Can the wedding guests fast while the bridegroom is with them?

The Son of man is Lord even of the sabbath.

Is it lawful on the sabbath to do good or to do harm, to save life or to kill?

These sayings—all of them in part or in whole christian formulations—have a vital bearing on the content of the gospel message and on the early church's understanding of its Lord.

Today's reading (2:1-12) is the first of the conflict-stories. The passage is composite, with vv.1-5a, 11-12 forming a coherent miracle-story, augmented by a section on the remission of sins (vv.5b-10). Mark has converted a miracle story into a controversy story. The evangelist is telling us that the cure of a paralytic was intended to manifest the sin-forgiving power of the Son of man. In the early kerygma the remission of sins was regarded as intrinsic to the experience of being a Christian. Thus Acts 10:43 states, "To him (Jesus) all the prophets bear witness that every one who believes in him receives forgiveness of sins through his name." In the light of this and similar texts it is evident that the early Christians proclaimed the forgiveness of sins as a present fact. This meant a head-on clash with Jewish belief which regarded forgiveness a future benefit to be hoped for.

The very presence of the forgiveness of sins debate in the gospel is an indication that it was a live issue for Mark's community. Their assertion of forgiveness of sins on earth was blasphemy to their Jewish adversaries. Their defence is their claim of a share of the authority of the eschatological Son of man (v.10). For Mark the full revelation of the Son of man is in his suffering, death and resurrection and so is accessible only to believers. When, however, those who believe in Jesus seek to live and act in the Spirit of Jesus, they participate in his power to forgive sins. The story is a vindication of the church's claim to declare the forgiveness of sins in the name of Jesus (cf. Jn 20:23), a forgiveness achieved in baptism.

Patristic Commentary

Clement of Alexandria (c.150-c.215)
Paidagogus, 1.2., SC 70., FOTC 23.6.

God alone is sinless. Yet we must strive, to the best of our ability, to be as sinless as we can. Nothing is more important for us than first to be rid of sins and weaknesses, and then to uproot any habitual sinful inclination. The highest perfection, of course, is never to sin in any way; but this can be said by us of God alone. The next highest is never deliberately to commit wrong; this is the state proper to the wise man. In the third place comes not sinning except on rare occasions; this marks a man who is well schooled by the Pedagogue. Finally, in the lowest degree, we must place delaying in sin for a brief moment; but even this, for those who are called to recover their loss and repent, is a step on the path to salvation.

The Word is our Pedagogue, who heals the unnatural passions of our soul with His counsel. The art of healing, strictly speaking, is the relief of the ills of the body, an art learned by man's wisdom. Yet, the only true divine Healer of human sickness, the holy Comforter of the soul when it is ill, is the Word of the Father. Scripture says: "Save Thy servant, O my God, who trusts in Thee. Be gracious to me, O Lord, because I have cried to Thee the whole day through." In the words of Democritus, "The healing art, cures the body of its diseases, but it is wisdom that rids the spirit of its ills." The good Pedagogue, however, Wisdom Himself, the Word of the Father, who created man, concerns Himself with the whole creature, and as the Physician of the whole man heals both body and soul.

"Arise," the Saviour said to the paralytic, "take up your pallet on which you are lying and go home." And immediately the sick man regained his health. To the man who was dead He said: "Lazarus, come forth." And the dead came forth from his tomb, the same as he had been before he underwent death, except for having tasted resurrection.

But the soul He heals in a way suitable to the nature of the soul: by His commandments and by His gifts. We would perhaps expect Him to heal with His counsels, but, generous with His gifts, He also says to us sinners: "Your sins are forgiven." With these words we have become little ones in spirit, for by them we share in the magnificent and unvarying order established by His providence. That providence begins by ordering the world and the heavens, the course of the sun's orbit and the movements of the other heavenly bodies, all for the sake of man. Then, it concerns itself with man himself, for whom it had undertaken all these other labors. And because it considers this as its most important work, it guides man's soul on the right path by the virtues of prudence and temperance, and equips his body with beauty and harmony. Finally, into the actions of mankind it infuses uprightness and some of its own good order.

Insights from the Documents of the Church

Forgiveness

Society can become "ever more human" only when we introduce into all the mutual relationships which form its moral aspect the moment of forgiveness, which is so much of the essence of the Gospel. Forgiveness demonstrates the presence in the world of *the love which is more powerful than sin*. Forgiveness is also the fundamental condition for reconciliation, not only in the relationship of God with man, but also in relationships between people. A world from which forgiveness was eliminated would be nothing but a world of cold and unfeeling justice, in the name of which each person would claim his or her own rights vis-à-vis others; the various kinds of selfishness latent in man would transform life and human society into a system of oppression of the weak by the strong, or into an arena of permanent strife between one group and another.

For this reason, the Church must consider it one of her principal duties—at every stage of history and especially in our modern age—*to proclaim and to introduce into life* the mystery of mercy, supremely revealed in Jesus Christ. Not only for the Church herself as the community of believers but also in a certain sense for all humanity, this mystery is the *source* of a life different from the life which can be built by man, who is exposed to the oppressive forces of the threefold concupiscence active within him. It is precisely in the name of this mystery that Christ teaches us to forgive always. How often we repeat the words of the prayer which he himself taught us, asking *"forgive us* our trespasses *as we forgive* those who trespass against us," which means those who are guilty of something in our regard! It is indeed difficult to express the profound value of the attitude which these words describe and inculcate. How many things these words say to every individual about others and also about himself! The consciousness of being trespassers against each other goes hand in hand with the call to fraternal solidarity, which Saint Paul expressed in his concise exhortation to "forbear one another in love." What a lesson of humility is to be found here with regard to man, with regard both to one's neighbour and to oneself! What a school of good will for daily living, in the various conditions of our existence! If we were to ignore this lesson, what would remain of any "humanist" programme of life and education? (John Paul II, On the Mercy of God [*Dives in Misericordia*])

EIGHTH SUNDAY OF THE YEAR

Scriptural Commentary

First Reading Hosea 2:16-17, 21-22.

Hosea, a younger contemporary of Amos, preached in the northern kingdom of Israel during the latter years of

Jeroboam II (783-743 B.C.) and during the turbulent years
that preceded the fall of Samaria in 721 B.C. Hosea was the
first to represent the covenant relation of Yahweh with his
people as a marriage. It is out of his own personal experience (Hos chs. 1,3) that the marriage image came to the
prophet and that he realized its aptness in describing the
relations between Yahweh and his people. He understood
that the psychology of human love can wonderfully illustrate the mystery of God's relations with mankind, the
reality and depth of his love. The divine Husband has been
betrayed by his spouse who has given herself to adultery
(to Baal worship). Yet he seeks only to win her again to him
and if he chastises her it is with that sole end in view. As a
last resort he determines to bring her back once more to
the conditions of the Exodus, the honeymoon period of
their love (2:16-17). In fact, he ultimately goes beyond
this and promises to bring her into the harmony of a new
garden of Eden (2:18) where their love will be the crowning
and fulfilment of the mutual love of the first human couple
(2:21-22). In Hosea's view, what God is calling for is a
restoration of his people's first fervour and simplicity.
She had been led from this first love through over-concern
with human affairs.

Second Reading 2 Cor 3:1-6.

Things had gone so badly between the Corinthians and
Paul that he, who had brought the faith to them, was now
expected to produce a letter of introduction! Paul is at his
most deadly when he is being ironical. The itinerant evangelists, his opponents, press their charge: "This man
commends *himself*, but we can show *our* letters of recommendation from other communities." Paul, devastatingly,
can retort that the Corinthian church itself, every man,
woman and child of it, is *his* letter of recommendation.
The Christians of Corinth are a sufficient recommendation
of Paul's authenticity. Christ delivers this letter, through
his work, with the help of the Spirit. It is not written on

stone like the old law. It is the "letter" of their faith in Christ, written by the Spirit on their hearts.

Paul is confident of the success of his work—because success comes from God. Of himself he can do nothing. He takes up now a key-idea which surfaced in Galatians and will run through Romans: he has been appointed minister of a new covenant, not based on a written law, but on the Spirit. The law showed what was wrong but could not, of itself, provide the dynamism which leads to right conduct. The Spirit is a principle of life which effects a new way of living. It is a transforming power.

Gospel Mk 2:18-22.

Ever so often one shakes one's head in puzzled disbelief at the insensitivity of the compilers of the Lectionary. Jesus' tablefellowship with sinners, the gospels proclaim, was his favoured manner of preaching hope to the hopeless and, at the same time, inevitably, was a red rag to his pharisaic opponents (cf. Lk 15:1-2)—and Mk 2:13-17 has been left aside!

Today's reading is made up of a pronouncement story (2:18-20) to which two sayings, on patches and wineskins, have been added (2:21-22). The fact that the disciples of Jesus did not fast brings home to those who can understand that the Bridegroom is with them. But those who do not recognize the signs of the times (cf. Mt 16:2-3) are scandalized by such conduct. The two appended sayings (vv.21-22) are designed to make clear that the new movement which Jesus inaugurated cannot be confined within the limits of the old religion.

The bridegroom is manifestly Jesus and his being "taken away" (v.30) is a veiled reference to his impending death. Like the disciples of John (cf. 6:29) the disciples of Jesus, too, will have their time of mourning (cf. Jn 16:20). The qualification "and they will fast in that day" would suggest that fasting had become a practice in the Marcan community.

Though the parabolic sayings (vv.21-22) certainly had an independent existence, it is clear that in their Marcan context they illustrate a contrast between the old spirit and the new. A patch of unshrunk cloth will shrink at the first wash and tear apart the weakened fabric of the old garment. Old wineskins become thin and brittle; the new fermenting wine would burst the skins and wine and skins would be lost. The new spirit is not a piece added to the old nor a new element poured into the old: it is a vivifying power which transforms the abiding teachings of the old revelation. This is what Jesus outlines in the Sermon on the Mount, the Gospel which Paul develops in his turn.

Patristic Commentary

Gaudentius of Brescia (4th-5th Cent.)
S.8, PL 20.896, Toal, Patristic Homilies, 1.313.

And they had no wine. Because the wedding wine was consumed, which means that the Gentiles had not the wine of the Holy Spirit. So what is here referred to is not the wine of these nuptials, but the wine of the preceding nuptials; for the nuptial wine of the Holy Spirit had ceased, since the prophets had ceased to speak, who before had ministered unto the people of Israel. For all the prophets and the Law had prophesied until the coming of John; nor was there any one to give spiritual drink to the Gentiles who thirsted; but the Lord Jesus was awaited, who would fill the new bottles with new wine, by His baptism; *For the old things have passed away: behold all things are made new.*

All things are made new, but so that their origin from the old remains, since wine is produced, not from nothingness, but from the ancient element of water. Neither think ye that the letter of the Law is to be despised, whence the Holy Spirit, by the operation of Jesus, is drawn forth by faithful servitors; and for that reason men perished in the ancient flood, and are now in Baptism reborn; *for the letter killeth, but the spirit quickeneth.* The letter alone killeth, but tempered by the Holy Spirit it regenerates.

It is known that all men of that time perished, save those who had merited to be in the Ark, which was a figure of the Church to come. Likewise even now they can not be saved who will have turned away from the Apostolic Faith and the Catholic Church. Let each one of you, therefore, strive most earnestly to remain within the house of the Lord, doing the things that are becoming to the grace that is within you, that you have received.

Let those reborn into *the new man* be on guard against your former sins. Safeguard, I beseech you, the new bottles, O Neophytes; lest returning to your old way of life, and breaking the bottles, you spill the new wine: *for the new wine will break the bottles, and the wine will be spilt.* Safeguard therefore the whole newness of the reborn man, and preserve the heavenly wine of grace in your vessels, so that your faith, being defended, will defend you, through the Saviour of all men, Jesus Christ Our Lord, reigning with the Father and the Holy Spirit before all things were, and now, and for ever and ever, Amen.

Insights from the Documents of the Church

Fasting; interior penitence

The word "penitence" recurs in many pages of Holy Scripture, it re-echoes on the lips of prophets and, finally, in a particularly eloquent way, on the lips of Jesus Christ himself: "Repent, for the kingdom of heaven is at hand." (Mt 3:2) It can be said that Christ introduced the tradition of fasting for forty days into the liturgical year of the Church, because he himself "fasted forty days and forty nights" (Mt 4:2) before beginning to teach. With this forty-day fast, the Church is, in a certain sense, called every year to follow her Master and Lord, if she wishes to preach his Gospel effectively.

Penitence in the evangelical sense means, above all, "conversion." From this point of view, the passage of the Gospel of Ash Wednesday is very significant. Jesus speaks of the carrying out of acts of penitence, known to and practised by his contemporaries, by the people of the Old Covenant. At the same time, however, he criticizes the purely external way in which these acts, charity, fasting, prayer, are carried out, because this is contrary to their special purpose. The purpose of the acts of penitence is a sincere turning to God so as to be able to meet him deep down in one's being, in the recesses of the heart (cf. Mt 6:2-6, 17-18). Therefore the first and principal meaning of penitence is interior, spiritual. The principal effort of penitence consists "in entering oneself," one's deepest being, entering this dimension of one's own humanity in which, in a certain sense, God is waiting for us. The "exterior" man must, I think, yield, in each of us, to the "interior" man and, somehow, "make way for him." These days, man does not live enough on the "interior" plane. Jesus Christ clearly indicates that even acts of devotion and penitence (such as fasting, charity, prayer) which because of their religious purpose are mainly "interior," may yield to the current "exteriorism," and can therefore be falsified. Penitence, on the contrary, as turning to God, requires above all that man should reject appearances, succeed in freeing himself from falsehood, and find himself again in all his interior truth. Even a rapid, summary look into the divine splendour of man's interior truth is an achievement in itself. It is necessary, however, to consolidate this success skilfully by means of systematic work on oneself. This work is called "ascesis" (it had already been given this name by the Greeks of the times of the origins of Christianity). Ascesis means an interior effort not to let oneself be swept along and pushed by the different "exterior" currents, in such a way as to remain always oneself and keep the dignity of one's own humanity.

But the Lord Jesus calls us to do something more. When he says "go into your room and shut the door," he is talking about an ascetic effort of the human spirit which must not be confined within oneself. This shutting-in of oneself is, at the same time, the deepest opening of the human heart. It is indispensable for the purpose of meeting the Father, and must be undertaken for this purpose. "Your Father who sees in secret will reward you." Here it is a question of acquiring again the simplicity of thought, of will, and of heart which is indispensable if one is to meet God in one's own "self." And God is waiting for this, in order to approach man who is absorbed interiorly and at the same time open to his word and his love! God wishes to communicate himself to the soul thus disposed. He wishes to give it truth and love, which have their real source in him. (John Paul II, Homily on Ash Wednesday, 1979)

NINTH SUNDAY OF THE YEAR

Scriptural Commentary

First Reading Dt 5:12-15.

We have two versions of the ten commandments, the "ten words" (Ex 20:2-17; Dt 5:6-21). Today's reading gives the deuteronomical text of the sabbath commandment. The sabbath probably goes back to the very origins of Yahwism. It was prescribed in the Code of the Covenant (Ex 23:12) and in the Yahwistic "ritual decalogue" (Ex 34:21). In both texts a settled, agrarian way of life is presupposed, but they are both adaptations of an earlier law. The sabbath is also found in both forms of the decalogue as the central commandment and the most developed. The developments date from a period when the sabbath had become one of the leading religious observances. The reasons given for the sabbath law are different in Exodus and in Deuteronomy. In the first the sabbath is said to be an initiation of Yahweh, who rested after his work of creation (Ex 20:11). In the other it serves to remind the people of deliverance from slavery in Egypt (Dt 5:15). The fact that there are two different explanations shows that the law was very old. In its simple form, every seventh day was "sanctified" and a day of rest. It was not a feast nor was it marked by any special rite. It was simply a day when everyday activities ceased.

In Jewish religion of the post-exilic period the sabbath became one of the great signs of the covenant, and its observance was more and more emphasized. This in turn led to meticulous discussion of what constituted the sabbath rest and of what kind of work was forbidden on the sabbath. Sabbath observance became an end in itself. It was against this attitude and such casuistry that Jesus spoke and acted.

Second Reading 2 Cor 4:6-11.

In his first letter to the Corinthians (1:18-30) Paul had spoken of the folly of the cross. The same idea runs through the present reading: God works through human weakness so that the success of the apostolate and the advance of the kingdom of God will be seen as the work of God, not of man. In v.6 it would seem that Paul refers not only to the creation of earthly light but also to the heavenly light of revelation granted him on the Damascus road (cf. Acts 26:13,18). Through this experience he recognized that the glory of God was to be seen rather on the face of Christ than on the face of Moses (3:7). This message is preached by weak "servants of the word" like himself to show that it is the power of God, and not themselves, which brings it to fruition. Their lives are paradox, revealing the intimate nature of their ministry which is to prolong in time the paschal mystery, the death and resurrection of Jesus. They may be worn down by the tribulations of the ministry but the life of Jesus flows from them to others. What was true of the apostolate in Paul's day remains true of the church in every generation. The all too human character of christian ministers is no indication that the church's mission will fail.

Gospel Mk 2:23 - 3:6.

Today's reading contains the last two of the five conflict stories. The passage 2:23-28 is made up of a pronouncement story (vv.23-26) to which the sayings of vv.27-28 have been appended. In Mark's version (unlike Matthew and Luke) what is at issue is not "work" on the sabbath but a comparison of David and Jesus. The intent is christological: Jesus, as God's Anointed, has the same freedom as David in respect of the law. The wisdom saying of v.27 has a rather close rabbinical parallel, "The sabbath is delivered unto you, and ye are not delivered to the sabbath." The meaning of the saying is that God ordained the sabbath for man's sake; it is a reaction against a false evaluation of the sabbath whereby man becomes a slave to sabbath observance. Mark's christological point is made in v.28: in the light of vv.23-27 ("so then") the Son of man is lord of the sabbath. Christians had begun to observe not the Jewish sabbath but the day of the resurrection, "the Lord's day" (Rev 1:10). They maintained that their Lord had set the sabbath free and their distinctive observance was traced back to his authority.

The fifth conflict-story (3:1-6) is the climax of the series. Here Jesus himself is more aggressive and the plot against him (v.6) points to the inevitable end of this persistent hostility. But the issue is, too, of immediate interest to Mark's community. If Christians had chosen to observe the Lord's day rather than the Jewish sabbath, they had thereby opted for some form of sabbath observance. The question then remained as to how far to push that observance and in what spirit. The challenge of Jesus (v.4) and his deed of mercy will have given them their principle and their pattern.

The Pharisees accuse Jesus of a breach of sabbath observance. He views the matter in a wholly different light and he challenges their attitude. To heal a man is to "do good"; to leave him in his infirmity is to "do evil." In forbidding healing on the sabbath the rabbis would equivalently admit that, on this day, moral values are reversed: it is forbidden to "do good" and prescribed to "do evil"! The real issue is no longer what one is permitted to do; it is the obligation of doing good at all times and in all circumstances. Jesus asks, "On the sabbath day should one rather do good than evil, rather save a life than kill?" How sad it is that the spirit of legalism has so often and so firmly asserted itself in the christian church. We had been so eager to observe rules, as well as to impose them, anxious to measure our Christianity by the punctiliousness or our "observance."

Patristic Commentary

St. Ambrose (c.340-397)
Isaac or the Soul, VI-VII, FOTC 65.46,
     PL 14.522.
The Soul that goes forth at his Word is searching for the Word . . . By her search she arouses his love for her, and she knows where to search for the Word. For he delays, she knows, among the prayers of his saints and remains close to them, and she understands that he feeds his Church and the souls of his just ones among the lilies. The Lord showed this mystery to you in the Gospel, when he led his disciples through the standing grain on the Sabbath. Moses led the people of the Jews through the desert; Christ leads them through the standing grain, Christ leads them through the lilies, because through his passion the desert blooms like a lily. Let us follow, therefore, so that we may gather the fruits on the Sabbath day, the great Sabbath day, on which there

is great rest. Do not be afraid that the Pharisees may accuse you of gathering standing grain. Even if they accuse, yet Christ excuses, and he makes the souls that he wishes, that follow him, like to David, who ate the loaves of proposition outside of the law—for even then he foresaw in his mind the prophetic mysteries of a new grace (1 Kg 21:6).

Accordingly, she is praised by the bridegroom, because she sought after him so well and so constantly, and now not only is she called sister, but also well-pleasing—for she is pleasing to him who was pleasing to the Father—and beautiful as Jerusalem, an object of admiration in her array. For she possesses all the mysteries of the heavenly city and arouses admiration in all who see her. Because she is like the full and perfect justice, having borrowed her splendor from the light of the Word, while she strives always toward him, she becomes terrible too as she advances in a certain array to the heights of virtue.

And so he says to her, as if to one who is perfect, "'Avert your eyes from me,' do not gaze at me." (Song 6:4). Out of an excess of faith and devotion, she has passed beyond the capacity of her own natural state, because it is a weighty matter to look directly upon the inaccessible light. "Avert your eyes from me," because she cannot withstand the fullness of his divinity and the splendor of the true light.

Yet we can also take "Avert your eyes from me" as follows: "Although you have been perfected, I must still redeem other souls and strengthen them. For you exalt me by looking upon me, but I have descended so that I may exalt all men. Although I have risen up and possess the throne of the Father, still I will not leave you orphans, bereft of a father's help, but by my presence I will strengthen you. You find this written in the Gospel: 'I am with you even unto the consummation of the world.' Avert your eyes from me, therefore, because you exalt me." The more anyone strives toward the Lord, the more he exalts the Lord and is himself exalted.

Insights from the Documents of the Church

The Sabbath

Holy Mother Church believes that it is for her to celebrate the saving work of her divine Spouse in a sacred commemoration on certain days throughout the course of the year. Once each week, on the day which she has called the Lord's Day, she keeps the memory of the Lord's resurrection. She also celebrates it once every year, together with his blessed passion, at Easter, that most solemn of all feasts....

By a tradition handed down from the apostles, which took its origin from the very day of Christ's resurrection, the Church celebrates the paschal mystery every seventh day, which day is appropriately called the Lord's Day or Sunday. For on this day Christ's faithful are bound to come together into one place. They should listen to the word of God and take part in the Eucharist, thus calling to mind the passion, resurrection, and glory of the Lord Jesus, and giving thanks to God who "has begotten them again, through the resurrection of Christ from the dead, unto a living hope" (1 Pet 1:3). The Lord's Day is the original feast day, and it should be proposed to the faithful and taught to them so that it may become in fact a day of joy and of freedom from work. Other celebrations, unless they be truly of the greatest importance, shall not have precedence over Sunday, which is the foundation and kernel of the whole liturgical year. (Vat. II, Constitution on the Liturgy, 102, 106)

Carrying the death of Jesus in our bodies

In the human nature united to himself, the son of God, by overcoming death through his own death and resurrection, redeemed man and changed him into a new creation (cf. Gal 6:15; 2 Cor 5:17). For by communicating his Spirit, Christ mystically constitutes as his body those brothers of his who are called together from every nation.

In that body the life of Christ is communicated to those who believe and who, through the sacraments, are united in a hidden and real way to Christ in his passion and glorification. Through baptism we are formed in the likeness of Christ: "For in one Spirit we were all baptized into one body"(1 Cor 12:13). In this sacred rite fellowship in Christ's death and resurrection is symbolized and is brought about: "For we were buried with him by means of baptism into death"; and if "we have been united with him in the likeness of his death, we shall be so in the likeness of his resurrection also" (Rom 6:4-5). Really sharing in the body of the Lord in the breaking of the eucharistic bread, we are taken up into communion with him and with one another. "Because the bread is one, we, though many, are one body, all of us who partake of the one bread" (1 Cor 10:17). In this way all of us are made members of his body (cf. 1 Cor 12:27), "but severally members one of another" (Rom 12:4). (Vat. II, Constitution on the Church, 7)

TENTH SUNDAY OF THE YEAR

Scriptural Commentary

First Reading Gen 3:9-15.

Genesis 3:1-7 tells the tragic story of Temptation and Fall; then (3:8-19) comes judgment on the Fall. In v.8 we see that the former familiarity with Yahweh (ch.2) is now gone. True, he comes as before, strolling in the garden, eminently accessible—but *they* are changed. The man and woman flee the very sound of God and hide or seem to hide, from him. He has come, as before, but because of *their* conduct he must now be Judge. They must face the consequence of responsibility. Man cannot remain hidden from

God, from the God he now fears (vv.9-10). So far, man and woman had experienced shame within themselves and fear before God. Fear and shame will henceforth be the common experience of mankind.

Man's reply to the second question of Yahweh witnesses to his desperate attempt to clear himself of guilt, to place responsibility for the results of his actions anywhere than at his own door (vv.11-12). First he blames the woman. Ultimately, he seeks to pin the blame on God: she is the woman "whom thou gavest to be with me." The attempt to involve God is pathetic (but it is still the way of mankind). More tragic is the breakdown between man and woman—here the man betrays the woman. Somehow—and it is perhaps the intent of the Yahwist who had already shown himself to be unconventional by his insistence on the importance of woman (2:18-25)—the woman emerges from this sorry episode with more dignity than the man.

V.15 has become famous in christian tradition. For an exegesis of this verse see above *The Immaculate Conception of Mary,* p. 24.

Second Reading 2 Cor 4:13 - 5:1.

In the preceding passage read last Sunday, Paul spoke of the trials and tribulations of his apostolic mission. In v.13 he gives the reason why he should submit to these sufferings. He is far from daunted because he has that faith which made the psalmist exclaim: "I believe, and so I spoke" (Ps 116:10). For him faith consists in the knowledge that God who has raised Jesus from the dead will raise the apostle to be with Jesus—and raise up, too, his Corinthian brethren. All, together, will come into the presence of God. Paul's apostolic concern is to bring more and more people within the influence of God's grace so that God may be more and more glorified as people acknowledge his graciousness.

"So we do not lose heart" (v.16) looks back to 4:1. Paul admits that his "outer nature," his self as subject to suffering, is being worn down, but he asserts that his "inner man," open to God, is being renewed all the time. With his eyes on the parousia and all that it entails his present suffering is a matter of small moment—because his present brief tribulation will be followed by eternal glory. Logically, then, his eyes are fixed not on the things and values of this world but on the age to come and its reality. He looks not to the present, visible, changeable world but to that which is future, invisible, eternal where God will provide us with a permanent dwelling in place of a temporary tent (5:1).

Gospel Mk 3:20-35.

Our reading aptly illustrates a statement in the prologue of the Fourth Gospel: "He came to his own home, and his own people received him not" (Jn 1:11). Here, the family of Jesus, and the religious leaders of his people, fail to recognize him and the true source of his activity. His relatives are not his real kindred, those who do the will of God; and the scribes who accuse him of being in league with the devil are guilty of the gravest sin of all—sin against the light. In his own way, Mark wrestles with the problem that tormented John: that men could choose darkness rather than light (Jn 3:19).

Mark's distinctive "sandwich" technique points us, unerringly, to a true understanding of the passage 3:20-35—the episode of the scribes is "sandwiched" between the two sections (vv.20-21 and 31-35) on the family of Jesus. It is his pointer to us that the "slices" and the "filling" have been blended into one.

In v.21 "friends" (RSV) should read "family"—the Nazareth family, concerned for Jesus, had come to "seize" him. They wanted to save him for himself: "he is beside himself." Then emerge the Jerusalem scribes: official Jewish reaction. Verse 20 contains two accusations: he is possessed by Beelzebul, an evil spirit; his exorcisms are wrought by the power of "the prince of demons," that is, Satan. The accusations are taken up in turn in vv.28-29 and v.27. The charge that Jesus casts out demons by the power of Satan

is answered by a denial that Satan is divided against himself
(vv.24-26)—there are no signs of the alleged civil war.
The explanatory editorial comment of the evangelist in v.30
shows that the saying on blasphemy against the Holy Spirit
(vv.28-29) is to be taken as Jesus' response to the accusa-
tion of being possessed by Beelzebul. The meaning of
"blasphemy against the Holy Spirit" is shown in v.30. It is
the act of attributing the exorcisms of Jesus (and, by
implication, his whole ministry), wrought by the power of
the Spirit, to the agency of Satan. The unpardonable
gravity of the sin comes from the fact that, in attributing
the activity of Jesus to a demonic influence (3:22a), one
refuses to admit that the kingdom of God has come. One
thus puts oneself outside of it, rejecting the kingdom.
The "sin" or "blasphemy" is not so much an offence against
the Spirit as man's refusal of the salvation which God offers
to him by the Spirit active in Jesus. The whole presence
and teaching of Jesus make abundantly clear that, from
God's side, there is no such thing as an unforgivable sin.

The pronouncement story (3:31-35) preserves the saying
of Jesus that his true kindred are those who do the will of
God. For Mark it is a continuation of vv.20-21. His insertion of the Beelzebul dispute establishes a relationship
between the attitude of the brethren of Jesus and the
attitude of the religious authorities—his own did not
receive him. The mother of Jesus (v.31) does not appear
again in Mark, but she is mentioned in 6:3. Those who
are sitting around Jesus are in the process of listening to
his teaching and thus of placing themselves in his "family."
Jesus subordinates the bond of kinship to the higher bond
of brotherhood. The will of the Father is the motive power
and guide of all Jesus' activity: "My food is to do the will
of him who sent me" (Jn 4:34). Those who similarly do the
will of God enter into a real relationship with Jesus, they
belong to the family of God. But the first requirement in
doing God's will is to know it. One must learn at the school
of Jesus.

Patristic Commentary

Tertullian (c.155-c.220)
Against Marcion IV, 19, CCL 1.593, ANF 3.377.

To what purpose could they have tempted Him by naming His mother and His brethren? If it was to ascertain whether He had been born or not—when was a question ever raised on this point, which they must resolve by tempting Him in this way? Who could doubt His having been born, when they saw Him before them a veritable man?—whom they had heard call Himself "Son of man?"—of whom they doubted whether He were God or Son of God, from seeing Him, as they did, in the perfect garb of human quality?—supposing Him rather to be a prophet, a great one indeed, but still one who had been born as man? Even if it had been necessary that He should thus be tempted in the investigation of His birth, surely any other proof would have better answered the trial than that to be obtained from mentioning those relatives which it was quite possible for Him, in spite of His true nativity, not at that moment to have had. For tell me now, does a mother live on contemporaneously with her sons in every case? Have all sons brothers born to them? May a man rather not have fathers and sisters living, or even no relatives at all? But there is historical proof that at this very time a *census* had been taken in Judaea by Sentius Saturninus, which might have satisfied their inquiry respecting the family and descent of Christ. Such a method of testing the point had therefore no consistency whatever in it and they "who were standing outside" were really "His mother and His brethren." It remains to examine His meaning when He resorts to non-literal words, saying "Who is my mother or my brethren?" It seems as if His language amounted to a denial of His relatives and His birth; but it arose actually from the absolute nature of the case, and the conditional sense in which His words were to be explained. He was justly indignant, that persons so very near to Him "stood outside,"

while strangers were *within* hanging on His words, especially as they wanted to call Him away from the solemn
work He had in hand. He did not so much deny as disavow
them. And therefore, when to the previous question, "Who
is my mother, and who are my brethren?" He added the
answer "Those only who hear my words and do them," He
transferred the names of blood-relationship to others,
whom He judged to be more closely related to Him by
reason of their faith.

Insights from the Documents of the Church

Mary, example of devotion and obedience

Mary is not only an example for the whole Church
in the exercise of divine worship but is also, clearly, a
teacher of the spiritual life for individual Christians.
The faithful at a very early date began to look to Mary
and to imitate her in making their lives an act of worship
of God and making their worship a commitment of their
lives. As early as the fourth century, Saint Ambrose, speaking to the people, expressed the hope that each of them
would have the spirit of Mary in order to glorify God: "May
the heart of Mary be in each Christian to proclaim the
greatness of the Lord; may her spirit be in everyone to exult
in God." But Mary is above all the example of that worship
that consists in making one's life an offering to God. This is
an ancient and ever new doctrine that each individual
can hear again by heeding the Church's teaching, but also
by heeding the very voice of the Virgin as she, anticipating
in herself the wonderful petition of the Lord's Prayer—
"Your will be done" (Mt 6:10)—replied to God's messenger:
"I am the handmaid of the Lord. Let what you have said be
done to me" (Lk 1:38). And Mary's "yes" is for all Christians a lesson and example of obedience to the will of the
Father, which is the way and means of one's own sanctification. (Paul VI, To Honour Mary, [*Marialis Cultus*] 21)

Mary, example of faith

Mary is *the attentive Virgin*, who receives the word of God with faith, that faith which in her case was the gateway and path to divine Motherhood, for, as Saint Augustine realized, "Blessed Mary by believing conceived him (Jesus) whom believing she brought forth." In fact, when she received from the angel the answer to her doubt (cf. Lk 1:34-37), "full of faith, and conceiving Christ in her mind before conceiving him in her womb, she said, 'I am the handmaid of the Lord, let what you have said be done to me' (Lk 1:38)." It was faith that was for her the cause of blessedness and certainty in the fulfilment of the promise: "Blessed is she who believed that the promise made her by the Lord would be fulfilled" (Lk 1:45). (Paul VI, ibid., 17.)

ELEVENTH SUNDAY OF THE YEAR

Scriptural Commentary

First Reading Ezek 17:22-24.

The allegory of the eagles (Ezek 17:1-10) is aimed at Zedekiah who had violated his oath of allegiance to Nebuchadnezzar; his punishment will be defeat and deportation (vv.16,20-21). A great eagle (Nebuchadnezzar) has broken off the topmost branch (Jehoiachin) of the cedar (Judah) and carried it off to Babylon—Jehoiachin was, in 597 B.C., taken into permanent exile. The "vine" set in his place was Zedekiah, now vassal of Nebuchadnezzar. He turned to another eagle (Egypt); the result was disaster. The riddle ends with the query: "Can the Davidic dynasty survive?"

In today's reading Yahweh promises that he will plant in Zion a twig from the top (*semereth*) of the cedar (v.22). The same term designates Zedekiah in v.3: Ezekiel hopes that God will raise up a Messiah from the descendants of

Jehoiachin. It must have seemed to his contemporaries that the transplanted twig could only shrivel and die. But that would be to ignore the protective power of God, the God who puts down the mighty from their thrones and raises up the lowly, the God who destroys mighty kings and nations ("the high tree") and raises up the weak ("the low tree"). The God of Israel would transplant the people of Israel in the land of their fathers. There would be a messianic age and a new Davidic dynasty—the "noble cedar" offering shelter to birds of every sort. The nations of the earth ("all the trees of the field") would recognize the presence of the might of God in this turn of events. The immediate restoration was not as Ezekiel had dreamed. But he had glimpsed a future son of David whose kingdom would be universal.

Second Reading 2 Cor 5:6-10.

The corresponding reading of last Sunday concluded with Paul's conviction that the death of the body will yield to resurrection and transformation (5:1-2). In today's section he switches to the image of being "at home" or "away from home." First of all, he acknowledges that earthly existence is separation from the Lord; he lives his life by faith. And, of course, he would prefer to be at home with the Lord. This is strikingly like Phil 1:23—"My desire is to depart and be with Christ, for that is far better." Still, in his present exile, Paul is steadfastly "of good courage." His one and only object is to please the Lord. Again note the close parallel in Philippians. Though his ardent desire was to be with the Lord he declares: "To remain in the flesh is more necessary on your account" (Phil 1:24)—in other words, he is pleasing the Lord. That is why *he* has no fear of appearing before Christ.

Gospel Mk 4:26-34.

The nucleus of Mark's parable section (4:1-34) is a group of three parables: the sower (3-9), the seed growing to harvest (26-29) and the mustard seed (30-32); the two latter comprise today's reading.

The parable of the seed growing to harvest (26-29) is peculiar to Mark. It seems best to take it as a parable of contrast between the inactivity of the sower and the certainty of the harvest. The sower goes his way; the seed sprouts and grows without his taking anxious thought. It is God who brings about the growth of the kingdom. Paul had learned the lesson of the parable: "I planted, Apollos watered, but God gave the growth" (1 Cor 3:6). It may be that, originally, it was Jesus' reply to those who looked, impatiently, for a forceful intervention of God; or it may have been meant to give assurance to those of the disciples who were discouraged because nothing seemed to be happening. Mark, at least, takes it in the latter sense. Jesus encourages his disciples: in spite of hindrance and apathy the seed was being sown. Its growth is the work of God who will bring it to harvest.

The parable of the mustard seed (30-32) is another parable of contrast; but again the idea of growth must be given due weight. The contrast between insignificant beginning and mighty achievement is primary—but the seed does grow into a plant. The detail of branches in which the birds of the air nest (v.32) manifestly recalls Ezek 17:23 (first reading). In Mark's view, the proclamation of the kingdom will bring all nations within its scope. The parable would have been the reply of Jesus to an objection, latent or expressed: could the kingdom really come from such inauspicious beginnings? His reply is that the little cell of disciples will indeed become a kingdom. And, in the last analysis, if the kingdom does reach its full dimension, that is not due to anything in the men and women who are the seed of the kingdom; the growth is due solely to the power of God. That is why Jesus can speak with utter confidence of the final stage of the kingdom. And that is why the parable is a call for patience.

Patristic Commentary

Origen (c.185-c.254)
Commentary on Song of Songs, Book 3.12,
    GCS 33.208, ACW 26.219.

And perhaps, just as God made man to His own image and likeness, so also did He create the other creatures after the likeness of some other heavenly images. And perhaps the correspondence between all things on earth and their celestial prototypes goes so far, that even *the grain of mustard seed, . . . which is the smallest of all seeds*, has something in heaven whose image and likeness it bears; and so, because the nature of this seed is such that, *though it is the smallest of all seeds, . . . it nevertheless becomes greater than all shrubs . . . so that the birds of the air come and dwell in the branches thereof*, the likeness that *it* bears is not merely that of some heavenly image, but of the kingdom of heaven itself.

In the same way, therefore, it is possible that other seeds too that are in the earth may have a likeness and relationship to something found in heaven. And, if this is so with seeds, it is doubtless the same with plants; and if with plants, undoubtedly with animals, whether they fly or creep or are quadrupeds.

And there is something further that can be understood. The grain of mustard seed resembles the kingdom of heaven because the birds dwell in its branches, but that is not its only likeness. It is an image also of the perfection of faith, so that if a man had *faith as a grain of mustard seed*, and told a mountain to move, then it would move away. This being so, it is possible that other things also bear the appearance and likeness of things heavenly, not in one respect only, but in several.

And although in a grain of mustard seed, for example, there are several qualities that reflect the likeness of things heavenly, yet its last and final use is to serve the bodily needs of them. So with the other seeds and plants and roots of herbs, and even with the animals, it is possible to think that though they do serve the bodily needs of men, yet they also have the shapes and likenesses of incorporeal things; and thus by them the soul may be instructed and taught how to contemplate those other things that are invisible and heavenly.

Insights from the Documents of the Church

From Creation to Resurrection

The entire world created out of nothing is the world in which salvation and redemption are in fact accomplished through Jesus Christ.

Already in the Old Testament the truth of God's creative action is not presented as an abstract philosophical principle; rather, it enters the minds of the Israelites, with the help of a notion of the oneness of God, as a message declaring the power and victory of Yahweh, as the basis for showing that the Lord remains always with his people (cf. Is 40:27-28; 51:9-13). The omnipotence of God the Creator is also manifested in a splendid way in Christ's resurrection, wherein is revealed "the immeasurable scope of his power" (Eph 1:19).

For this reason the truth of creation is not to be presented simply as a truth standing by itself, torn from the rest, but as something which is in fact ordered to the salvation wrought by Jesus Christ. The creation of visible and invisible things, of the world and of angels, is the beginning of the mystery of salvation; the creation of man (cf. Pius XII, Encycl. *Humani generis, AAS*, 1950, p.575; GS, 12,14) is to be regarded as the first gift and the first call that leads to glorification in Christ (cf. Rom 8:29-30). When a Christian hears the explanation of the doctrine about creation, besides thinking about the first act whereby God "created the heavens and the earth" (Gen 1:1), he should turn his mind to all the salvific undertakings of God. These things are always present in the history of man and of the world; they also shine forth especially in the history of Israel; they lead to the supreme event of Christ's resurrection; and, finally, they will be brought to completion at the end of the world, when there will be "new heavens and a new earth" (cf. 2 Pet 3:13). (General Catechetical Directory, 51)

Growth of the Church

The Son, accordingly, came, sent by the Father who, before the foundation of the world, chose us and predestined us in him for adoptive sonship. For it is in him that it pleased the Father to restore all things (cf. Eph 1:4-5 and 10). To carry out the will of the Father Christ inaugurated the kingdom of heaven on earth and revealed to us his mystery; by his obedience he brought about our redemption. The Church—that is, the kingdom of Christ—already present in mystery, grows visibly through the power of God in the world. The origin and growth of the Church are symbolized by the blood and water which flowed from the open side of the crucified Jesus (cf. Jn 19:34), and are foretold in the words of the Lord referring to his death on the cross: "And I, if I be lifted up from the earth, will draw all men to myself" (Jn 12:32; Gk). As often as the sacrifice of the cross by which "Christ our Pasch is sacrificed" (1 Cor 5:7) is celebrated on the altar, the work of our redemption is carried out. Likewise, in the sacrament of the eucharistic bread, the unity of believers, who from one body in Christ (cf. 1 Cor 10:17), is both expressed and brought about. All men are called to this union with Christ, who is the light of the world, from whom we go forth, through whom we live, and towards whom our whole life is directed. (Vat. II, The Church, 3)

TWELFTH SUNDAY OF THE YEAR

Scriptural Commentary

First Reading Job 38:1, 8-11.

The dialogues of Job (chs. 3-31) were necessarily inconclusive (the speeches of Elihu, chs. 32-37, are a later attempt to restate the traditional theology maintained by the friends). The answer to Job's problem is given by Yahweh himself (chs. 38-39). Job had not understood the ways of God in his regard; the long litany of questions presents him with the transcendence of the mystery of God. In highly dramatic form these chapters are a restatement of Is 55:9—"As the heavens are higher than the earth, so are my ways higher than your ways." It is not for man to question the wisdom or the justice of God's behaviour. God understands the workings of the world which he himself has created. Man is in the dark.

Today's passage (chosen with the gospel reading in mind) stresses God's mastery of the watery chaos. It reflects the old Semitic myths of the origin of the world—the world was created out of a primeval watery chaos, an evil force which would withstand God. With this background in mind we can better appreciate the force of the poetic imagery where the violent power of the sea is so overwhelmed by God's might that he treats it as a new-born baby ("swaddling band") and places it securely within its play-pen (v.11). From this image of effortless authority we may gain a deepened sense of God's creative might which implies his unlimited and effective concern for the world.

Second Reading 2 Cor 5:14-17.

Our appreciation of Paul will be increased when we understand that what is central to him is not so much a doctrinal position as his experience of the boundless love of Christ. This is the driving force behind his passionate, at times polemical, interest in the christian communities for which he feels himself responsible. Today's reading brings us close to the heart of Paul. The love of God stirs him and he, in his turn, proclaims Christ, dead and risen again. Here he gives the reason for Jesus' death not in cultic terms (a sacrifice for sin) but in terms of human existence: Christ died so that we should live a Christ-centred and no longer a self-centred life. In v.17 he uses a stronger expression: accepting Christ means entering a new creation. This radical newness is a here-and-now reality for those who are "in Christ," that is to say, for those who have accepted Christ and the outgoing power of his love as the norm of their existence.

Paul mentions one result of this new life in his own case; he no longer judges anyone by worldly standards and conventions. This goes, supremely, for his understanding of Christ (v.16). Before his conversion Paul would have looked upon Jesus as a man among men, "according to the flesh." On the Damascus road he encountered the risen Saviour. Within the context of the situation in the Corinthian church of the time there is a polemical note to Paul's remark about "a human point of view." He implies that the rival preachers who operate in Corinth do in fact follow worldly standards of prestige-seeking and are not permeated by a vivid realization of the all-embracing love of Christ.

Gospel Mk 4:35-41.

Certain Old Testament ideas and passages form the background of this miracle-story. Control over the sea and the calming of storms are characteristic signs of divine power (Job 7:12; 38:8-11; Pss 74:13; 89:8-9; Is 51:9-10). Calming of a storm at sea is a major proof of God's loving care (Ps 107:23-32). It is also noteworthy that calm and untroubled sleep is a mark of perfect trust in God (cf. Prov 3:23-24; Pss 3:5; 4:8; Job 11:18-19). Mark's narrative is a miracle-story with a catechetical point. In view of the Old

Testament background, it might be expected that the story would have closed with praise of God "who had given such power to men"; instead, the limelight is on Jesus. The disciples had seen a work that only God can accomplish. They ask, in awe and perplexity, who this man is who can do a work of God (v.41).

When all is said and done, it is not the little handful of disciples in that lake drama who are chiefly in question. The cry, "Master, are we to perish for all you care?" (v.38) suggesting that the disciples are awake and in danger while their Master "sleeps" reflects the post-Easter experience of the church. Christians may feel that the Lord has no care for them, has abandoned them, and the church may seem to be at the mercy of forces pitted against it. Individuals and communities who 'feel so earn the rebuke: "Have you no faith?" It is enough that he should "awaken," that they should have faith and trust in his presence, for the storm of their fear to be stilled. Mark has painted an episode in the life of Jesus in colours of early Christianity.

Patristic Commentary

Tertullian (c.155-c.220)
On Baptism c.12, SC 35.82.

It is laid down as a rule that no one can be saved without Baptism. The principal basis for this is the Lord's statement which says, "Unless a man is born of water he shall not have life." Because of this some shallow and rash people ask how, in the light of this rule, the Apostles could be saved, seeing that with the one exception of Paul we have no record that any of them were baptized in the Lord.

Others advance the theory, obviously farfetched, that the drenching and buffeting they received from the waves while in the boat supplied for Baptism in the case of the Apostles; Peter, at any rate, they say, certainly received sufficient immersion when he walked on the waters. But, in my opinion, it is one thing to be drenched or engulfed by an angry sea, another thing to be baptized by an ordinance of religion. Besides, the boat has stood as a type of the Church which on the sea of the world is tossed about by the waves of persecution and temptation, while the patient Lord continues to sleep calmly, until, roused at last by the prayers of the saints he restores peace to His own.

Now, whether they were baptized in some way or whether, in fact they never were (in which latter case what the Lord said at Peter's feet about one baptism sufficing concerns us alone,) it is rash to speculate about the salvation of the Apostles. Because for them, the privilege of being the first to be called, and then the fact of their being on terms of closest personal familiarity with Christ, could well take the place of Baptism.

Insights from the Documents of the Church

Who can this be? Christ's hope for Modern Man

The dichotomy affecting the modern world is, in fact, a symptom of the deeper dichotomy that is in man himself. He is the meeting point of many conflicting forces. In his condition as a created being he is subject to a thousand shortcomings, but feels untrammeled in his inclinations and destined for a higher form of life. Torn by a welter of anxieties he is compelled to choose between them and repudiate some among them. Worse still, feeble and sinful as he is, he often does the very thing he hates and does not do what he wants. And so he feels himself divided, and the result is a host of discords in social life. Many, it is true, fail to see the dramatic nature of this state of affairs in all its clarity for their vision is in fact blurred by materialism, or they are prevented from even thinking about it by the wretchedness of their plight. Others delude themselves that they have found peace in a world-view now fashionable. There are still others whose hopes are set on a genuine and total emancipation of mankind through human effort alone and look forward to some future earthly paradise where all the desires of their hearts will be fulfilled. Nor is it unusual to find people who having lost faith in life extol the kind of foolhardiness which would empty life of all significance in itself and invest it with a meaning of their own devising. Nonetheless, in the face of modern developments there is a growing body of men who are asking the most fundamental of all questions or are glimpsing them with a keener insight: What is man? What is the meaning of suffering, evil, death, which have not been eliminated by all this progress? What is the purpose of these achievements, purchased at so high a price? What can man contribute to society? What can he expect from it? What happens after this earthly life is ended?

The Church believes that Christ, who died and was raised for the sake of all, can show man the way and strengthen him through the Spirit in order to be worthy of his destiny: nor is there any other name under heaven given among men by which they can be saved. The Church likewise believes that the key, the center and the purpose of the whole of man's history is to be found in its Lord and Master. She also maintains that beneath all that changes there is much that is unchanging, much that has its ultimate foundation in Christ, who is the same yesterday, and today, and forever. And that is why the Council, relying on the inspiration of Christ, the image of the invisible God, the firstborn of all creation, proposes to speak to all men in order to unfold the mystery that is man and cooperate in tackling the main problems facing the world today. (Vat. II, Constitution on the Church in the Modern World, 10)

THIRTEENTH SUNDAY OF THE YEAR

Scriptural Commentary

First Reading Wis 1:13-15, 2:23-24.

This reading has been chosen to give background to the message of the Gospel today: that Jesus' saving power can dominate death itself. The author of the Book of Wisdom lived in the middle of the first century B.C., almost certainly in the hellenistic city of Alexandria in Egypt. He had fully assimilated the insight that some had reached about a century earlier, that of the blessed immortality of the just with God beyond death. For the author of Wisdom, man is mortal by virtue of his earthly origin (7:1) and he takes physical death for granted. In our reading, then, he is not speaking of physical death but of "spiritual" death, what Revelation calls "the second death" (Rev 2:11; 21:8), definitive separation from God. He asserts that God is good and wants man's happiness. V.14 does little more than spell out the conviction of Gen 1:31—"And God saw everything that he had made, and behold, it was very good." One of the precious lessons of the Old Testament that we Christians could take wholly to heart is that God's world is *good*. The rather enigmatic v.15 ("for righteousness is immortal") means that righteousness leads to immortality. When the author takes up the "image of God" of Gen 1:26, he connects it with the blessed immortality for which man is destined, but which he can forfeit by sin (2:23). And 2:24 makes very clear that he understands "death" not as physical death but as spiritual death. Still looking to Genesis, this time Gen 3:1-7, he interprets the "serpent" there as the "devil"— Satan—of later Jewish speculation, and he states that "death" is something that the wicked ("those who belong to his party") experience.

What our reading says, in short, is this: (1) God's plan is that mankind should enjoy a blessed immortality which is God's gift; God did not create man in order to destroy him. (2) The full bitterness of death as the total wreck of human existence will be experienced by those who are "of the devil's party."

Second Reading 2 Cor 8:7,9,13-15.

Chapters 8 and 9 of 2 Corinthians are, each of them, concerned with a collection for the Jerusalem church. This matter of a collection on behalf of the "saints" of Jerusalem was of great importance in Paul's eyes (cf. Gal 2:10; 1 Cor 16:1-3; 2 Cor 8-9; Rom 15:25-27). Since, for him, the Christian is a member of the Body, and life in Christ is the life of the people of God, the unity of the church is essential. He developed his theology of unity especially in the face of differences between Judaeo-Christian and Gentile converts and under the impetus of internal strife in the Corinthian community. In view of this, and of his high regard for Jerusalem, the collection was much more than a work of charity.

Two preoccupations dominate his appeal in 2 Cor 8: (1) that the Corinthians be as generous as can reasonably be expected and (2) that they feel themselves entirely free, not under pressure of Paul's authority, for "God loves a cheerful giver" (9:7). Christian generosity is appealed to in a context of christian maturity. Paul offers two reasons why the Corinthians should respond generously. Firstly, the Corinthians obviously prided themselves on the abundance of charismatic gifts which they enjoyed (v.7; cf. 1 Cor 12-14); all the more reason that they should excel in generosity too. Charismatic gifts, if genuinely from the Holy Spirit, must give their recipients an even greater sensitivity to the practical needs of fellow-Christians. Secondly, Paul sets before the Corinthians the example of the Lord Jesus (v.9) who emptied himself in his incarnation (cf. Phil 2:5-11) in order to fill up our emptiness. This must surely serve as a stimulus to them. While the Corinthians are not expected to impoverish themselves they ought give generously whatever they can spare. Christian love should find it intolerable that one community could live in affluence while another is in material need.

Gospel Mark 5:21-43.

The dovetailing of one story with another is a feature of Mark's style; it is his "sandwich" technique. But nowhere else does an insertion so clearly separate two parts of a single story as it does here (5:21-24a, [24b-34], 35-43). Each "sandwich" is a carefully constructed unit and should be read as such. The ideas of salvation and faith are the major themes of our twin narrative. Jairus is persuaded that at Jesus' touch his daughter will be "made well" (v.23) and the woman is convinced that if she touches Jesus' garments she will be "made well" (v.28). Each time the verb is *sōzō* which means also "to save." More pointedly still, in v.34, Jesus reassures the woman, telling her, "your faith has made you well—has saved you." Mark has in mind more than bodily healing. Salvation stands in close relation to faith. Jesus, then, exhorts the father of the dead girl, "Do not fear, only believe" (v.36). Furthermore, the evangelist lets it be understood that the narrative of the daughter of Jairus has to do with resurrection. The verbs "to arise" and "to rise up" in 5:41-42 are used to describe the resurrection of Jesus (14:28; 16:6 and 8:31; 9:9-10; 10:34). A confirmation of the theological significance of the raising accomplished by Jesus is the exclusive presence of the three privileged witnesses, Peter, James and John (5:37) who are also alone with Jesus at the Transfiguration (9:2), in Gethsemane (14:33) and (with Andrew) on the Mount of Olives as hearers of the farewell discourse (13:3). Each time their presence is a pointer to the reader: here is something especially significant. Jesus raises the dead girl to life because he is "the resurrection and the life" (Jn 11:25). For Mark and his readers he is the Lord, the source of saving power (Mk 5:30). And the narrative is a lesson in salvation by faith.

Faith comes to fulfilment only in personal encounter with Jesus, only when one enters into dialogue with him. Jairus believed that Jesus had power to heal one at the point of death, when all earthly means had failed. But

Jesus looks for a deeper faith: faith in him as one who could raise from the dead, a faith that must find expression in the midst of unbelief. The woman, too, had faith in the power of Jesus. She, too, is asked to have a deeper, fuller faith in him; she meets his gaze and comes to kneel at his feet. And through faith in Jesus she and the little girl are *saved*. The lesson cannot be missed. The Christian is asked to recognize that faith in Jesus can transform life and is a victory over death. But this faith is not something vague or impersonal. One must come to him, seek him out. One must kneel at his feet, not abjectly, but in the intensity of one's pleading (v.22) or in humble thankfulness (v.33). This Jesus will give to him who believes that peace the world cannot give (v.34). He will assure him of life beyond death (v.41).

Patristic Commentary

Eusebius (d. 371)
Proof of the Gospel, Book 3, Chapter 4, GCS 23.113.

Let us now proceed to review the number and character of the marvellous works He performed while living among men: how He cleansed by His divine power those leprous in body, how He drove demons out of men by His word of command, and how again He cured ungrudgingly those who were sick and laboring under all kinds of infirmity. As, for instance, one day He said to a paralytic, "Arise, take up thy bed, and walk," and he did what he was ordered. Or again He bestowed on the blind the blessing of seeing the light; and once, too, a woman with a flow of blood, worn down for many long years by suffering, when she saw great crowds surrounding Him, which altogether prevented her approaching Him in order to kneel and beg from Him the cure of her suffering, taking it into her head that if she could only touch the hem of His garment she would recover, she stole through, and taking hold of His garment, at the same

moment took hold of the cure of her illness. She became
whole that instant, and exhibited the greatest of proof
to our Saviour's power.' And another, an official who had a
sick son, besought Jesus, and at once received him safe
and well.

Another, again, had a sick daughter, and he was a chief
ruler of a Synagogue of the Jews, and He restored her
though she was already dead. Why need I tell how a man
four days dead was raised up by the power of Jesus? Or
how He made His way upon the sea, as upon the earth
we tread, while His disciples were sailing?—and how when
they were overtaken by the storm He rebuked the sea, and
the waves, and the winds, and they all were still at once,
as fearing their Master's voice? . . . Such were the far-famed
wonders of our Saviour's power. Such were the proofs of
His divinity. And we ourselves have marvelled at them
with sober reasoning, and received them after subjecting
them to the tests and inquiries of a critical judgment. We
have inquired into and tested them not only by other plain
facts which make the whole subject clear, by which our Lord
still shows to those, whom He thinks worthy, some slight
evidences of His power, but also by the more logical method
which we are accustomed to use in arguing with those who
do not accept what we have said, and either completely
disbelieve in it, and deny that such things were done by
Him at all, or hold that if they were done, they were done
by wizardry for the leading astray of the spectators, as
deceivers often do.

Insights from the Documents of the Church

Death and Christ's Death

Justice is also brought to bear upon death, which from
the beginning of man's history had been allied to sin. Death
has justice done to it at the price of the death of the one
who was without sin and who alone was able—by means of

his own death—to inflict death upon death. In this way *the Cross of Christ*, on which the Son, consubstantial with the Father, *renders full justice to God*, is also *a radical revelation of mercy*, or rather of the love that goes against what constitutes the very root of evil in the history of man: against sin and death. (John Paul II, On the Mercy of God. [*Dives in Misericordia*])

The Christian attitude to death

The Church celebrates the paschal mystery of Christ in the funerals of its children, so that they who in baptism have become one with the dead and risen Christ will pass with him from death to life, to be purified in their spirit and taken to heaven with the saints and the elect, in their body looking forward to the blessed hope of Christ's coming and to the resurrection of the dead.

It is for this reason that the Church offers the eucharistic sacrifice of Christ's Passover for the dead and offers prayers and supplications for them so that, with the faithful united in Christ, all will reap an advantage: (the dead) spiritual help and (the mourners) consolation.

When they celebrate the funeral rites of their brothers and sisters, Christians certainly intend to affirm their hope of eternal life, but in such a way that they do not seem to be unaware of or to disregard that attitude of their own time and place towards the dead, or their customs. Free use may be made of whatever is good in family traditions, local customs or societies set up to look after funerals. However, whatever appears contrary to the gospel they should endeavour to transform so that Christian funerals may truly manifest the paschal faith and the spirit of the gospel.

Without indulging in pomp or ostentation, it is right to honour the bodies of the faithful, which were temples of the Holy Spirit. It is right, therefore, that at least at the most important moments between death and burial, faith in eternal life be re-affirmed and prayers and supplications be offered. (Introduction to the Rite of Funerals)

FOURTEENTH SUNDAY OF THE YEAR

Scriptural Commentary

First Reading Ezek 2:2-5.

The typical Israelite prophet is a man who has received a divine call to be a messenger and interpreter of the word of God. He is a man who has met with God; the word which comes to him *is* word of God. Armed with this conviction, the prophet was outspoken, a merciless critic of the people and of the establishment. Ezekiel was called to be a "watcher" for the house of Israel, a pastor of his people (Ezek 33:1-9). He had not only to deliver the divine "word" of prophecy; he was also like a sentinel on a city wall who must warn the people of approaching danger, who would give Israel a chance to "turn," to repent. The verses of our reading, from the account of his call, underline what an uphill task was his.

When, in 597 B.C., Nebuchadnezzar had, after a short siege of Jerusalem, accepted Jehoiachin's surrender, he had the king, together with leading citizens, deported to Babylon. Among those exiles was Ezekiel. In Babylon (ch.1) he received his call. The word of the Lord to him is a hard word (2:1-5) for the hearts of the people are far from God. But it is at the same time a word of love, for it means that God will not abandon his people. Whether they listen or refuse to listen, the prophet will be sent. Ezekiel had to become wholly indifferent to public opinion, "like adamant harder than flint" (3:9), as he uncompromisingly delivered God's word. What mattered was that the people should know without possibility of evasion that "there has been a prophet among them," that their God was still concerned over them. Ezekiel's life and mission hold the abiding lesson that the proclaiming of God's word is a serious and demanding task. God's spokesmen must be prepared for misunderstanding, opposition and rejection. It was so for the Old Testament prophets, it was so for Jesus himself (see today's gospel), it must be so for the prophets of our time. The call and the sending come from God and he gives his Spirit to enlighten and strengthen those who accept the task.

Second Reading 2 Cor 12:7-10.

Chapters 10-13 of 2 Corinthians is Paul's letter written "out of much affliction and anguish of heart and with many tears" (2:4)—a stirring and emotional defence of his apostolate and gospel. The Lord has called him to the apostolic ministry; this is approbation and praise enough; self-praise would sound foolish beside it (ch.10). Much of ch.11 is bitingly sarcastic. Paul had been called a "fool"; let them put up with his "folly" then! He had been driven to self-defence by the fickleness of the Corinthians who were ready to accept a different gospel. Although boasting about visions is out of place, Paul is compelled to recall an extraordinary experience he had: he had found himself caught up to the divine presence (12:1-4). A keen reminder of his human weakness kept him from being carried away by the experience (vv.5-7). We do not know the nature of the "thorn in the flesh"; most likely it was a recurring illness. He regarded his infirmity as an impediment to the effectiveness of his ministry and prayed to be rid of it. This was not to be and Paul realized that God's mysterious ways of salvation were at work in his own person. What was important to him above all was the Lord's answer to his prayer: "My grace is sufficient for you, for my power is made perfect in weakness." The human limitations and disabilities of the sincere and generous apostle are not an obstacle to apostolic work because the power of Christ within him "is able to do far more abundantly than all that we ask or think" (Eph 3:20). Indeed, insult, persecution, even calamity, may be vehicles of that power, a power all the more manifest because it works through the frailty of the apostle.

These are comforting words and challenging words for Christians and especially for those entrusted with the

ongoing proclamation of Christ's message. To acknowledge
our human weakness should not be an excuse for lapsing
into a comfortable mediocrity. The love of Christ must be
a driving force (cf. 2 Cor 5:14) for his power is at its best in
weakness. Paul's words proclaim to Christians that the
enemy of the apostle is not humbling self-knowledge but
thoughtless self-sufficiency.

Gospel Mk 6:1-6.

The episode of the rejection of Jesus at Nazareth (6:1-6a)
has deep meaning for Mark and he has placed it deliberately
at this point in his gospel. A poignant problem in the early
days of the church was the fact that while many Gentiles
were accepting the Good News, the Jewish people resisted
it (cf. Rom 9-11). Already, in Mark, the bitter opposition
of the authorities has been demonstrated (2:1 - 3:6); and
Jesus was misunderstood even by his own family (3:20-35).
Now, at the close of the Galilean ministry, his own townspeople are challenged to make up their minds about his
claim, and they take offence at him. Their rejection of him
is an anticipation of his rejection by the Jewish nation
(15:11-15). That final rejection of him is possible because the
blindness of men to God's revelation had been present
from the start (cf. Jn 1:10-11). The issue is one of faith or
unfaith in Jesus; or, in christian terms, faith in or rejection
of the Lord.

Today's reading lays bear one of the roots of this unbelief.
Jesus' fellow-townsmen react in astonishment to his
teaching. They wonder at the origin ("where") of his teaching and the nature ("what") of his wisdom. They had heard
of his mighty works. They are on the verge of asking the
right question about him. But they make the mistake of
imagining that they already have all the answers to their
own questions. That attitude is fatal to faith. Besides, they
cannot bring themselves to believe in the greatness or in
the mission of a man who is one of themselves. They "took
offence" at him: by Mark's time *skandalon* had practically
become a technical term to describe the obstacle which

some found in Christ and which prevented them from passing on to full christian faith and discipleship (cf. Rom 9:32-33; 1 Pet 2:8; 1 Cor 1:23). The proverb of v.4, in one form or another, was current in the ancient world; Jesus implicitly assumes the role of prophet. His word must have fortified the early church against the enigmatic refusal of the chosen people as a whole to accept the message of Jesus. Christian communities down the ages must beware that the proverb does not fit them. Prophets are never comfortable people to have around and we are adept at finding ways of discrediting them.

"He could do no mighty work there": Jesus always demanded faith in himself when he worked a miracle— because a miracle is a sign of the kingdom and without faith would lack significance. Want of faith in Nazareth meant that an opportunity of doing a "mighty work" was not there. The decisive thing is that a man bow in acceptance before the mystery of the person of Jesus. The people of Nazareth failed to do this because they thought their own natural knowledge of Jesus was adequate. Their unbelief was, humanly speaking, so surprising that Jesus' amazement is stressed by the evangelist. His message seems to be that if Christians of his day were understandably troubled by Israel's lack of faith, they must remember that their Master, too, had marvelled at this unbelief. Christians today may often be amazed and puzzled at the unbelief of people who have heard the message of Jesus. More important than seeking reasons is not to be discouraged by disbelief. Jesus continued his work after the Nazareth disappointment.

Patristic Commentary

St. John Chrysostom (c.347-407).
Hom. 48 on Matt., PG 58.487, NPNF 10.296-297.

He is moreover continually frequenting the synagogues, lest if He were always abiding in the wilderness, they should the more accuse Him as making a schism, and fighting against their polity.

Being amazed therefore, and in perplexity, they said, "Whence hath this man this wisdom, and these powers?" either calling the miracles powers, or even the wisdom itself. "Is not this the carpenter's son?" The greater then the marvel, and the more abundant the ground of amaze. "Is not His mother called Mary, and His brethren James, and Joses, and Simon, and Judas? and His sisters, are they not all with us? Whence hath this man these things? And they were offended in Him."

Seest thou that Nazareth was where He was discoursing? "Are not his brethren," it is said, "such a one, and such a one?"

What then saith Christ unto them? "A prophet," saith He, "is not without honor, save in his own country, and in his own house: and He did not," it is said, "many mighty works, because of their unbelief." But Luke saith, "And He did not there many miracles." And yet it was to be expected He should have done them. For if the feeling of wonder towards Him was gaining ground (for indeed even there He was marvelled at), wherefore did He not do them? Because He looked not to the display of Himself, but to their profit. Therefore when this succeeded not, He overlooked what concerned Himself, in order not to aggravate their punishment.

And yet see after how long a time He came to them, and after how great a display of miracles: but not even so did they endure it, but were inflamed again with envy.

Wherefore then did He yet do a few miracles? That they might not say, "Physician, heal thyself." That they might not say, "He is a foe and an enemy to us, and overlooks His own"; that they might not say, "If miracles had been wrought, we also should have believed." Therefore He both wrought them, and stayed: the one, that He might fulfill His own part; the other, that He might not condemn them the more.

And consider thou the power of His words, herein at least, that possessed as they were by envy, they did yet admire. And as with regard to His works, they do not find fault with what is done, but feign causes which have no existence, saying, "In Beelzebub He casteth out the devils"; even so here too, they find no fault with the teaching, but take refuge in the meanness of His race.

But mark thou, I pray thee, the Master's gentleness, how He reviles them not, but with great mildness saith, "A prophet is not without honor, save in his own country." And neither here did He stop, but added, "And in his own house." To me it appears, that with covert reference to His very own brethren, He made this addition.

Insights from the Documents of the Church

Dissent in the Church

The Church that I—through John Paul I—have had entrusted to me almost immediately after him is admittedly not free of internal difficulties and tension. At the same time, however, she is internally more strengthened against the excesses of self-criticism: she can be said to be more critical with regard to the various thoughtless criticisms, more resistent with respect to the various "novelties," more mature in her spirit of discerning, better able to bring out of her everlasting treasure "what is new and what is old," more intent on her own mystery, and because of all that more serviceable for her mission of salvation for all: God "desires all men to be saved and to come to the knowledge of the truth." (John Paul II, *Redemptor Hominis*)

He was amazed at their lack of faith

Many baptized persons have withdrawn so far from their religion that they profess a form of indifferentism or something close to atheism. "Still, many of our contemporaries recognize in no way this intimate and vital link with God, or else they explicitly reject it. Thus atheism must be accounted among the most serious problems of this age, and must be subjected to closer examination"(GS, 19).

The Second Vatican Council gave the matter careful consideration (cf. GS, 19-20) and dealt expressly with remedies to be applied: "The remedy which must be applied to atheism, however, is to be sought in a proper presentation of the Church's teaching as well as in the integral life of the Church and her members. For it is a function of the Church to make God the Father and his incarnate Son present and in a sense visible by ceaselessly renewing and purifying herself under the guidance of the Holy Spirit. This result is achieved chiefly by the witness of a living and mature Faith, namely, one trained to see difficulties clearly and to master them" (GS, 21).

There are also cases in which the Christian Faith is found contaminated with a new form of paganism, even though some religious sense and some faith in a Supreme Being persist. A religious disposition can exist far from the influence of the word of God and from the practice of the sacraments, but be nourished by the practice of super-stition and magic; moral life can fall back into pre-Christian ethics. Sometimes elements of nature worship, animism, and divination are introduced into the Christian religion, and thus in some places a lapse into syncretism can occur. Moreover, religious sects are being propagated which mingle together the Christian mysteries and elements of fables from antiquity.

In these cases, there is the greatest possible need for the ministry of the word, especially evangelization and cate-chesis, to be renewed in accord with the *Decree on the Missionary Activity of the Church*, nn. 13, 14, 21, 22. (General Catechetical Directory)

FIFTEENTH SUNDAY OF THE YEAR

Scriptural Commentary

First Reading Amos 7:12-15.

Amos was the great champion of justice. He castigated the disorders that prevailed in an era of hectic prosperity (the reign of Jeroboam II in Israel—783-743 B.C.). To his eyes the symptoms of social decay were glaring. Wealth, concentrated in the hands of a few, and these the leaders of the people, had corrupted its possessors; oppression of the poor was rife; the richly-endowed national religion, with its elaborate ritual, provided a comfortable, self-righteous atmosphere. It was this dangerous complacency that the prophet set out to shatter. His preoccupation sounds sharply in a ringing declaration like the following: "Take away from me the noise of your songs; to the melody of your harps I will not listen. But let justice roll down like waters, and righteousness like an everflowing stream" (5:23-24).

Our reading is an historical interlude between visions of the prophet (7:1 - 9:15). Amos, a native of Judah, was preaching in the northern kingdom of Israel. He does not pull his punches; his warnings reach a climax in the verse immediately preceding our passage: "The high places of Isaac shall be made desolate, and the sanctuaries of Israel shall be laid waste, and I will rise against the house of Jeroboam with the sword" (7:9). This is too much for Amaziah, chief priest of the shrine of Bethel; he peremptorily ordered Amos to get back to his own country. Amos' reply, which underlines the clash of charismatic prophethood and institutional priesthood, is a definition of the true prophet. He is not a court prophet nor one of a group of "ecstatic" prophets—he is prophet by divine call. In his case the call had come to a poor, unsophisticated shepherd and "dresser of sycamore trees," a total outsider to the ranks of the professional prophets. Choice of such as he has its own wisdom. Such a one enjoys the freedom to be honest to a degree that one identified with an institution can rarely manage. It is in its attempt to suppress the cry of honesty that the institution sins most grievously.

Second Reading Eph 1:3-14.

It is generally accepted today that this letter was not originally addressed to the church at Ephesus. Arguing from the marked differences in style and doctrine between this work and the unquestionably Pauline letters, many scholars maintain that Paul is not the author. Others, with justice, maintain that arguments against Pauline authorship are not conclusive. We shall refer to "the author," or to "Paul" (in quotation marks). Unlike the other letters, Ephesians does not appear to have been written in response to a particular need; in it "Paul" displays a detached and contemplative mood. Ephesians is more a treatise or a homily than a letter proper. (Ephesians is read until the Twenty-first Sunday inclusive).

After addressing his readers (1:1-2), the author pronounces a long prayer or blessing in which he thanks God for the blessing which he has bestowed on us in Christ. Like the Jewish *berakah* ("blessing") on which it is based, it is also an announcement of God's great works in favour of his people. It is a veritable summary of God's plan of salvation, beginning before the foundation of the world and looking forward to the fulness of time when the universe will be reconciled in Christ. Throughout the prayer the emphasis is on God's initiative and Christ's mediation.

Election (1:4). God's choice of his elect is an act of love ("in love" should be attached to v.4), a choice that obliges them to live holy and blameless lives. "Before the foundation of the world": the choice is not casual but is God's plan from the beginning.

Adoption (5-6). Through Christ the elect become children of God; and this divine filiation, like the other blessings of God, has its source in the divine goodness and its end in the exaltation of his glory by his creatures. In this plan everything comes from him and returns to him. A recurrent theme in Ephesians is that men, understanding God's plan, should praise him and give thanks.

Redemption (7-8). Redemption is achieved by the blood of the beloved Son shed on the cross. Redemption is the setting free of an individual or a group held in bondage; in the New Testament Christ is the liberator who sets men free from the bondage of sin. So, here, "redemption" is to be understood as "the forgiveness of our trespasses."

Revelation (9-10). The fourth blessing is the revelation to the apostles, and by them to all humankind, of the "mystery" of the universal supremacy of Christ. In Ephesians the divine plan of salvation is presented as the "mystery," that is, a secret long hidden in God but now revealed: the mystery is God's plan to create a community of men and women in Christ. Further, that plan is the re-capitulation of all things in Christ—in other words the unification of all things and their submission to Christ as to their head.

In Christ, Israel, a chosen people, had been set apart in order to keep alive in a fallen world the expectation of the Messiah and the hope of salvation through him (11-12). The sixth stage is the call of the Gentiles to share the salvation formerly reserved for Israel, a salvation assured by the gift of the Holy Spirit long ago promised by the prophets (13-14). The motifs of this blessing will recur throughout the rest of the letter.

Gospel Mk 6:7-13.

Jesus had been rejected by his own people (gospel of last Sunday). Now he turns his attention to the twelve. He had chosen them "to be with him" (3:14) and so he had concentrated on instructing them. But he had chosen them, too, "to be sent out to preach"; the time has come for them to take an active part in the ministry. Mark evidently meant the incident, though preparatory and provisional, to be seen as the basis of christian missionary activity. He carefully avoids the statement, present in Matthew and Luke, that the disciples proclaimed the kingdom of God because, in Mark's perspective, the disciples have not yet understood the true nature of the kingdom. Like the Baptist (1:4) they preached "that men should repent."

The sending out the disciples "two by two" follows Jewish practice. They are to take nothing with them for the journey. If they are not received in a village they will give a solemn warning. "Shake off the dust that is on your feet": this is a symbolic action indicating that the place is as good as heathen. Jews shook off heathen dust on re-entering Palestine. "For a testimony against them," that is, as a warning to them: the gesture is intended to make them think again and lead them to repentance.

In a summarizing passage (12-13) Mark's reference to a preaching of repentance is deliberate: in his plan the preaching of the imminence of the kingdom is reserved to Jesus; the disciples, like the Baptist, prepare for Jesus' proclamation. Besides, Mark may wish to distinguish their "preaching" from the full christian gospel which can be proclaimed only after the Easter event. They also shared in the exorcising and healing work of Jesus. Oil was used in medical treatment (cf. Lk 10:34), hence its symbolical value in miraculous healing. James (5:14-15) shows that healing by anointing was known in the early church. The practice attested here may well be at the origin of the later practice, and eventually of the sacrament of the anointing of the sick.

Patristic Commentary

St. Peter Chrysologus (c.406-450).
S.170, PL 52.646, FOTC 17.281.

"And he gave them authority over the unclean spirits," the text says. This is a badge of divine power. This is the trophy of an outstanding triumph. The pirate himself is now handed over to his prey, the captive himself to his own captives, and the Devil, bound himself, is surrendered to those he once held bound, in order that he should be subjected to the sway of those over whom he once acted as slave master and tyrant. Rightly does he grieve, rightly does he groan, rightly does he howl. He who had long been persuading men by lies that he was a god now perceives himself struck down by the sentence of men and the power of men.

"And he charged them to take nothing for their journey, but a staff only—no wallet, no bread, no money in their belts." When a man invites laborers to work, he supplies not merely the necessities of food, but even banquets with extensive preparations. He desires the banquet provided by the human kindness he lavishes to win a victory over the burden and toil of the work. If God invites a man to work, and the man comes burdened and anxious with a wallet, bread, and wages, how inhuman he believes God to be! That unbelieving man approaches the work either as a tired or sluggish worker, or perhaps he cannot even approach! God promises abundant rewards, by His numerous signed bonds and His witnesses. He promises a generous reward. Do you think that, in a niggardly spirit, He will supply neither bread nor clothing? He granted you existence when you were not. Whatever you have, O man, He gave to you. When you were living for yourself and your own pleasures, He did not refuse the necessities of food. Do you think that He will not give bread or clothing to one applying himself to His virtues and tasks? Who gave you the very contents of your wallet and belt? Why do you hasten to insult Him over His own gifts? He knows that you are rich.

O man, give up your resources! Divine poverty is enough for you. Put off the packs of your riches; a burdened man cannot make his way along the narrow road all the way to the work of the Lord's harvest. Come unencumbered.

come free to the tasks, before you get stripped and robbed, and arrested for punishment as a worker unfaithful to all. For, as it is written: "Riches do not go along with a dying man." (Ps 49:17)

Let your conscience be your wallet, let your life be your bread, in order that the true bread in your life can be Christ, who said: "I am the bread." Regard your heavenly reward as your salary. For, if in order to follow Christ a man has dispossessed himself of everything and faithfully scorned and despised what he had, he can ask a reward from Christ without any anxiety.

Insights from the Documents of the Church

All things brought together in Christ

Christ Jesus, the incarnate Word of God, since he is the supreme reason why God intervenes in the world and manifests himself to men, is the centre of the Gospel message within salvation history.

He is "the image of the invisible God, the first-born of all creation. In him everything . . . was created" (Col 1:15). For he stands out as the one mighty Mediator through whom God draws near to man and man is led to God (cf. 1 Tim 2:5). In him the Church has its foundation. In him all things are brought together (cf. Eph 1:10). For this reason, created things and the conscience of men and the genuine values which are found in other religions and the diverse signs of the times are all to be thought of, though not univocally, as paths and steps by which it is possible to draw near to God, under the influence of grace and with an ordering to the Church of Christ (cf. LG, 16). (General Catechetical Directory, 40)

Take nothing for the journey: evangelical poverty practised by some religious today

How then will the cry of the poor find an echo in your lives? That cry must, first of all, bar you from whatever would be a compromise with any form of social injustice. It obliges you also to awaken consciences to the drama of misery and to the demands of social justice made by the Gospel and the Church. It leads some of you to join the poor in their situation and to share their bitter cares. Furthermore, it calls many of your institutes to rededicate for the good of the poor some of their works—something which many have already done with generosity. Finally, it enjoins on you a use of goods limited to what is required for the fulfilment of the functions to which you are called. It is necessary that in your daily lives you should give proof, even externally, of authentic poverty. (Paul VI, Apostolic Exhortation on the Renewal of Religious Life [*Evangelica Testificatio*], 18)

SIXTEENTH SUNDAY OF THE YEAR

Scriptural Commentary

First Reading Jer 23:1-6.

The book of Jeremiah is complex. The great bulk of the material is authentic but some passages are later than the prophet's time. This seems to be the case with the first of the two brief oracles (23:1-4, 5-6) that make up this first reading. In its present form, at least, it seems to presuppose the Babylonian Exile (v.3). At the same time, the oracle squares with Jeremiah's view that the radical reason for his people's disastrous course is the culpable irresponsibility of its leaders. Having the role of guides or "shepherds," they have failed to keep the people together; they will be punished for their infidelity. But God will not let his people languish in exile. A faithful shepherd himself, he will gather his flock together again and entrust it to good and faithful shepherds. Cf. Ezek 34.

The second oracle (vv.5-6) announcing the future (ideal) king of David's line is authentic. Its date in the reign of Zedekiah is assured by the play on the name of that king. The term "Branch," derived from Is 11:1, designates the ideal (Messianic) king (cf. Zech 3:8; 6:12). The new reign will be marked, in an eminent degree, by wisdom, justice, and righteousness, and in the days of the new king the reunited land will again know peace. The name of the promised king, *Yahweh-sidqenu* ("Yahweh is our righteousness") is almost the same as Zedekiah (*Sidqiyahu*— "Yahweh is my vindication"). Jeremiah is only too well aware that Zedekiah is a living contradiction of the promise of his name. But he is sure that the Lord will raise up one who will worthily bear that reassuring name.

Second Reading Eph 2:13-18.

Addressing himself mainly to the Gentile members of the community (2:11-12), the author reminds them that they were previously separated from Israel and, therefore, from all the hopes and ambitions associated with God's people (vv.11-12). Christ's death on the cross, however, has served as a peace offering between the two factions of mankind (v.13). Moreover, this death represents an end to the Jewish law and cult which constituted a division within mankind. In Christ all mankind—Jews and Gentiles alike—is united through one body and in one body. God's plan for mankind, realised in Christ, is a unity so profound that it can be described in terms of "one new man" (13-17). This unity is assured by our access to the one Father (v.18).

The reconciling of Jew and Gentile was not something that had in fact taken place during the author's lifetime—it cannot be said to have ever happened to any significant extent. What is here stated is a matter of principle—and of hope. The heritage of the Old Testament belongs to the church, but the church goes beyond the narrow bounds of that heritage to gather *all* humankind and so "reconcile them to God" (v.16). The point is that it is the church which is the focus of unity. Throughout the reading the author typifies this ecclesial unity in one word—peace (v.14,15,17). And peace is no mere absence of conflict; it is the dynamic reconciliation of men in one community. Reconciliation is a costly business; sacrifices have to be made. We are united "by the blood of Christ" (v.13), "through the cross" (v.15). All who truly work for reconciliation will know the cost—but will not count the cost.

Gospel Mark 6:30-34.

In this short passage Mark first rounds off (vv.30-31) his account of the mission of the twelve (last Sunday's reading). Emphasis has shifted to the instruction of the disciples and Jesus' desire to be alone with them. This desire prepares for the retiral to a "desert place" where the miracle of the loaves will take place. Here only in Mark are the twelve called "apostles." It might seem that the missionary journey had achieved their advancement from discipleship to apostolate. But they will be fully apostles only when they are sent out by the risen Lord. After their missionary labours the twelve needed to rest. More significant is the fact that Jesus wants them to be "by themselves." This Greek expression (*kat' idian*) occurs seven times in Mark (4:34; 6:31,32; 7:33; 9:2,28; 13:3) always in a redactional passage and is each time used in reference to a revelation or an instruction reserved for the disciples. Each time the *reader* is being nudged to special attention.

The details of vv.32-34 are quite vague and the destination is unknown. For the evangelist the important factor is that the disciples reach a "desert" place (a fitting Exodus setting for the bread miracle) and that they are "by themselves." Jesus' attempt to seek solitude for himself is frustrated, but he is not annoyed. Instead, he is deeply moved by the earnestness of the crowd and by their need. The image of a shepherdless people is found in Num 27:17; 1 Kgs 22:17. Jesus sees himself in their regard as the messianic shepherd (Ezek 34; Jn 10:1-18) who will feed his sheep (Ezek 34:13-14;

Jn 10:9; cf. Jer 23:1-4). The motif of the sheep without a shepherd foreshadows the moment when the shepherd will be stricken and his sheep scattered (Mk 14:27). The people's most pressing hunger was spiritual and Jesus began to teach them. It is interesting that in John's first discourse on the bread of life (Jn 6:35-50) the "bread" is Jesus' teaching, his revelation.

Patristic Commentary

St. Basil the Great (c.330-379).
Ep. 2, PG 32.224, FOTC 13.6.

The mind of man is incapable of perceiving the truth clearly, if it is distracted by innumerable worldly cares. Wild desires, unruly impulses, and passionate yearnings greatly disturb him who is not yet united in the bonds of wedlock; and a tumultuous throng of different cares awaits him who already has taken a wife: the longing for children, if he is childless; the solicitude for their training, if he has children; the watchfulness over his wife, the care of his home, the protection of his servants, the losses on contracts, the contentions with his neighbors, the lawsuits, the business risks, the farm work. Each day, as it comes, brings its own shadow for the soul, and the nights, taking over the troubles of the day, beguile the mind with the same phantasies.

There is but one escape from these distractions, a complete separation from the world. Withdrawing from the world, however, does not mean mere bodily absence, but implies a disengagement of spirit from sympathy with the body, a renunciation of city, home, personal possessions, love of friends, property, means of livelihood, business, social relations, and learning acquired by human teachings; also, a readiness to receive in one's heart the impressions produced there by divine instruction. And this disposition follows the unlearning of worldly teachings which previously held possession of the heart. Just as it is not possible to write in wax without first smoothing down the letters already engraved upon it, so it is impossible to impart the divine teachings to the soul without first removing from it the conceptions arising from worldly experiences.

Now, solitude provides us with the greatest help toward this achievement, quieting our passions, and giving leisure to our reason to uproot them completely from the soul. Just as animals, if they are stroked, are more easily subdued, so desires, wraths, fears, and griefs, the venomous evils of the soul, if they have been lulled to sleep by silence and have not been kept aflame by constant provocation, are more easily overcome by reason. Therefore, choose a place removed from association with men, so that nothing from the outside will interrupt the constant practices of the ascetic life. When the mind is not engaged by external affairs, nor diffused through the senses over the whole world, it retires within itself. Then, it ascends spontaneously to the consideration of God. Illumined by that splendor, it becomes forgetful of its own nature.

Insights from the Documents of the Church

Shepherds of the Flock

To put the whole matter in a few words, the minister of the word should be honestly aware of the mission assigned to him. It is to stir up a lively Faith which turns the mind to God, impels conformance with his action, leads to a living knowledge of the expressions of tradition, and speaks and manifests the true significance of the world and human existence.

The ministry of the word is the communication of the message of salvation: it brings the Gospel to men. The mystery which has been announced and handed down deeply influences that will to have life, that innermost desire for attaining fulfilment, and that expectation of future happiness which God has implanted in the heart of every man and which by his grace he raises to the supernatural order.

The truths to be believed include God's love. He created all things for the sake of Christ and restored us to life in Christ Jesus. The various aspects of the mystery are to be explained in such a way that the central fact, Jesus, as he is God's greatest gift to men, holds first place, and that from him the other truths of Catholic teaching derive their order and hierarchy from the educational point of view.

Shepherds of souls should always keep in mind the obligation they have of safeguarding and promoting the enlightenment of Christian existence through the word of God for people of all ages and in all historical circumstances (cf. CD, 14), so that it may be possible to have contact with every individual and community in the spiritual state in which each one is.

They should also remember that catechesis for adults, since it deals with persons who are capable of an adherence that is fully responsible, must be considered the chief form of catechesis. All the other forms, which are indeed always necessary, are in some way oriented to it. In obedience to the norms of the Second Vatican Council, shepherds of souls should also strive "to establish or better adapt the instruction of adult catechumens" (CD, 14; cf. AG, 14). (General Catechetical Directory, 16, 20)

SEVENTEENTH SUNDAY OF THE YEAR

Scriptural Commentary

First Reading 2 Kgs 4:42-44.

The Elisha cycle of stories (2 Kgs 2-13) is an anthology, popular in style, and with complacent stress on the miraculous. Today's anecdote is typical and, obviously, prepares for the gospel story of the multiplication of loaves. The setting of the miracle is the famine mentioned in 4:38. The core of the prophetic message (for it is as such that the miracle must be seen) is that the feeding of a hundred men with a few loaves is a token of the concern of God for his people—a point underlined by the fact that the bread which Elisha distributes is the bread of the first-fruits. He does not offer it to God but gives it to the people as a sign that God is truly with his people in the person of his prophet. The doubts of the servant are overcome by the assurance that it is the Lord who wishes to provide. The left-overs stress the Lord's generosity.

Ever since the manna in the desert the people of Israel believed that God would provide bread for the hungry, bread from heaven. In the course of time this bread came to be understood in a metaphorical sense and the bread of heaven was taken to be the word of God. Such is the history of the expression as it journeyed through the Wisdom literature and into John's gospel.

Second Reading Eph 4:1-6.

Having opened his heart to his readers in his prayer to God (1:3 - 3:21) "Paul" now begs them to lead a life which corresponds to the gospel which they have heard. "Thus we can detect a very fine balance in his thought between the objective fact of men's salvation and their subjective appropriation of this reality. It is as if the readers are being exhorted to become what they are already by God's grace. Particular stress is laid upon unity and harmony within the community which should correspond to the unity of God himself" (L. Swain). Again it is by a dynamic peace that this unity is achieved (see last Sunday's second reading, Eph 3:13-18), a peace which is typified not by any grand gestures but by the "ordinary" charities of "lowliness and meekness, with patience" (v.2). The context is that of simple daily life. But we touch the hem of a great mystery—for it is not just a matter of people living together harmoniously, but of preserving "the unity of the Spirit" (v.3). The Holy

Spirit is the principle of unity for the church as he is the principle of unity between man and God (2:18,22). The author underscores his teaching by heaping up expression after expression of this fundamental christian oneness: ". . . one body, one Spirit . . . one Lord, one faith, one baptism . . ." (vv.4-5). All comes from "one God and Father of us all, who is above all and through all and in all" (v.6). He has woven a trinitarian pattern (one Spirit . . . one Lord . . . one God and Father) through these insistent expressions of christian unity.

Gospel John 6:1-15.

Last Sunday's gospel reading brought us to Mark's introduction to his narrative of the feeding of the five thousand. The Lectionary switches to John's gospel, and his chapter six is read over Sundays Eighteen through Twenty-One. All four gospels carry the story of the multiplication of loaves: Mark (6:32-44; 8:1-10; cf. Lk 9:10-17) and Matthew (14:13-21; 15:29-38) have two accounts of a miraculous feeding. There are several arguments for regarding these two accounts in Matthew and Mark as variant forms of the same incident. And it seems best to take it that the fourth evangelist (Jn 6:1-15) drew on an independent tradition quite like that of Mark's and Matthew's second account.

Like Elisha—the prophet of the old covenant—Jesus, the prophet of the new, feeds the hungry crowds, only more astonishingly. The introductory sentences (6:1-3) bring together motifs which belong to the common substance of the Gospel tradition: a journey across the Sea of Galilee, the pressure of the crowd, the reputation of Jesus as a healer, his withdrawal to "the mountain" with his disciples. In v.4 we meet a distinctively Johannine trait: the reference to the festival of Passover. The christian reader could hardly miss this hint of the eucharistic significance of the following narrative. "How are we to buy bread . . ." (v.5)—a reaction like that of Moses (Num 11:13; 21-22; cf. 2 Kgs 4:43).

While in the synoptics the disciples distribute the bread, John has Jesus himself do it, which reminds us of the circumstances of the Last Supper. Only in John is the gathering of the fragments given as a command of Jesus, and in the Didache the same word *synagein*, is used for the gathering of the Eucharist. John is again introducing the theme of the Eucharist which will be dealt with explicitly in 6:51-58.

The crowds, however, do not understand the proper meaning of Jesus' sign (vv.14-15). They take Jesus to be the one—prophet and king—who will fulfil their material hopes and ambitions. This is a view of his miracles which Jesus violently rejects as he retires from the scene. He is God's spokesman and the true Messiah but not as understood by his contemporaries. Christians must beware that our understanding of Christ is not tainted by triumphalism.

Patristic Commentary

Novatian (c.200-c.258)
On Jewish Foods, c.5, CCL 4.98,
    FOTC 67.152.

God is not worshipped by the belly nor by foods, which the Lord says will perish and are discharged into the privy in accordance with the natural law of life. (cf. Mt 15:17). The man who worships God with foods is almost like one who has God as his belly. (cf. Phil 3:19).

True and holy and pure food, I maintain, is an upright faith, immaculate conscience, and innocent spirit. Whoever partakes of food in this manner eats with Christ. One who dines thus is a guest of God. This is the food of angels, the banquet which makes martyrs. Accordingly, we have the pronouncement of the Law: "Not by bread alone does man live, but by every word that comes forth from the mouth of the Lord."(Deut 8:3). Christ says: "My food is to do the will of the one who sent Me, and to complete His work." (Jn 4:34). And again he says: "You seek Me, not because you have seen signs, but because you have eaten of my loaves and have been filled. Do not labor for the food that perishes but for that which endures unto life everlasting, that which the Son of Man will give you. For upon Him the Father, God Himself, has set His seal."(Jn 6:26-27)

I maintain that God is worshipped by righteousness, and moderation, and the other virtues. Zechariah also states: "And when you eat or drink, do you not yourselves eat or drink?" (Zech 7:6) He wants to say that food and drink are things proper to man, not to God, because God is not made of flesh. God is not pleased by flesh meat nor is He intent upon enjoying the pleasure of our foods. God only delights in our faith, our innocence, our truthfulness, those virtues of ours which dwell in the soul, not the stomach. Fear of God and heavenly awe, not earthly perishable food, obtain these virtues for us.

Insights from the Documents of the Church

Dispositions required for receiving the Eucharist, food for our souls

The blessed Sacrament, by virtue of which the paschal mystery of Christ is ever present among men, is the source of all grace and of pardon for sins. But those who wish to receive the Body of the Lord in order to share in the fruits of the paschal sacrament must approach it with a pure conscience and the proper dispositions. In particular the Church prescribes that "no one who is conscious of being guilty of mortal sin, however repentant he may feel, may receive Holy Communion until he has received sacramental absolution."

If there are urgent reasons for receiving Holy Communion and no confessor is available, a communicant should make a perfect act of contrition with the intention of confessing every mortal sin of which he is guilty, when the opportunity offers.

Those who receive Holy Communion daily or very frequently should receive the sacrament of Penance at suitable times, according to their individual circumstances.

But the faithful should consider the blessed Sacrament as a remedy by which they are absolved from their daily venial faults and are preserved from mortal sin. They should appreciate the value of the penitential elements in the Liturgy and especially in the Mass.

The faithful may not receive Holy Communion unless they have abstained for at least one hour from all food and drink except water.

The time prescribed for abstinence from food or alcohol is reduced to a quarter of an hour for:

(a) The sick in hospital or at home, even though they are not confined to bed;

(b) The faithful advanced in age who are either confined to the house on account of their age or are living in homes for the elderly;

(c) Priests who are ill, even though they are not confined to bed or advanced in age, who wish to celebrate Mass or to receive Holy Communion;

(d) Those engaged in the care of the sick or aged and their relatives, who wish to receive Holy Communion with their patients whenever it would be difficult for them to observe the fast of one hour.

Union with Christ, which is the object of the sacrament, should extend to the whole Christian life. The faithful, therefore, being ever mindful of the gift they have received, should live their daily lives in a spirit of gratitude under the guidance of the Holy Spirit and thus derive more abundant fruits of charity.

In order the better to maintain this spirit of gratitude, which is so admirably expressed to God in the Mass, it is recommended that all those who receive Holy Communion should spend some time in prayer afterwards. (On Holy Communion and the Worship of the Eucharistic Mystery Outside of Man, 23-25)

EIGHTEENTH SUNDAY OF THE YEAR

Scriptural Commentary

First Reading Ex 16:2-4, 12-15.

This reading is about the murmuring of the people of Israel in the desert and God's promise of manna and quails. In Numbers 11:4-34 we are told that the people had grown tired of the monotonous manna and longed for meat, whereupon God sent the quails; in Exodus 16 quails and manna are provided together. Focus, however, is on the manna, with the quails getting only a brief mention.

The story of quails and manna is probably based on phenomena which may still be observed in the Sinai peninsula. Quail, in the course of their long migrations between Africa and Europe are frequently forced down to rest there and are then easily caught. The manna is probably a sweet resinous substance exuded by the desert tree called *tamarix mannifera*—though it appears only in small quantities. Memory of this food, found and eaten occasionally in the desert, was built up in Hebrew tradition into the classic instance of God's care for his people (cf. Ps 78:24-25—"the grain of heaven . . . the bread of angels"; Ps 105:40—"bread from heaven"; Wis 16:20—"the food of angels . . . providing every pleasure").

God had heard his people's cry in Egypt. He hears them still, even though they, ungraciously, hankered after the fleshpots of Egypt. In the wilderness, a place universally associated with the absence of life and life-giving resources, he provides bread and meat for his people. This feeding with quail and manna is much more than a mere satisfying of hunger. It is one aspect of the covenant relationship set up between Yahweh and his people and is a sign and promise of his abiding concern.

Second Reading Eph 4:17, 20-24.

The author of Ephesians has already reminded his largely Gentile readers that, in Christ, they have become co-heirs with the Jews in God's promises. Now he exhorts them to live accordingly. In the first place they must break with their pagan past (v.17). Throughout the section 4:17 - 5:20 the radical conversion of those who have been re-created in Christ is described and quite specific demands are made. The demands will, of course, be lived out only if Christians had grasped the transforming truth—the truth that is *Christ* and not some teaching about him (20-21). If Christ, by his death, has created in himself (of Jew and Gentile) one new man (2:15), the Christian, in accepting the work of Christ, must "put on" this new man by a fresh moral behaviour. The "new man" is none other than Christ. The particular value of the metaphor of clothing ("put on") "is that it expresses *our* participation in the work of our salvation: we really do change our whole way of life. This is a real renewal in our minds. This conversion is symbolized by the changing of clothes connected with baptism. Paul is probably referring to this practice while intimating that what is being changed is not so much a garment as a whole way of life. It is when we 'put on' Christ in this way that we achieve our true destiny as the image of God (Gen 1:26)" (L. Swain, *Ephesians*, 89-90).

Gospel Jn 6:24-35.

In Jn 6 we have two discourses on the Bread of Life: 35-50 in which "bread of life" is primarily the revelation of Jesus and 51-59 in which "bread of life" is now the Eucharist. Our reading (25-34) is a preface to the present two-fold discourse.

Jesus begins (v.26) by pointing out the difference between a "miracle" and a "sign": the multitude may have eaten the miraculous bread but unless they realized its underlying signification it had no lasting effect for them. In v.27 he begins to press the lesson home in terms of familiar Johannine dualism: perishable food and the food that lasts for eternal life—that abiding food should be the object of their striving. Striving, literally "working," for the abiding food leads to a play on "work." The crowd wants to know what works they should do; Jesus puts the emphasis on faith (v.29)—having faith is a "work"; it is the all-important work of God. The crowd still thinks in terms of works and begins to question Jesus' claims on that basis. They had seen in him the prophet-like-Moses (6:14); now they challenge him to produce manna: a sign of the End-time (vv.30-31). Jesus' reply is that he himself is the true bread of heaven prefigured in the manna. It was not Moses who *gave*; it is the Father who *gives* the genuine (*alēthinos*) heavenly bread. And that bread is Jesus himself. Therein lies his power to feed the multitude (6:5-13): he gives bread because he is the bread of life. The crowd asks for this bread (v.34) but in typically Johannine fashion—like the Samaritan woman, 4:15—without understanding what it is they really ask for. In that they are not unlike a goodly number of Christians.

Patristic Commentary

St. Caesarius of Arles (c.470-542)
S.102, CCL 103.422, FOTC 47.105.

Notice, brethren, that on the Jewish sabbath God never rained any manna at all, nor did the Jews deserve that grace should come down to them from heaven on their sabbath. However, on our Sunday, not only does manna always come to us, but the very beginning of its coming originated on that day. Therefore, God always rains manna from heaven for us: there are those heavenly discourses which are spoken to us, and from God descend those words which are read to us. Thus, when we receive such manna, it is always given to us from heaven. For this reason the unhappy Jews are to be deplored and bewailed, because they do not merit to receive manna as their fathers did. They never eat manna, because they are unable to eat what is small like a seed of coriander or white as snow. The unfortunate Jews find in the word of God nothing small, nothing fine, nothing spiritual, but everything rich and solid; "For heavy is the heart of this people." (Isa 6:10). Now an examination of the word tells us the same thing. Manna is interpreted as "What is this?" See whether the very power of the name does not provoke you to learn it, so that when you hear the law of God read in church you may always ask and say to the teachers: What is this? This it is that the manna indicates. Therefore, if you want to eat the manna, that is, if you desire to receive the word of God, konw that it is small and very fine like the seed of the coriander.

Therefore, let us now hasten to receive the heavenly manna. Indeed, according as each one receives it, such a taste it creates in his mouth. Moreover, listen to the Lord say to those who approach Him: "Be it done to thee according to thy faith." (Mt 8:13). If, then, you receive God's word which is preached in church with all faith and devotion, that same word will do for you whatever you desire. For example, if you are troubled, it will console you by saying: "A heart contrite and humbled God does not despise." (Ps 50:19). If you rejoice in hopes for the future, it will increase your joys with the words: "Be glad in the Lord and rejoice, you just." (Ps 31:11). If you are angry, it will soothe you by saying: "Give up your anger, and forsake wrath." (Ps 36:8). If you are in pain, it cures you with the words: "The Lord heals all your ills." (Ps 102:3). If you are consumed with poverty, it consoles you by saying: "The Lord raises up the lowly from the dust; from the dunghill he lifts up the poor." (Ps 112:7). Thus, then, the manna of God's word brings to your mouth whatever taste you desire.

Insights from the Documents of the Church

The call to Holiness

The Lord Jesus, divine teacher and model of all perfection, preached holiness of life (of which he is the author and maker) to each and every one of his disciples without distinction: "You, therefore, must be perfect, as your heavenly Father is perfect" (Mt 5:48). For he sent the Holy Spirit to all to move them interiorly to love God with their whole heart, with their whole soul, with their whole understanding, and with their whole strength (cf. Mk 12:30), and to love one another as Christ loved them (cf. Jn 13:34; 15:12). The followers of Christ, called by God not in virtue of their works but by his design and grace, and justified in the Lord Jesus, have been made sons of God in the baptism of faith and partakers of the divine nature, and so are truly sanctified. They must therefore hold on to and perfect in their lives that sanctification which they have received from God. They are told by the apostle to live "as is fitting among saints" (Eph 5:3), and to put on "as God's chosen ones, holy and beloved, compassion, kindness, lowliness, meekness, and patience" (Col 3:12), to have the fruits of the Spirit for their sanctification (cf. Gal 5:22; Rom 6:22). But since we all offend in many ways (cf. Jas 3:2), we constantly need God's mercy and must pray every day: "And forgive us our debts" (Mt 6:12).

It is therefore quite clear that all Christians in any state or walk of life are called to the fullness of Christian life and to the perfection of love, and by this holiness a more human manner of life is fostered also in earthly society. In order to reach this perfection the faithful should use the strength dealt out to them by Christ's gift, so that, following in his footsteps and conformed to his image, doing the will of God in everything, they may wholeheartedly devote themselves to the glory of God and to the service of their neighbor. Thus the holiness of the People of God will grow in fruitful abundance, as is clearly shown in the history of the Church through the life of so many saints.

The forms and tasks of life are many but holiness is one—that sanctity which is cultivated by all who act under God's Spirit and, obeying the Father's voice and adoring

God the Father in spirit and in truth, follow Christ, poor, humble and cross-bearing, that they may deserve to be partakers of his glory. Each one, however, according to his own gifts and duties must steadfastly advance along the way of a living faith, which arouses hope and works through love. (Vat. II, Constitution on the Church, 39-41)

NINETEENTH SUNDAY OF THE YEAR

Scriptural Commentary

First Reading 1 Kings 19:4-8.

In his zeal for Yahweh, Elijah had confronted and defeated the prophets of Baal at Mount Carmel (1 Kgs 18:20-40) and even had the whole band of them put to death (v.40). This won for him the implacable hostility of Ahab's queen, Jezebel, a formidable woman fanatically attached to her native Phoenician Baal religion. She vowed to have the prophet's life (19:2). We find Elijah resting in the desert as he flees for his life (vv.4-7). We find him, the erstwhile bold champion of Yahweh, a broken, dispirited man (v.4); but his journey of despair will end in a meeting with his God (vv.9-13). In the meantime, he is sustained by his God. Like the Israelites of the Exodus he fled into the desert and like them his flagging hope was restored by "bread from heaven." In the strength of this food he can continue his journey to the holy mountain for his meeting with God (v.8).

Second Reading Eph 4:30 - 5:2.

Christian life is not all plain sailing; that is made abundantly clear in the candid passage Eph 4:25-32. Unsocial behaviour is a lack ot respect and reverence for the Spirit who dwells in the Christian (v.30)—the Spirit who is the pledge of future glory. There is no place for bitterness in christian life; Christians should be remarkable for generous forgiveness. That is not only because of a word of Jesus (Mt 18:21-22); it is, more fundamentally, because of God's forgiveness: "God shows his love for us in that while we were yet sinners Christ died for us" (Rom 5:8). As children of God, Christians must be imitators of their Father. Because the whole of God's saving word can be summed up in the action of divine filiation (1:5) the whole of christian morality can be summed up in the imitation of God. God's way has been brought near to us in the loving example of Christ. We are to walk in love and that means, as Christ has shown, self-giving service to the point of death (5:2). Christ's self-giving love was the sacrifice wholly pleasing to God; our first worship of God is in the service of our fellows. "This is not just a form of worship among several others. It is the *only* form suitable for a God who *is* Father, that is who is himself totally 'for' the others who are his children" (Lionel Swain).

Gospel Jn 6:41-51.

The Constitution on the Liturgy has stipulated that there should be a homily "at those Masses which are celebrated with the assistance of the people on Sundays and holidays of obligation" (art. 52). Our gospel reading today already is a homily! We know that later Palestinian homiletic preaching followed a clearly-defined pattern. The starting-point always was a Scripture text, usually from the Pentateuch—followed by a paraphrase of the text. Then came the homily, which took account not only of the text but of the whole passage which formed its context. Commonly, within the homily there was a subordinate quotation (usually from the Prophets or Writings) to which a few lines of commentary were devoted—the whole by way of a development of the main commentary. The closing statements referred back to the main statement at the beginning and at the same time summed up points from the homily. Jn 6:31-50 is a typical example of this homiletic pattern.

The Scripture quotation which forms the starting-point of the Johannine homily is: "He gave them bread from heaven to eat" (v.31), which contains elements from Ex 16:4,15, in accordance with the practice of employing the whole context. Verses 32-33 constitute Jesus' paraphrase of the citation: "I tell you most solemnly, it is not Moses who gave you bread from heaven, it is my Father who gives you the bread from heaven, the true bread; for the bread of God is that which comes down from heaven and gives life to the world." Then, in 35-50, we find his homily on this Scripture text: first on the theme of "bread"(vv.35-40), then on the theme "from heaven" (vv.44-48), and finally, on the theme of eating (vv.49-50). The subordinate quotation ("They will all be taught by God"—Is 54:13), with its brief commentary, occurs in v.45. And, according to the homiletic rules, the statement which opened the homily (v.35) is repeated at the end (v.48): "I am the bread of life." For that matter, even the Scripture quotation and its paraphrase are taken up again (in vv.49-50). Significantly, Jesus is represented as speaking in a synagogue in Capernaum (v.59). Fittingly, John has him following the accepted homiletic style of synagogue preachers.

In vv.35-50 the fundamental reaction to Jesus' presentation of himself as bread is that of belief (35,36,40,47) or of coming to him, which is a synonym of belief (35,37,44-45). Only once (v.50) is it said that anyone must eat the bread of life; it is in vv.51-58 that "eating" appears insistently. In vv.35-50 "the bread of life" is, primarily, the revelation given to men by Jesus; at a secondary level, it does envisage the Eucharist.

Patristic Commentary

St. John Chrysostom (c.347-c.420)
Homily 46 on Gospel of John, PG 59.257,
    FOTC 33.462.
"The Jews therefore murmured at him because he had said: I am the bread that has come down from heaven.

And they kept saying: 'Is this not the son of Joseph, whose father and mother we know? How, then, does he say: I have come down from heaven?'"

"Their god is the belly, their glory is in their shame," (Phil 3:19) said Paul, writing to the Philippians about certain men. Now, it is clear from what had gone before that the Jews were just like these men, and this is likewise clear from the words they addressed to Christ as they approached Him. When, indeed, He gave them bread and satisfied their hunger, they kept calling Him a prophet and sought to make Him king. But when He taught them about their spiritual food, about life everlasting, when He led them away from things of sense, when He spoke to them of the resurrection, and elevated their thoughts, when, in short, they ought most of all to have admired Him, then they murmured and went away.

Now, if He was in truth the Prophet, as they had just said "This is indeed he about whom Moses said, 'The Lord thy God will raise up to thee a prophet of thy brethren like unto me: him shalt thou hear,'" they ought to have listened to Him when He said: "I have come down from heaven." On the contrary, they did not listen to Him, but murmured. Of course, they still held Him in awe because of the recent miracle of the loaves. That is why they did not oppose Him openly, but by murmuring they showed that they resented it, because He did not give them the table which they desired. And as they murmured, they kept saying: "Is this not the son of Joseph?"

From this it is clear that they did not yet know His marvelous and strange generation. That is why they still called Him the son of Joseph. Yet, He did not reprove them or say to them: "I am not the son of Joseph." This was not, to be sure, because He was the son of Joseph, but because they were not yet able to hear of His wonderful Incarnation. And if they were not ready for a clear revelation of His birth according to the flesh, much more was that the case with that ineffable one from above. If He did not reveal the humble one, much less would He have treated of the other. And though it scandalized them very much to think that He was of a lowly and ordinary father, He nevertheless did not reveal His true parentage, in order that, in removing one scandal, He might not cause another.

What, then, did He reply when they murmured? "No one can come to me unless the Father who sent me draws him." He here was pointing out that it is not anyone who happens to do so that comes to Him, but that it is a person enjoying the benefit of much assistance who comes.

In the next place, He also pointed out the manner by which He draws him. In order that they might not suspect of God some purely material operation, He added: "Not that anyone has seen the Father except him who is from God, he has seen the Father." (Jn 6:46).

Insights from the Documents of the Church

Fostering Reverence for the Eucharist

The other table of the Eucharistic mystery, that of the Bread of the Lord, also requires reflection from the viewpoint of the present-day liturgical renewal. This is a question of the greatest importance, since it concerns a special act of living faith, and indeed, as has been attested since the earliest centuries, it is a manifestation of *worship of Christ, who in Eucharistic communion entrusts himself to each one of us,* to our hearts, our consciences, our lips and our mouths, in the form of food. Therefore there is special need, with regard to this question, for the watchfulness spoken of by the Gospel, on the part of the pastors who have charge of Eucharistic worship and on the part of the People of God, whose "sense of the faith" must be very alert and acute particularly in this area.

I therefore wish to entrust this question to the heart of each one of you, venerable and dear Brothers in the Episcopate. You must above all make it part of your care for all the Churches entrusted to you. I ask this of you in the name of the unity that we have received from the Apostles as our heritage, collegial unity. This unity came to birth, in a sense, at the table of the Bread of the Lord on Holy Thursday. With the help of your brothers in the priesthood, do all you can to *safeguard the sacred dignity of the Eucharistic ministry and that deep spirit of Eucharistic communion* which belongs in a special way to the Church as the People of God, and which is also a particular heritage transmitted to us from the Apostles, by various liturgical traditions, and by unnumbered generations of the faithful, who were often heroic witnesses to Christ, educated in "the school of the Cross" (Redemption) and of the Eucharist.

It must be remembered that the Eucharist as the table of the Bread of the Lord is a continuous invitation. This is *shown in the liturgy when the celebrant says: "This is the Lamb of God. Happy are those who are called to his supper";* it is also shown by the familiar Gospel parable about the guests invited to the marriage banquet. Let us remember that in this parable there are many who excuse themselves from accepting the invitation for various reasons. (John Paul II, The Holy Eucharist)

TWENTIETH SUNDAY OF THE YEAR

Scriptural Commentary

First Reading Proverbs 9:1-6.

Chapter 9 of Proverbs contrasts Dame Wisdom (1-6) with Dame Folly (13-18) [the diptych is upset by the insertion of six independent proverbs (7-12)]. Personified Wisdom and Folly each has prepared her banquet and each is on the lookout for the "simple." Proverbs conceives a world divided into two distinct categories: the wise and the foolish. An intermediate category is that of the uncommitted, the simple or inexperienced who have yet to fall under the influence of one of the two groups and join one or other of them. The contrast "wise-foolish" (and not "wise-ignorant") is significant: even the highly-skilled, cultured man is a "fool" if he does not grasp the true meaning and purpose of life. Today's reading tells us what Wisdom offers: a splendid mansion in which a sumptuous banquet has been prepared. "Seven" is the traditional figure for completeness and perfection. Spices were mixed with wine (v.2) to make it more pleasant to the palate. Meat and wine are festive foods and the bread and wine of v.5 are symbols of the teaching and experience offered by Wisdom. To a Jew the text would suggest the eschatological banquet promised by Yahweh (Is 25:6; 55:1-5), but a Christian will readily see here a foreshadowing of the eucharistic invitation (Lk 22:15).

Second Reading Eph 5:15-20.

In 5:3-20 the author of Ephesians bids Christians walk as children of light—there are some kinds of behaviour which are not compatible with holiness. Though, in a sense, we stand in the "fulness of time" (1:10), the church is still waiting for the final accomplishment of God's saving plan. The wise Christian will make the most of this present time. He will not be a "fool" (see first reading) but will be alert to the will of the Lord, and shape his conduct accordingly. The further exhortation: "do not get drunk with wine . . . but be filled with the Spirit" (v.18) might well be rendered, in modern terms: "do not get high on spirits, but on the Spirit." And, in the setting of christian fellowship (19-20) it is firmly suggested that the Spirit is the source of joyful fellowship.

Gospel Jn 6:51-58.

This is a duplicate of the preceding discourse on the bread of life (35-50—see previous Sunday); but now the theme is exclusively eucharistic. The discourse begins (v.51) with a reiteration of the statement, "I am the living bread which came down from heaven" (cf. v.41) and goes on to draw out its logical consequence. If Jesus is both the Bread and the Giver of bread, then what he gives is himself—his flesh and blood. "The question, 'How can this man give us his flesh to eat?' receives no direct answer, any more than did Nicodemus' question, 'How can a man be born again?' The instructed christian reader cannot miss the reference to the sacrament of the Eucharist. Indeed, the Johannine expression, 'I am the bread of life . . . the bread which I shall give for the life of the world is my flesh', amounts to an expanded transcription of the words of 'institution,' 'this is my body which is for you' as we have it in 1 Cor 11:24 (written at Ephesus), and John's ultimate answer to the question 'How?' would undoubtedly have been given in sacramental terms" (C. H. Dodd).

In 53-55 the language is very realistic. "Flesh . . . blood"—the Hebrew idiom "flesh and blood" means the whole man: it is necessary to reveal the whole Christ. The word "to eat" (*trogein*) had a crude connotation—something like "gnaw" or "munch." Used in a metaphorical sense, "to eat someone's flesh" implies hostile action (Ps 27:2; Zech 11:9). The drinking of blood was strictly forbidden (Gen 9:4; Lev 3:17; Dt 22:23); its transferred meaning was that of brutal murder (Jer 46:10). If Jesus' words are to have a favourable meaning—as in the context they should have—they must refer to the Eucharist.

Throughout his words on the bread of life, John does not overlook the sacrificial aspect of the eucharist. Jesus tells us that "the bread which I shall give for the life of the world is my flesh" (v.51). The food of eternal life is the flesh of Christ offered in sacrifice for the world. Likewise, reference to his blood which must be drunk evokes the "blood poured out for many" of Paul and the synoptists. Nor is John unaware of the eschatological aspect of the sacrament. Indeed, for him, the Eucharist is *par excellence* the sacrament of eternal life; in it the Christian finds, in anticipation, the gift of life, and has the gage of final resurrection: "he who eats my flesh and drinks my blood abides in me, and I in him." Yet, in relation to this idea of life, John organizes everything around the notions of food and of bread: the Eucharist is "the bread of life" or "the bread which came down from heaven." And, all the while, the mystery of the living bread is only one aspect of the mystery of the Incarnation itself. It is significant that John does not speak of "body" but of "flesh"—we must eat the "flesh" of Jesus. We are reminded of the evangelist's description of the Incarnation: "the Word became flesh and dwelt among us" (1:14). The Eucharist is the memorial of the redemptive Incarnation.

Patristic Commentary

St. Cyril of Alexandria (c.375-444)
Comm. on John's Gospel, PG 73.593,
LFC 43.406.

This is the Bread Which Came Down from Heaven, not such as Your Fathers ate the Manna and Died; He That eats This Bread shall Live Forever (v.58).

Great (says he) ought to be the effects of great things, and the gifts of the grace from above should appear God-befitting and worthy of the divine munificence. For if you have wholly received in faith that *the bread came down from heaven*, let it produce continuous life in them that long for it, and have the unceasing operation of immortality. For this will be a clear proof of its being *the bread from heaven*, that is from God: since we say that it befits the eternal to give what is eternal, and not the enjoyment of temporary food, which is barely able to last for the least moment. For one will no longer wisely suppose that that was the bread from God and from above, which our forefathers eating, were overcome by death, and repelled not the evil of corruption, and no wonder; for that was not the bread which avails to render immortal. Hence neither will it be rightly conceived and said by any to be from heaven. For it was a work befitting that which came down thence, to render its partakers superior to death and decay. By undoubted proof again will it be confirmed, that this was *the bread from heaven*, that namely through Christ, that is, his body. For it makes him that tastes thereof to live forever. Herein too is seen a great pledge of the divine nature, which vouchsafes not to give a little thing, but everything wonderful, even surpassing our understanding, so as for the greatness of the grace, to be even disbelieved by the more simple. For with so wealthy a hand how should not the will to give largely be present? Wherefore Paul too says in amazement, *eye has not seen, nor ear heard, neither has it entered into the heart of man, to conceive the things which God has prepared for them that love him* (1 Cor 2, 9). By little examples was the Law typifying great ones, *having the shadow of the good things to come, not the very image of these things* (Heb 10, 1), as it is written: as in the food of manna is seen the blessing that is through Christ. For *the shadow of the good things to come* was prefigured to them of old.

Insights from the Documents of the Church

Receiving Holy Communion

Our Catholic communities certainly do not lack people who *could participate* in Eucharistic Communion *and do not*, even though they have no serious sin on their conscience as an obstacle. To tell the truth, this attitude, which in some people is linked with an exaggerated severity, has changed in the present century, though it is still to be found here and there. In fact what one finds most often is not so much a feeling of unworthiness as a certain lack of interior willingness, if one may use this expression, a lack of Eucharistic "hunger" and "thirst," which is also a sign of lack of adequate sensitivity towards the great Sacrament of love and a lack of understanding of its nature.

However, we also find in recent years another phenomenon. Sometimes, indeed quite frequently, everybody participating in the Eucharistic assembly goes to communion; and on some such occasions, as experienced pastors confirm, there has not been due care to approach the Sacrament of Penance so as to purify one's conscience. This can of course mean that those approaching the Lord's Table find nothing on their conscience, according to the objective law of God, to keep them from this sublime and joyful act of being sacramentally united with Christ. But there can also be, at least at times, another idea behind this: the idea of the Mass as *only* a banquet in which one shares by *receiving the Body of Christ in order to manifest, above all else, fraternal communion.* It is not hard to add to these reasons a certain human respect and mere "conformity."

This phenomenon demands from us watchful attention and a theological and pastoral analysis guided by a sense of great responsibility. We cannot allow the life of our communities to lose the good quality of sensitiveness of Christian conscience, guided solely by respect for Christ, who, when he is received in the Eucharist, should find in the heart of each of us a worthy abode. This question is closely linked not only with the practice of the Sacrament of Penance but also with a correct sense of responsibility for the whole deposit of moral teaching and for the precise distinction between good and evil, a distinction which then becomes for each person sharing in the Eucharist the basis for a correct judgment of self to be made in the depths of the personal conscience. Saint Paul's words, "Let a man examine himself," are well known; this judgment is an indispensable condition for a personal decision whether to approach Eucharistic communion or to abstain. (John Paul II, The Holy Eucharist)

TWENTY-FIRST SUNDAY OF THE YEAR

Scriptural Commentary

First Reading Joshua 24:1-2, 15-18.

Chapter 24 stands as an epilogue to the book of Joshua. It deals with a covenant-renewal ceremony that took place at Shechem shortly after the Hebrews from Egypt had entered the promised land. Moses had led the people to the borders of Canaan; it was left to Joshua to bring them into the land (Jos 1:2-3). More significant than the idealized picture of Jos 10-11 (which casts back into the age of Joshua the conquest of David) is the account of the Shechem assembly (Jos 24). The Shechem covenant covers a vital stage of the development of Israel: groups who did not experience the exodus or Sinai joined the Yahwistic group at Shechem. A study of the narrative of the exodus from Egypt reveals two distinct episodes involving two groups: an exodus-flight and an exodus-expulsion, and the situation may have been more involved. Those who entered Canaan would have found groups who had never been in Egypt. Some of these were willing to acknowledge the God, Yahweh, of the Moses-group. The Shechem assembly marks this amalgamation. While the account of the Shechem covenant is overlaid with deuteronomic theology, it is not a creation of the deuteronomists but is far older. At Shechem "all the tribes of Israel" made the solemn declaration: "We will serve Yahweh, for he is our God" (24:18,24) "So Joshua made a covenant with the people that day, and made statutes and ordinances with them at Shechem" (24:25). The "people of Yahweh" of Moses had grown into the people of Israel. In the excerpts from the chapter that form our reading, the main emphasis is on the vital decision that the people are called upon to make—the decision whether or not to serve Yahweh. Being reminded of everything he has done for them since the Exodus, they make a decision for the Lord. They commit themselves to serve Yahweh in covenant relationship.

Second Reading Eph 5:21-32.

It is the precise relationship between the church and Christ which provides the basis for the author's exhortation to wives and husbands (5:21-33). The opening verse (21) is a general exhortation and the following verse is almost the same as Col 3:18. But, at this point (vv.23-24), in Ephesians, a striking motive is added: the fact that Christ is the "head" of the church. By being subject to their husbands, (and "subjection" means the loving service characteristic of *agape*) wives are realizing this truth. The author has realized that the marriage image strikingly expresses the intimate union of Christ and his church. So he has set up a parallel between the husband-wife relationship and the union of Christ and his church: husband and wife, in their marriage, verify this union and make it manifest in their personal relations. The Christ-Church relationship is thus the archetype of christian marriage and it is precisely in view of the archetype (he explains) that the wife is "subject" to her husband. Already, in v.21, he had urged all Christians: "Be subject to one another out of reverence for Christ"; the "subjection" to which he exhorts wives is a specific form of that universal service. All Christians are disciples of the one who came "to serve" (Mk 10:45).

The recommendation to husbands: "love your wives" sounds banal—until we realize that "Paul" is not talking of *eros* (sensual love) nor of *philia* (friendship) but of *agape* self-giving, unselfish service. If this is his "love" for his wife, then the husband is quite as much "subject" to her as she is to him. For both of them, the model and inspiration of their love is the generous love of Christ. The argument in vv.28-32 comes to this: Husbands should love their wives as they love their own bodies. Everyone loves his own flesh; so also Christ loves the church, his Body. This is the meaning of Gen 2:24 when one sees there a type of Christ and the church. This is precisely the great mystery of which he speaks —great not because of its mysteriousness but because of its significance and sublimity. And in the measure in which each earthly marriage reflects the mystery of the marriage of Christ and his church, it shares in that mystery. Only christian marriage (which is truly such) can hope to reproduce with any fidelity the perfect lines of the archetype.

Coming after this, the last verse (23) must sound an anticlimax; instead it strikingly brings out the essentially practical nature of Christianity. Christians may have their eyes raised to heaven but they must strive to give bone and flesh to sublime ideals in a world that is the home of men, not of angels. The parting admonition is not banal but shows a spirit of realism and an appreciation of actual conditions that forcefully sets off the foregoing teaching. "However, for your part, let each one of you love your wife as yourself, and let the wife see that she reveres her husband" (33). Once again, as at the beginning, love and reverence are recommended. For on both of these, on love and reverence, mutually expressed, is marriage founded and sustained.

Gospel Jn 6:60-69.

The long chapter 6 of John is rounded off by reactions to the discourse on the Bread of Life. The first thing one must determine is whether the passage (60-71) refers to the whole discourse (35-58) or only to the "original" discourse (35-50). Always, v.63 has been seen to raise a problem: it would seem that "flesh" there must refer to the eucharistic flesh of 51-58 and thus involve a contradiction. Let us suppose that v.60 followed immediately on v.50 (in other words acknowledge that 51-59 is another, parallel, discourse, inserted, later, into the complex). In v.50 Jesus claimed to be the bread come down from heaven; in v.60 the disciples murmur about this as the Jews murmured about the same claim (v.41). The disciples refuse *to listen*: all the references in 60-71 concern hearing or believing Jesus' doctrine. There is not a single reference to refusal to eat his flesh or drink his blood—which must surprise after the great emphasis on eating and drinking in vv.51-59. Reference to the "ascending" of the Son of Man evidently envisages the claim that he has "come down from heaven" (vv.41,50). All in all, one agrees with Raymond E. Brown: "We have interpreted 60-71 as if these verses had no reference to 51-58; this agrees with our theory that 51-58 is a later editorial insertion of Johannine material breaking up the unity that once existed between 35-50 and 60-71. But one may ask, even if this theory is correct, does not the final form of the chapter where 60-71 *now* follow 51-58 require that 60-71 have some secondary reference to the Eucharist? We are not convinced that it does; for we believe that the editor or final redactor added 51-58 to bring out the secondary eucharistic motifs of 35-50, but did not make any real attempt to give a new orientation to 60-71 in light of this addition" (*The Gospel According to John*, New York, 1966, p.302).

What then does v.63 mean? The first notable feature is the reappearance of *pneuma* ("spirit"). In the Nicodemus passage of ch.3 we are told that the realm of "the above" is the sphere of "spirit" and that rebirth into the eternal life of the higher realm is birth "of the Spirit" (3:3-8). And there is the forceful statement: "That which is born of the flesh is flesh, and that which is born of the Spirit is spirit" (v.6). Similarly here (6:33) the point is made that only one "born of spirit" can accept that Jesus has come from heaven and can receive his revelation. One "born of the flesh," and so open only to the merely human, cannot know him or his teaching. If "flesh" here has nothing to do with the eucharist, neither then does the emphasis on Spirit have anything to do with a spiritual interpretation of the eucharistic presence of Jesus.

Just as the synoptic account of the ministry in Galilee ended on a note of disbelief (cf. Mk 6:1-6) so, here, the final reaction of the disciples is one of unbelief (v.66). In the passage 67-69, which turns our attention to the different reaction of the Twelve who believe in Jesus, we have John's parallel to the synoptic scene at Caesarea Philippi (Mk 8:27-32, parr.). The chapter ends on a sombre note (70-71):

Jesus, Bread of Life—the life-giver—will be brought to death by unbelief and betrayal.

Patristic Commentary

St. John Chrysostom (c.347-407)
Homily 47 on John, PG 59.266, FOTC 33.480-481.

What did Peter then say? "To whom shall we go? Thou hast the words of everlasting life, and we have come to believe and to know that thou art the Christ, the Son of the living God." Do you perceive that it was not really His words that were scandalous but the inattentiveness and apathy and ignorance of His hearers? I say this because, even if He had said nothing, they would have been scandalized and would not have ceased to be so, since their thoughts were always centered on bodily nourishment and riveted to things of earth. Moreover, those who were with the Twelve also heard Him; nevertheless, they showed a feeling just the opposite of theirs when they said: "To whom shall we go?" These words were indicative of a great and tender love, for they showed that their Master was dearer to them than all else—father and mother and all the rest—and that, if they departed from Him, they had nowhere to go.

Next, lest Peter might seem to have said the words: "To whom shall we go?" because they had no other refuge, he at once added: "Thou hast the words of everlasting life." Some, to be sure, had listened to Him carnally, and with human reasonings, but these heard Him spiritually and entrusted all to faith. That is why Christ said: "The words that I have spoken to you are spirit"; that is: "Do not conceive the notion that My doctrine is subject to the sequence of events and the necessity of human things. Spiritual things are not of this kind and are not constrained to be enslaved by the laws of earth. Paul also makes this clear when he says: "Do not say in thy heart, Who shall ascend into heaven? (that is, to bring down Christ); or, Who shall descend into the abyss? (that is, to bring up Christ from the dead)." (Rom 10:6).

"Thou hast the words of everlasting life." They had already accepted the resurrection and all that will be appointed therein. And see how this lover of his brethren, this warm-hearted friend, spoke out in the name of the whole group, for he did not say: "I know" but "We know." And more than this, notice how he came near using the very words of the Master, not the same ones as the Jews. They had said: "This is the son of Joseph," while he said: "Thou art the Christ, the Son of the living God," and "Thou hast the words of everlasting life," perhaps because he had often heard Him saying: "He who believes in me has everlasting life." Indeed, by recalling His very words he showed that he cherished all that Christ said.

Insights from the Documents of the Church

Second Reading: Christian Marriage

Dear brothers and sisters! On the indispensable foundation and premises of what has been said, we wish to turn now to the deepest mystery of marriage and the family. From the point of view of our faith, marriage is a *sacrament* of Jesus Christ. Love and conjugal fidelity are understood and sustained by the love and fidelity of God in Jesus Christ. The power of his cross and of his resurrection sustains and sanctifies Christian spouses.

As the recent Synod of Bishops stressed in its Message to Christian Families in the Modern World, the Christian family is called in particular to collaborate in God's salvific plan, since it helps its members "to become agents of the history of salvation and at the same time living signs of God's loving plan for the world" (Sect. III, n.8).

As a "Church in miniature," sacramentally founded, or domestic Church, marriage and the family must be a school of faith and a place of common prayer. I attribute great significance precisely to prayer in the family. It gives strength to overcome the many problems and difficulties. In marriage and in the family, the fundamental human and Christian attitudes, without which the Church and society cannot exist, must grow and mature. This is the first place for the Christian apostolate of the laity and of the common priesthood of all the baptized. Such marriages and families, imbued with the Christian spirit, are also the real seminaries, that is, seedbeds for spiritual vocations for the priestly and religious state.

Dear spouses and parents, dear families! What could I more heartily wish you on the occasion of today's Eucharistic meeting than this: *that all of you and every single family may be such a "domestic Church,"* a Church in miniature! That the parable of the kingdom of God may be realized in you! That you may experience the presence of the kingdom of God, in that you are yourselves a living "net," which unites and supports and gives refuge for yourselves and for many around you.

This is my good wish and blessing, which I express as your guest and pilgrim and as the servant of your salvation. (John Paul II at Cologne, Germany, 15 Nov., 1980)

TWENTY-SECOND SUNDAY OF THE YEAR

Scriptural Commentary

First Reading Dt 4:1-2, 6-8.

The Book of Deuteronomy purports to offer three addresses of Moses just before the entry of Israel into the promised land (the book is, of course, very much later than Moses). The first address comprises 1:1 - 4:43; our reading, taken from the close of it, opens a prologue to the promulgation of the Law to all Israel (4:1-34). Two motives urge obedience to the law: it is a source of *life*, and it is a *teaching* of divine origin. Israel's distinguishing trait in the world's eyes will be her wisdom and discernment derived from the Law. Thus, it is crucial that Israel never forget what happened at Horeb (Sinai). The words "law," "commands," "statutes," "ordinances" are all synonymous in Deuteronomy: they represent the full expression of God's will. The law is not seen as a burden to be suffered but as a gift, a source of life and wisdom and righteousness. It is not easy to maintain such an open and sophisticated attitude to law and doctrine. A drift to legalism and stifling orthodoxy is fatally easy.

Second Reading James 1:17-18, 21-22,27.

The letter of James will be read over five Sundays, beginning today. The James named in the address as the author of the writing is James "the brother of the Lord," leader of the Jewish Christian community of Jerusalem. If authentic, the letter would date from the end of James' life, between 57 and 62 A.D. Many scholars would date it instead in the last decade of the first century. The letter is addressed to a milieu in which social differences are marked. There are the rich who expect, and receive, deferential treatment even in the liturgical assemblies (2:1-3), men who are prodigal of generous words that cost them nothing (2:16). Entirely absorbed in their business affairs (4:13-17), they do not hesitate to cheat their workers and to squeeze the poor (5:1-6). These same poor receive scant attention even from those who are supposed to be their shepherds and ought to be their servants (2:2-6). Such conduct cannot but give rise to dissension: jealousy (3:14; 4:2), anger (1:19), murmuring (5:9), and cursing (4:11). The exasperated poor may be driven to rebel against their lot (4:2), or they may, enviously, be seized by the desire for worldly possessions. All James' sympathy goes to the afflicted and to the weak; he has written mainly for them. Like the Old Testament prophets, he takes issue with social injustice; at the same time, however, he considers poverty to have a religious value which makes of the unfortunate the privileged friends of God—the *anawim*. And if he could, and did, turn to the sages and the psalmists to find expression of this outlook, his words have a fresh vigour from the practice and teaching of Jesus.

In our reading (and the whole passage, 16-27, should be read) James firmly asserts that God is the giver of good and perfect gifts (16-18). His greatest gift to men is rebirth through the Gospel; v.18 (cf. 1 Pet 1:22-23) seems to refer to a baptismal liturgy. Nevertheless, one must be prepared to listen, to check hasty speech, to put away wickedness, and to attend with docility to the word of the Law written on the heart (1:19-21). In Judaism, the Law was not regarded as a burden; in a much truer sense the Gospel, fulfilment of the Old Testament, is a law of liberty which is gladly obeyed (1:22-25). It is all too easy to imagine oneself a "religious" person; failure to control one's tongue (cf. 3:1-12) gives the lie to such an illusion. Genuine religion shows itself in the service of those in need and by repudiation of the life-style of the world, that is, of those who make pleasure and self-seeking their goal.

Gospel Mk 7:1-8, 14-15, 21-23.

Having completed the reading of John 6, we return to the gospel of Mark. (See Sixteenth Sunday). A precise incident lies behind Jesus' dispute with the Pharisees and scribes (Mk 7:1-23): they had observed that the disciples of Jesus did not observe the ritual washing of hands before meals. In their eyes this constituted a transgression of the "tradition of the elders," the oral law. (These Pharisaic traditions claimed to interpret and complete the Mosaic law and were considered equally authoritative and binding. Later rabbis would claim that "the ancestral" laws constituted a second, oral law, given, together with the written law, to Moses on Sinai). In responding to their criticism of neglecting one observance (v.5), Jesus turns the debate on to the wider issue: the relative worth of oral law and the

Mosaic law. He cites Is 29:13 (in its Greek form!) against the Pharisees, drawing a parallel between the "precepts of man" of which Isaiah spoke and the "traditions of men" on which the Pharisees count. Jesus rejects the oral law because it is the work of men (not word of God) and because it can and does conflict with the law of God. The oral law had put casuistry above love. He instances (9-13) the manner in which a son could avoid all obligations to his parents by fictitiously dedicating to the Temple treasury the money that should go to their support; this was an overturning of a precept of the Decalogue. Thus, by their tradition, the Pharisees had "made void the word of God."

The principle of clean and unclean was at the root of Pharisaic preoccupation with ritual purification. A saying of Jesus: "There is *nothing* outside a man which by going into him can defile him; but the things that come out of a man are what defile him" (v.15) strikes at the very distinction of clean and unclean, of sacred and secular. It is a flat denial that any external things or circumstances can separate one from God (cf. Rom 8:38-39). We can be separated from God only by our own attitude and behaviour. In a Gentile-Christian setting this saying was provided with a commentary. The first half of v.15—nothing outside a man can defile him—is explained in verses 18b-19, and the second part of the verse—it is what comes out of a man that makes him unclean—is developed in vv.20-23. In this way it is made clear to Gentile Christians that being followers of Christ does not involve them in the observance of Jewish practices. "The Way" (cf. Acts 9:2; 19:9,23) is truly open to all men and women.

Patristic Commentary

St. Gregory of Nyssa (c.330-c.395)
On the Lord's Prayer, S.5, PG 44.1185,
    ACW 18.77.
As our life is lived in this world on many levels, partly in the sphere of soul and intellect, partly in that of the

bodily senses, it is difficult, so it seems to me, or even altogether impossible, that one should not at least acquiesce in one sinful passion. For example: Since the life which the body enjoys is divided into our senses, but that of the soul is regarded as the impulse given by the mind and the movement of the free will—who is of so surpassingly noble character as to remain free from the stain of evil in both? Whose eye is without sin, whose sense of hearing without reproach? Who is a stranger to the brutish pleasure of gluttony, who is pure from the sins occasioned by touch? Who does not understand the symbolic sense of the Scriptural saying, *Death has come in through the windows?* (Jer 9:21). What Scripture calls windows are the senses, through which the soul issues forth to the things outside and lays hold of those it likes; and thus these windows, as Scripture says, make an entrance for death. Truly, the eye is often an entry for many a death. If it sees someone angry, it is incited to the same passion; if it observes one enjoying greater prosperity than he deserves, it burns with envy. It may see someone arrogant and rage with hatred, something of lovely colour or beautiful shape and be completely carried away with desire for the pleasing object. So the ear, too, opens windows to death. Through what it hears it admits many passions into the soul: fear, sorrow, wrath, pleasure, desire, bursts of laughter, and suchlike things. And the pleasure of taste is, one may well say, the mother of each individual evil. For who does not know that indulgence of the palate is pretty nearly the root of the sins committed in the physical life? Likewise the sense of touch is the last of the senses by which sin can be committed. For all things that pleasure-lovers practise on the body are diseases of the perception of touch, which it would take too long to enumerate in detail. Nor would it be seemly to get all the sins of touch entangled with our serious considerations.

But as to the swarm of sins of the soul and of free will, what sermon could enumerate them? *From within*, He says, *proceed evil thoughts*, (Mk 7:21) and He adds a catalogue of thoughts that defile us. If, therefore, the nets of sin are thus spread around us on every side, through all the senses and through the interior movements of the soul, *Who shall glory*, as Wisdom says, *that his heart is clean?* (Prov 20:9) Or, as Job testifies to the same, *Who is clear from filth?* (Job 14:4, LXX). Filth on the purity of the soul is sensual pleasure, which is mixed up with human life in manifold ways, through soul and body, through thoughts and senses, through deliberate movements and bodily actions.

Insights from the Documents of the Church

God's Word

Under special inspiration of the Holy Spirit, divine revelation has also been expressed in writings, that is, in the sacred books of the Old and New Testaments, books which contain and present divinely revealed truth.

The Church, guardian and interpreter of the Sacred Scriptures, learns from them, by constantly meditating on and penetrating more and more into their teaching. Remaining faithful in tradition, the ministry of the word finds its nourishment and its norm in Sacred Scripture. For in the sacred books the Father, who is in heaven, very lovingly meets with his children and speaks with them.

But if it takes its norm for thinking from Sacred Scripture, the Church, inspired by the Spirit, interprets that same Scripture: "and the sacred writings themselves are more profoundly understood and unceasingly made active in her."

The ministry of the word, therefore, takes its beginning from Holy Writ and from the preaching of the apostles, as these are understood, explained, and applied in concrete situations by the Church.

By faith man accepts revelation, and through it he consciously becomes a sharer in the gift of God.

The obedience of faith must be offered to the God who reveals. By this, man, with full homage of his mind and will, freely assents to the Gospel of the grace of God (cf. Acts 20:24). Instructed by Faith, man, through the gift of the Spirit, comes to contemplate and savour the God of love, the God who has made known the riches of his glory in Christ (cf. Col 1:26). Indeed, a living Faith is the beginning in us of eternal life in which the mysteries of God (cf. 1 Cor 2:10) will at last be seen unveiled. Informed of God's plan of salvation, Faith leads man to full discernment of the divine will towards us in this world, and to co-operation with his grace. "For Faith throws a new light on everything, manifests God's design for man's total vocation, and thus directs the mind to solutions which are fully human" (GS, 11). (Gen. Catechetical Directory)

Faith and Customs

The Faith of many Christians is strained to a critical point in those places where religion was seeming to favour the prerogatives of certain social classes to an excessive degree, or where it was depending too much on ancestral customs and on regional unanimity in religious profession.

Great numbers are drifting little by little into religious indifferentism, or are continuing in danger of keeping the Faith without the dynamism that is necessary, a Faith without effective influence on their actual lives. The question now is not one of merely preserving traditional religious customs, but rather one of also fostering an appropriate re-evangelization of men, obtaining their reconversion, and giving them a deeper and more mature education in the Faith.

By no means, however, is the above to be interpreted in such a way that it results in neglect of the genuine Faith which is preserved within groups in a culture that is traditionally Christian, or in a low estimation of the popular religious sense. Despite the growth of secularization, a religious sense continues to flourish in the various parts of the Church. No one can fail to note it, for it is expressed in ordinary life by a very large number of people, and for the most part in a sincere and authentic way. In fact, the popular religious sense provides an opportunity or starting point for proclaiming the Faith. The question is, as is clear, only one of purifying it and of correctly appraising its valid elements, so that no one will be content with forms of pastoral action which today have become unequal to the task, altogether unsuitable, and perhaps even irrelevant. (General Catechetical Directory)

TWENTY-THIRD SUNDAY OF THE YEAR

Scriptual Commentary

First Reading Is 35:4-7.

Though it is found in the first part of the Isaiah-book (1-39) which consists, predominantly, of oracles of the eighth-century prophet, the triumphant poem of Is 35 dates from the Exile and describes, in idyllic terms, Israel's return from exile. It is shot through with the joy of restoration, of good fortune, felt by the one who was absolutely certain that, in the end, God would not sell his people short. Our reading bids those who were losing heart to take courage. For God will come to vindicate and save his people. And his coming will reverse their situation of suffering and oppression. As the prophet puts it: "Then the eyes of the blind shall be opened, and the ears of the deaf unstopped ... and the tongue of the dumb sing for joy." Mark, in his account of the cure of a man who "had an impediment in his speech" (Gospel reading) had this Isaian passage in mind. He uses the rare word *mogilalos* ("stammerer") taken, surely, from the Greek text of Is 35:6. For that matter, the Isaian reference to the opening of the eyes of the blind will be developed by the evangelist in the parallel miracle of 8:22-26, the cure of a blind man.

Second Reading James 2:1-5.

The passage 2:1-13 is concerned with class distinction: it deplores a favouring of the rich and a slighting of the poor. "Partiality" towards the rich is the wisdom of the "world" (1:27), whereas God's wisdom (that is; his way of acting) is partiality towards the oppressed and the poor (cf. Is 35; Ps 145:7-9). The christian standard is to reflect God's standard, otherwise Christians become "judges with evil thoughts" (v.4). The different treatment meted out to rich and poor is especially reprehensible in liturgical assemblies (cf. 1 Cor 11). Besides, the *anawim* (the "poor") are the heirs of God's promise. The Bible's emphasis on God's concern for the poor does not imply that God loves them simply because they are poor, as if poverty were a virtue. Here, as elsewhere, the background is that of the law-court in which justice was perverted and the poor were abused by the wealthy (v.6). The bible (apart from Luke) sees the rich man and the poor man as oppressor and oppressed respectively. And God is determined to vindicate the oppressed. This is the only passage in James (apart from the address 1:1) in which Jesus is named and his title here is solemn: "Our Lord Jesus Christ, the Lord of glory" (v.1). It is a confession of christian faith based on the early credal liturgical acclamation: "Jesus Christ is Lord!" It proclaims the christian belief that Jesus of Nazareth who was crucified is the promised Messiah (Christ) and the Lord who has been glorified through resurrection from the dead.

The Gospel Mk 7:31-37.

Mark has set the healing of a deaf-mute in the region of Decapolis; as in the previous episode (the healing of a

Gentile woman's daughter [7:24-30]), he is concerned with Jesus' attitude to the Gentiles. In that story, the casting out of the unclean spirit which possessed the gentile girl shows Jesus hearkening to the Gentiles and setting them free. This time the spirit (cf. 9:17) not only departs but the man recovers his faculty of hearing and speaking. The healing has the symbolic intent of showing that the Gentiles, once deaf and dumb towards God, are now capable of hearing God and paying him homage. They, too, have become heirs of the eschatological promise to Israel: "The ears of the deaf will be opened and the tongue of the dumb will cry for joy" (Is 36:5-6).

Jesus' action of putting his fingers into the man's ears and touching his tongue with spittle are common to the technique of Greek and Jewish healers. Here the gestures have a certain "sacramental" quality (cf. 8:23). "Looking up to heaven," as in 6:41, implies Jesus' intimacy with God. "Sigh" expresses his deep feeling for the sufferer (cf. 1:41). "Be opened": characteristically, Mark translates the Aramaic word *ephphata*. (Noteworthy is Ezek 24:26: "Your mouth will be opened, and you shall speak and shall no longer be dumb," where the same Greek verb occurs). Both the word *ephphata* and the use of saliva passed at an early date into the baptismal ritual.

The description of this cure (v.35) is given a solemn cast (the parallel cure in chapter 8 will be described, too, in three clauses [8:25]). The fact that the injunction to preserve silence is disobeyed is put very strongly (v.36). As in 1:45 the deed is "proclaimed": the deeds of Jesus cannot but speak the good news. Astonishment is "beyond measure," the strongest statement of astonishment in Mark. The miracle has exceptional significance. "He has done all things well" recalls Gen 1:31. We may also see in the Greek chorus of the crowd (v.37) the response in faith of the christian community who perceive in the works of Jesus the time of fulfilment announced by the prophet.

Patristic Commentary

Origen (c.185-c.254)
Comm. on Mt, XIII, PG 13.1105, 1110,
ANF 9.478.

But the dumb and deaf spirit, who was cast out by the Word, must be figuratively understood as the irrational impulses, even towards that which seems to be good, so that, what things any man once did by irrational impulse which seemed to onlookers to be good, he may do no longer irrationally but according to the reason of the teaching of Jesus. Under the inspiration of this Paul also said, "If I have all faith so as to remove mountains;" for he, who has all faith, which is as a grain of mustard seed, removes not one mountain only, but also several analogous to it; for although faith is despised by men and appears to be something very little and contemptible; yet when it meets with good ground, that is the soul, which is able fittingly to receive such seed, it becomes a great tree, so that no one of those things which have no wings, but the birds of heaven which are winged spiritually, are able to lodge in the branches of faith so great.

But you will inquire whether there are such disorders in spirits as well as in men; so that some of them speak, but some of them are speechless, and some of them hear, but some are deaf; for as in them will be found the cause of their being impure, so also, because of their freedom of will, they are condemned to be speechless and deaf; for some men will suffer such condemnation if the prayer of the prophet, as spoken by the Holy Spirit, shall be given heed to, in which it is said of certain sinners, "Let the lying lips be put to silence." (Ps 30:19). And so, perhaps, those who make a bad use of their hearing, and admit the hearing of vanities, will be rendered deaf by Him who said, "Who hath made the stone-deaf and the deaf," (Ex 4:11) so that they may no longer lend an ear to vain things.

Insights from the Documents of the Church

God chose the Poor

Before his own townspeople, in Nazareth, Christ refers to the words of the prophet Isaiah: "The Spirit of the Lord is upon me, because he has anointed me to preach good news to the poor. He has sent me to proclaim release to the captives and recovering of sight to the blind, to set at liberty those who are oppressed, to proclaim the acceptable year of the Lord." These phrases, according to Luke, are *his first messianic declaration.* They are followed by the actions and words known through the Gospel. By these actions and words Christ makes the Father present among men. It is very significant that the people in question are especially the poor, those without means of subsistence, those deprived of their freedom, the blind who cannot see the beauty of creation, those living with broken hearts, or suffering from social injustice, and finally sinners. It is especially for these last that the Messiah becomes a particularly clear sign of God who is love, a sign of the Father. In this visible sign the people of our own time, just like the people then, can see the Father.

It is significant that, when the messengers sent by John the Baptist came to Jesus to ask him: "Are you he who is to come, or shall we look for another?", he answered by referring to the same testimony with which he had begun his teaching at Nazareth: "Go and tell John what it is that you have seen and heard: the blind receive their sight, the lame walk, lepers are cleansed, and the deaf hear, the dead are raised up, the poor have good news preached to them." He then ended with the words: "And blessed is he who takes no offence at me!"

Especially through his life-style and through his actions, Jesus revealed that *love is present in the world* in which we live—an effective love, a love that addresses itself to man and embraces everything that makes up his humanity. This love makes itself particularly noticed in contact with suffering, injustice and poverty—in contact with the whole historical "human condition," which in various ways manifests man's limitation and frailty, both physical and moral. It is precisely the mode and sphere in which love manifests itself that in biblical language is called "mercy." (John Paul II, On the Mercy of God, [*Dives in Misericordia*])

TWENTY-FOURTH SUNDAY OF THE YEAR

Scriptural Commentary

First Reading Is 50:5-9.

This reading is an excerpt from the third of Isaiah's four Servant Songs. In this song the Servant speaks of the suffering and persecution he encountered in his effort to bring about justice on earth and to teach people the ways of God. Despite the opposition and the persecution of his fellows the Servant knows (because he is the Servant *of the Lord*) that the Lord will vindicate and deliver him—all the more because he suffers not in spite of his innocence but precisely because of it and, further, because of his preaching and teaching mission. With courageous gentleness, he offers no resistance. Although it is not possible to identify the Servant with any historical figure, he is clearly a type of the suffering just man, the person who is oppressed by others. The New Testament sees Jesus as this servant. For us, in our time, he is too a type of many suffering just people. (See Passion Sunday).

Second Reading Jas 2:14-18.

"You see that a man is justified by works and not by faith alone" (Jas 2:24). "We hold that a man is justified by faith apart from works of law" (Rom 3:28; cf. Gal 2:16). So speak James and Paul and, at the same time, offer apparently diametrically opposed interpretations of the justification of Abraham. James asks: "Was not Abraham our father justified by works, when he offered his son Isaac upon the altar?" (2:21); and Paul flatly asserts that Abraham was justified not by works but by his faith (Gal 15:6; Rom 4:2-3). It can hardly be doubted that James is challenging the Pauline slogan "faith apart from works." It is evident that he has not read Paul's letters and is opposing the use of Paul's slogan by teachers who were promoting moral permissiveness on the basis of the apostle's thesis of justification by faith.

We find that while Jesus and Paul use the same words, the meaning of the words is different in each case. When Paul puts his readers on their guard against a vain confidence in works, he has in view specific works, those of the Mosaic law. He states emphatically that justification is an absolutely free gift of God which cannot be merited by works of the Law—or by any works. The works envisaged by James are of a different order; they are good deeds which sanctify christian life (2:15-17,25,22). Paul sets just as much store by the practice of these virtues (cf. Rom 11:9-12; Gal 5:22). And when James seems to minimize faith to the profit of works, he has in view a merely speculative assent without repercussion on daily living, a faith that is incapable of saving (2:14), that is dead (2:17-18); the demons believe in this manner (2:19). Unlike Paul, he does not consider the gratuitousness of faith. His concern is to encourage Christians to observe the commandments and to lead lives that conform to the divine will. Paul is concerned to demonstrate that at the moment of his conversion, the unjustified man is justified independently of observance of the Mosaic law or of his personal merits.

Although he has no conflict with Paul, the fact remains that James does insist on the value and necessity of works. Authentic religion consists just as much in help given to orphans and widows in their need (1:27) as in cultic practices; otherwise, ritual observance is a vain and empty thing. James wants to prevent just that. He is concerned with liturgy and with the common life of the christian assembly; this is why he insists on the need of social justice and works of mercy. An economic divide splits the members of the community; hence the need for insisting on the dignity of the poor before God (2:5) and for censuring the attitude of the rich (2:6-7)—all in a liturgical context. Similarly, the liturgical salutation, "Go in peace," is cruel derision when not accompanied by effective help (2:14-16). James' no-nonsense approach proposes a lesson that cannot be driven home too often. Is is a message that John has formulated with characteristic directness: "Little children, let us not love in word or speech but in deed and in truth" (1 Jn 3:18).

Gospel Mk 8:27-35.

In the evangelist's eyes, the unique significance of Peter's confession (8:27-30) rests upon the fact that here, for the *first* time, the disciples speak with Jesus as to what he is in their estimation. Jesus takes the initiative and asks the disciples about the opinion of "men"—"those outside" (4:11)—and learns that they would regard him not as a messianic figure but, at most, as a forerunner of the Messiah. It is very clear that not only was his teaching riddlesome to them but that they had missed, too, the import of his works. Peter, however, has at last begun to see: "You are the Messiah." The sequel will show that this is but the first stage of his enlightenment; it is the risen Lord who will open his eyes fully. Again the disciples are bidden to keep silence but now, for the first time, the prohibition is related to Jesus' own person. Mark, indeed, looks beyond Peter and the disciples to the christian community of his concern and bids his Christians take care that they really understand who their Christ is. And they are reminded that only the Lord can grant understanding.

The passage, in truth, is occupied not primarily with the historical situation of the ministry of Jesus but with the historical situation of the church for which Mark is writing.

Historically, Jesus and Peter engage in dialogue. At a deeper level, "Jesus" is the Lord addressing his church and "Peter" represents fallible believers who confess correctly but then interpret their confession mistakenly. Similarly, the "multitude" (v.34) is the people of God for whom the general teaching (8:34 - 9:1) is meant. Thus, a story about Jesus and his disciples has a further purpose in terms of the risen Lord and his church.

"Peter . . . began to rebuke him." Peter has spoken for all of us. Jesus confirms this: "You are on the side of men"— you think the thoughts of men. Not the thoughts of the proud, the arrogant, but the natural reaction of those who shrink from a way of suffering. Have we, at bottom, any different idea of salvation from that of Peter? Can we really conceive of salvation other than in categories of victory? We experience the saying of Jesus again and again as contradiction. The word of Jesus asserts, unequivocally, that the disciples of the Son of man (v.31) must necessarily walk in his path. Only one who is willing to be called as a disciple and truly answers that call really understands Jesus. The loyal disciple cannot be preoccupied with his personal interests but will be faithful unto death in a sustained faithfulness to Jesus (v.34). The way of discipleship is not easy and one may be tempted to shrink from what it entails. But to seek thus to evade the risk and save one's life is to suffer the loss of one's true self. Only one who is prepared and willing to risk all for Jesus and for his gospel will attain to authentic selfhood (v.35).

Patristic Commentary

St. Leo the Great (d.461)
Tract 62, CCL 138A.377.

Deservedly was the blessed Apostle Peter praised on his confession; who, when our Lord asked what His disciples understood concerning Him, with all speed anticipated the voices of them all, saying, "Thou art the Christ, the Son of the living God." Which indeed he saw, not by flesh and blood explaining it (for their interposition might have been a hindrance to the inward eyes) but by the very Spirit of the Father working in his believing heart; so that, being prepared for the government of the whole Church, he might first learn what he had to teach, and on account of the firmness of that faith which he was to proclaim, might hear it said, "Thou art Peter, and upon this rock I will build My Church, and the gates of hell shall not prevail against it." Accordingly, the strength of Christian faith, which, being built on an impregnable rock, fears not the gates of death, confesses one Lord Jesus Christ, both very God and very Man: believing the same to be the Virgin's Son Who is the Maker of His Mother; the same to have been born in the close of ages, Who is the Creator of times; the same to be Lord of all powers, and one of the race of mortals; the same to have "known no sin," and to have been sacrificed for sinners "in the likeness of sinful flesh."

And even towards His slayers so strong was His feeling of tenderness, that in His prayer to the Father from the Cross, He asked not that He should be avenged, but that they should be pardoned. saving. "Father, forgive them, for they know not what they do." And the might of that prayer had this result, that the hearts of many of those who said, "His blood be on us and on our children," were converted to repentance by the preaching of Peter the Apostle, and in one day "about three thousand" Jews were baptized; and they all became "of one heart and of one soul," prepared already to die for Him Whose crucifixion they had demanded.

Insights from the Documents of the Church

Giving to the poor

"Repent and give alms" (cf. Mk 1:15 and Lk 12:33).

Today we do not like to listen to the word "alms." We feel that there is something humiliating about it. The word seems to presuppose a social system in which there is injustice and an unequal distribution of goods, a system which should be changed by adequate reforms. And if these reforms were not carried out, the need for radical changes, especially in the sphere of social relations, would then loom up on the horizon. We find the same conviction in the texts of the Prophets of the Old Testament, on which the liturgy often draws during Lent. The Prophets consider this problem at the religious level: there is no true conversion to God, there can be no real "religion," without putting right offences and injustices in relations among men, in social life. Yet in this context the Prophets also exhort us to almsdeeds. They do not even use the word "alms," which, moreover, is "sedaqah" in Hebrew which means "justice." They ask for help for those who are victims of injustice and for the needy: not so much by virtue of mercy, but rather by virtue of the duty of active charity.

"Is not this the fast that I choose: to loose the bonds of wickedness, to undo the thongs of the yoke, to let the oppressed go free, and to break every yoke? Is it not to share your bread with the hungry, and bring the homeless poor into your house; when you see the naked, to cover him, and not to hide yourself from your own flesh?" (Is 58:6-7) . . . .

When the Lord Jesus speaks of alms, when he asks for almsdeeds to be practised, he always does so in the sense of bringing help to those who need it and sharing one's own goods with the needy, that is, in the simple and essential sense, which does not permit us to doubt the value of the act we call "almsdeeds," but, on the contrary, urges us to approve it as a good act, as an expression of love for one's neighbour and as a salvific act.

Moreover, at a moment of particular importance, Christ utters these significant words: "The poor you always have with you" (Jn 12:8). He does not mean by these words that changes in social and economic structures are not important and that we should not try to eliminate injustice, humiliation, want and hunger. He merely means that man will always have needs which cannot be satisfied except by help for the needy and by sharing one's own goods with others.

What sort of help are we speaking about? What do we mean exactly by "sharing"? Is it only a question of "alms," understood in the form of money, of material aid? Certainly, Christ does not remove alms from our field of vision. He also thinks of pecuniary, material alms, but in his own way. The most eloquent expression of this is the example of the poor widow, who put a few small coins into the treasury of the temple: from the material point of view, an offering that could hardly be compared with the offerings given by others. Yet Christ said: "This poor widow has put in . . . all the living that she had" (Lk 21:3-4). So it is, above all, the interior value of the gift that counts; the readiness to share everything, the readiness to give oneself.

Let us here recall St. Paul: "If I give away all I have . . . but have not love, I gain nothing" (1 Cor 13:3). St. Augustine, too, writes well in this connection: "If you stretch out your hand to give, but have not mercy in your heart, you have not done anything; but if you have mercy in your heart, even when you have nothing to give with your hand, God accepts your alms" (*Enarr. in* Ps 125, 5). (John Paul II, General Audience, 28 March, 1980)

TWENTY-FIFTH SUNDAY OF THE YEAR

Scriptural Commentary

First Reading Wisdom 2:12,17-20.

Wisdom 1-5 represents the climax of Old Testament thought on the suffering and righteous man at the hands of the wicked. The setting is the life of the faithful Jew in Alexandria surrounded by pagans, and by Jews who have turned from their Jewish ways. The "ungodly men" here are such Jews, disenchanted with traditional wisdom, who have resorted to hedonism: "Come, let us enjoy the good things that exist, and make use of the creation to the full as in youth" (2:6). The "righteous" are those who, despite the problems that the tradition must have raised for them, nevertheless (like Job) hold on to their faith in God and obey his commandments. Their faithfulness cuts the ungodly to the quick and threatens their existence: "Let us lie in wait for the righteous man, because he is inconvenient to us and opposes our actions" (2:12). Verses 17-20 present suffering as a test or trial, primarily for the benefit of the ungodly who want to prove their own thesis, but also for the righteous whose true mettle is revealed in their affliction: "Having been disciplined a little, they will receive great good, because God tested them, and found them worthy of himself" (3:5). The passage has been seen in christian tradition as anticipating hostility to Jesus, the suffering just one *par excellence*. It forms a unified theme with the Gospel reading and with the reading from James.

Second Reading James 3:16 - 4:3.
From the start of his letter, James has insisted that true wisdom (1:5) comes from God (1:17) and is modelled on Jesus' behaviour. True wisdom is the leading of a christian life: "Who is wise and understanding among you? By his good life let him show his works in the meekness of wisdom" (3:13). This is clearly the wisdom of the righteous, depicted in Wis 1-5, as opposed to the "wisdom" of the ungodly, and is necessarily translated into action: peace, gentleness, reasonableness, mercy, certainty and sincerity (3:17). The "harvest" or righteousness (3:18), which is the expression of God's righteousness (1:20), is the effect of peace (3:18). True justice can be based only on peace. By contract, James turns from peace to warfare (4:1-12). Strife is caused by unruly passions and uncontrolled desires; even prayer can be wrongly motivated (4:1-3). In short, the "wisdom" which is of man gives rise to wars, ambitious rivalry, cut-throat competition, and injustices of all kinds. This is so

because man is basically selfish and self-seeking. He needs
to open his heart to God in prayer, and submit his desires
to God's purifying word.

Gospel Mk 9:30-37.

Mark 9:30-32 presents Jesus' second prediction of his
suffering death and resurrection (cf. 8:31-32; 10:33-34). On
the fateful journey to Jerusalem, Jesus "was teaching" his
disciples; Mark thus stresses both the importance of the
lesson and the difficulty which the hearers experienced
in grasping it. The disciples are warned of the fate that
awaits their Master in the city. It is a revelation granted to
them alone, but they do not understand and are afraid.
"The Son of man will be delivered into the hands of men":
this is likely to be close to the form of the original passion-
saying which underlines the developed versions of the
three passion-predictions. In Aramaic it would run something like: "God will (soon) deliver up the son of man to the
sons of men." The disciples' thoughts are still the thoughts
of men (cf. 8:33) and they cannot understand this teaching
which is a revelation of God.

In vv.33-34 their lack of understanding appears at its
most blatant. They, disciples of a Master so soon to suffer
bitter humiliation and death are all too humanly involved
in petty squabbling over precedence. The caressing of the
child—"taking him in his arms," proper to Mark, a vivid
touch in his style—is a symbolic gesture in the manner of
the prophets. "Receives" (= "welcomes"): the loving
service of the weaker members of the community, those
who stand in greatest need of being served. A Christian
is one baptized "into the name of" Jesus (Mt 28:19; 1 Cor
1:13,15), so becoming his. That is why one meets (serves)
Christ himself in the disciple, and the Father in Christ.
This, then, is the dignity of christian service. Mark has
made the point that the revelation of Jesus cannot be
received by one who is not ready to enter into the spirit of
discipleship and thereby become "last" and "servant."

Perhaps the reader of today is once again attuned to the unambiguous message of this word of Jesus: greatness in his church is found in *diakonia*, service, and only there. Our first step is to have relearned this. It is high time for us to act accordingly, at all times, and at all levels.

Patristic Commentary

St. Maximus of Turin (+408-420)
h.54, CCL 23.218.

The Pasch in Hebrew means "passage" or "departure," doubtless because through this mystery there is a passage from evil to good. It is a good passage to pass from sin to justice, from vice to virtue, from infancy to old age. I refer to infancy of simplicity, not of years. For virtue too has its ages. By our previous falls we were established in the seniority of sin, but by Christ's resurrection we were renewed in the innocence of little children. For Christian simplicity also has its infancy; just as an infant does not know how to be angry, or cheat, or does not dare to strike back, so also among Christians infancy is not perturbed by those who do us injuries, or does not offer resistance to or does not fight against those who kill. In a word, as the Lord has ordered, it even prays for its enemy, lets go its shirt to those who would take its coat, offers the other cheek to one slapping it on the face, except that in this Christ's infancy is better than normal infancy: the latter does not know how to sin, the former rises above it, the latter is harmless through weakness, the former is innocent through virtue. And so he is more praiseworthy in being not so much incapable of committing sin as unwilling to commit it.

But the Lord said to the apostles already well on in years: *Unless you become like this little child you will not enter into the Kingdom of Heaven* (Mt 18:3). He recalls them then to the source of their beginning, so that of course, though old and fragile in body, they might be reborn in innocence of character, as the Savior says: *unless a man be born again of water and the spirit he cannot enter the Kingdom of God* (John 3,5). Therefore, the apostleş are told, *unless you return and become like this little child.* He does not say "like these little children" but "like this little child," he selects and proposes just one.

Let us see, then, who is so great as to be proposed for imitation to the disciples. I do not think this is an ordinary individual, a man in the street, one of the multitude, especially as he is proposed as an example of sanctity to the whole world through the apostles. As I say, I do not think he is from the street, but from heaven. For he is the boy from Heaven of whom Isaiah, the prophet, spoke: *For a child is born to us, a son is given us* (Isa 9,5). Assuredly he like an innocent boy did not curse back when he was cursed, did not strike back when he was struck, nay rather during his very passion he prayed for his enemies saying: *Father, forgive them, for they know not what they do* (Luke 23,34). So, the simplicity, which is nature's gift to the young, was crowned with goodness by the Lord of mercy. Therefore, he is the boy who is to be imitated and followed.

Insights from the Documents of the Church

War and the Arms Race

Undoubtedly, armaments are not amassed merely for use in wartime. Since the defensive strength of any nation is thought to depend on its capacity for immediate retaliation, the stockpiling of arms which grows from year to year serves, in a way hitherto unthought of, as a deterrent to potential attackers. Many people look upon this as the most effective way known at the present time for maintaining some sort of peace among nations.

Whatever one may think of this form of deterrent, people are convinced that the arms race, which quite a few countries have entered, is no infallible way of maintaining real peace and that the resulting so-called balance of power is no sure and genuine path to achieving it. Rather than eliminate the causes of war, the arms race serves only to aggravate the position. As long as extravagant sums of money are poured into the development of new weapons, it is impossible to devote adequate aid in tackling the misery which prevails at the present day in the world. Instead of eradicating international conflict once and for all, the contagion is spreading to other parts of the world. New approaches, based on reformed attitudes, will have to be chosen in order to remove this stumbling block, to free the earth from its pressing anxieties, and give back to the world a genuine peace.

Therefore, we declare once again: the arms race is one of the greatest curses on the human race and the harm it inflicts on the poor is more than can be endured. And there is every reason to fear that if it continues it will bring forth those lethal disasters which are already in preparation. Warned by the possibility of the catastrophes that man has created, let us profit by the respite we now enjoy, thanks to the divine favor, to take stock of our responsibilities and find ways of resolving controversies in a manner worthy of human beings. Providence urgently demands of us that we free ourselves from the age-old slavery of war. If we refuse to make this effort, there is no knowing where we will be led on the fatal path we have taken.

It is our clear duty to spare no effort in order to work for the moment when all war will be completely outlawed by international agreement. This goal, of course, requires the establishment of a universally acknowledged public authority vested with the effective power to ensure security for all, regard for justice, and respect for law. But before this desirable authority can be constituted, it is necessary for existing international bodies to devote themselves resolutely to the exploration of better means for obtaining common security. But since peace must be born of mutual trust between peoples instead of being forced on nations through dread of arms, all must work to put an end to the arms race and make a real beginning of disarmament, not unilaterally indeed but at an equal rate on all sides, on the basis of agreements and backed up by genuine and effective guarantees. (Vat. II, The Church in the Modern World, 81, 82)

TWENTY-SIXTH SUNDAY OF THE YEAR

Scriptural Commentary

First Reading Num 11:25-29.

This passage tells of the institution of seventy elders who were to assist Moses in ruling the people of Israel (cf. 11:14). They were endowed with the spirit of leadership, a participation in Moses' charism of leadership, and with the spirit of prophecy, that they might speak on behalf of the Lord. Though Eldad and Medad were not in the group thus commissioned they, too, were inspired by God to exercise leadership and to speak on his behalf. Joshua objects to these "interlopers." This leads Moses to underline what is the main point of the reading: God's choice is not a personal privilege to be jealousy guarded. It is rather a call to serve his people. Would that as many as possible were engaged in that service! And Moses fervently wishes: "Would that all the Lord's people were prophets!"

Second Reading James 5:1-6.

The passage Jas 4:13 - 5:6 is a warning to the wealthy. First, boastful self-confidence is censured (4:13-17; cf. 1:10-11; 2:9). Because, in the Bible, "rich" is regularly a pejorative term; here, for James, the "rich man" is the type of the unrighteous man. He stresses two factors: (i) The ultimate worthlessness of wealth. Whatever comfort and luxury it affords is transitory; in the end it is vanity. (ii) Acquiring and retaining wealth more often than not involves acting unjustly and exploiting the weak and the innocent. And further, the rich tend to use their wealth selfishly. In view of the judgment which is the permanent background to James' letter, the wealthy had better repent before they reap the harvest of what they have sown (cf. 3:18). The warning speaks not only to wealthy individuals but to structures sustained by exploitation.

Gospel Mk 9:38-43, 45, 47-48.

As a correlative of a belief in demons, the practice of exorcism was widespread in the hellenistic period among Jews and gentiles. The apostolic church found itself faced with the problem of its attitude to non-christian exorcists who invoked the name of Jesus (cf. Acts 19:13-16). Mk 9:38-43 gives one answer. The fact of casting out demons "in the name of Jesus" shows that the exorcist recognized the power of Jesus; he is not against Jesus and his disciples even if he is not joined to them. The saying of Jesus (v.39) offers his disciples a directive: they are not to forbid one who acts so. The presumption is that one who does a good deed in the name of Jesus cannot be an enemy of his; the saying of v.40 suits the context perfectly. In a christian setting the statement means that one is a member of Jesus' church as long as one does categorically separate oneself from him. Linked by the catchword "in the name of" v.41 asserts that the smallest act of kindness shown to a disciple on the ground of his connection with Christ will not fail to have its reward. Presupposed is God's kindness which will not overlook the slightest deed of generosity. "Reward" is not something we win for ourselves; it is always a free gift of a generous God.

Jesus had come to seek out and save the lost. Now he utters a grim warning against any who would hurt those "little ones," who would shake their faith in him. Deliberately to lead others astray, to snatch from them the hope that he has given them, is seen by Jesus as the blackest sin: the very denial of his demand of love (9:42). But a man's own enemy, his stumbling-block, may lie in himself (cf. 7:20-23). Occasions of sin are to be ruthlessly cut off (43-48). With the compelling emphasis of startling metaphor and threefold repetition the Lord urges men to make the costliest sacrifices in order to avoid sin and enter into life. "Hell," is, literally, "gehenna." Gehenna was a ravine south of Jerusalem, where infants were offered in sacrifice to Moloch (Jer 7:31; 19:5-6; 39:35). It was desecrated by Josiah (2 Kgs 23:10) and was henceforth used as a dump for offal and refuse. Jeremiah warned that there the faithless ones of Israel would be destroyed by fire. As a site of ill-omen, it came to symbolize the place of future punishment. Only crass literalism could have led to the later notion of hell as a place of fiery torment.

Patristic Commentary

St. Clement of Rome (fl. c. 96)
ep. ad Corinth, cc. 45, 46, SC 167.174,
    FOTC 1.44.

Brothers, be eager and zealous for the things that pertain to salvation. You have studied the Holy Scriptures, which are true and inspired by the Holy Spirit. You know that nothing contrary to justice or truth has been written in them. You will not find that just men have been expelled by holy men. Just men were persecuted, but by wicked men. They were imprisoned, but by impious men. They were stoned by breakers of the laws; they were killed by men who had conceived a foul and wicked jealousy. Although suffering such things, they endured nobly. What shall we say, brothers? Was Daniel cast into the lions' den by men who feared God?

Or were Ananias, Azarias, and Misael shut up in the fiery furnace by men who observed the great and glorious worship of the Most High? Not at all. Who, then, were the men who did these acts? They were detestable men, filled with all wickedness, who were carried to such fury that they heaped torture on those who served God in holiness and purity of intention.

And so, brothers, we, too, must cling to suitable models. For it is written: "Cling to the saints, for they who cleave to them shall become saints." And again in another place: "With the innocent man, Thou shalt be innocent; and with the elect man, Thou shalt be elect; and with the perverse man, Thou shalt be perverse." Let us cling, then, to the innocent and the just, for they are God's elect. Why are there quarrels and ill will and dissensions and schism and fighting among you? Do we not have one God and one Christ, and one Spirit of Grace poured out upon us? And is there not one calling in Christ? Why do we wrench and tear apart the members of Christ, and revolt against our own body, and reach such folly as to forget that we are members one of another? Remember the words of the Lord Jesus: For He said: "Woe to that man! It were better for him if he had not been born, rather than scandalize one of My elect. It were better for him that a millstone were tied to him, and that he be cast into the sea, than that he should pervert one of My chosen ones."

Insights from the Documents of the Church

An answer for the Rich

All this is happening *against the background of the gigantic remorse* caused by the fact that, side by side with wealthy and surfeited people and societies, living in plenty and ruled by consumerism and pleasure, the same human family contains individuals and groups *that are suffering from hunger.* There are babies dying of hunger under their mothers' eyes. In various parts of the world, in various socio-economic systems, there exist entire areas of poverty, shortage and underdevelopment. This fact is universally known. *The state of inequality* between individuals and between nations not only still exists; it is increasing. It still happens that side by side with those who are wealthy and living in plenty there exist those who are living in want, suffering misery and often actually dying of hunger; and their number reaches tens, even hundreds of millions. This is why moral uneasiness is destined to become even more acute. It is obvious that a fundamental defect, or rather a series of defects, indeed a defective machinery is at the root of contemporary economics and materialistic civilization, which does not allow the human family to break free from such radically unjust situations.

This picture of today's world in which there is so much evil both physical and moral, so as to make of it a world entangled in contradictions and tensions, and at the same time full of threats to human freedom, conscience and religion—this picture explains the uneasiness felt by contemporary man. This uneasiness is experienced not only by those who are disadvantaged or oppressed, but also by those who possess the privileges of wealth, progress and power. And, although there is no lack of people trying to understand the causes of this uneasiness, or trying to react against it with the temporary means offered by technology, wealth or power, still in the very depth of the human spirit *this uneasiness is stronger than all temporary means.* This uneasiness concerns—as the analyses of the Second Vatican Council rightly pointed out—the fundamental problems of all human existence. It is linked with the very sense of man's existence in the world, and is an uneasiness for the future of man and all humanity; it demands decisive solutions, which now seem to be forcing themselves upon the human race. (John Paul II, On the Mercy of God [*Dives in Misericordia*])

TWENTY-SEVENTH SUNDAY OF THE YEAR
Scriptural Commentary
First Reading Gen 2:18-24.

The Yahwist's charming, and theologically important, story of the creation of woman. God recognizes that solitude is "not good" for man; he is determined to provide "a helper fit for him." Thus, something more than solitude is involved: there is helplessness too. Cf. Sir 36:24-25—"He who acquires a wife gets his best possession, a helper fit for him and a pillar of support . . . Where there is no wife, a man will wander about and sigh." "A helper fit for him": the word *ezer*, "helper," "standby," is normally applied to God himself—as in many of the psalms. The name-giving in 19-20 expresses the dominion over the animal kingdom that is explicitly attributed to man in 1:26-28. But the fact that man and the animals are made from a common clay has not sufficed to establish any real bond between them; man's helpmate must be more intimately bound to him: she will be formed from part of him. This alone will assure the desired conformity between them (21-22). Yahweh himself, "like a father of the bride," leads the woman to the man. As she stands before his delighted gaze, the man bursts into song— the first lovesong! Her very name *ishsha* (woman) indicates her relationship to *ish* (man). This is a typical Hebrew word-play; the etymology is popular only, it is not exact.

The underlying story in v.24 is aetiological: it is told to answer a definite question: whence this attraction of man and woman, this drive of the sexes to each other; why do a man and woman now leave home and cleave to each other to become one flesh with each and in the child? The story gives the answer. Man, who has lost his rib, feels incomplete and will feel so until he gets his "rib" back, until he finds a woman. Obviously, the woman, too, yearns for the man from which she, the "rib," was taken. The Yahwist, as usual, goes beyond the ancient story and stresses the complementary nature of man and woman in relation to marriage: it is because Yahweh made them for each other from the beginning that man and woman will break all other ties and join in marriage. Centuries later a greater than the Yahwist will add his comment and bring out the full explanation of the earlier text: "So they are no longer two but one flesh. What, therefore, God has joined together let no man put asunder" (Mt 19:6). Cf. 1 Cor 6:16; Eph 5:31.

Second Reading Heb 2:9-11.

From today until the Thirty-Third Sunday inclusive, second readings are from the letter to the Hebrews. The prologue of the letter (Heb 1:1-4) announces the great themes to follow: the superiority of the new order of revelation to the old which it replaces; the divinity shared by the Son and manifested to us in him; his place in the cosmos; his role in achieving salvation for us by his passion and return to the heavenly world. The message of the letter is twofold: the meaning of the Christ-event; the consequences of that event for the believer. The author views the history of the old covenant as a futile striving to attain forgiveness of sin: law, cult and sacrifices of the Old Testament are ineffectual. This underlines the efficacy of Jesus' sacrifice: in him God has, once for all, forgiven the sin of mankind. Because Jesus effected this in his gift of himself in death, the believer can now approach God. The barrier of sin which stood between God and his people has been swept aside.

Christ is presented in Hebrews as the Perfect Priest. The various arguments serve, now from one angle now from another, to emphasize this truth. This priesthood is strictly according to definition; in its type and in itself it is superior to the levitical priesthood; it is eternal, not transferable, set up by divine oath, the fulfilment of prophecy. Christ is priest by his incarnation. Though the efficacy of his priesthood flows from his divine Sonship, he can be priest only as man. An outstanding trait of his High Priest is compassion for his brethren, a sympathy founded on his experience of human suffering. Through him, our mediator, we can advance boldly to the throne of God's mercy; we find him there interceding for us.

As priest he offers sacrifice. The blood that flows is not any more the blood of animals but the blood of Jesus. That blood is wholly efficacious: there is no longer an offering for sin. Beyond the forgiveness of sins, the new permanent covenant of God with his people is sealed in the blood of Christ. The priesthood according to the order of Melchisedek, the eternal priesthood of Christ, finds its true place in heaven. He has entered the heavenly sanctuary, as the high priest entered the holy of holies, in virtue of blood. There, "when he had offered for all time a single sacrifice for sins, he sat down at the right hand of God" (10:12).

(Heb 2:9-11). The author of Hebrews begins his work by demonstrating that Jesus, Son of God, is superior to the angels (1:5 - 2:18). In 2:5-18 he faces up to the paradox that Jesus, as brother of humankind, was for a time less than the angels. Our reading begins with his exegesis of Ps 8:4-6 (cited by him in 2:6-8). While noting that the universe, though in principle subject to the dominion of Christ, is not yet totally subjected to him, he argues that Christ's humiliation is a necessary step towards his exaltation. By entering fully into human life, by calling all men his brothers (v.11), and by experiencing the bitterness of death like them (v.9), he became the source of their salvation and sanctification. It was "by the grace of God" (v.9), that is, by God's purpose of grace and love, that Jesus suffered and died for all mankind. The same idea is implied in the phrase "it was fitting" (v.10): by God's freely ordained plan of salvation. The death of Jesus was not accidental; it was part of God's plan for him and it was through obedience and suffering that he became perfect. Jesus is the pioneer and leader of our salvation: pointing the way and leading the way along his road of obedience and suffering. Hebrew's theology sees a thorough correspondence between Saviour and saved, Son and "sons," Sanctifier and sanctified. Jesus is happy to call all men and women his brothers and sisters.

Gospel Mk 10:2-16.

New Testament teaching on divorce has come under special scrutiny in recent times and Mk 10:2-12 figures prominently in all studies of the subject. In rabbinical style, question (v.2) is matched by counter-question (v.3). Nowhere in the written Torah is the permission of divorce explicitly spelled out; rather it seems to have been a custom taken for granted, a right given only to the, husband to repudiate his wife without her having any redress (cf. Dt 24:1-4). Jesus (v.5) does not question their interpretation of the Law; but he does declare that Moses had written the "commandment" on divorce on account of man's *sklerokardia*, "hardness of heart"—his unteachableness, his failure to acknowledge God's moral demands and to obey the higher law contained in Genesis. Jesus carries his argument further (vv.6-9) by asserting that, from the beginning, God had no divorce in mind; by creating male and female God intended marriage to be for one man and one woman bound together in the indissoluble union implied by "one flesh" (Gen 1:27; 2:24). This monogamous union, moreover, was indeed indissoluble and unbreakable not only by reason of the two being one, but also because God himself brings the partners together and is the author of the marriage union: "What, therefore, God has joined together, let not man put asunder" (v.9).

An appendix (vv.10-12) to the pronouncement story is presented as an exposition which Jesus gives his disciples in private. V.11 declares that not only is divorce forbidden but also the marriage following divorce constitutes adultery because the first marriage bond has never been broken. The words "against her," referring to a man's first wife, go beyond Jewish law which did not consider that a man could commit adultery against his own wife. The statement in v.12 goes quite beyond Jewish law since a woman was not allowed to divorce her husband. Mark has expanded the teaching of Jesus so as to meet the needs of gentile Christians living under Greco-Roman law.

The passage 10:13-16 is a pronouncement story showing Jesus' attitude to children; its place here is on topical grounds, due, very likely, to the preceding teaching on marriage. Mark has delightfully brought the little scene to life: mothers anxious to present their children to the renowned Rabbi and wonderworker; the disciples officiously intervening; Jesus indignant at their rebuff to children; his taking them into his arms. The point of the narrative lies in the sayings: children, better than any other, are suited for the kingdom since the kingdom is a gift which must be received with simplicity. Jesus himself, in a true sense, is the kingdom; that is why children have a right of access to him. No one can enter upon the blessings of the kingdom who is not open and willing to receive the kingdom as a gift. It is probable that the story may have been influential in determining the early church's attitude to the practice of infant baptism.

Patristic Commentary

St. Augustine (354-430)
On Adulterous Marriage, Bk. 2.8, PL 40.475,
FOTC 27.109.

I am definitely speaking to Christians who heed faithfully the words: "A husband is head of the wife," (Eph 5:23) whereby they realize they are to be the leaders; their wives, on the other hand, followers. Therefore, the husband must avoid entering upon a path of conduct which he may fear his wife will follow in imitation. However, there are some who are not pleased at the fact that, in the matter of chastity, there is a single standard for both husband and wife. In this matter, particularly, they would rather be subject to the standard of the world than the laws of Christ, because civil law does not seem to restrict men with the same bonds of chastity as it does women. They should read the decree, passed by the Emperor Antoninus, who certainly was not a Christian. In the decree, he did not allow the husband whose conduct did not furnish an example of chastity to accuse his wife of the crime of adultery. As a result, both were condemned if the investigation proved that both were equally unchaste.

If these things are to be observed for the decorum of the earthly city, how much more chaste should be men who seek the heavenly fatherland and the company of the angels. Since this is the case, is this proud and licentious boasting on the part of men a lesser, or rather, a greater and more debased, form of unchastity? Therefore, let not men be shocked because Christ forgave the adulteress; let them, rather, realize their own danger, and let them, struggling as they are with the same disease, flee with pious supplication to that same Saviour. Let them acknowledge that they also require what they read was accomplished in that woman; let them receive the remedy of their own adulteries; let them now cease to commit adultery; let them praise the forbearance of God shown to them; let them perform works of penance, receive pardon, and finally, let them alter their opinion of the punishment of women and their own impunity.

Insights from the Documents of the Church

First Reading and Gospel: Christian Marriage

Through the work of the Holy Spirit, you have become a unity of two. The power that unites you is love. This human love of yours, which matured in your hearts and decisions, was manifested before the altar, when, to the words of the priest who called upon you to express your generous and definitive consent, you replied with your mutual "I will," and you gave each other the blessed ring, the symbol of your perennial fidelity in love.

Love is formed in the human person, embraces body and soul, matures in the heart and in the will; to be "human," love must comprise the person in his physical, psychical and spiritual totality.

Simultaneously "God's love has been poured into our hearts through the Holy Spirit who has been given to us" (Rom 5:5).

The reciprocal compenetration of divine love and human love lasts from the day of your marriage. Divine love, in fact, penetrates into human love, giving it a new dimension: it makes it deep, pure and generous; it develops it towards fullness, ennobles it, spiritualizes it, makes it ready even for sacrifices and self-denial, and at the same time enables it to produce peace and joy as its fruit.

By means of this love you constitute unity in God: the *communio personarum*. You constitute the unity of the two gathered in his name and he is in your midst (cf. Mt 18:20).

This unity in Christ spontaneously seeks, in a way, expression in prayer. Love, in fact, is a gift and it is a commandment: it is a gift from God, because he first loved us (cf. 1 Jn 4:10) and it is also the fundamental commandment of all moral orientation. As I said in the Homily at the Mass for Families, on 12 October of last year: "To carry out the commandment of love means accomplishing all the duties of the Christian family: fidelity and conjugal virtue, responsible parenthood and education. The "little Church"—the domestic Church—means the family living in the spirit of the commandment of love; its interior truth, its daily toil, its spiritual beauty and its power." But to live this poem of love and unity in this way you absolutely need to pray. In this sense prayer becomes really essential for love and unity: in fact, prayer strengthens, relieves, purifies, exalts, helps to find light and advice, deepens the respect that spouses in particular must mutually nourish for their hearts, their conscience and their bodies, by means of which they are so close to each other. The Second Vatican Council aptly writes in this connection: "Outstanding courage is required for the constant fulfilment of the duties of this Christian calling: spouses, therefore, will need grace for leading a holy life: they will eagerly practice a love that is firm, generous, and prompt to sacrifice, and will ask for it in their prayers" (*Gaudium et Spes*, n.49).

My wish for you today is that the Emmaus event may constantly be repeated in your lives: that you may know Christ in the breaking of bread and that you may always find him present in your midst, in your hearts, after this "breaking of bread"!

And I commend you all, every couple, to Christ, who wants to accompany you along your way, just as he accompanied the disciples along the way to Emmaus. I entrust you all to Christ, who knows human hearts! (John Paul II, Address to World Congress on 'The Family and Love.' Rome, 3 May 1981)

TWENTY-EIGHTH SUNDAY OF THE YEAR

Scriptural Commentary

First Reading Wis 7:7-11.

The long passage 7:1 - 8:21, presented as a speech of Solomon, is a hymn of praise of wisdom. The inspiration of the poem is the prayer which Solomon made when he began his reign (cf. 1 Kgs 3:6-9; 2 Chr 1:8-10). He had asked for wisdom: "Give thy servant an understanding mind to govern thy people, that I may discern between good and evil" (1 Kg 3:9). The wisdom Solomon prayed for and was granted in abundance is a vision of the way things really are. It is gained not by intense intellectual exercise but is total dedication to God. It is a revelation of God's goodness, present in the act of creation and manifest in the world of men and women. And it engenders in the "wise" man an attitude of mind and heart that enables him to feel at home with divine and created reality. Since the fear of the Lord was regarded as the beginning of wisdom (cf. Prov 1:7), true wisdom was impossible without right relationship with God and without submission to his will.

Second Reading Heb 4:12-13.

The author of Hebrews frequently refers to the word of God, a word which covers the whole range of God's activities in relation to mankind. It is God's word which creates, reveals, makes demands, strengthens and saves. Ultimately, it was spoken, perfectly and completely, for man's benefit, in the person of God's Son, Jesus Christ (1:1-3). And it continues to be spoken in our day. Our reading makes use of a cluster of images and metaphors to describe the vital force of that word of God. This word is "living and active": *living* in the sense that through the power of the Spirit it gives life and leads to eternal life; *active* in that it inspires those who hear it to live christian lives. The word is "sharp" and "piercing" in that it penetrates to man's intimate being. The word discerns "the thoughts and intentions of the heart": it tests one's moral worth because it evaluates one's dispositions. The qualities of the word of God are such that there is no escape from its authority, no hope of shirking one's responsibility towards it. The *logos* is boldly personified, and though the context is against the view of its being identified with the personal Logos, yet the word of God's revelation is so authoritative as to be ultimately interchangeable (v.13) with the God who speaks it. He is the one "with whom we have to do" in the long run. We ought, here and now, if we are wise, regulate our lives according to his word so that we may stand with confidence before his throne of grace (4:16).

Gospel Mk 10:17-30.

This is the saddest story in the gospel, this story (10:17-22) of the refusal of one whom Jesus loved to answer his call. Entry into the kingdom is the matter and issue as Jesus is asked what one must do to inherit eternal life. He begins to answer the question by pointing to the duties towards one's neighbour prescribed in the decalogue; but he knows that observance of the law is not the whole answer. He was drawn to the man and invited him to become his disciple. But this aspiring disciple has to learn that discipleship is costly: he, a wealthy man, is asked to surrender the former basis of his security and find his security in Jesus' word. He cannot see that following Jesus is the true treasure, the one pearl of great price (Mt 13:44,46) beyond all his great possessions. He cannot face the stern challenge of loving in deed and in truth by opening his heart to his brother in need (cf. 1 Jn 3:17-18).

The rich man's sad departure (v.22) was dramatic witness that riches could come between a man and the following of Jesus; the words of Jesus (23-27) drive the message home. Jesus begins by stressing the difficulty of access to the kingdom for the wealthy (v.23) and passes quickly to the difficulty of entering the kingdom at all (v.24). The vivid example of the impossible (v.25)—contrast of the largest beast of burden known in Palestine with the smallest of domestic apertures—applied as it is to the rich, would come more logically before v.24. The point is that salvation is ever God's achievement, not man's (v.27). It is the only answer, the confident answer, to the helpless question, "Then who can be saved?"

Patristic Commentary

St. Augustine (354-430)
Confessions, 13.19, CSEL 33.1, 363,
    FOTC 21.429.

That rich man asked the Good Teacher what he should do to gain eternal life. The Good Teacher, whom he thought a man and nothing more—but He is good because He is God—let our Good Teacher say to him that, if he wishes to enter into life, he should keep the commandments; that he should remove from himself the bitterness of malice and wickedness; that he should not kill, or commit adultery, or steal, or bear false witness, in order that dry land may appear and bring forth the honour of mother and father and the love of our neighbour. "I have done all these things," he says. Whence, then, so many thorns, if the earth is fruitful? Go, root out the bushy thickets of avarice, "sell what thou hast" and grow rich in fruits by giving to the poor and thou shalt have treasure in heaven, and follow the Lord, if thou dost wish to be perfect, as a companion of them amongst whom He speaks of wisdom, He who knows what to assign to the day and to the night—do so that thou mayest also know it, and that, for thee, too, lights may be made in the firmament of heaven. And this will not be done, unless thy heart be there. This, again, will not be done, unless thy treasure be there, just as thou hast heard from the Good Teacher. But, the barren earth was grieved, and the thorns choked out the Word. (Mt 13:7).

But, you, "a chosen race," the weak things of the world, who have left all to follow the Lord, go, follow after Him and confound the strong; go, follow after Him: your feet are beautiful, and shine in the firmament, that the heavens may show forth His glory, distinguishing between the light of the perfect who are not yet like the angels and the darknesses of the little ones who are not desperate. Shine over every part of the earth, and let the day, lighted by the sun, give forth to the day the word of wisdom, and the night, lighted by the moon, announce to the night the word of knowledge. The moon and stars shine for the night, but the night does not obscure them, for they illuminate it according to its measure. For behold, as if God were saying: "Let there be lights made in the firmament of heaven," "suddenly there came a sound from heaven, as a violent wind coming, and there appeared parted tongues as of fire, which settled upon each of them," and lights were made in the firmament of heaven, "holding fast the word of life." Run in every direction, O holy fires, O beautiful fires! For, "you are the light of the world," nor are you "under the bushel" (Mt 5:15). He, to whom you have held fast, has been exalted and He has exalted you. Run, and make it known to all nations.

Insights from the Documents of the Church

The Church loves the sacred scriptures and wishes to acquire a deeper understanding of truth and to provide nourishment for its own life by studying them. The Second Vatican Council spoke of the bible as a source of renewal for God's people and directed that "more abundant, more varied and appropriate reading from the sacred scripture" be provided in the renewed liturgy. The council directed, further, that "the treasures of the bible be opened up more lavishly so that a richer fare may be provided for the faithful at the table of the Lord's word. In this way a more representative part of the sacred scriptures will be read to the people in the course of a prescribed number of years." (Const. on the Liturgy, 51)

It is clear why the council made such provisions. Through the reading of sacred scripture during the liturgy of the word and its explanation in the homily. "God speaks to his people, reveals to them the mysteries of redemption and salvation, and provides them with spiritual nourishment: and Christ himself, in the form of his word, is present in the midst of the faithful" (General Instruction on the Roman Missal, 33). Thus the Church at Mass "partakes of the bread of life and offers it to the faithful from the one table of the Word of God and the Body of the Lord." (Divine Revelation, 21) Introduction to the Lectionary.

Sell what you have

The Church bears in mind too the apostle's admonition when calling the faithful to charity and exhorting them to have the same mind which Christ Jesus showed, who "emptied himself, taking the form of a servant . . . and became obedient unto death" (Phil 2:7-8) and for our sakes "became poor, though he was rich" (2 Cor 8:9). Since the disciples must always imitate this love and humility of Christ and bear witness of it, Mother Church rejoices that she has within herself many men and women who pursue more closely the Saviour's self-emptying and show it forth more clearly, by undertaking poverty with the freedom of God's sons, and renouncing their own will: they subject themselves to man for the love of God, thus going beyond what is of precept in the matter of perfection, so as to conform themselves more fully to the obedient Christ.

Therefore all the faithful are invited and obliged to holiness and the perfection of their own state of life. Accordingly let all of them see that they direct their affections rightly, lest they be hindered in their pursuit of perfect love by the use of worldly things and by an adherence to riches which is contrary to the spirit of evangelical poverty, following the apostle's advice: Let those who use this world not fix their abode in it, for the form of this world is passing away (cf. 1 Cor 7:31, Greek text). (Vat. II, Constitution on the Church, 42)

TWENTY-NINTH SUNDAY OF THE YEAR

Scriptural Commentary

First Reading Is 53:10-11.

This reading is a short excerpt from the fourth Servant Song (52:13 - 53:12). Already, the Servant has been described as one "smitten by God, afflicted" (53:4). But his sufferings are vicarious: "bruised for our iniquities" (v.5), with "the iniquity of us all" laid upon him (v.6). Our reading stresses, again, that it was "the will of the Lord to bruise him" (v.10)—and then draws an unexpected and startling conclusion from his death. Offered as a sacrifice of atonement for the sins of others, it is a veritable triumph of failure. The Servant carries out his mission for mankind in and through his sufferings and death. And death marks the beginning of glorification for him. For others it will be the source of many blessings; it will be their "justification" (v.11). By reflection on this and similar passages, the early Christians came to an understanding of the saving achievement of the suffering and death of Jesus. (See Good Friday).

Second Reading Heb 4:14-16.

Jesus the high priest who has entered the heavenly sanctuary (6:20; 7:26; 8:1; 9:11) offers solid motivation indeed for holding fast to the faith we profess. Our high priest has already passed through all the heavens to penetrate into the highest of them where God dwells. The high priest is named: Jesus, the true Son of God. The religion which has such a priest, the very Son of God, is such a sanctuary, is a religion to which we must cling despite all difficulties. But may not this surprising greatness of the high priest imply an aloofness towards human misery? Not so: our high priest can sympathize with us in all our trials and sufferings. Jesus had suffered trials as we do, and throughout his life. "Without sinning" indeed—but this fact does not make him less our brother.

Having such a high priest, Christians can advance with full confidence to present themselves before God. The "throne of grace" is the throne of God's mercy. It is precisely because it is accessible to sinners that it is throne of grace; access is through the priesthood of Christ, the link between God and mankind. Christians who approach the throne encounter the loving mercy of God who bestows on them his favour (*charis*). The sympathy of Jesus is "seasonable," "opportune"; it is expressed in practical aid to those who are tempted, accommodated to their situation and suitable above all because timely. Our high priest has entered heaven but he is united to us still by his understanding of our trials and difficulties. The distance between us, abolished by the incarnation, has not been broadened again by the ascension, he is always ready and able to help us because he is always our compassionate high priest. (See Good Friday).

Gospel Mk 10:35-45.

In 10:33-34 we have the third and most detailed prediction of the passion in this gospel. Sadly, the stark words fall on ears deafened by selfish ambition. Jesus asks of one who would follow him a readiness to face and share his sufferings. The power of the risen Lord will in due course break through the present self-seeking of James and John and give backbone to their facile enthusiasm; they will indeed manfully walk in the way of their Master. As it is, their request for the first places in the kingdom is one which Jesus not only will not but cannot grant: these are at the disposition of the Father who is no respecter of persons. Lack of understanding persists in the resentment of the other disciples who feel that the brothers have tried to "pull a quick one" on them. This leads to Jesus' earnest repetition (cf. 9:35) of his teaching on true greatness. He had come as the servant of all, as one who would lay down his life to rescue mankind from the oppression and slavery of sin. Authority in his church must wear the unmistakable livery of *diakonia*, service. Any suggestion of dominance, any vestige of oppression, must stand as a denial of him and of all he represents.

The ground of the paradoxical behaviour required of disciples is to be found in the example of the Son of Man himself (v.45). That saying specifies in what sense Jesus is to "serve" men: he will give his life as a ransom for them. *Lytron* ("ransom") was originally a commercial term: the ransom is the price that must be paid to redeem a pledge, to recover a pawned object, or to free a slave. In the Septuagint the term is predicated metaphorically of God who is frequently said to have bought, acquired, purchased, ransomed his people (e.g. Ps 49:8; Is 63:4). In its Marcan form the saying is related to Is 53:10-11 and "ransom" is to be understood in the sense of the Hebrew word *asham* of Is 53:10, "an offering for sin," an atonement offering. By laying down his life for a mankind enslaved to sin. Jesus fulfils the saying about the Servant in Is 53:10-11. Jesus has paid the universal debt: he has given his life to redeem all others. But this is metaphor, not crude commerce. The death of Jesus, in the Father's purpose and in the Son's acceptance, is a gesture of sheer love. Any suggestion that the death of the Son is, in any sense at all, the literal payment of a debt, the placating of an offended God, is blasphemy. God is ever motivated by *love*, not "justice."

Patristic Commentary

St. Irenaeus (c.130-200)
Frag. 55, ANF 1.577.

"Then drew near unto Him the mother of Zebedee's children, with her sons, worshipping, and seeking a certain thing from Him." (Mt 20:20). These people are certainly not void of understanding, nor are the words set forth in that passage of no signification: being stated beforehand like a preface, they have some agreement with those points formerly expounded.

"Then drew near." Sometimes virtue excites our admiration, not merely on account of the display which is given of it, but also of the occasion when it was manifested.

Now, with regard to that mother of Zebedee's children, do not admire merely what she said, but also the time at which she uttered these words. For when was it that she drew near to the Redeemer? Not after the resurrection, nor after the preaching of His name, nor after the establishment of His kingdom; but it was when the Lord said, "Behold, we go up to Jerusalem, and the Son of man shall be delivered to the chief priests and the scribes; and they shall kill Him, and on the third day He shall rise again."

These things the Saviour told in reference to His sufferings and cross; to those persons He predicted His passion. Nor did He conceal the fact that it should be of a most ignominious kind, at the hands of the chief priests. This woman, however, had attached another meaning to the dispensation of His sufferings. The Saviour was foretelling death; and she asked for the glory of immortality. The Lord was asserting that He must stand arraigned before impious judges; but she, taking no note of that judgment, requested as of the judge: "Grant," she said, "that these my two sons may sit, one on the right hand, and the other on the left, in Thy glory." In the one case the passion is referred to, in the other the kingdom is understood. The Saviour was speaking of the cross, while he had in view the glory which admits no suffering. This woman, therefore, as I have already said, is worthy of our admiration, not merely for what she sought, but also for the occasion of her making the request.

She did indeed suffer, not merely as a pious person, but also as a woman. For, having been instructed by His words, she considered and believed that it would come to pass, that the kingdom of Christ should flourish in glory, and walk in its vastness throughout the world, and be increased by the preaching of piety. She understood that He who appeared in a lowly guise had delivered and received every promise. I will inquire upon another occasion, when I come to treat upon this humility, whether the Lord rejected her petition concerning His kingdom. But she thought that the same confidence would not be possessed by her, when, at the appearance of the angels. He should be ministered to by the angels, and receive service from the entire heavenly host. Taking the Saviour, therefore, apart in a retired place, she earnestly desired of Him those things which transcend every human nature.

Insights from the Documents of the Church

Poverty, obedience, service

The mission of the Church is carried out by means of that activity through which, in obedience to Christ's command and moved by the grace and love of the Holy Spirit, the Church makes itself fully present to all men and peoples in order to lead them to the faith, freedom and peace of Christ by the example of its life and teaching, by the sacraments and other means of grace. Its aim is to open up for all men a free and sure path to full participation in the mystery of Christ.

Since this mission continues and, in the course of history, unfolds the mission of Christ, who was sent to evangelize the poor, then the Church, urged on by the Spirit of Christ, must walk the road Christ himself walked, a way of poverty and obedience, of service and self-sacrifice even to death, a death from which he emerged victorious by his resurrection. So it was that the apostles walked in hope and by much trouble and suffering filled up what was lacking in the sufferings of Christ for his body, which is the Church. Often, too, the seed was the blood of Christians. (Vat. II, Decree on the Church's Missionary Activity, 6)

Holiness, mutual support and suffering

Christian married couples and parents, following their own way, should support one another in grace all through life with faithful love, and should train their children (lovingly received from God) in Christian doctrine and evangelical virtues. Because in this way they present to all an example of unfailing and generous love, they build up the brotherhood of charity, and they stand as witnesses and co-operators of the fruitfulness of mother Church, as a sign of, and a share in that love with which Christ loved his bride and gave himself for her. In a different way, a similar example is given by widows and single people, who can also greatly contribute to the holiness and activity of the

Church. And those who engage in human work, often of a heavy kind, should perfect themselves through it, help their fellow-citizens, and promote the betterment of the whole of human society and the whole of creation; indeed, with their active charity, rejoicing in hope and bearing one another's burdens, they should imitate Christ who plied his hands with carpenter's tools and is always working with the Father for the salvation of all; and they should rise to a higher sanctity, truly apostolic, by their everyday work itself.

In a special way also, those who are weighed down by poverty, infirmity, sickness and other hardships should realize that they are united to Christ, who suffers for the salvation of the world; let those feel the same who suffer persecution for the sake of justice, those whom the Lord declared blessed in the Gospel and whom "the God of all grace, who has called us to his eternal glory in Christ Jesus, will himself restore, establish, strengthen and settle" (1 Pet 5:10).

Accordingly, all Christians, in the conditions, duties and circumstances of their life and through all these, will sanctify themselves more and more if they receive all things with faith from the hand of the heavenly Father and cooperate with the divine will, thus showing forth in that temporal service the love with which God has loved the world. (Vat. II, Constitution on the Church, 41)

THIRTIETH SUNDAY OF THE YEAR

Spiritual Commentary

First Reading Jer 31:7-9.

It was Jeremiah's conviction that faithless Jerusalem would fall, a conviction voiced (as elsewhere) in his letter to those exiled to Babylon in 598 (29:16-20). Yet, in the same context, he can frame a promise: "For I know the plans I have for you, says the Lord, plans for welfare and not for evil, to give you a future and a hope" (29:11). This hope is held out not to those left behind in Jerusalem but to the exiles—a point more forcefully expressed in the vision of two baskets of figs (24:5-7). There is, then, the remarkable feature that the same Jeremiah who so pitilessly demolished false hope yet put before his people a positive hope for the future. His efforts to bring his people to their senses had failed, but it is the greatness of the man and the grandeur of his faith, that precisely during the most tragic moment of his life he spoke his optimistic oracles, notably those of chapters 30-33, "The Book of Consolation."

This collection includes earlier oracles of Jeremiah originally addressed to northern Israel (which had been devastated by the Assyrians in 721). Our passage (31:7-9) appears to be an adaptation of such an earlier oracle of Jeremiah to the situation of the exiles in Babylon. It is certainly reminiscent of Second Isaiah and may have been influenced by the Isaian tradition. At any rate, it carries a message of hopeful joy. It first presents God as a good shepherd gathering together his scattered flock; and ends with Yahweh as "a father to Israel" who will not allow his "first-born" to be totally destroyed. The "remnant," purified by frustration and suffering, will constitute the new people of God; and all this by God's gracious mercy and not through any merit of their own. Even the most helpless of the people, the blind, the lame, and women with child, will share in the joyful event of salvation. Such a great redemption will be a matter for the world to know about (v.7).

Second Reading Heb 5:1-6.

In the passage 5:1-10 the author of Hebrews sets out to show that Christ has perfectly met the requirements of priesthood—he argues in terms of the levitical high priesthood. In v.1 he states that a high priest is a man officially instituted as a mediator between God and mankind, who defends the cause of men before God, and offers the gifts of men to God, especially sacrifice for sin. Then, in v.2, he demands that the priest must be compassionate. Such a requirement is nowhere demanded of priests in general: the author is thinking of Christ. Hence he can specify that the priest be indulgent towards the ignorant and erring who sin because they are human; all the more because he, too, as human, is "beset with weakness." The reference in v.3 is to the obligation of the high priest on the Day of Atonement to offer sacrifices for his own sins, for those of the priests, and only then for the sins of the people (Lev 16:16-17). A presupposition of priesthood is divine vocation (v.4). That a high priest must have this call is proved by the history of Aaron and his sons who were chosen and designated by Yahweh (Ex 28:1; 29:5,10-15). Therefore, a true high priest must: a) show great benevolence and indulgence to sinners; b) be chosen and called by God.

In proving that Christ possesses these qualities the author proceeds in inverse order, dealing first with his vocation (5-6) and then with his fellowship in human suffering (7-10). For the author, Ps 2:7 gives the ground of the priesthood of Christ and Ps 110:4 the explicit and solemn declaration of his priesthood (5-6). The priesthood of Christ flows not from his passion alone but from his passion crowned by his exaltation. (Curiously, our reading stops at v.6—the reader should certainly go on to v.10). Our Saviour, confronted with imminent suffering and death, prayed to his Father "who was able to save him from death," but according to Jn 12:27-28,32; 17:5; Acts 2:25-31, this deliverance from death went beyond deliverance from tasting death to deliverance from the grip of death, through resurrection and glorification. "Being made perfect" recalls the cry of Jesus: "It is fulfilled" (Jn 19:30): by his passion and death Jesus was perfected in his priestly office. So perfected, he has become to all who believe in him the author or cause of salvation (v.9). Christ, then, has the qualities of high priest. The most decisive proof is the declaration of his Father. He has designated his Son as high priest according to the order of Melchizedek—that is, an eternal high priest (v.10). (See Fifth Sunday of Lent).

Gospel Mk 10:46-52.

This narrative focuses on the blind man, who is thereby presented as a model of faith in Jesus in spite of discouragement and as one who eagerly answers the call of the Master and follows him in the way of discipleship. For Mark the story sounds a new departure in the self-manifestation of Jesus. He finds himself acclaimed, repeatedly, as "Son of David," a messianic title. Far from imposing silence, as hitherto, he calls the man to his presence and openly restores his sight. The way is being prepared for the manifestation of the humble Messiah (11:1-10). The days are near for him to be delivered up and he set his face to go to Jerusalem (10:32). God's purpose is already working itself out. Very soon the true nature of his messiahship will be clearly seen.

In v.51 Jesus challenges the man to make his request. His question is the same as that to James and John (v.36) [See previous Sunday]. The simple and humble request of Bartimaeus is so different from their selfish demands; he understands so much better than they the authority of Jesus who does not dominate but has come to serve (vv.42-45). Unlike them (v.39) he is aware of his need and of his helplessness and finds his only hope in Jesus' nearness. And Jesus responds to his need: "your faith has made you well." "Faith" is confident trust in God and in the healing power of Jesus (cf. 5:34). "Made you well," literally "saved you" has the same overtones of salvation as in 5:28,34. "Followed him on the way" could mean that the man joined the crowd on the way to Jerusalem. There can be no doubt that Mark means: he followed Jesus on the way of christian discipleship. The phrase "on the way" and the following of Jesus form an inclusion with v.32. Only one of faith, enlightened by Jesus, can walk his way without consternation and without fear.

Patristic Commentary

St. Jerome (c.347-c.420)
Homily on St. Mark 8.22-26, PLS 2.147,
   FOTC 57.155.

"They brought to him a blind man." This is the blind man who was sitting by the wayside in Jericho; not in the road, but by the wayside; not in the true law, but in the law of the letter. They entreat the Lord to touch the man. When the man in Jericho heard Jesus passing by, he began to cry out and say: "Son of David, have mercy on me," and those who were passing by tried to silence him. But Jesus does not rebuke him, for He has not come except to the lost sheep of the house of Israel. (Mt 15:24) Jesus commanded that he should be brought to Him. He hearing that Jesus was calling for him: "sprang to his feet, and throwing off his cloak ran to him." (Mk 10:50) He could not go to Him in his garments. Why did he throw off his cloak and run without it to Jesus? He could not go in his old clothes: naked he ran to the Lord. He was blind; his garments were soiled and tattered; so he ran like a blind man, and he was healed. Now, just as there was in Jericho this blind man on the wayside who was healed, a blind man is healed also, in Bethsaida. (Mk 8:22-26).

"Entreated him to touch him." The disciples entreated the Lord Savior to touch him; because of his blindness, he did not know the way; he could not walk up to Christ to touch Him. The apostles entreat Jesus and say: Touch him, and he will be healed. Why, I ask, should He go to Bethsaida and why should a blind man be brought before Him? He does not cure him in the village, but outside, for he cannot be healed of his blindness in the Law, but in the Gospel. If this very day, Jesus should enter Bethsaida, the synagogue of the Jews, if Jesus—I mean the Divine Word—should go into the synagogue of the Jews, into the council of the Jews, as long as that blind man is in the synagogue, in the letter of the law, he cannot be healed unless he is led outside . . .

"Then again he laid his hands upon the man's eyes, and he began to see." Note: He laid His hand upon his eyes and the man began to see. If it were merely a matter of human power, surely, even if he had sight, he could not see if hands were covering up his eyes, but the hand of the Lord is clearer than all eyes. He laid His hands upon his eyes, and he began to see: "and was restored so that he saw all things plainly," all things—I repeat—that we see; so that he discerned the mystery of the Trinity and perceived all the secret mysteries that are in the Gospel. "So that he saw plainly." Unless there were some who could see, but not clearly, Scripture would never say: "so that he saw plainly." Now, what he saw clearly, we all, likewise, see, for we believe in Christ who is the true Light.

Insights from the Documents of the Church

Christ's word cures our blindness

Christ is the light of humanity; and it is, accordingly, the heart-felt desire of this sacred Council, being gathered together in the Holy Spirit, that, by proclaiming his Gospel to every creature (cf. Mk 16:15), it may bring to all men that light of Christ which shines out visibly from the Church. Since the Church, in Christ, is in the nature of sacrament—a sign and instrument, that is, of communion with God and of unity among all men—she here purposes, for the benefit of the faithful and of the whole world, to set forth, as clearly as possible, and in the tradition laid down by earlier Councils, her own nature and universal mission.

The condition of the modern world lends greater urgency to this duty of the Church; for, while men of the present day are drawn ever more closely together by social, technical and cultural bonds, it still remains for them to achieve full unity in Christ.

The eternal Father, in accordance with the utterly gratuitous and mysterious design of his wisdom and goodness, created the whole universe, and chose to raise up men to share in his own divine life; and when they had fallen in Adam, he did not abandon them, but at all times held out to them the means of salvation, bestowed in consideration of Christ, the Redeemer, "who is the image of the invisible God, the firstborn of every creature" and predestined before time began "to become conformed to the image of his Son, that he should be the firstborn among many brethren" (Rom 8:29). He determined to call together in a holy Church those who should believe in Christ. Already present in figure at the beginning of the world, this Church was prepared in marvellous fashion in the history of the people of Israel and in the old Alliance. Established in this last age of the world, and made manifest in the outpouring of the Spirit, it will be brought to glorious completion at the end of time. At that moment, as the Fathers put it, all the just from the time of Adam, "from Abel, the just one, to the last of the elect" will be gathered together with the Father in the universal Church. (Vat. II, Constitution on the Church, 1)

Revelation is the manifestation of the mystery of God and of his saving action in history. It takes place through a personal communication from God to man. The content of this communication constitutes the message of salvation which is to be preached to all men.

It is, consequently, the supreme and absolutely necessary function of the Church's prophetic ministry to make the content of this message intelligible to men of all times, in order that they may be converted to God through Christ, that they may interpret their whole life in the light of Faith, having considered the special conditions of events and times in which that life develops, and that they may lead a life in keeping with the dignity which the message of salvation has brought them and that Faith has revealed to them. (General Catechetical Directory, 37)

THIRTY-FIRST SUNDAY OF THE YEAR

Scriptural Commentary

First Reading Dt 6:2-6.

The section 6:1-19 of Deuteronomy 6 is a commentary on 5:1-10 (the first part of the decalogue); it reaffirms the obligation to reject all other gods. There is, however, a shift of emphasis: the love of God has become the first great imperative. The decalogue is no longer merely a law. It becomes the living words of Moses—"this day"(v.6). This blend of old and new law claims an obedience (vv.20-25) which is founded on one basic premise: "we *were* Pharaoh's slaves . . ." (v.21) A land "flowing with milk and honey" (v.3)—a Canaanite phrase. Coming from the desert, the Hebrews must have been dumbfounded by the fertility of the land of Canaan. This fact created a problem for them as is clear in the northern prophets like Hosea. And, spiritually, Deuteronomy is heir of Hosea.

"Hear" (v.4) is *shema*; the word gave its name to the Shema, the "creed" which every Israelite man (women and children were dispensed!) recited morning and evening; it opens with this passage from Deuteronomy. Verse 4 asserts that Yahweh is (the) "one Yahweh." Israel owes undivided loyalty, with her whole being, to this unique God. In Deuteronomy this is the meaning of "love of God." The context is always one of faithful adherence to God, walking in his ways, keeping or doing his commandments, heeding his voice, and serving him—it is convenantal love.

Second Reading Heb 7:23-28.

In chapter 7 the author of Hebrews intends to prove the superiority of Christ over the levitical priests. He begins by showing the excellence of the type of this priesthood of Christ, that of Melchizedek (7:1-10), and passes to direct contrast between Christ and the levitical priests. Our reading (23-28) is the conclusion of his argument. In v.23 the uniqueness and permanence of Christ's priesthood is set against the multiplicity and impermanence of priests whom death prevented from maintaining office. V.25 forms a transition: it concludes the argument of 7:20-24 and introduces the peroration of 26-28; it is an excellent definition of the priestly office of Christ. The salvation brought by him is not transitory but permanent (and therefore marked with perfection): he is a perfect Saviour and everlasting Advocate (cf. Jn 12:34; 1 Jn 2:1-2).

Christ is pious, saintly, without falsehood or malice, without vice or moral imperfection: the language suggests a contrast between the deep ethical purity of Jesus and the ritual purity of the levitical priests (v.26). V.27 is a reference to *yom kippur*. On that Day of Atonement emphasis was on sacrifices of expiation, and the high priest had to sacrifice for his own sins before sacrificing for the people—in fact he stands in need of daily sacrifice even for himself. What a contrast with the perfection of Christ who has offered his sacrifice once for all, and not for himself but for the people only. The concluding verse (28) sounds a note of triumph: the Law sets up as priests men subject to sin and mortality, but the solemn word bolstered by a divine oath (Ps 110:4) proclaimed through the mouth of David long after the Law, sets up one who is Son and whose perfection is consummated in priestly achievement and glory.

Gospel Mk 12:28-34.

In this pronouncement story, Jesus gives the answer to the question, "Which commandment is the first of all?" It was a question the rabbis sought to answer. They looked for the commandment that outweighed all others, the one that might be regarded as a basic principle on which the whole Law was grounded. Because this scribe's question is an honest question by one well-disposed (vv.32-34) Jesus answers directly. He begins by quoting the opening formula (Dt 6:4) of the *Shema*, and joins to it Lev 19:18 on the love of the Neighbour. He had been asked to name the first commandment; he responds by naming two commandments. That is because, for him, the one flows directly and necessarily from the other. Love for neighbour arises'out of love for God. He had taken and welded the two precepts into one.

In the synoptic gospels, only here and in Lk 11:42 is there word of man's love for God, and it appears sparingly in the rest of the New Testament. Usually, the emphasis is on God's love for man. And this is as it should be. It is because God has first loved us that we love God (Rom 5:5,8; 1 Jn 4:11). Indeed, love for one another is the test of the reality of our love of God (1 Jn 4:20-21). Jesus himself showed in his life and death the quality of this twofold love. His love of God motivated his total dedication to his mission: his love of humankind marked him as one who had come to serve the saving purpose of God, one who had laid down his life as a ransom for mankind (10:45).

The scribe's reply (32-33) is proper to Mark. He agrees fully with Jesus' answer and further specifies that the true love of God and the loving service of others is more important than elaborate cult. His insistence on love with the whole heart is a recognition that love cannot be measured. Love is incompatible with a legalism that sets limits, that specifies what one must do and must avoid. Jesus' assurance that this scribe is not far from the kingdom of God is, in truth, an invitation. And we sense that this time the invitation will not be in vain (cf. 10:17-23). Nowhere else in the gospels does a scribe emerge in such a favourable light.

Patristic Commentary

Clement of Alexandria (c.150-c.215)
Paidagogos, 2.5, GCS Clemens 1.157,
FOTC 23.97.

An Agape is in reality heavenly food, a banquet of the Word. The Agape, or charity, "bears all things, endures all things, hopes all things; charity never fails." (1 Cor 13:7) "Blessed is he who eats bread in the kingdom of God." (Lk 14-15) Surely, of all downfalls, the most unlikely is for charity, which faileth not, to be cast down from heaven to earth among all these dainty seasonings. Do you still imagine that I refer to a meal that is to be destroyed? "If I distribute my goods to the poor and have not charity," Scripture says, "I am nothing." (1 Cor 13:3)

On this charity depend the whole Law and the word. If you love the Lord thy God and thy neighbour, there will be a feast, a heavenly one, in heaven. The earthly feast, as we have proved from Scripture, is called a supper, one permeated with love, yet not identified with it, but an expression of mutual and generous good will.

"Let not then our good be reviled," the Apostle says, "for the kingdom of God does not consist in food and drink," meaning the daily meal, "but justice and peace and joy in the Holy Spirit." (Rom 14:17) Whoever eats of this feast is put in possession of the most wonderful of all things, the kingdom of God, and takes his place in the holy assembly of love, the heavenly Church.

Certainly, love is pure, worthy of God, and its fruit is giving. "The care of discipline is love," Wisdom says, "and love is the keeping of the laws. (Wis 6:18) Festive gatherings of themselves do contain some spark of love, for from food taken at a common table we become accustomed to the food of eternity. Assuredly, the dinner itself is not an Agape, yet let the feasting be rooted in love. "Thy children, O Lord," it is said, "whom Thou lovest, know that it is not the

growing of fruit that nourishest men, but Thy word preserves them that believe in Thee." (Wis 16:26) "For it is not
on bread that the just man will live." (Mt 4:4)

Insights from the Documents of the Church

Love of God and Neighbour

Jesus Christ and he alone also satisfied that fatherhood
of God and that love which man in a way rejected by breaking the first Covenant and the later covenants that God
"again and again offered to man." The redemption of the
world—this tremendous mystery of love in which creation is
renewed—is, at its deepest root, the fullness of justice in a
human Heart—the Heart of the First-born Son—in order
that it may become justice in the hearts of many human
beings, predestined from eternity in the First-born Son
to be children of God and called to grace, called to love. The
Cross on Calvary, through which Jesus Christ—a Man, the
Son of the Virgin Mary, thought to be the son of Joseph
of Nazareth—"leaves" this world, is also a fresh manifestation of the eternal fatherhood of God, who in him draws
near again to humanity, to each human being, giving him
the thrice holy "Spirit of truth." . . . .
Man cannot live without love. He remains a being that
is incomprehensible for himself, his life is senseless, if love
is not revealed to him, if he does not encounter love, if he
does not experience it and make it his own, if he does not
participate intimately in it. This, as has already been said,
is why Christ the Redeemer "fully reveals man to himself."
If we may use the expression, this is the human dimension
of the mystery of the Redemption. In this dimension man
finds again his greatness, dignity and value. (John Paul II,
Redemptor Hominis)
In his fatherly care for all of us, God desired that all
men should form one family and deal with each other in a

spirit of brotherhood. All, in fact, are destined to the very same end, namely God himself, since they have been created in the likeness of God who "made from one every nation of men who live on all the face of the earth" (Acts 17:26). Love of God and of one's neighbor, then, is the first and greatest commandment. Scripture teaches us that love of God cannot be separated from love of one's neighbor: "Any other commandment [is] summed up in this sentence: "You shall love your neighbor as yourself . . ." therefore love is the fulfilling of the law" (Rom 13:9-10; cf. 1 Jn 4:20). It goes without saying that this is a matter of the utmost importance to men who are coming to rely more and more on each other and to a world which is becoming more unified every day.

Furthermore, the Lord Jesus, when praying to the Father "that they may all be one . . . even as we are one" (Jn 17:21-22), has opened up new horizons closed to human reason by implying that there is a certain parallel between the union existing among the divine persons and the union of the sons of God in truth and love. It follows, then, that if man is the only creature on earth that God has wanted for its own sake, man can fully discover his true self only in sincere giving of himself. (Vat. II, The Church in the Modern World, 24)

THIRTY-SECOND SUNDAY OF THE YEAR

Scriptural Commentary

First Reading 1 Kings 17:10-16.

A story from the Elijah cycle (1 Kgs 17 - 2 Kgs 2); its setting is the great drought (1 Kgs 17-18) that devastated the land of Israel and beyond. A widow of Zarephath in Phoenicia (modern Lebanon) was down to her last ration of food: a handful of meal and a drop of olive oil. After that she and her child must starve. Yet, at the word of the prophet, she made a cake for him out of his meagre provisions. She took the prophet at his word and the abundance promised her, the never-ending supply of flour and oil, became hers. She stands out as one of the poor of the Lord, one of those who place all their trust in him, despite poverty and oppression. In its liturgical use the incident becomes a fitting commentary on today's gospel reading.

Second Reading Heb 9:24-28.

The christian High Priest does not officiate in an earthly sanctuary; his rightful place is in heaven itself. There he appears, now and forever, before God on our behalf. Blood-sprinkling by the high priest in the holy of holies was the actual rite of expiation in the old ritual (Lev 16:14-16). By analogy the consummation of Christ's saving work has taken place in the heavenly Holy of Holies. Hebrews uses three images to express the work of Christ in the heavenly sanctuary: 1) ritual of the Day of Atonement, which reconciles God and the people (v.23); 2) appearance in the presence of God (25-26); 3) "intercession" (v.25). All three images are combined in v.24. The theological reality behind these images is that of the presence of the glorified humanity (once a suffering humanity) of Christ with God, and the new people of a heavenly calling. Verses 25-26 offer a recapitulation of ideas expressed in 7:23-24; 9:12,24. Christ does not offer himself again and again to effect a periodical expiation, like the annual expiation of *yom kippur*—otherwise he would have suffered many times over since the beginning of the world: a *reductio ad absurdum*. But now once, and once only, at the consummation of the ages (messianic age), he has appeared for the destruction, through the sacrifice of himself, of sin and the power of hell. V.27 notes the moments of man's destiny: death and judgment. And v.28 notes Christ's single sacrifice of atonement for the sins of all and his return for the final moment of destiny at the end of time.

Gospel Mk 12:38-44.

Censure of the scribes (38-40). The scribes prided themselves on their theological learning and—most of them being Pharisees—on their meticulous religious observance. On both scores they invited and received deference; to that end they affected distinctive dress. It should surely be of more than academic interest that the authentic Jesus-tradition is critical of distinctive "churchly" garb. The "best seats" in the synagogue: directly in front of the ark containing the sacred scrolls and facing the people. The charge in v.40 is more serious. Not only do they make an ostentatious display of long-winded prayer, they are shown to be greedy and exploiters of the helpless. Judaism has some scathing condemnation of unscrupulous scribes. However, the sweeping character of the charges here reflects the animosity between the church and official Judaism, an animosity more trenchantly expressed in Mt 23.

The Widow's Mite (41-44). This charming vignette may have found its setting here partly because of the catchword *widow* (vv.40,42). More importantly it is in place because, as an example of true Jewish piety, it contrasts with the counterfeit piety of the scribes. The poor widow who receives Jesus' approbation represents the common people. The "copper coin" (*lepton*) was the smallest in circulation. Mention of two coins is important: the woman would have kept one for herself. Wealthy people had been generous (v.41); yet this poor widow's mite is an immeasurably greater gift than theirs for she has given of her all—her "whole living" (4:44). She had let go of every shred of security and had committed herself wholly to God.

Patristic Commentary

St. Gregory Thaumaturgos (c.213-c.270)
Panegyric on Origen, 3, PG 10.1057, ANF 6.23.

Ingratitude appears to me to be a dire evil, indeed, the direst of evils. For when one has received some benefit, his failing to attempt to make any return by at least the oral expression of thanks, where anyting else is beyond his power, marks him out either as an utterly irrational person, or as one devoid of the sense of obligations conferred, or as a man without any remembrance. And, again, though one is possessed naturally and at once by the sense and the knowledge of benefits received, yet, unless he also carries the memory of these obligations to future days, and offers some evidence of gratitude to his benefactor, such a person is a dull, and ungrateful, and impious fellow and he commits an offence which can be excused neither to the great not the small. Upon the great, therefore, and those who excel in powers of mind, it is incumbent, as out of their greater abundance and larger wealth, to render greater and worthier praise, according to their capacity, to their benefactors.

But the humble also, and those in narrow circumstances, neither should neglect those who do them service, nor take their services carelessly, nor flag in heart as if they could offer nothing worthy or perfect; but as poor indeed, and yet as of good feeling, and as measuring, not the capacity of him whom they honor, but only their own, they ought to pay him honor according to the present measure of their power,—a tribute which will probably be grateful and pleasant to him who is honored, and in no less consideration with him than it would have been had it been some great and splendid offering, if it is only presented with decided earnestness, and with a sincere mind.

Thus is it laid down in the sacred scriptures, that a certain poor and lowly woman, who was with the rich and powerful that were contributing largely and richly out of their wealth, alone and by herself cast in a small, indeed, the very smallest offering, which was, however, all her substance, and received the testimony of having presented the largest offering. For, as I judge, the sacred word has not set up the large outward quantity of the substance given, but rather the mind and disposition of the giver, as the standard by which the worth and the magnificence of the offering are to be measured. Wherefore it is not fitting even for us by any means to shrink from this duty, through the fear that our thanksgiving be not adequate to our obligations; but, on the contrary, we ought to venture and attempt everything, so as to offer thanksgiving, if not adequate, at least such as we have it in our power to exhibit, as in due return.

Insights from the Documents of the Church

Proclaiming Christ Jesus

This great mystery, namely, Christ as Head and Lord of the universe, "has been manifested in the flesh" (1 Tim 3:16) to men. The man, Jesus Christ, who dwelt among men—the one who as man worked with his hands, thought with a human mind, acted with a human will, loved with a human heart—he is truly the Word and the Son of God, who through the incarnation in a certain way joined himself with every single man (GS, 22).

Catechesis must proclaim Jesus in his concrete existence and in his message, that is, it must open the way for men to the wonderful perfection of his humanity in such a way that they will be able to acknowledge the mystery of his divinity. Christ Jesus, for a fact, who was united with the Father in a constant and unique practice of prayer, always lived in close communion with men. By his goodness he embraced all men, the just and the sinners, the poor and the rich, fellow-citizens and foreigners. If he loved some more particularly than others, this predilection was showered on the sick, the poor, the lowly. For the human person he had a reverence and a solicitude such as no one before him had ever manifested.

Catechesis ought daily to defend and strengthen belief in the divinity of Jesus Christ, in order that he may be accepted not merely for his admirable human life, but that men might recognize him through his words and signs as

God's only-begotten Son (cf.Jn 1:18), "God from God, light from light, true God from true God, begotten not made, consubstantial with the Father" (Dz-Sch., 150). The correct explanation of the mystery of the incarnation developed in Christian tradition: through a diligent understanding of the Faith, the Fathers and the Councils made efforts to determine more precisely the concepts, to explain more profoundly the peculiar nature of Christ's mystery, to investigate the hidden connections that bind him to his heavenly Father and to men. Besides, there was the witness of the Christian life about this truth—a witness that the Church presented throughout the centuries: that God's communion with men, which is had in Christ, is the source of joy and inexhaustible hope. In Christ there is all fullness of divinity; through him God's love for men is shown forth.

St. Ignatius wrote to the Ephesians: "There is only one physician, both in body and in spirit, born and unborn, God become man, true life in death; sprung both from Mary and from God, first capable of suffering and then incapable of it, Jesus Christ our Lord" (*Enchiridion patristicum*, 39). (General Catechetical Directory, 53)

THIRTY-THIRD SUNDAY OF THE YEAR

Scriptural Commentary

First Reading Daniel 12:1-3.

The second part of the book of Daniel (chs. 7-12) is apocalyptic, and consists of four visions. The fourth is the great Vision: a) The Time of Anger (chs. 10-11); b) The Time of the End (ch. 12). Chapter 11 is a veiled description of the history of the Ptolemies and Seleucids, culminating in the profanation of the Temple by Antiochus IV. This sparked-off the Maccabaean revolt which is the setting of the composition of Daniel. The last vision (ch.12) leaves the sphere of politics and moves to a higher plane. The goal of history is God's kingdom, which will come solely by God's own power and in his good time. Despite the tribulations of the eschatological crisis the elect of God, whose "names shall be found written in the book" of life will be saved. This "book of life" is mentioned in Ex 32:32-33; it expresses the idea that the Lord has a list of the elect (cf. Ps 69:29; Apoc 20:12-15). Our passage is remarkable for the earliest clear statement of belief in the resurrection of the dead and the first mention in the Bible of "everlasting life." And it firmly introduces the notion of retribution *after death* (2-3). It is a theologically significant text.

Second Reading Heb 10:11-14, 18.

The section 10:1-18 of Hebrews is a recapitulation; the author again insists on the superiority of the sacrifice of Christ over the Mosaic sacrifices. In 10:11-14 he treats of the replacement of the standing priests by the priest enthroned. As before, the multiplicity of futile actions is contrasted with the single, permanently effective, action of Christ. While the heavenly high priest is already present with God (v.12) the universe is still incompletely subjected to his dominion before his future coming (v.13). But now that Christ is "perfected" as priest (5:9), the "sanctifier" has "perfected" those "who are sanctified." The new covenant suffices from now on without need of further sacrifice (15-18). The sacrifice of Christ has been made once for all, and the forgiveness it achieved has been achieved once for all. There is no more sacrifice to be made for sins. There remains only to apply the sacrifice of Christ through the sacramental order—"proclaiming the Lord's death until he comes" (1 Cor 11:26).

Gospel Mk 13:24-32.

In Mark, Jesus' farewell discourse (ch.13), after the introduction (13:1-4), falls into three parts: The Signs of the Parousia (5-23); The Parousia of the Son of Man (24-27); The Nearness of the Parousia (28-37). Our reading includes the second part and most of the third part.

Mark certainly believes in a parousia (advent) of the Son of Man and is convinced that it is imminent; in this he shows the common expectation of early Christians. The passage 24-27 is a collage of prophetic texts. The cosmic signs which accompany the parousia (24-25) are part and parcel of Jewish apocalyptic descriptions of the Day of the Lord. The parousia marks the definitive manifestation of the Son of Man. Then he *will be seen*: seen in fulness instead of being dimly perceived. This is the real message of hope for Christians. This promise and this hope they cling to while the Lord is absent (2:20; 13:34). It is this that enables them, no matter what their present situation, to endure to the end (13:9-13). Already 8:38 had warned that only those who, here and now, in this vale of tears, are not "ashamed" of a suffering Son of Man will rejoice in his glorious coming. That is why Mark will go on, insistently, to urge watching and readiness for the coming (33-37). And, for the faithful ones, that coming will be joy indeed. The Son of Man will not come to execute judgment. The one purpose of his appearing will be to gather *his* elect. After his comforting presentation of the parousia, Mark continues that encouragement by stressing its nearness. But he insists that the intervening time must be spent in watchfulness (28-32). There can never be room for complacency in the life of the Christian.

There can be no doubting that Mark earnestly expected ·an imminent parousia (9:1; 13:30). Was he, then, mistaken? In one sense, obviously, yes; the parousia of the Son of Man did not happen in his generation, nor has it occurred nineteen centuries later. Yet, we can find a basic truth in Mark's conviction. The death and rising of Jesus did usher in the last age. Besides, "parousia" is an apocalyptic symbol which gives dramatic expression to the belief that God's saving plan is perfectly rounded. While we cannot share

Mark's view that the End is very near, nor look for a coming of the Son of Man in clouds, we do share his faith in God's victory in Christ. And, for each of us, the "parousia" will be our meeting with the Son of Man when we pass out of this life into the life of God. It should be our christian hope that we stand among the elect to be fondly welcomed by him.

Patristic Commentary

Methodius (d.c.311)
On the Resurrection, 1.47, (GCS, Methodius, p.298, XXVII, ANF VI.365).

The creation, then, after being restored to a better and more seemly state, remains, rejoicing and exulting over the children of God at the resurrection; for whose sake it now groans and travails, waiting itself also for our redemption from the corruption of the body, that, when we have risen and shaken off the mortality of the flesh, according to that which is written, "Shake off the dust, and arise, and sit down, O Jerusalem," (Is 52:2) and have been set free from sin, it also shall be freed from corruption and be subject no longer to vanity, but to righteousness... Isaiah says, too, "For as the new heaven and the new earth which I make, remaineth before me, saith the Lord, so shall your seed and your name be;" (Is 66:22) and again, "Thus saith the Lord that created the heaven, it is He who prepared the earth and created it, He sets its boundaries; He created it not empty but formed it to be inhabited." (Is 45:18). For in reality God did not establish the universe in vain, or to no purpose for destruction, as those weak-minded men say, but to exist, and be inhabited, and continue. Wherefore the earth and the heaven must exist again ater the conflagration and destruction of all things.

But if our opponents say, How then is it, if the universe be not destroyed, that the Lord says that "heaven and earth shall pass away;" and the prophet, that "the heaven shall perish as smoke, and the earth shall grow old as a garment;" (Is 51:6) we answer, because it is usual for the Scriptures to call the change of the word from its present condition to a better and more glorious one, destruction; as its earlier form is lost in the change of all things to a state of greater splendor; for there is no contradiction nor absurdity in the Holy Scriptures. For not "the world" but the "fashion of this world" passeth away, it is said; so it is usual for the Scriptures to call the change from an earlier form to a better and more comely state, destruction; just as when one calls by the name of destruction the change from a childish form into a perfect man, as the stature of the child is turned into *manly* size and beauty. We may expect that the creation will pass away, as if it were to perish in the burning, in order that it may be renewed, not however that it will be destroyed, that we who are renewed may dwell in a renewed world without taste of sorrow; according as it is said, "When Thou lettest Thy breath go forth, they shall be created, and Thou shalt renew the face of the earth. (Ps 104:30)

Insights from the Documents of the Church

The Day of Judgment

In Christ Jesus and through his mystery, the faithful already in this earthly life hopefully await "our Lord Jesus Christ, who will give a new form to this lowly body of ours and remake it according to the pattern of his glorified body" (Phil 3:21; cf. 1 Cor 15). The very last realities, however, will become manifest and perfect when and only when Christ comes with power, as Judge of the living and the dead, to bring history to its end and to hand over his people to the Father, so that "God may be all in all" (1 Cor 15:24-28). Until "the Lord comes in his majesty, and all the angels with him, and until death is destroyed and all things are subject to him, some of his disciples are pilgrims on earth, some have finished this life and are being purified, and others are in glory, beholding clearly God himself, three and one, as he is" (LG, 49).

On the day of the Lord's coming, the entire Church will reach her perfection and enter into the fullness of God. This is the very foundation of the hope and prayer of Christians ("Thy kingdom come"). Catechesis on the subject of the last things should, on the one hand, be taught under the aspect of consolation, of hope, and of salutary fear (cf. 1 Thess 4:18), of which modern men have such great need; on the other hand, it should be imparted in such a way that the whole truth can be seen. It is not right to minimize the grave responsibility which every one has regarding his future destiny. Catechesis cannot pass over in silence the judgment after death of each man, or the expiatory punishments of Purgatory, or the sad and lamentable reality of eternal death, or the final judgment. On that day each man will fully arrive at his destiny, because all of us will be revealed "before the tribunal of Christ, so that each one may receive the recompense, good or bad, according to his life in the body" (2 Cor 5:10), and "those who have done right shall rise to live; the evildoers shall rise to be damned" (Jn 5:29; cf. LG, 48). (The General Catechetical Directory, 69)

Christ's Single Offering

The mystery of Christ appears in the history of men and of the world—a history subject to sin—not only as the mystery of the incarnation but also as the mystery of salvation and redemption.

God so loved sinners that he gave his Son, reconciling the world to himself (cf. 2 Cor 5:19). Jesus therefore as the Firstborn among many brethren (cf. Rom 8:29), holy, innocent, undefiled (cf. Heb 7:26), being obedient to his Father freely and out of filial love (cf. Phl 2:8), on behalf of his brethren, sinners that they were, and as their Mediator, accepted the death which is for them the wages of

sin (cf. Rom 6:23; GS, 18). By this his most holy death he
redeemed mankind from the slavery of sin and of the devil,
and he poured out on it the spirit of adoption, thus creating
in himself a new humanity. (General Catechetical Directory, 54)

THIRTY-FOURTH SUNDAY OF THE YEAR

SOLEMNITY OF OUR LORD JESUS CHRIST UNIVERSAL KING

Scriptural Commentary

First Reading Daniel 7:13-14.

In the first of the apocalyptic visions of the book of
Daniel (ch. 7), the seer saw four beasts rising out of the sea
(the abode of things evil); an angel explained that these
beasts were four successive empires (Babylonian, Mediah,
Persian and Greek [Seleucid]). Then, in contrast to the
beasts, appears one "like a son of man" (that is, a human
figure); again, in contrast to the beasts' origin in the
depths of the sea, he appears "on the clouds of heaven"
(v.13). The "son of man" is presented to the "Ancient of
Days" (God) and receives universal and everlasting dominion
(V.14). In keeping with the technique of apocalyptic, the
vision is explained to the seer by a heavenly messenger
(vv.26-27) and now it emerges that the "son of man" of
the vision symbolized "the saints of the Most High"—the
faithful people of the kingdom. In a later period the Danielic
"son of man" was understood in individualistic terms and,
in apocalyptic literature, became a title for the future
redeemer. It is not clear that Jesus referred to himself as
"Son of Man" in this apocalyptic sense. It is certain that the
early church, in its christological endeavour, did give him
the title, so understood (cf. Mk 13:26; 14:62).

Second Reading Rev 1:5-8.

Revelation 1:4-8 is the introduction to "The Letters to the Seven Churches" (1:4 - 3:22). The titles given to Jesus (v.5a) are suggested by Ps 89:27,37. The threefold title—witness, firstborn, ruler—answers to the threefold purpose of the Apocalypse, which is at once a divine testimony, a revelation of the Risen Lord, and a forecast of the issues of history. Vv. 5b-6 are the first of many doxologies in the book. The love of Christ for his own is a constant theme; this "ruler of kings" holds no terror for them. By him they have been made a kingdom, each member of which is a priest: a royal house of priests (cf. Ex 19:6; 1 Pet 2:9), inheriting the privilege of the chosen people. From the redemption wrought by Christ in time, John looks to his coming at the end of time (v.7). His text is based on a combination of Dan 7:13 and Zech 12:10, a combination which occurs also in Mt 24:30. In v.8 the speaker is God. In 21:6 and 22:13 the expression "the Alpha and the Omega" is explained: God is the first and the last, the beginning and the end. God is "the Almighty": all-ruler, the sovereign Lord—a reminder to Christians that their God and his Christ hold supreme power, even over the arrogant "rulers of the earth."

Gospel John 18:33-37.

The Johannine scenario of the trial before Pilate (18:28 - 19:16) is involved and dramatic. John has two stage settings. The *outer court* of the praetorium where the Jews vociferously put pressure on Pilate to find Jesus guilty. *Within the praetorium* where Jesus is held prisoner, in an atmosphere of calm reason, the innocence of Jesus becomes clearer to Pilate. In seven carefully balanced episodes, Pilate passes back and forth from one setting to the other, his movement giving expression to the struggle within himself.

And Pilate's struggle between his conviction of Jesus' innocence and political pressure to declare him guilty is evident. On the inner stage, where Jesus and Pilate dialogue, is where the real drama unfolds. From the first, the roles have been reversed: it is Pilate, not Jesus, who is on trial. Pilate, like any other, must take a stand for or against the Light. After he had assured Pilate that he does not constitute a political danger because his kingship "is not of this world" (v.36), Jesus goes on to challenge him to recognize the truth (v.37): "Everyone who is of the truth hears my voice." Because Pilate will not meet the challenge of deciding for the Truth in Jesus and against the Jews, he thinks he can persuade the Jews to accept a solution that will make it unnecessary for him to decide for Jesus. This is the Johannine view of the episodes of Barabbas, the scourging, and the handing over of Jesus as "your King." For John, the trial scene is our own tragic history of temporizing and indecision. Pilate, the would-be neutral man, is frustrated by outside pressure. He, and all who would act like him, end up enslaved to the "world." We should face up, honestly, to the Pilate in us.

Patristic Commentary

St. Augustine (354-430)
On the Gospel of St. John, Tractate CXV,
    c.18, CCL 36.644, NPNF7.423.

Hear then, ye Jews and Gentiles; hear, O circumcision; hear, O uncircumcision; hear, all ye kingdoms of the earth: I interfere not with your government in this world, "My kingdom is not of this world." Cherish not the utterly vain terror that threw Herod the elder into consternation when the birth of Christ was announced, and led him to the murder of so many infants in the hope of including Christ in the fatal number, made more cruel by his fear than by his anger: "My kingdom," He said, "is not of this world." And when He proved this by saying, "If my kingdom were of this world, then would my servants fight, that I should not be delivered to the Jews," He saith not, "But now is my kingdom not" here, but, "is not from hence." For His kingdom is here until the end of the world, having tares intermingled therewith until the harvest; for the harvest is the end of the world, when the reapers, that is to say, the angels, shall come and gather out of His kingdom everything that offendeth; which certainly would not be done, were it not that His kingdom is here. But still it is not from hence; for it only sojourns as a stranger in the world; because He says to His kingdom, "Ye are not of the world, but I have chosen you out of the world." They were therefore of the world, so long as they were not His kingdom, but belonged to the prince of this world. Of the world therefore are all mankind, created indeed by the true God, but generated from Adam as a vitiated and condemned stock; and there are made into a kingdom no longer of the world, all from thence that have been regenerated in Christ. For so did God rescue us from the power of darkness, and translate us into the kingdom of the Son of His love: and of this kingdom it is that He saith, "My kingdom is not of this world;" or, "My kingdom is not from hence."

Insights from the Documents of the Church

Jesus, Universal King

A Christian recognizes that in Jesus Christ he is linked with all of history and is in communion with all men. The history of salvation is being accomplished in the midst of the history of the world. By this history of salvation God fulfils his plan, and thus the People of God, that is, "the whole Christ," is being perfected in time. The Christian acknowledges with simplicity and sincerity that he has a role in such work, which through the power of Jesus the Saviour is aimed at having creation give the greatest possible glory to God (cf. 1 Cor 15:28).

The building up of human society, human progress, and the ongoing execution of human plans stimulate the concern of the men of our era (cf. GS,4). Faith should by no means keep itself as it were outside that human progress. Joined with that progress there are indeed even now serious aberrations. Accordingly, the Gospel message should pass judgment of this state of affairs and tell men what it means.

The ministry of the word, through an ever-deeper study of the divine and human calling of man, must permit the Gospel to spread its own vital seeds of genuine freedom and progress (cf. AG, 8,12) and to stimulate a desire for promoting the growth of the human person and for contending against that way of acting and thinking which tends toward fatalism.

What has been said above is meant merely to show how today's ministry of the word ought to direct its activity toward this world: . . . it is demanded from the Church that she inject the perennial, vital, divine power of the Gospel into the human society of today" (John XXIII, Apost. Const. *Humanae salutis, AAS*, 1962, p.6).

That form of civilization which is called scientific, technical, industrial, and urban not infrequently diverts the attention of men from matters divine and makes their concerns with regard to religion more difficult. Many feel that God is less present, and less needed, and God seems to them less able to explain things in both personal and social life. Hence a religious crisis can easily arise. (General Catechetical Directory, 52, 4, 5)

The Church believes that Christ, who died and was raised for the sake of all, can show man the way and strengthen him through the Spirit in order to be worthy of his destiny: nor is there any other name under heaven given among men by which they can be saved. The Church likewise believes that the key, the center and the purpose of the whole of man's history is to be found in its Lord and Master. She also maintains that beneath all that changes there is much that is unchanging, much that has its ultimate foundation in Christ, who is the same yesterday, and today, and forever. And that is why the Council, relying on the inspiration of Christ, the image of the invisible God, the firstborn of all creation, proposes to speak to all men in order to unfold the mystery that is man and cooperate in tackling the main problems facing the world today. (Vat. II, The Church in the Modern World, 23)

THE SOLEMNITIES
OF THE LORD

THE MOST HOLY TRINITY.
SUNDAY AFTER PENTECOST.

Scriptural Commentary

First Reading Dt 4:32-34, 39-40.

It is no easy matter to choose a fitting reading from the Old Testament for the feast of the Holy Trinity since this mystery of our religion was not revealed in the Old Testament at all. The chosen text speaks about the power and glory of God and of his nonetheless close relationship with his people. No other nation ever enjoyed such an intimate relationship with its gods. No other people could claim that the God who created heaven and earth involved himself in their history and remained present to them through his word.

Privilege, however, carries with it obligation and the second part of today's reading reminds the Israelites of the duties that spring from their relationship with God. They can never forget the moral standards which their status as God's people imposes on them. They can never ignore the laws and commandments which formulate the demands of their religion and which enables Israelites of all generations to discern the kind of conduct that pleases God and ensures his continued favour. This is the relationship of love that God wants to exist between himself and his children. Later revelation will show that it reflects the intimate relationship that exists, within God himself, between Father and Son. In and through the Son we are brought into a relationship of sonship with God, our Father, by the power of the Holy Spirit.

Second Reading Rom 8:14-17.

The whole of chapter 8 of Romans is taken up with the theme of life in the Spirit. The Christian who lives in Christ (8:1) also lives in the sphere of the work of the Spirit who reveals Christ and imparts salvation (8:9). By the indwelling Spirit, Christians are made children of God, sharing the divine life; this is the reason why they can address their Father with the intimate title used by Jesus himself: *Abba* (8:14-16). Now the undreamt-of effect of God's gift of his Spirit emerges: it is our adoption as God's children, our participation in the sonship of Christ. The Spirit who animates and activates Christians, who is the source of our new life, makes us children of God. The "Spirit" of God (or of Christ) is not a "spirit" of slavery, slave-mentality—a play on the word *pneuma*. It is the Spirit who brings men into a union of brotherhood with Christ and establishes them in a special relationship of sonship to the Father. Not surprisingly, the Spirit must bring the Christian to an awareness of this extraordinary situation, one beyond the bounds of human expectation. It is an exercise of divine condescension. The God who has adopted us as his children awakens in us an awareness of that fact, and then gently helps us in our wondering acknowledgement of that fact: Abba! It has about it something of the flavour of a mother teaching her little child to pray. There is the same quality of love that strips the exercise of any condescension. The close of v.17 brings us firmly down to earth. True, we are indeed children of God and fellow heirs with Christ—but, "provided we suffer with him"! That is his way: "Was it not necessary that the Christ should suffer these things and enter into his glory?" (Lk 24:26). There is no *christian* way to glory other than his.

Gospel Mt 28:16-20.

The glorious Son of Man commissions his church. A "mountain" is a place of revelation—an apt setting. The "eleven" adored their Lord—yet some "doubted": Matthew is drawing for his community a picture of every christian community—believers caught between adoration and doubt. Jesus solemnly declares that, by his death-resurrection, he has been given, by the Father, total power over the universe. He is, therefore, in a position to launch a universal mission, and he duly commissions his representatives who are to achieve his task. Consequently, he sends them into the world to make disciples of "all nations." During *his* ministry Jesus limited his concern to Israel; in this new era the good news is for *all*.

One become a *disciple* through baptism in the name of Father, Son, and Spirit—a trinitarian formula which doubtless reflects the baptismal liturgy of Matthew's church. Disciples must be taught Jesus' commands. "The teaching of Jesus will encompass much of what was in the Mosaic Law. But the church teaches these commands not because they come from Moses but because they come from Jesus . . . The command of Jesus—one might almost say Jesus himself—is the ultimate law of morality, the criterion, the criterion for deciding what is will of God" (J. Meier, *Matthew*, 372). Matthew skillfully rounds off his gospel by catching up the God-with-us (1:23) of his prologue: the all-powerful Son of Man promises to be with us always. It is an encouraging word to the church of our day—a church seemingly lost in a mass of humanity.

It is important to be clear that this solemn commission, so theologically important, is *not* historically a command of Jesus to his church at its beginning. Acts 1-15 and Gal 2 show that the reception of Gentiles and the mission to them were bitterly resisted. This commission voices the experience of a church that had become open to all, a church tranquilly convinced that it had become what the Lord had meant it to be.

Patristic Commentary

St. Gregory Nazianzus (c. 329-388)
OR XLI, On Pentecost, IX, PG 36.441,
LNPF 7².382.

The Holy Spirit, then, always existed, and exists, and always will exist. He neither had a beginning, nor will He have an end; but He was everlastingly joined with and numbered with the Father and the Son. For it was not ever fitting that either the Son should be wanting to the Father, or the Spirit to the Son. For then Godhood would be shorn of Its Glory in its greatest respect, for It would seem to have arrived at the consummation of perfection as if by an afterthought. Therefore He was ever being partaken, but not partaking; perfecting, not being perfected; sanctifying, not being sanctified; deifying, not being deified; Himself ever the same with Himself, and with Those with Whom He is joined; invisible, eternal, incomprehensible, unchangeable, without quality, without quantity, without form, impalpable, self-moving, eternally moving, with free-will, self-powerful. All-powerful (even though all that is of the Spirit if referable to the First Cause, just as is all that is of the Only-begotten); Life and Lifegiver; Light and Lightgiver; absolute Good, and Spring of Goodness; the Right, the Princely Spirit; the Lord, the Sender, the Separator; Builder of His own Temple; leading, working as He wills; distributing His own Gifts; the Spirit of Adoption, of Truth, of Wisdom, of Understanding, of Knowledge, of Godliness, of Counsel, of Fear (which are ascribed to Him) (Is 11:12) by Whom the Father is known and the Son is glorified; and by Whom *alone* He is known; one class, one service, worship, power, perfection, sanctification. Why make a long discourse of it? All that the Father has the Son has also, except the being Unbegotten; and all that the Son has the Spirit has also, except the Generation. And these two matters do not divide the Substance, as I understand it, but rather are divisions within the Substance.

Insights from the Documents of the Church

The Blessed Trinity and Human Salvation

Just as Christ is the centre of the history of salvation, so the mystery of God is the centre from which this history takes its origin and to which it is ordered as to its last end. The crucified and risen Christ leads men to the Father by sending the Holy Spirit upon the People of God. For this reason the structure of the whole content of catechesis must be theocentric and trinitarian: through Christ, to the Father, in the Spirit.

Through Christ: The entire economy of salvation receives its meaning from the incarnate Word. It prepared his coming; it manifests and extends his kingdom on earth from the time of his death and resurrection up to his second glorious coming, which will complete the work of God. So it is that the mystery of Christ illumines the whole content of catechesis. The diverse elements—biblical, evangelical, ecclesial, human, and even cosmic—which catechetical education must take up and expound are all to be referred to the incarnate Son of God.

To the Father: The supreme purpose of the incarnation of the Word and of the whole economy of salvation consists in this: that all men be led to the Father. Catechesis, therefore, since it must help to an ever-deeper understanding of this plan of love of the heavenly Father, must take care to show that the supreme meaning of human life is this: to acknowledge God and to glorify him by doing his will, as Christ taught us by his words and the example of his life, and thus to come to eternal life.

In the Spirit: The knowledge of the mystery of Christ and the way to the Father are realized in the Holy Spirit. Therefore, catechesis, when expounding the content of the Christian message, must always put in clear light this presence of the Holy Spirit, by which men are continually moved to have communion with God and men and to fulfil their duties.

If catechesis lacks these three elements or neglects their close relationship, the Christian message can certainly lose its proper character.

The theocentric-trinitarian purpose of the economy of salvation cannot be separated from its objective, which is this: that men, set free from sin and its consequences, should be made as much like Christ as possible (cf. LG,39). As the incarnation of the Word, so every revealed truth is for us men and for our salvation. To view the diverse Christian truths in their relation to the ultimate end of man is one of the conditions needed for a most fruitful understanding of them (cf. First Vatican Council, Dogm. Const. *Dei Filius*, Dz.-Sch., 3016).

Catechesis must, then, show clearly the very close connection of the mystery of God and Christ with man's existence and his ultimate end. This method in no way implies any contempt for the earthly goals which men are divinely called to pursue by individual or common efforts; it does, however, clearly teach that man's ultimate end is not confined to these temporal goals, but rather surpasses them beyond all expectation, to a degree that only God's love for men could make possible. (General Catechetical Directory, 41, 42)

CORPUS CHRISTI
Thursday after Holy Trinity.

Scriptural Commentary

First Reading Ex 24:3-8.

This passage describes the ratification of the Sinai covenant between God and Israel. Two dominant ideas emerge, namely the significance of the sacrificial blood, and the place of the word of God in the ceremony. The constant pattern of word and event throughout the Old

Testament is well illustrated in this passage. Blood, symbol of life, belonged exclusively to God. Here the blood of the sacrificed animals is sprinkled by Moses, half of it on the altar of God and half on the people. The prophetic word spoken by Moses interpreted this event for the people. The word of the Lord is accepted by the people in their promise to observe all the commands of their God—not the acceptance of a legal system, but an acceptance in faith of the gift of life. By this response in faith the people bind themselves to God. He is their God who has manifested himself to them and has chosen them on his people.

The phrase which explains the choice of this passage for today's Mass is "the blood of the covenant," a phrase which is repeated in the gospel reading. On Sinai the blood was, in some sort, a sacramental sign of the relationship that now existed between God and his chosen people. At the Last Supper, where a new people of God was established and a new covenant sealed, a new relationship between the Lord and his people was ratified with the sacrificial blood of Christ, and a rite was instituted which would be a perpetual reminder of the saving death of Christ and of the intimate bond of fellowship that exists between him and his covenant community.

Second Reading Heb 9:11-15.

In 9:11-28 the author of Hebrews presents the sacrifice of Christ as being efficacious and definitive. The perfection of Christ's priesthood and cult is contrasted, typologically with the imperfection of the old levitical priesthood, and, in a framework of typology and imagery drawn from the Old Testament, a typology of the saving word of Christ is propounded. The great barrier of access to God is sin and Hebrews uses details of the ritual of the Day of Atonement to draw typological parallels with the "heavenly liturgy" of Christ—his work of salvation.

The "greater and more perfect tent not made with hands" is either the heavens through which Christ passed in order to arrive before God in the Holy of Holies; of Christ's glorified body in which he entered heaven (v.11). If it is by virtue of his own blood that he has entered into the heavenly sanctuary once for all, it is by the same means that he has won for us an eternal salvation—"eternal" because it belongs to the heavenly, eternal source of perfect efficaciousness (v.12). Verses 13-14 constitute an argument *a fortiori*: if the old liturgy with its animal victims could achieve a reconciliation with God which affected the "outer man," so much more will the effects of Christ's liturgy with himself as victim reach the "inner man." "Through an eternal spirit": the divine power, the principle behind Christ's work. Jesus had become priest "by the power of an indestructible life" (7:16); it is to this life which cannot be destroyed that "the eternal spirit" corresponds. What the statement means is that Jesus' self-offering is a heavenly, not an earthly, reality. It is offered through an eternal spirit because it is offered in that new, heavenly sphere of existence that he entered at the time of his resurrection and exaltation. And it is this same "eternal spirit" permeating the saving work of Christ which is the ultimate reason for that work being able not only to cleanse the "flesh" of men like the liturgy of the old "fleshly" ordinances but to bring about that internal, spiritual renovation of conscience and newness of heart (8:10) which enable us to come to heavenly glory.

Gospel Mk 14:12-16, 22-26.

The account of preparation for the passover (12-16) is quite like that of preparation for the entry to Jerusalem (11:1-6). Here, as there, two disciples are sent off with a precise description of the situation they will encounter and are told exactly that to say. And here, too, all turned out as the Teacher had assured them. Here only in Mark is the last supper designated a passover meal.

The phrase, "And as they were eating" (v.22) resumes the meal episode after the warning of betrayal (17-21). Jesus "took bread," "blessed," "broke," "gave": the same actions and the very same words as in both feeding stories (6:41; 8:6). Then the disciples "did not understand about the loaves" (6:52; cf. 8:17-21); now the mystery is being revealed. Jesus is the "one loaf" (cf. 8:14) for Jews and Gentiles because, as he tells them, his body is being given and his blood poured out for Jew and Gentile (23-24).

"This is my body"; Paul (1 Cor 11:22) adds "which is for you." But this is already firmly implied in Mark both through the repeated references to Jesus' death since the beginning of the passion narrative and the explicit statement in the cup saying. "This is my blood of the covenant"— Ex 24:8 is certainly in mind: "Behold the blood of the covenant which the Lord has made with you." By the sprinkling of sacrificial blood the people of Israel shared in the blessings of the covenant given at Sinai. Likewise this blood of the cup will be poured out "for many" (a semitism, meaning "all"): a new covenant is being forged and sealed whose blessings are offered to all. The death of Jesus founds the new community. The Last Supper helps us to understand the meaning of Jesus' death on Calvary.

The whole of the Supper narrative (22-25) is based on the eucharistic liturgical tradition of Mark's church. While less explicit than the Pauline tradition (1 Cor 11:23-26) it has the same meaning. In both the body and blood are given: the context is sacrificial death. In both the blood seals a new covenant. In both the eucharistic meal anticipates the eschatological banquet of the kingdom. And if Mark does not have Paul's "Do this in remembrance of me," the eucharistic liturgy of his church was the living fulfilment of that word.

Patristic Commentary

Cyril of Jerusalem (c.315-386)
Mystery Lect. IV., PG 33.1097, FOTC 64.181.

Once at Cana in Galilee He changed water which is akin to blood into wine; is it not credible, then, that He changed

wine into blood? If as a guest at a physical marriage He
performed this stupendous miracle, shall He not far more
readily be confessed to have bestowed on "the friends of the
bridegroom" (Mt 9:15) the fruition of His own Body and
Blood?

With perfect confidence, then, let us partake of the Body
and Blood of Christ. For in the figure of bread His Body is
given to you, and in the figure of wine His Blood, that by
partaking of the Body and Blood of Christ you may become
the same body and blood with Him. For when His Body and
Blood become the tissue of our members, we become
Christ-bearers and as the blessed Peter said, "partakers of
the divine nature." (2 Pet 1:4).

Once, speaking to the Jews, Christ said: "Unless you
eat my flesh and drink my blood, you can have no life in
you." (Jn 6:53) Not understanding His words spiritually,
they "were shocked and drew back," imagining that He was
proposing the eating of human flesh.

The Old Testament had its loaves of proposition, but
they, as belonging to the Testament, have come to an end.
The New Testament has its heavenly bread and cup of
salvation, to sanctify both body and soul. For as the bread
is for the body, the Word suits the soul.

Do not then think of the elements as bare bread and
wine; they are, according to the Lord's declaration, the
Body and Blood of Christ. Though sense suggests the
contrary, let faith be your stay. Instead of judging the
matter by taste, let faith give you an unwavering confidence
that you have been privileged to receive the Body and Blood
of Christ.

Insights from the Documents of the Church

The Eucharist

The Church lives an authentic life when she *professes
and proclaims mercy*—the most stupendous attribute of

the Creator and of the Redeemer—and when she brings people close to the sources of the Saviour's mercy, of which she is the trustee and dispenser. Of great significance in this area is constant meditation on the word of God, and above all conscious and mature participation *in the Eucharist* and *in the sacrament of penance or reconciliation.* The Eucharist brings us ever nearer to that *love* which is more powerful than death: "For as often as we eat this bread and drink this cup," we proclaim not only the death of the Redeemer but also his Resurrection, "until he comes" in glory. The same Eucharistic rite, celebrated in memory of him who in his messianic mission revealed the Father to us by means of his words and his Cross, attests to the inexhaustible *love* by virtue of which he desires always to be united with us and present in our midst, coming to meet every human heart. (John Paul II, On the Mercy of God [*Dives in Misericordia*])

The primacy of the Eucharist over all the other sacraments is unquestionable, as is also its supreme efficacy in building up the Church (cf. LG 11, 17; Instruction, *Eucharisticum mysterium*, nn.5-15).

For the Eucharist, when the words of consecration have been pronounced, the profound (not the phenomenal) reality of bread and wine is changed into the Body and Blood of Christ, and this wonderful change has in the Church come to be called "transubstantiation." Accordingly, under the appearances (that is, the phenomenal reality) of the bread and wine, the humanity of Christ, not only by its power but by itself (that is, substantially), united with his divine Person, lies hidden in an altogether mysterious way (cf. Paul VI, Encycl. *Mysterium fidei, AAS,* 1965, p.766).

This sacrifice is not merely a rite commemorating a past sacrifice. For in it Christ by the ministry of the priests perpetuates the sacrifice of the cross in an unbloody manner through the course of the centuries (cf. SC,47). In it too he nourishes the faithful with himself, the Bread of Life, in order that, filled with love of God and neighbour, they may become more and more a people acceptable to God.

Having been nourished with the Victim of the sacrifice of the Cross, the faithful should by a genuine and active love remove the prejudices because of which they are at times accused of a sterile worship that keeps them from being brotherly and from cooperating with other people. By its nature the Eucharistic banquet is meant to help the faithful to unite their hearts with God more each day in frequent prayer, and thence to acknowledge and love other men as brothers of Christ and sons of God the Father. (General Catechetical Directory, 58)

THE MOST SACRED HEART OF JESUS
Friday After the Second Sunday after Pentecost

Scriptural Commentary

First Reading Hosea 11:1, 3-4, 8-9.

Hosea has to warn his nation, Israel, of approaching Assyrian danger; he has to speak of judgment. But his lead idea remains the divine goodness (*hesed*) which explains the origin of Israel (11:1-9) and which will have the last word. Israel is Yahweh's own son, born to him in Egypt. In bold imagery the prophet shows the divine parent as a doting father playing with and feeding and guiding the faltering steps of his precious first-born. What he gets in return is base ingratitude (vv.2,7). The heart of God is wounded, not in resentment but with anguished love for a people set on self-destruction. "How can I give you up!" Paul knew the same God as Hosea. When he, in his turn, agonised over the obduracy of his people he can ask: "Has God rejected his people?" and answers with the whole conviction: "God has not rejected his people whom he fore-knew"(Rom 11:1-2). Hosea and Paul had taken with utmost seriousness the declaration of their God: "I am God and not man . . . and I will not come to destroy" (Hos 11:9). It is tragic that so much of christian tradition has looked to a "God" who is all too "human." And that despite the fact that the true humanness of God-made-man under-writes the truth of Hosea's declaration.

Second Reading Eph 3:8-12, 14-19.

Ephesians 3:1-19 is a prayer of intercession. The object of the prayer is not expressed until v.16; before that "Paul" speaks of his apostolic role (2-13). His demand on his readers' behalf (v.16) is similar to that of 1:17-19. It is a prayer for their progress in faith and love and their com-prehension of the "mystery" so that they may accomplish their vocation as the "fulness" of God, that is, as Church (16-19). "Paul" makes three petitions, as he prays for strength (v.16), faith and love (v.17), understanding (vv.18-19).

"That he may grant you to be strengthened with might through his spirit in the inner man" (v.16). This is a strength that comes to us as gift through the Spirit of God—"the Spirit helps us in our weakness" (Rom 8:26). It is a strength that is an empowerment of the inner man, in the true core of his personality, at the point where he relates directly with God. "That Christ may dwell in your hearts through faith; and that you may be rooted and grounded in love" (v.17). Christ—faith—love: these three words belong together; they cannot exist apart from one another. Through faith and love, Christ *dwells* in our hearts. "That we may understand the love of Christ which surpasses all understanding" (v.19). "I am loved": that is the under-standing which surpasses all others. That love was made visible to us on the cross. And if we attain this under-standing—rather, if it is granted to us—then our response must echo that of Paul: "I count everything as loss because

of the surpassing worth of knowing Christ Jesus my Lord"
(Phil 2:8).

Gospel Jn 19:31-37.

The Beloved Disciple speaks here as a witness to a
revelation that is important for all the Christians whom he
symbolizes. It is very probable that in this flow of water
from the side of Jesus (from within him) John saw the
fulfilment of Jesus' prophecy. For the flow of water
coloured by Jesus' blood fulfils the promise of 7:38-39:
"As the Scripture says, 'From within him shall flow rivers
of living water' Here he was referring to the Spirit . . .".
Thus for John the flow of water is another prophetic
symbol of the giving of the Spirit, carrying on the theme
of v.30. On a secondary level the flow of blood and water
symbolizes the origin of the sacraments of Eucharist and
Baptism through which the life of Jesus is communicated
to the Christian. Blood and water flow from the *dead*
Jesus. The drama of the cross does not end in death but in a
flow of life that comes from earth. The death of Jesus on the
cross is the beginning of christian life. Finally, reference
to the passover lamb of which "not a bone could be broken"
(Ex 12:10,46) forms an inclusion with the "Lamb of God"
heralded by the Baptist at the beginning of the gospel (1:29).

Patristic Commentary

St. John Chrysostom (c.347-407)
Baptismal Instructions, 3, SC 50.159,
    ACW 31.60.

On that day in Egypt, the destroying angel saw the blood
smeared on the doors and did not dare to burst in. Today,
will the devil not check himself all the more if he sees, not
the blood of the type smeared on the doors, but the blood of
the truth smeared on the mouths of the faithful, since these

mouths have become doors of a temple which holds Christ? If the angel stood in awe when he saw the type, much more likely is it that the devil will flee when he sees the truth.

Do you wish to learn from another source as well the strength of this blood? Look from where it first flowed and where it had its source! It flowed down from the cross, from the Master's side. The Evangelist says that, when Christ was dead but still on the cross, the soldier came and pierced His side with a lance, and straightway there came out water and blood. (Jn 19:34) The one was a symbol of baptism, and the other of the mysteries. Therefore, he did not say: *There came out blood and water*, but first water came forth and then blood, since first comes baptism and then the mysteries. It was the soldier, then, who opened Christ's side and dug through the rampart of the holy temple, but I am the one who has found the treasure and received the wealth. So it was with the lamb. The Jews sacrificed the victim, but I reaped the reward of salvation which came from their sacrifice.

Insights from the Documents of the Church

Revelation of Love

This revelation of the Father and outpouring of the Holy Spirit, which stamp an indelible seal on the mystery of the Redemption, explain the meaning of the Cross and death of Christ. The God of creation is revealed as the God of redemption, as the God who is "faithful to himself," and faithful to his love for man and the world, which he revealed on the day of creation. His is a love that does not draw back before anything that justice requires in him. Therefore "for our sake (God) made him (the Son) to be sin who knew no sin." If he "made to be sin" him who was without any sin whatever, it was to reveal the love that is always greater than the whole of creation, the love that is he

himself, since "God is love." Above all, love is greater
than sin, than weakness, than the "futility of creation";
it is stronger than death; it is a love always ready to raise
up and forgive, always ready to go to meet the prodigal son,
always looking for "the revealing of the sons of God," who
are called to the glory that is to be revealed." This revelation
of love is also described as mercy; and in man's history
this revelation of love and mercy has taken a form and a
name: that of Jesus Christ. (John Paul II, *Redemptor
Hominis*)

"He who has seen me has seen the Father." The Church
professes the mercy of God, the Church lives by it in her
wide experience of faith and also in her teaching, constantly
contemplating Christ, concentrating on him, on his life and
on his Gospel, on his Cross and Resurrection, on his
whole mystery. Everything that forms the "vision" of Christ
in the Church's living faith and teaching brings us nearer
to the "vision of the Father" in the holiness of his mercy.
The Church seems in a particular way to profess the mercy
of God and to venerate it when she directs herself to the
Heart of Christ. In fact, it is precisely this drawing close
to Christ in the mystery of his Heart which enables us to
dwell on this point—a point in a sense central and also
most accessible on the human level—on the revelation of the
merciful love of the Father, a revelation which constituted
the central content of the messianic mission of the Son
of Man. (John Paul II, On the Mercy of God [*Dives in
Misericordia*])

OLD TESTAMENT MESSAGE:
A BIBLICAL-THEOLOGICAL COMMENTARY

Appreciating the spiritual and pastoral needs of the Christian community, twenty-one biblical scholars have written this up-to-date theological commentary on the Old Testament. The primary purpose is to stress and elucidate the message, not just to duplicate what is already available in other commentaries.

Each volume presents the great insights and achievements of modern biblical scholarship—clearly and pastorally. So, the *Old Testament Message* should be welcomed by all who preach, teach or study the word of God.

Editors
CARROLL STUHLMUELLER, C.P. and MARTIN McNAMARA, M.S.C.

- *Set of 23 Volumes: Quality Paperback. . .$135; Cloth Edition. . .$198*